THE PENGUIN DICTIONARY OF

ENGLISH IDIOMS

DAPHNE M. GULLAND
AND DAVID HINDS-HOWELL

PENGUIN BOOKS

PENGUIN BOOKS

Published by the Penguin Group
Penguin Books Ltd, 80 Strand, London WC2R 0RL, England
Penguin Putnam Inc., 375 Hudson Street, New York, New York 10014, USA
Penguin Books Australia Ltd, Ringwood, Victoria, Australia
Penguin Books Canada Ltd, 10 Alcorn Avenue, Toronto, Ontario, Canada M4V 3B2
Penguin Books India (P) Ltd, 11 Community Centre, Panchsheel Park, New Delhi – 110 017, India
Penguin Books (NZ) Ltd, Cnr Rosedale and Airborne Roads, Albany, Auckland, New Zealand
Penguin Books (South Africa) (Pty) Ltd, 24 Sturdee Avenue, Rosebank 2196, South Africa

Penguin Books Ltd, Registered Offices: 80 Strand, London WC2R 0RL, England

www.penguin.com

First published 1986
Reprinted with revisions and an additional category 1994
18

Translated into Greek by Agricultural Cooperative
Publications, Athens, Greece

Printed in England by Clays Ltd, St Ives plc
Typeset in Linotron Times

PENGUIN REFERENCE

THE PENGUIN DICTIONARY OF ENGLISH IDIOMS

Daphne Gulland was born in 1953. She was educated at Fidelis Grammar School in London. In 1975 she graduated with Honours in English and German at Bedford College, University of London. For many years she has been engaged in research into the origins of the most common idioms in the language, breaking new ground with her system of categorization for *The Penguin Dictionary of English Idioms*. She is married with four children. Her hobbies are gardening, walking, reading and history.

David Hinds-Howell was born in 1916. He was educated at Marlborough College, and obtained a Master of Arts degree in philosophy, politics and economics at Oxford University in 1938. After practising as a barrister, he had a long and distinguished career as director of the Hillcrest School of English (1952–1981) and as a teacher of English at advanced and intermediate level. He died in 1995.

PREFACE

The Penguin Dictionary of English Idioms will be of absorbing interest to foreign and native speakers of English alike. Its aims are twofold: to provide a wide selection of the most commonly used idiomatic phrases in the English language; and, with the help of copious examples taken from real life, to offer guidance on the most effective way to use them.

The English language is rich in idioms, and although it is possible to converse correctly in non-idiomatic English, a student with only a superficial knowledge of English idioms will find himself at a serious disadvantage in his reading, and even more so when he takes part in discussions and debates. Finding idioms in a general dictionary is a slow and laborious task, so it is hoped that this dictionary of idioms will provide assistance in a practical and interesting way.

What then is an idiom? We would define an idiom as a combination of words with a special meaning that cannot be inferred from its separate parts. The examples that follow will help to make the matter clear:

1. 'John couldn't say boo to a goose!' On the face of it, this is a very strange thing to say. Of course it is quite possible to say boo to a goose, but who would want to do such a thing? However, the statement has an idiomatic meaning, namely that John is so timid that he wouldn't dare to make even the mildest protest, however badly he was treated. Clearly, it is impossible to deduce this meaning from the separate words in the sentence above. In other words, the meaning of the whole is different from the parts. The sentence then has two meanings – a literal meaning which means very little, and a metaphorical one which is the idiom.
2. 'Shall we go Dutch?' Unlike the first example, this one has no literal meaning at all, only an idiomatic one: 'I suggest that you pay for your meal, and I'll pay for mine?' Again, it is impossible to infer the meaning of the idiom from the separate words in the question.

Every idiom belongs either to the first group or to the second as described above.

Traditionally, dictionaries of idioms present idiomatic expressions in alphabetical order; but we believe that the aims we have set ourselves can be achieved more efficiently by categorizing idioms, i.e. by grouping them round a limited number of key-words and putting them in the appropriate categories. For example, the first category, Colours (see the list of Categories on page 9), contains 14 different colours: red, blue, green, yellow, white, white and black, black, brown, grey, purple, scarlet, pink, golden and silver. Each of these colours (key-words) is used to form an idiom or idioms. The key-word 'red', for instance, is included in 13 idioms, as in 'to paint the town red', 'a red rag to a bull', 'to see red', and so on. All the 'red' idioms make up a group. 'Colours' itself, the name of the category, makes up a group of 17 idioms, as in 'to see someone in his true colours', 'with flying colours', and so on. The total number of groups make up the complete category with altogether 130 idioms. The same principle applies to the remaining 33 categories.

Categorizing idioms in this way has a number of important advantages over the alphabetical system. First, idioms that include the same key-word will be concentrated in greater numbers than is possible with the alphabetical system. For instance, there are 37 idioms in the 'dog' group, 88 idioms in the 'hand' and 47 in the 'heart' groups. By concentrating idioms in such large numbers, the reader is in a position to make a systematic study of all the idioms in a given group, and to compare and distinguish them in a way that would not be possible were they scattered over a whole dictionary. Secondly, categorizing makes it possible to introduce idioms in a coherent, logical order instead of the arbitrary, inconsequential order of the alphabet; and this makes for more interesting reading for students who like to browse through a dictionary. Finally, the use of categories will enable students to complete their study of a selected category with the minimum of effort, since all the items in which they are interested have already been assembled for them. The student is, of course, free to start wherever he wishes. As he proceeds through this *Dictionary*, category by category, he will find his knowledge of idioms growing until finally he has acquired a mastery of the subject.

HOW TO USE THE INDEX

We have provided an Index of idioms at the back of the *Dictionary*. The order of the idioms in the Index is strictly alphabetical. When you look an idiom up in the Index, look for it first under the noun, if there is one. If there are two or more nouns, look for the idiom under the first noun. If there are no nouns, then look for it under the first verb; if there is no verb, then under the first adjective.

Please note that if the idiom has two nouns standing next to each other, it will be indexed under both nouns, even if the first noun is a possessive, e.g. 'the lion's share' will be indexed under both 'lion's', and 'share'. Also note that idioms are not indexed under pronouns, e.g. 'one', 'someone', 'anyone', 'oneself', 'himself', etc., or the verb 'to be'.

Every idiom has a reference consisting of two numbers divided by a stroke, e.g. **000/0**. The first number of the pair, **000**, refers to the page on which the idiom you are looking for appears; the second number, **0**, refers to the actual idiom: 'to be too big for one's boots'. Here are some more idioms for you to look up, followed by the correct answers which you can check for yourself:

1. 'to sail against the wind'. There is one noun in this idiom, namely 'wind', so it will appear under 'wind' with the reference number **180/6**.
2. 'to pull the rug from under one's feet'. There are two nouns in this idiom, so it will be indexed under the first noun of the two, 'rug', with the reference number **152/5**.
3. 'to read the riot act'. In this idiom there are two nouns, 'riot' and 'act', that stand next to each other. The idiom can therefore be found in the Index under either of them. The reference number for this idiom is **231/14**.
4. 'at arm's length'. There are two nouns in this phrase, one next to the other, so this idiom can be found in the Index under 'arm's' (a possessive) or 'length', with the reference number **91/13**.
5. 'to do someone proud'. There is no noun here, but there is the verb 'to do', so this idiom will appear under 'do' in the Index with the reference number **119/10**.
6. 'fair, fat and forty'. As this phrase contains no noun or verb, it will appear under an adjective. There are, however, three adjectives, so, according to our rule, the phrase will appear under the first adjective, 'fair', with the reference number **219/16**.
7. 'Nobody's poodle'. 'Nobody' is a pronoun (which we have excluded) so the idiom will appear under 'poodle' which has the reference number **54/13**.

A number of variations on the idioms are listed in the Index; these appear immediately under the appropriate entry in the text.

When an idiom bears a close relation to one in a different category, it is given a cross-reference at the end of the note and the reader can follow this up, if he wishes, for further information. Apart from this, no cross-references are used and, once the reader has obtained the reference number of the idiom he is looking for from the Index, he can be sure of finding the idiom required without being referred to other parts of the *Dictionary*.

A number of proverbs have been included when the content of the proverb is idiomatic, as for example: 'Charity begins at home', and 'Don't look a gift-horse in the mouth'.

We hope that our readers will find as much interest in learning and using these idioms as we have had in collecting them.

Daphne Gulland
David Hinds-Howell
1986

CATEGORIES

1. COLOURS

COLOURS

1. to see someone in his **true colours** – to understand someone's true character, often for the first time. 'As soon as he made a fuss about returning her money, I saw him in his true colours.'

   to **show oneself in one's true colours** – to reveal one's true nature. 'When he lost his temper, he showed himself in his true colours.'

2. to **give/lend colour to** – to make (an account, story, explanation, etc.) more credible or more plausible. 'The broken window on the ground floor lent colour to Mrs Brown's story that her house had been burgled.'

3. with **flying colours** – with great success, with distinction. 'We were all expecting him to fail, but he passed with flying colours.'

4. to sail under **false colours** – to assume a false identity in order to conceal one's true purpose.

5. to paint in **bright/dark colours** – to describe something in a flattering or unflattering way. 'My brother wanted us all to emigrate to America and painted his life there in the brightest colours.'

6. to **win one's colours** – to win recognition for one's achievements. 'The young Minister won his colours with a brilliant defence of the government's policy.' Literally, to win a place in one's school or college team, which entitles one to wear the school or college colours. cf. 'to **win one's spurs**' **252/7**.

7. to **nail (one's) colours to the mast** – to make absolutely clear what one's views are in a very forthright manner. 'Now he has nailed his colours to the mast, he cannot change his mind.'

8. (to join) **the colours** (slightly old-fashioned) – to join the army.

   to be **called to the colours** – to be conscripted into the army.

9. to look through **rose-coloured/tinted spectacles** – to see things in a flattering or over-optimistic light. 'Anne always enjoys her visits because she sees everything through rose-coloured spectacles, but she would feel differently if she had to live there.'

10. to be **colourless** – to lack personality, to be uninteresting or nondescript. 'We talked for over half an hour together, but nothing that he said stands out in my memory. I'm afraid he's a dull, colourless man.'

11. To be **off colour** – to be not quite at one's best, to feel queasy or slightly ill. 'She's a little off colour today; she was up very late last night and may have had a little too much to drink!'

12. **under colour of** – in the guise of, under the pretext of. 'Under colour of consulting the kidney specialist, the newspaper man wormed a lot of information out of him for the television programme.'

13. **local colour** – background information about a place or event.

14. to **have one's views coloured by** – to have one's ideas and opinions changed by external influences. 'Like everyone else, his views were coloured by his background and upbringing.'

15. to see the **colour of** (someone's) **money** – to take some money in advance before parting with one's goods or services.

16. **colour bar** – discrimination against black and coloured people in favour of the whites, legally, socially or economically.

17. a **highly coloured** report – a report that is exaggerated or biased.

RED

1. to catch someone **red-handed** – to catch someone in the act of committing a crime, usually a theft. 'Caught you red-handed! I saw you take the money out of the box.' The reference is to the blood still on the hands of the criminal after stabbing his victim to death. The phrase is used now for less serious crimes.
2. to **paint the town red** (of American origin) – to celebrate by running wild, drinking and making a commotion. 'Richard has passed his exam. We are going to paint the town red tonight, so don't be surprised if we come home very late.'
3. a **red rag to a bull** – a source of violent anger to someone. 'Mention of animal experiments was like a red rag to a bull to the anti-vivisectionist.' The phrase originated in the belief that any red-coloured object will infuriate a bull.

   like a red rag to someone – has the same meaning. 'Property developers were like a red rag to the Prime Minister.'
4. **'Reds under the bed'** – the reds are everywhere. An ironic allusion to the obsession some people have that there are reds (communists) everywhere, plotting violent revolution.
5. **red in tooth and claw** – a violent revolutionary who shows no mercy and makes no compromises. Originally used as a description of Nature: Alfred Lord Tennyson, *In Memoriam*, Part LVI, Stanza 4: 'Nature, red in tooth and claw'.
6. to **see red** – to react with uncontrollable rage against an object of one's hatred. The object is usually a stereotype, for example civil servants, businessmen, Jews, blacks. 'The sight of demonstrators marching past his house made Stephen see red.' The idiom originated in the idea that red symbolizes both violent revolution and the colour of blood; however, it has shed its political motivation and is associated now with any person or thing that excites strong disapproval.
7. **red tape** – bureaucratic delay, excessive attention to rules and regulations, often resulting in injustice to the ordinary citizen. The 'red tape' is the red ribbon with which the civil servant ties his papers together.
8. a **red-letter day** – a day of special importance, for example a wedding, the celebration of a victory or the receiving of a great honour. The phrase originates in the custom of recording saints' days and holidays on calendars in red ink.
9. The **red-light** district – that part of the town which is given over to brothels and prostitution. The red light over the front door advertises the presence of prostitutes in the house.
10. to **see the red light** – to recognize approaching danger, the red light being a danger signal. 'When the doctor warned his patient that further drinking would damage his liver, the man saw the red light.' The phrase usually implies that the warning was heeded.
11. to be shown the **red card** – to be dismissed from one's job. 'The accountant was shown the red card for defrauding the company.' The phrase derives from football: a footballer is shown the red card by the referee for committing an offence after he has been warned and may be barred from playing for his side in future matches. cf. 'to be shown the **yellow card' 18/11**.
12. to be **in the red** – to have an overdraft, to be in debt. 'Oh, dear, I am overdrawn again. I hate being in the red.' The idiom originated in the banks' custom of showing the amount overdrawn in red type. Overdrafts are

shown in black today. cf. 'to be **in the black' 21/1**.

1. a **redneck** (American colloquialism) – a coarse, insensitive person.

BLUE

2. to **blue one's money** – spend money wildly. 'Peter has blued all the money you gave him on gambling and drink.'
3. to **look/feel blue** – to look/feel depressed or discontented. 'Now my girlfriend has left me, things are looking blue.' Blue is associated with gloom and depression in such expressions as having the blues, feeling blue, a fit of the blues.
4. in a **blue funk** – in a state of cowardly fear. 'John is in a blue funk about fighting Jackson in the boxing tournament tomorrow.' The word 'funk' is a slang word first used by an Oxford undergraduate in the eighteenth century. The word probably comes from Flemish 'fonck', meaning agitation, alarm.
5. **once in a blue moon** – extremely rarely, only once in a life-time. 'What does it matter what your uncle thinks of you? He only visits you once in a blue moon.'
6. to appear **out of the blue** – to arrive unexpectedly, usually after a long absence. 'My brother suddenly appeared out of the blue yesterday. We hadn't seen him for years and had given him up for dead.'

   a **bolt from the blue** – some unexpected bad news. 'We had no idea that their marriage was breaking up. The news came like a bolt from the blue.' A bolt was originally an arrow from a cross-bow, and is probably derived from Latin 'catapulta'. 'Out of the blue' meant out of a blue sky; hence, a blow struck without warning.
7. **to make the air turn blue** – to give vent to one's rage by swearing violently. 'When the engineer heard that his plans had been rejected, he fairly made the air turn blue.'
8. to shout/scream **blue murder** – to protest most violently at an injustice. 'If you take away the baby's toy, he'll shout blue murder.'
9. to talk, argue, complain, protest, etc., until you are **blue in the face** – to make a huge but vain effort to win a person's agreement. 'You can argue with Harry until you are blue in the face, but you will never get him to change his mind.' 'Until you are blue in the face' means 'for ever'. cf. **'until the cows come home' 58/4**.
10. **blue riband/ribbon** – the blue riband was an accolade awarded to the ship that made the fastest crossing of the Atlantic. Riband and ribbon are etymologically the same word.
11. a **blue-stocking** – a woman who is more interested in learning and an academic career than in marriage and bringing up children. 'I don't want to go out with that blue stocking. She is only interested in books!' The phrase has a derogatory meaning and dates back to the 1750s, when Mrs Montagu gave parties for literary reading and discussions instead of card-playing. These parties were also attended by men, who wore blue worsted stockings instead of black silk ones.
12. **blue blood / blue-blooded** – of the nobility or aristocracy. The phrase is of Spanish origin.
13. **men/boys in blue** – the police, from the colour of their uniform.
14. **a blue-eyed boy** – a boy/young man who has been singled out for special favours by someone in authority. Derogatory, since it implies that he has won favour by flattery and tale-bearing. 'Roger is Smith's blue-eyed boy; he can do no wrong.'

1. a **true blue** – one whose loyalty can always be counted on.
   a **true blue Conservative** – a person who holds strong Conservative convictions.
2. to **be a blue / get one's blue** – to represent Oxford or Cambridge University at games or sports. Dark blue stands for Oxford, and light blue for Cambridge.
3. to **blue pencil** – to censor. 'Most of my report on the treatment of the political prisoners was blue pencilled by the authorities.'
4. a **blue film** – a pornographic film, so called after the brothels of pre-revolutionary China which were painted blue outside to advertise the presence of prostitutes within.

GREEN

5. to **be green** – to be inexperienced or untried, from which comes the phrase 'to **be as green as grass'** – to be naïve, totally inexperienced in the ways of the world. 'You cannot expect Mary to do business with such people. She is only eighteen and as green as grass.'
6. to be **green with envy** – to feel extremely envious. 'If you buy that car, you'll make your friends green with envy.' At one time, a greenish complexion was believed to indicate jealousy. Shakespeare expresses the same idea in *Othello*: 'Beware of jealousy, it is a green-eyed monster' (III, iii, 165).
7. to have **green fingers** – to be blessed with luck in the growing of plants and flowers. 'She has green fingers! Everything she plants turns out well.'
8. a **green old age** (literary) – an old age in which a person's mental and physical powers are still strong and vigorous. 'I hope she will live to a green old age.' cf. 'a **ripe old age' 38/9**.
9. to **give the green light to** – to give permission to go ahead; to encourage or approve an enterprise. 'The boss has given us the green light. We can make a start on the project straight away.'

YELLOW

10. to **be yellow** – to be cowardly. Yellow is the traditional symbol of cowardice. 'You don't want to fight, do you? You are yellow.' cf. 'to be **yellow-livered' 114/5**.
    to **show a yellow streak** – to show cowardice.
11. to be shown the **yellow card** – to receive a warning that disciplinary action will be taken if an offence is repeated. 'I was shown the yellow card by the manager for coming in late to work.' The phrase derives from football: a player is shown the yellow card by a referee for committing an offence. cf. 'to be shown the **red card' 16/11**.

WHITE

12. **whiter than white** – too pure to be true, hypocritical.
    a **whited sepulchre** – innocent and pure in appearance, but dirty and corrupt within. An allusion by Jesus Christ to the hypocrisy of the Pharisees (Matthew XXIII, 27). Jesus meant that one should judge someone by his inner self, not by his outward appearance. (Tombs in biblical times were whitened to make them conspicuous.)
13. **lily white** – of great purity and delicacy.
14. a **white wedding** – a wedding in church, so called because the bride is dressed in white, the symbol of chastity.
15. to **white-wash** – to exonerate someone

by ignoring the evidence against him. 'It's no good complaining to the Post Office about the telephone engineer. They will only white-wash him.'

1. to **bleed** someone **white** – to extort all of someone's money, to overcharge grossly for a service. 'Why do you let Thompson blackmail you like this? He has bled you white!'
2. a **white lie** – a harmless or well-intentioned lie. This is generally not considered morally wrong because the motive is to spare the feelings of the person lied to. 'It is better to tell a white lie than to lose a friend.'
3. as **white as a sheet** – in a state of very great fear. 'Have you seen a ghost? Your face is as white as a sheet.'
4. **white heat** – the most intense energy, dynamic expansion. 'The white heat of the technological revolution' (the slogan of the Labour Party in the General Election of 1964).
5. to show the **white feather** – to act in a cowardly way. In the Great War of 1914–18, young women used to seek out men who were dressed in civilian clothes and place a white feather in their coats in order to humiliate them for not having enlisted.
6. to **hang out / show the white flag** – when approaching the enemy, you show the white flag to indicate (1) that you have come to negotiate a peace and your mission is a peaceful one (it is an unwritten law that the enemy will not fire at you) or (2) that you wish to surrender and have no desire to continue resistance.
7. 'Hold your fire until you see **the whites of their eyes**' – wait until the last possible moment before firing on the enemy. Fire is at its most effective when delivered at maximum proximity to the enemy.
8. **white slave traffic** – the selling of girls into prostitution. This is often effected by luring them abroad with promises of employment in night clubs and cabarets, and then cancelling their contracts or withholding their wages.
9. a **white elephant** – a very big and useless possession which costs a lot of money to maintain and may prove to be a source of financial ruin. 'You have bought yourself a white elephant: this house is far too isolated. No one will stay here and the upkeep will ruin you.' A king of Siam is said to have given white elephants to his enemies in order to ruin them.
10. **white horses** – white waves, so called because they appear to be galloping forward on to the shore like horses.
11. a **white Christmas** – a Christmas when snow has fallen and the countryside is white.
12. a **white-collar worker** – the professional or office worker who wears a shirt with a white collar, as opposed to the manual or factory worker who wears overalls.
13. **white man's burden** – a phrase from Rudyard Kipling. He meant that the white colonialist has the duty and responsibility to educate and protect the primitive peoples. Not unnaturally, the phrase has aroused much resentment among coloured people.
14. **white trash** – white people living in the Southern States of America after the Civil War who were as destitute as the blacks, and were treated with the same contempt.

WHITE AND BLACK

15. **white or black?** – with milk or without (in coffee).
16. **in black and white** – reduced to writing. Unless this has been done, some agreements are unenforceable in law. 'If you come to any agreement

with him, be sure to get it in black and white; you can't trust him.'

1. to **see** (everything) **in black and white** – to characterize everything and everyone as either very good or very bad, without any intermediate qualities.
2. to **swear black is white** – to perjure oneself or swear any falsehood, no matter how glaring.
3. **two blacks don't make a white** – two wrongs don't make a right. 'Just because Haines has cheated you, that's no reason why you should cheat his daughter; two blacks don't make a white.'

BLACK

4. **black and blue** – very badly bruised. 'The muggers beat the old woman black and blue.'
5. things are **looking black** – the prospects are very bad.
6. **black looks** – angry or revengeful looks. 'I got some black looks from the shopkeeper when I cancelled my order.'
7. to look **on the black side** – to see everything in a pessimistic light, to have gloomy forebodings.
   to be in a **black mood** – to be very depressed. 'George has been in a black mood ever since he lost his job.'
8. to **blacken** someone's **character** – to make someone appear worse than he really is by exaggerating his faults. 'Since you have blackened Miles' character, I shall give him the opportunity of defending himself.'
9. to be on the **black list** – to be on a list of persons under suspicion, who have committed crimes, or incurred the disapproval of the authorities. cf. **'to blackball' 21/7**.
10. **black art** – Satanic or devilish practices.
11. **black mass** – a travesty of the Christian Mass celebrated by practitioners of black magic and members of a Satanic cult.
12. the **black sheep (of the family)** – a member of the family who has disgraced himself, one whose name is generally not mentioned in the family circle.
13. the **Black Country** – the industrial Midlands of England, formerly discoloured by soot from its many open chimneys.
14. a **blackleg** – someone who continues to work during a strike in defiance of his union's instructions; hence **blackleg labour**, workers who refuse to come out when a strike has been called and who cross the picket lines to get to their work.
15. a **black eye** – an eye that is bruised and swollen as the result of a blow or a collision.
16. a **black-out** – (1) a sudden loss of consciousness. 'The accused told the judge that he couldn't remember what happened next because at that moment he had a black-out.' (2) concealing all source of light (in wartime) (3) total loss of electric power in a district.
17. a **black comedy** – a story or play in which the theme is sad or tragic, but the treatment is comic.
18. a **black economy** – that part of a country's economy which is carried on without the knowledge of the authorities for the purpose of avoiding tax. 'Despite the efforts of the government, the black economy continues to grow.'
19. to **black** (goods) – to refuse to handle goods coming from a source which has incurred the disapproval of the trade union responsible for their carriage. Such goods are said to be 'blacked'.
20. the **black market** – illegal buying and

selling of products that have been rationed by the government.

1. to be **in the black** – to be in credit. 'After making losses for the last six years, we are at last in the black.' cf. **'in the red' 16/12**.
2. to be **in** someone's **black books** – to have incurred the strong disapproval or enmity of someone. 'The boy was in the teacher's black books for having been disobedient.'
3. the **blackboard jungle** – lawlessness and violence in the classroom, with the pupils threatening and defying the teacher. (The term has been imported from America.)
4. as **black as thunder** – in a rage or fury. 'When I stood up to him, his face went as black as thunder.'
5. **black ice** – a layer of ice on the road which is invisible and therefore very dangerous.
6. **Black Power** – a militant organization of black people that uses force in furtherance of its struggle against the white establishment.
7. **to blackball** – to vote against a person's election to an organization when admission has to be by unanimous vote of its members. A white ball is dropped into the ballot box to signify a member's acceptance of the candidate, and a black ball, his rejection. cf. 'to be on the **black list' 20/9**.

BROWN

8. to be as **brown as a berry** – to be pleasantly tanned by the sun. 'The children are as brown as berries after three weeks at the seaside.'
9. to be **browned off** – to be bored, disgruntled. 'I am browned off with this place – there's nothing to do.'
10. to be in a **brown study** – to be in a reverie, a dreamy, distracted state of mind, unaware of one's surroundings.

GREY

11. **a grey-beard** – an old man. Often used in a derogatory sense. 'I don't want to spend my holiday with a lot of grey-beards!'
12. to **grow grey** (in the service) – to remain in one occupation (usually the army, navy or a government department) for most of one's working life.
13. **grey matter** (colloquial) – the brain. 'Alan hasn't got much in the way of grey matter, but intelligence isn't everything.' The phrase comes from the fact that the active part of the brain is coloured grey.
14. a **grey area** – an indeterminate area between two branches of learning, not covered by either, a kind of intellectual no man's land. 'Philosophy is the grey area between science and religion.'

PURPLE

15. Purple symbolized the monarchy and high rank in ancient Greece, the Roman Emperors, Consuls, Magistrates and Generals being dressed in purple robes. Hence there are a number of idioms derived from purple: (1) to be **born in/to the purple** – to be born the child of a king. (2) to **marry into the purple** – to marry a king or prince. (3) to be **raised to the purple** – to be created a cardinal in the Roman Catholic Church.
16. **purple passages/patches/prose** – passages in a book written in a florid, ornate style, contrasting with the style of the rest of the work, such as is to be found in the writings of Gibbon, Macaulay, Pater, Burke and sometimes Churchill.

SCARLET

17. a **scarlet woman** – a woman notorious for her many seductions of men; a

whore. The scarlet woman was seen by St John in a vision (Revelation XVII, 3–4).

PINK

1. to be **tickled pink** – to be very much amused, to relish a comical situation. 'He was tickled pink at the idea of taking a month's holiday at the expense of his company.'
2. the **pink of perfection** – sheer perfection, perfect to the smallest detail. 'Her skating was marvellous – graceful, elegant and stylish – the pink of perfection!'
3. in the **pink of condition / in the pink** – at peak fitness, often used in reference to athletes, racehorses or greyhounds.
4. a **pink socialist** – one who is less extreme than a full-blooded socialist. Sometimes used in contrast to a 'conviction socialist', and has largely been replaced by Labour Moderate.
5. **pink elephants** – frightening hallucinations experienced during withdrawal from alcohol, when the patient is suffering an attack of delirium tremens (D.T.s) and thinks that he sees pink elephants or other impossible objects in the room.
6. to **pink** – a swordsman was 'pinked' when he was pricked just deep enough to draw blood. The pinking was often regarded as an initiation ceremony.

GOLDEN (see also GOLD in Chapter 31)

7. a **golden opportunity** – a wonderful opportunity that may never recur.
8. the **golden rule** – a wise rule, the best rule. 'Never to let yourself be rushed into a decision you may afterwards regret is a golden rule.' The Golden Rule is found in Leviticus XIX, 34: 'do unto others as you would like them to do to you'.
9. a **golden handshake** – a lump-sum of money paid to a retiring director or manager, or to a redundant worker.
10. **golden opinions** – the highest praise. 'Peter's first book won golden opinions from the critics.'
11. a **golden boy** – a young man idolized for an outstanding skill, usually in sport, or for his good looks. 'Boris Becker, the youngest player ever to have won the men's singles at Wimbledon, was the golden boy of tennis in 1985.'
12. The **Golden Age** – (1) the first of the four ages when men were happy and innocent, the other three being the Silver, Bronze and Iron; (2) the finest period in a country's history and literature. 'The seventeenth century was the Golden Age of France.'
13. the **golden mean** – moderation in all things, a principle advocated by the Epicureans, a philosophic sect in Ancient Greece.
14. to worship the **golden calf** – to worship money, to subordinate everything else to mercenary considerations. The reference is to the wrath of God at the worship by the children of Israel of false idols (Exodus XXXII).
15. a **Golden Jubilee** – celebration of the fiftieth anniversary of an important event, such as the 50 years of Queen Victoria's reign in 1887.

    Golden wedding – the fiftieth anniversary of the wedding day.

SILVER

16. a **Silver Jubilee** – celebration of the twenty-fifth anniversary of an important event, such as the twenty-fifth year after the accession of George V, in 1935.

Silver wedding – the twenty-fifth anniversary of the wedding day.

1. the **silver screen** – the cinema. 'Valentino was one of the earliest stars of the silver screen.'

2. a **silver / silvery tongue** – eloquence, persuasiveness and charm.

3. **born with a silver spoon in one's mouth** – born into a wealthy family, with all the advantages that that can give a child. 'I have to work for my living; I wasn't born like you with a silver spoon in my mouth.' The reference is to the custom of the godparents giving the child a silver spoon at the christening.

2. ELEMENTS

ELEMENT

1. **in one's element** – in the conditions best suited to a person's tastes or abilities, enjoying oneself enormously. 'The sergeant-major is in his element drilling the young recruits.'
2. to **brave the elements** – to defy very bad weather. Used facetiously to mean simply going out in the rain. 'Well, I suppose I had better brave the elements or I shall miss my train.'

AIR

3. to vanish/disappear **into thin air** – to disappear completely without leaving any trace. 'We used to see a lot of our next-door neighbours, then one day, without any warning, they vanished into thin air.'

   out of thin air – out of nothing at all. 'Where do you imagine I can find £500 – out of thin air? I'm not a magician!'
4. you could **cut the air/atmosphere with a knife** – to sense at once a state of nervous tension, resentment or suppressed anger. 'When I went into the dining-room, there was an uncomfortable silence; you could have cut the air with a knife.'
5. to **air one's views** – to express one's opinions very freely, often in inappropriate situations. 'When we visit Aunt Mary, I hope you won't air your views the way you did last time. You will only annoy her if you do.'
6. to **put on airs / give oneself airs** – to behave as if one were socially superior to other people. 'She had better not give herself airs when she comes to live with us. My wife won't like it.' cf. **'airs and graces' 25/3**.
7. **airy-fairy** – lofty and impractical. 'Jean wouldn't have these airy-fairy ideas if she had to work for a living.'
8. **a fresh-air fiend** – a fanatical believer in the importance of fresh air to one's health. 'My father was a terrible fresh-air fiend. Whenever he came into a room, he would throw all the windows wide open.'
9. **hot air** – bombastic nonsense. 'Don't take any notice of Hammond's letters; they are nothing but hot air.'
10. to **clear the air** – to remove any previous misunderstanding by open and frank discussion. 'I'm so glad we've had this talk, Irene; it has really cleared the air.'
11. to **give public airing** to something – to raise a question publicly so that the facts may be fully disclosed and debated.
12. **on/off the air** – to broadcast / to cease broadcasting. 'The first time I went on the air, I thought I would be terribly nervous, but when the time came I was perfectly all right.'
13. **castles in the air** – dreams or hopes that will never be realized. 'I am afraid that all Tom's schemes will come to nothing; they are just castles in the air.' cf. **'castles in Spain' 186/8** and **'pie in the sky' 160/15**, which mean the same.
14. to **walk/dance on air** – to be in a state of exaltation. 'Since Simon and Lilian have got engaged, they have been walking on air.'
15. to **go up in the air** – to become furiously angry. 'My parents went up in the air when I told them that I wanted to move out into a flat.' cf. 'to **fly off the handle' 156/8**.
16. **in the air** – of plans, undecided, uncertain. 'We haven't made up our minds

yet where we are going to live; our plans are still in the air.'

1. something **in the air** – rumours that something important is going to happen. 'The clerks were whispering together in the office today; something is in the air.'
2. **as free as (the) air** – without any burden or obligation. 'Now that I have passed my exams, I feel as free as the air and can do whatever I like.'
3. **airs and graces** – affected manners which are intended to impress other people. 'I have never met your sister before; does she always give herself such airs and graces?' cf. 'to **put on airs' 24/6**.

WATER

4. to **water down** – to soften (the language or tone), to dilute. 'You'll have to water down your article if you want me to publish it. At present the wording is far too strong.' Alcoholic drinks can be watered down by the addition of water.
5. to be **on the (water) wagon** (colloquial) – to abstain from alcohol, usually on doctor's orders. 'Thank you very much, but I'm on the water wagon; I'll have an orangeade.'
6. a **watershed** – a decisive turning-point. 'The general elections in 1979 and 1983 were a watershed in Britain's post-war history.' The watershed is the line which separates waters flowing into different river basins or seas.
7. **water-tight** – irrefutable. The analogy is with water-tight clothing or water-tight shoes which protect the wearer from the water, just as a water-tight alibi protects the accused from conviction or a water-tight case admits of no doubt.
8. to pour **oil on troubled waters** – to resolve a quarrel by the exercise of tact and diplomacy. 'Mandy and Ned do nothing but quarrel. What a pity Uncle Tom isn't here to pour oil on troubled waters.'
9. to **pour cold water** (on a scheme or idea) – to find fault with, disparage. 'I wish Father weren't so negative; he pours cold water on all my ideas.' cf. 'to **put a damper on' 123/4**.
10. **dull as ditchwater** – uninteresting, boring. 'The play we saw last night was as dull as ditchwater.'
11. to **hold water** – to be valid, tenable; used with reference to theories, arguments or explanations; in fact anything that is open to debate. 'At first the prisoner's explanation seemed reasonable enough, but under cross-examination it didn't hold water.'
12. to **pass water** – to urinate.
13. to **tread water** – to be inactive or static. 'You've done nothing but tread water for the last six months. Isn't it time you took a job?' Literally, to keep one's head above water in swimming by moving one's hands and feet up and down. cf. **'mark time' 33/13**.
14. in **hot water** – in serious trouble. 'Jack has had to change his address. He's in hot water with the police again!'
15. **in deep water** – in difficulties. 'We are in deep water; we may have to sell the house to pay our debts.'
16. to **make a hole in the water** – to commit suicide by drowning.
17. of the **first water** – of the finest quality. 'Rubinstein was a musician of the first water, absolutely superb.' The phrase is derived from the custom of valuing diamonds according to their 'waters'. The 'water' is the colour or lustre of the diamond.
18. to **turn on the waterworks** – to weep.

'Susan can turn on the waterworks whenever she wants to.'

FIRE

1. a **fire-eater** – someone who is eager for a fight, who quarrels on the slightest pretext. 'What a fire-eater you are, Joe; you aren't happy unless you are fighting with someone, are you?' The reference is to the 'fire-eaters' at the circus.
2. to go **through fire and water** – to undergo any danger, for another's sake. 'You know I would go through fire and water, Elizabeth, to be with you.'
3. **'Fire away!'** – 'Say whatever you want to.' 'I am ready to listen to you now. Fire away!'
4. to **fire off questions** – to ask questions very fast, one after the other. 'They were firing off questions at me from all sides.'
5. to **hang fire** (of plans, arrangements) – to be delayed, to make no progress. 'Our plans to emigrate are hanging fire, but we are determined to go just the same.' The allusion is to a gun which is slow in detonating.
6. to **add fuel to the fire** – to aggravate someone's rage, to make someone still angrier. 'Philip added fuel to the fire by telling Jane that it was her own fault he had missed his date with her.' cf. 'to **fan the flames' 26/14**.
7. to **catch fire** – to arouse interest, excitement. 'Roger's play was well written and very realistic, but somehow it failed to catch fire.'
8. to have many/several/other **irons in the fire** – to have more than one interest at the same time. 'Don't worry if we have to close the shop; I have other irons in the fire.'
9. to **play with fire** – to take a needless risk, often by meddling in other people's affairs. 'I wouldn't advise Kate what to do when she and her husband quarrel; you'll be playing with fire if you do.'
10. to **pull the chestnuts out of the fire** – to get someone out of a predicament, often at some risk to oneself. 'I don't see why I should pull the chestnuts out of the fire for Andrew. He has only got himself to blame for the difficulty he is in.'
11. to **spread like wild fire** – to circulate very rapidly; said of scandal, gossip and news (particularly bad news). 'The news of the Minister's offer to resign spread like wild fire, although he hadn't discussed it with his staff.'
12. to threaten / call down **fire and brimstone** – to threaten dire penalties; generally in a humorous sense. 'Peter is threatening us with fire and brimstone if we don't pay him back the £10 he lent us by the end of the week.' Fire and brimstone is a biblical phrase, meaning the punishment in hell that awaits the sinner on his death.

FLAME

13. **an old flame** – a former girl/boyfriend. 'Was that an old flame you were speaking to on the telephone? You seemed very pleased to hear her voice!'
14. to **fan the flames** – to worsen existing ill-feeling by one's words or actions. 'The thieves seem to have taken most of Marion's jewellery, but you are only fanning the flames by exaggerating its value.' cf. 'to **add fuel to the fire' 26/6**.

EARTH

15. **down-to-earth** – practical, sensible; concerned with facts, not theories. 'I am surprised that a down-to-earth

character like Jim should suddenly start taking an interest in astrology.'

1. to **come down to earth** – to abandon one's dreams and take a realistic view of life. 'One of these days, Alan will have to come down to earth; no amount of theorizing will pay the bills.'

   to **bring** someone **down to earth** – to force someone to abandon his dreams and take a realistic view of life.

2. who/what/why/how, etc., **on earth** – whoever/whatever/whyever/however, etc. 'What on earth have you done to your face? Have you been in a fight?' The addition of 'on earth' to the interrogative is an emphatic way of asking a question and may express surprise or annoyance.

3. to **go to earth/ground** – to seek refuge in a hiding place. 'The film star eventually went to earth in a small, out-of-the-way cottage in Rottingdean.'

   to **run** someone **to earth/ground** – to discover someone in his hiding place after a lengthy search.

   These two phrases have been taken from hunting when the quarry 'goes to earth' or 'is run to earth'.

4. to **pay the earth** for – to pay a very large sum of money for something. 'You must have paid the earth for that mink coat!'

5. **no earthly reason** – no reason at all. 'There's no earthly reason why you should always follow your brother's advice.' This phrase is often used to express mild irritation.

6. not to have an **earthly chance** / an **earthly** – to have no chance of success at all. 'Swimming the Channel? In weather like this, she won't have an earthly chance of breaking the record.'

7. **like nothing on earth** (colloquial) – ghastly, awful. The phrase can be used with the verbs: look, feel, sound, taste and smell. 'You look like nothing on earth in that ridiculous outfit.'

8. to **move heaven and earth** – to do everything humanly possible to achieve one's aim. 'We have moved heaven and earth to get the squatters out of our house, but so far without success.'

MUD

9. a **stick-in-the-mud** – someone without initiative who never takes a chance. 'My husband has been working as a clerk in that firm for the last twenty years. He has no ambition – he's a real stick-in-the-mud.'

3. WEATHER

WEATHER

1. a **fair-weather friend** – a friend only for as long as things are going well.
2. to be/feel **under the weather** – to feel unwell, depressed or out of sorts. 'I'm afraid John was out celebrating last night and didn't get home till late, so he's feeling a bit under the weather this morning.'
3. to **make heavy weather** of something – to take excessive pains over a relatively simple task, to exaggerate its difficulties. 'He made terribly heavy weather of mending the puncture; it only took a few minutes when he finally did it.'
4. to **weather the storm** – to overcome a crisis, often financial. 'If we cut out all unnecessary expenses, we shall have a reasonable chance of weathering the storm.'
5. to **keep a weather eye open** – originally a seaman's phrase, meaning to be watchful – now used generally, as well as on board ship.
6. to **change like a weather-cock** – to be for ever changing one's mind, to be easily influenced. The weather-cock moves round according to the prevailing wind, and like the wind is always changing direction.

RAIN

7. to be/feel **as right as rain** – to be perfectly well again. The phrase implies that the speaker has been ill, or met with some accident, from which he has completely recovered. Often used with the object of reassuring the inquirer. 'Ann has got over her 'flu. She's as right as rain now!'
8. to **rain cats and dogs** – to pour with rain. The raindrops are compared with cats and dogs fighting one another.

   to rain in buckets has the same meaning: it rains so hard that the raindrops feel as though water were being poured out of buckets.
9. a **rainy day** – bad times when it will be difficult to make a living. 'Here's £50 for a rainy day. If things go wrong, it may come in handy.'

   to **put something by for a rainy day** – to save money against the day one is too old or ill to work, or has lost one's job.
10. **come rain or shine** – whatever happens. 'Come rain or shine, Caroline always visits her husband in hospital after her work.'
11. a **drop in the ocean** – only a tiny fraction of what is needed. 'We need £70,000 to clear our debts. I'm afraid the £5,000 Ted has offered us is only a drop in the ocean.' In this phrase, the 'drop' is a raindrop.

SNOW

12. **pure as the driven snow** – absolutely pure in one's moral character and behaviour. 'How Mary has changed! When she was a teenager, she was as pure as the driven snow.'
13. to be **snowed under** – to be overwhelmed. 'Since we issued our latest prospectus, we have been snowed under with inquiries.'

ICE

14. to **cut no ice** – to make no impression at all, to fail to produce the desired effect. 'Peter's success at school and college cut no ice with the selection committee. They were not impressed with academic attainments but wanted a man with practical

experience.' The idiom comes from the cutting of the ice with the edge of the skate.

1. to **skate on thin ice** – to introduce a subject about which someone is especially sensitive. 'You were skating on thin ice, weren't you, when you praised his brother's book. Didn't you know they have nothing to do with each other!'
2. to **break the ice** – to overcome someone's shyness or reserve, usually in a social setting. 'I didn't know how to break the ice with him. We were both shy and had nothing in common.'
3. to **put on ice** – to defer a project for the time being while preserving it for future use. 'I'm sorry, Alan, but we've had to put your plan on ice. We'll have another look at it in six months' time.'
4. the **tip of the iceberg** – evidence that a great deal more exists but remains hidden. 'The police have uncovered a bad case of corruption, but they believe it is only the tip of the iceberg.' Only a small part of the iceberg is visible, nine-tenths or so remaining hidden from view below the surface of the water.

CHILL

5. to **cast a chill on/over** – to depress or sadden. 'The news of her daughter's illness cast a chill over the party, and we all sat about in gloomy silence.'

SHIVERS

6. to **give one the shivers** – to embarrass. 'He is so uneducated; it gives me the shivers to see him showing off in front of the guests.'

FLOOD

7. **before the Flood** – a facetious comment on anything that is old-fashioned or out of date. 'Karen's room badly needs redecorating; the wallpaper looks as if it had been put up before the Flood.' 'Before the Flood' refers to before Noah and the Great Flood.

FOG

8. to be (all) **in a fog** – to be confused, nonplussed. 'When I saw Jack this morning, he was all in a fog about what to do next.'
9. to have not **the foggiest (idea)** – to have not the least idea. This is sometimes abbreviated in colloquial language to **'not the foggiest'**. 'I haven't the foggiest idea what you are talking about.' 'I haven't the foggiest either; I was only practising my French.'

RAY

10. a **ray of hope** – some grounds for hope. The negative form is often used – **not a ray of hope** – not the slightest hope. 'I am so sorry but the doctor didn't offer a ray of hope; it's very sad.'

CLOUD

11. **Every cloud has a silver lining** (proverb) – however unfortunate one's circumstances, there is always some consolation to be found. 'William has lost his job, which is a great blow to him, but his redundancy payment is very substantial. Every cloud has a silver lining.'
12. to **cast a cloud** over – to sadden, to fill with gloom, to mar one's pleasure. 'The news of her father's illness cast a cloud over Mary's honeymoon.'
13. to be **under a cloud** – to be the object of someone's suspicion. 'Gerald has

been under a cloud at the office ever since the petty cash went missing.'

1. **on Cloud Nine** (American colloquialism) – very happy, joyful. 'Since her engagement to Peter, Joan has been on Cloud Nine.' Cloud Nine was originally Cloud Seven, which was probably derived from 'the seventh heaven'. cf. 'in the **seventh heaven**' **218/11**.
2. to **be** / to **have one's head in the clouds** – to be out of touch with reality. 'It's no good asking him what to do. He has his head in the clouds.'
3. to have **a cloud lifted** from over one – to be cleared of suspicion, to end a period of depression, to be restored to favour. 'Now that the cloud over Richard has been lifted, he will be much happier at the office.'
4. **wait till the clouds roll by** – wait until the difficulties have eased. 'I am sure our difficulties are only temporary. We must wait until the clouds roll by.'
5. to **live in Cloud-cuckoo-land** – to live in one's imagination in a world that bears no relation to reality. 'If you think Judy's scheme would ever work, then the two of you must be living in Cloud-cuckoo-land!' From Aristophanes' comedy, *The Birds*, written in fifth-century BC. Athens, which depicts the building of an imaginary city in the air by the birds.
6. a **cloud no bigger than a man's hand** – a distant, insignificant threat, but one that may become dangerous in the course of time.

SQUALLS

7. **look out for squalls** – be on your guard against trouble. A nautical phrase, meaning a sudden gust of wind that may capsize your boat if you are not careful.

WIND

8. a **fair wind** – favourable conditions (for a project or enterprise).

   to **wish** something or someone **a fair wind** – to wish something or someone success. 'Neil Kinnock, leader of the Labour Party, wished the new legislation against football hooliganism a fair wind.'
9. to **whistle in the wind** – to talk to someone without obtaining a sensible reply. 'You might just as well whistle in the wind as talk to Larry.'
10. **the wind of change** – a new outlook, a fresh point of view. The phrase was first used by Harold Macmillan in reference to political developments in Africa.
11. to know **which way the wind is blowing** – to foresee the general drift of events, to know in advance what is likely to happen, to make a correct prediction. A variant is **'wait and see which way the wind blows'** – to await developments before making up one's mind. 'I shall wait and see which way the wind is blowing before committing myself.' Much used in political comment.
12. to sail **close to the wind** – to verge on the improper or the illegal, to stop just short of breaking the social code. 'The comedian sailed close to the wind. Some ladies in the audience were looking distinctly uneasy.'
13. to **take the wind out of** someone's **sails** – to embarrass someone by forestalling him, anticipating his actions. 'Counsel for the accused was about to address the jury when he had the wind taken out of his sails by his client, who blurted out that he was guilty.' Literally, the phrase means to take the wind out of another ship's sails by sailing close to it on its windward side. cf. 'to **cut the ground from under one's feet' 104/13**, 'to **pull the rug from under one's feet' 152/5**.

1. to **sow the wind and reap the whirlwind** (proverb) – to suffer catastrophic consequences for one's wrong-doing. 'The French aristocracy were punished a hundredfold for their callous neglect of the poor; they sowed the wind and reaped the whirlwind.' (From the Bible: Hosea VII, 7.)
2. to get one's **second wind** – to regain one's energy, to acquire fresh strength. 'After a bad start, Paul got his second wind and tried again.'
3. **in the teeth of the wind** – literally, moving against the wind, despite the wind, and hence figuratively against any opposition. The wind can be a strong hindrance to the progress of a sailing ship.
4. **in the wind's eye** – directly facing the wind.
5. to **get to windward of** – to attack from a favourable angle.
6. to **put the wind up** someone – to alarm or frighten someone. 'You put the wind up me, telephoning at three in the morning. I thought that something terrible had happened.'

   to **get the wind up** – to become alarmed or frightened. 'We all got the wind up when the bride didn't arrive at the church. We thought she must have changed her mind, but she was only late.'
7. to **throw caution to the winds** – to take bold action without considering one's own safety.
8. to **get wind of** – to receive early warning of imminent events, often from a confidential source. 'We got wind of his resignation a week before it was announced in the newspapers.' This is on the analogy of an animal that scents danger in the wind.
9. **there is something in the wind** – something is about to happen; one suspects that something important is going to happen without knowing what. 'The clerks in the office have been exchanging knowing glances for the last week, and there's been a lot of whispering going on. Something is in the wind.'

   What's in the wind? – What's up? What's going on? The same idiom as above in the interrogative form.
10. to **raise the wind** – to obtain the necessary finance.
11. a **windfall** – an unexpected stroke of good luck, for example a legacy from a distant relative. The literal meaning is fruit blown from the tree to the ground which can be eaten without being picked.
12. a **windbag** – someone who is talkative but incapable of action.
13. **long-winded** – verbose, using several words when one would have done. Here are some examples taken from a memorandum of the British Tourist Authority on the teaching of English, BLE/1980: 'an integrated programme of studies' *instead of* 'a curriculum'; 'suitably graded groups for teaching purposes' – *instead of* 'classes'; 'teachers with appropriate training and relevant experience' *instead of* 'qualified teachers'; 'transfer of students between one group and another' *instead of* 'promotion'.
14. to **tilt at windmills** – to fight imaginary enemies, hence to squander one's energy uselessly. 'Why do you always attack the landlords, Jack? There are hardly any private landlords left in London. You are tilting at windmills.' From Cervantes' *Don Quixote* (1605) in which an elderly knight attacked windmills, in the mistaken belief that they were giants who had imprisoned innocent girls.

STORM

15. **the calm before the storm** – a period of quiet before an upheaval or crisis.

1. to **take by storm** – to exert an irresistible fascination over something (a woman, city, country, etc.). 'Caruso took all America by storm.'
2. to **ride the storm** – to confront a crisis resolutely. 'I refuse to resign; I shall ride the storm, no matter how long it lasts.'
3. to **bow before the storm** – to submit to public indignation and protest. 'There was such an outcry when the Government put forward its proposals that it was forced to bow before the storm and withdraw them.'
4. a **storm in a tea-cup** – a violent agitation over a trifle. 'Father was furious with Geoff for doing the *Times* crossword puzzle before he came down to breakfast, but they were soon friends again. It was all a storm in a tea-cup.'

THUNDER

5. to **steal** someone's **thunder** – to divert attention from the person expecting it to oneself by adopting his methods. This happens when a minor actor overshadows the leading player, and receives the applause the other was expecting. 'Although Philip had only a minor role, he completely overshadowed the leading player and stole all his thunder.'
6. **blood and thunder** – violent, melodramatic. Almost always applied to plays and stories. 'There were at least six murders in that blood-and-thunder story.'

LIGHTNING

7. **like (greased) lightning / like a streak of lightning** – with the speed of lightning; so fast that you barely have time to see it. 'I've never seen anyone move so fast. He ran like lightning across the field.'
8. a **lightning strike** – a strike that is called without warning.

4. TIME

TIME

1. **high time** – the time has come when delay is no longer possible. 'It's high time you got ready or you will miss your train.'
2. to have a **rough time** – to be treated severely, to have a run of bad luck.
3. to have **the time of one's life** – to have a wonderfully happy time. 'James was dreading his military service but now he is in the army, he is having the time of his life.'
4. a **good-time girl** – a girl who lives for pleasure, a loose woman.
5. to be **born before/ahead of one's time** – to be born before people are in a position to appreciate one's true worth. Many important scientists and artists have died in obscurity.
6. **for the sake of old times / for old times' sake** – to honour past friendships, to do someone a favour. 'I've only got the afternoon between flights, but I had to see you for old times' sake.'
7. **time out of mind** – time immemorial, beyond human memory. 'Some are born to rule, and others are born to serve; so it has always been, time out of mind.'
8. **more times than I've had hot dinners** – more times than I can remember. 'I've shown tourists round the Houses of Parliament more times than I've had hot dinners.'
9. **behind the times** – out of date in one's ideas. 'Why, Grandfather, you haven't got a colour TV set. You *are* behind the times!'
10. to **take one's time** – to do something at one's own pace without hurrying. 'Our builder is taking his time, isn't he? He's been three days on that job already.'
11. to **fritter away** one's time, energy, money – to divide one's attention among a number of activities so that time, energy and money are wasted. 'If you hadn't frittered your time away on so many useless projects, you would have qualified by now.'
12. to **bide one's time** – to wait for the right moment to take one's revenge, or carry out a plan.
13. to **mark time** – to delay taking action until everyone else is ready; from the military command 'Mark time!' – to stamp the feet on the same spot without advancing. cf. 'to **tread water**' **25/13**.
14. to have a **rare time** (colloquial) – to have exceptional fun.
15. **time(s) without number** – many, many times. Often used to express impatience or annoyance. 'I have warned you time without number not to accept lifts from strangers.' Literally, so many times that they can no longer be counted.
16. **time is of the essence** – time is the most important consideration. A condition is sometimes made in a contract that time shall be of the essence, meaning that the work must be completed by a definite date, otherwise the contract is cancelled.
17. to be **pushed/pressed for time** – to have little or no time to spare, to be in a hurry.
18. **time is running out** – there is little time left. 'We have only three shopping days left till Christmas. Time is running out.' Time is here compared with sand running through an hour-glass.
19. to **live on borrowed time** – to regard each year exceeding the normal life-span as not one's own but for temporary use only.
20. **(dead) on time** – absolutely punctual.
21. **in the nick of time** – at the very last

moment, with no time to spare. 'I caught my aeroplane in the nick of time.'

1. **near her time** – approaching the moment when her baby will be born.
2. to **make up for lost time** – to work extra hard to compensate for time wasted.
3. to take **time off** – to absent oneself from work, often for a particular reason. 'I took time off this morning to visit my sister in hospital. I'll make it up this evening.'
4. to have **time on one's hands** – to have nothing to do, to be idle. 'Why don't you ask Tony round for a game? During the holidays he will have time on his hands.'
5. **How time drags!** – How slowly the time passes! What a boring time we are having!
6. to **kill (the) time** – to do anything, however trivial, to pass the time and so avoid being bored. 'We had an hour's wait, so we played cards to kill the time.'
7. to **serve one's time** – to work for the prescribed number of years in a service (army, navy, civil service, etc.).
8. to **do time** – to serve a prison sentence.
9. a **race against time** – a rush to get a task finished within a given time.
10. a **time-server** – someone who adopts the principles of his or her superiors in order to gain advancement.
11. a **time-lag** – the interval between a cause and its effect. For example, there is always a time-lag between the printing of money by the government and the resulting rise in prices.
12. **time-consuming** – requiring a great deal of time. 'It was time-consuming work, going through all the Jessops in the telephone directory, but we tracked him down in the end.'
13. a **question/matter of time** – sooner or later. 'It's only a question (or matter) of time before you are caught!'
14. **in the fullness of time** – at the proper time, in the end. 'In the fullness of time, your contribution to physics will be recognized; have patience and do not despair.'
15. to **have no time for** – to disapprove strongly of. 'I have no time for people who preach equality and then take their holidays in the Bahamas.'
16. to **make time** – to spare time, even when one is busy, for an additional duty. 'I know you have a lot to do, but you must make time for Henry. He's an old friend of yours.'
17. to **play for time** – to try to delay some undesirable action in the hope that conditions will meanwhile improve. 'They want their money at once, but if your uncle is coming back on Tuesday, I can play for time until then.'
18. to **march/move/keep up with the times** – to keep one's attitude and methods up to date. 'If we don't march with the times, our customers will go elsewhere.'

YEAR, YEARS

19. **year in, year out** – repeatedly over a long period of time. The phrase is often used of fixed habits. 'Year in, year out, Mr Masters would make his way to his local pub on the stroke of one.'
20. the **man of the year** – the most talked-of man of the year, in a good sense, cf. **'the man of the day' 36/10**.
21. to be **light years away** from someone – to have nothing in common with someone, to hold views that cannot be reconciled with the other person's. The analogy is with the time light takes to travel, implying a vast distance.

1. the **lost years** – wasted years that can never be made up.
2. **years of discretion** – the age at which a boy or girl is old enough to make moral judgements.

SEASON

3. **in season** – at the right time, at an opportune time. 'Why can't we have peaches? They are in season, aren't they?'

   out of season – at the wrong time, during the close season when game may not be shot.
4. a **word in season** – a timely piece of advice.
5. the **silly season** – the time of the year when Parliament is in recess, and newspapers, having little news to report, start idle theoretical discussions in their columns.

THE SEASONS: SPRING, SUMMER, AUTUMN AND WINTER

6. to **spring clean** – to clean and redecorate one's house, when the winter is over.
7. an **Indian summer** – a period of great happiness that comes late in a person's life. Literally, a late summer, a spell of warm sunshine in October. (Late summers are common in the West of the USA, which was mostly settled by Red Indians when this phrase was first used.)
8. the **autumn of one's life** – well into middle age, with the best years behind one.
9. England's **Winter of Discontent** – the winter of 1979 when strikes broke out all over England, resulting in much hardship and suffering, especially in hospitals and schools. The reference is to Shakespeare's *King Richard III*, I, i, 1: 'Now is the winter of our discontent.'

MONTHS: APRIL, MAY

10. to make an **April fool** of someone – to play a joke on someone on the morning of 1 April.
11. a **may-day warning** – an international call for help, a signal transmitted by ships and aeroplanes warning of impending danger. 'May-day' has nothing to do with the month of May but is a corruption of the French international signal, 'M'aider', meaning 'Help me'.

DAYS OF THE WEEK: MONDAY, FRIDAY AND SUNDAY

12. that **Monday morning feeling** – a feeling of depression when people have to return to work after the weekend holiday.
13. **Black Monday** – the first day of the school term when lessons are resumed.
14. **Man Friday** – a faithful servant and companion. From Defoe's *Robinson Crusoe*.

    Girl Friday – a personal assistant in an office, the phrase having been coined from Man Friday (see above).
15. not in a **month of Sundays** – not for a long time, far longer than is necessary; usually said in an exasperated or impatient tone. 'That won't be ready in a month of Sundays.'
16. one's **Sunday best** – one's best clothes.

DAY

17. **day in, day out** – day after day without any interruption.
18. **one of these (fine) days** – before long.

The phrase is used in predicting some (unpleasant) event. 'One of these fine days you'll get run over if you don't take care.'

1. an **off-day** – a day when one works badly. 'Pauline must have had an off-day; her typing is full of mistakes.'
2. it's **not my day** – everything is going wrong for me today.
   just **one of those days** – a day when everything goes wrong; said in a tone of resignation.
3. **not to have all day** – not to have any more time to spare for somebody. 'I do wish you'd tell me exactly what you want – I haven't got all day.' Used to express the speaker's impatience or exasperation (impolite).
4. **late in the day** – too late. The expression is often used as a reproach: 'It's a bit late in the day for you to cancel the booking; I've made all the arrangements.'
5. to **call it a day** – (1) to stop working, often said when the workers feel they have done enough for one day. (2) It can also mean that it would be better to put an end to an arrangement. 'I suggested to my partner that, since we didn't agree, we should call it a day.'
6. it's **early days** yet – it's too early to judge. 'Wait until you have got used to the work before you make up your mind. You've only been there a few days. It's early days yet.'
7. **'That will be the day!'** – used ironically to indicate a desirable event that will never occur. 'When Peter finishes his book, did you say? That'll be the day!'
8. to **make** someone's **day** – to delight someone, often in an unexpected way. 'Receiving a call from her daughter in Australia made Pamela's day.'
9. at the **end of the day** – ultimately, when the battle or campaign is over. 'At the end of the day, I am sure our policies will have been justified.'
10. to be the **man of the day** – to be the outstanding man of his time. cf. **'man of the year' 34/20**.
    the **man of his day** – the outstanding man of his time.
11. to **carry/win the day** – to triumph over one's adversary, to win the struggle.
12. a **field day** – a highly successful occasion when full advantage is taken of every opportunity, especially an opportunity to ridicule or punish an opponent. 'When Jennifer took over her father's firm, she had a field day dismissing her old colleagues on the office staff.' 'Your new book is full of mistakes; the critics will have a field day!' Originally a military term for allocating a special day to army exercises.
13. to have **had one's day** – to be past one's best.
14. a **hey-day** – the best days, the prime. 'The early nineteenth century was the hey-day of English romantic poetry.' 'hey' may be a corruption of 'high'. cf. 'in the **halcyon days' 70/4**, which has the same meaning.
15. **open as the day** – transparently honest, without subterfuge.
16. a **day's grace** – grace days are those allowed by law or by the creditor for the payment of a debt. Hence, an extra period of time allowed before being called to account. 'grace' in this idiomatic sense may apply to a number of days or months, or even to a year.
17. to **fall on evil days** – to live in poverty after having enjoyed better times.
18. in the **cold light of day** – in a mood of sober realism, as opposed to one of uncritical enthusiasm (frequently used with reference to ideas and plans that have been put forward). 'We discussed my idea at dinner and my

boss became terribly excited about it. However, in the cold light of day, he saw many objections to it.'

1. a **black day** – a day that has disastrous consequences. 'It was a black day for us when Harris joined the firm. He has done nothing but make trouble for us ever since.'
2. the **order of the day** – (1) the day's routine or programme. 'Swimming is the order of the day.' (2) It can also mean the way things are: 'Open prisons are the order of the day.'
3. **all in the day's work** – all part of one's normal duties. '"I am so grateful to you for giving my little girl first aid." "That's quite all right; it's all in the day's work."'
4. to **name the day** – to fix the date for the wedding.
5. **early-closing day** – one afternoon in the week, usually Wednesday or Thursday, when the shops are closed.
6. the **daily grind** – the monotonous routine of everyday life.
7. the **day of reckoning** – the time when one is obliged to answer for one's misdeeds. 'There will be a day of reckoning for what you have done to me!' The phrase comes from the biblical Day of Judgement.

DAYLIGHT

8. to **see daylight** – to gain an insight into a problem. 'After months of work, we are beginning to see daylight.'
9. **daylight robbery** – a shameless swindle. 'Charging you £200 for that simple repair was daylight robbery.'
10. to **frighten/scare the living daylights** out of someone – to terrify someone almost to death, by threats and intimidation.
11. to **beat the living daylights** out of someone – to give someone a severe beating.

YESTERDAY

12. not **born yesterday** – old or wise enough not to be easily taken in. 'You won't fool me with that trick. I wasn't born yesterday.'

NIGHT

13. to **burn the midnight oil** – to work late into the night.
14. a **fly-by-night** operator – someone who sets up business for only a short time in order to make a big profit, and then moves on.

HOUR

15. in the **small hours** of the morning – in the early hours of the morning.
16. at **all hours** – at an unusual time, often used in a censorious manner. 'The neighbours have parties at all hours.'
17. a **good hour** – at the very least one hour, probably more.
18. a **solid hour** – a full hour, often used when the time passes slowly. 'We waited for you a solid hour.'
19. to **improve the shining hour** – to make oneself useful. Used humorously: 'You can improve the shining hour by cleaning the car, Tom.'
20. the **question of the hour** – currently the most debated question.
21. in one's **hour of need** – at a time when help is most urgently required. 'Yes, £100 will be most useful. Thank you for helping me in my hour of need.'
22. the **rush hour** – the time of day when people travelling to and from their work are crowding the buses and trains.

MOMENT

23. **on the spur of the moment** – on a sudden impulse, without premeditation.

1. **in the heat of the moment** – at a moment when one's anger has been aroused. 'In the heat of the moment I suppose I might attack an armed burglar, but never in cold blood.'
2. the **man of the moment** – one who enjoys public acclaim, but only for a short time.
3. in an **unguarded moment** – in an indiscreet moment. 'In an unguarded moment Alison told me she had been convicted of shop-lifting many years ago.'
4. to **have its moments** – to be good, exciting, interesting, but only occasionally. 'The cruise was disappointing although it had its moments. I shall always remember our day in Madeira.'
5. The **moment of truth** – the moment of crisis when one learns the truth about oneself. 'I have often wondered how I would react if I saw a girl in the street being attacked by a gang of hooligans. For me, that would be the moment of truth.'
6. the **psychological moment** – the most propitious time, the best time to seize an opportunity. 'He was on the point of proposing to Karen when the telephone rang. The psychological moment had passed.'

AGE

7. to **come of age** – to attain the legal age of manhood/womanhood.
8. the **age of consent** – the age when a girl may lawfully consent to have sexual intercourse. The age of consent in Britain is sixteen. Below that age, her consent, even if freely given, is deemed by law to be unreal, and the man is guilty of the crime of rape.
9. at a **ripe old age** – very old. 'He lived to a ripe old age.' cf. **'a green old age' 18/8**.
10. to take/be **an age** – to take a long time over something, to keep someone waiting. 'What an age you've been, Simon!'
11. **it's ages since . . .** – it's a very long time since . . . 'It's ages since we met.'
12. to **be one's age** – to behave like a grown-up person. 'For heaven's sake, be your age, Martin! You are eighteen, not eight!'
13. to **show one's age** – to betray one's age by trying to look younger than one really is. 'She showed her age when she dressed like a teenager.'

DATE

14. to **date** something – (1) to establish the date an object was made, implying that it is the product of an earlier age. (2) Also used in reference to elderly people. 'His manners and speech date him.'
15. to **have a date** – to arrange a meeting with a member of the opposite sex. 'I've just made a date with Philip. We are going to the theatre tomorrow evening.'

CLOCK

16. to work **round the clock** – to work without ceasing at a task until it is finished. 'For that money I'm prepared to work all round the clock.'
17. a **clock-watcher** – someone who has lost interest in his work and does the absolute minimum required. 'Alan was an enthusiastic teacher when he started here, but now he is a clock-watcher – just like the rest of the staff.'
18. to **put the clock back** – to recapture an earlier period of time. 'You can't order young people about any more. Times have changed, and it is useless trying to put the clock back.'

1. to go **like clockwork** – to go exactly according to plan. 'We got the group to Edinburgh without the least difficulty. Everyone co-operated, and it all went like clockwork.'

BY-GONES

2. **let by-gones be by-gones** – let's forgive and forget.

5. LIFE AND DEATH

LIFE

1. a **walk of life** – an occupation or profession. 'I have travelled all over the world and have met people from every walk of life.'
2. **for the life of me** – even if my life depended on it. 'I can't for the life of me see why you should take your holiday in Yorkshire just because you were born there.' The phrase is used negatively, generally with 'can't' or 'couldn't'.
3. **as large as life** – in person. 'I had just posted a letter to James in Cologne – when suddenly there he was, as large as life, standing right in front of me!'
4. a **fact of life** – a truth which must be accepted, no matter how unfair or unreasonable it may seem. 'I'm sorry that you find the rule unreasonable, but there is nothing I can do about it; it is a fact of life.'
5. **not on your life!** – in no circumstances, certainly not. An emphatic way of refusing a request. '"If you are going to the theatre this evening, would you mind very much taking my aunt along?" "Not on your life!"'
6. **you (can) bet your life** – you can be absolutely certain. This phrase is often used ironically of people who are expected to act in a particular way, judging by what one knows of their past behaviour. 'You can bet your life that, if Edward comes, Mary will come too. She won't let him out of her sight for a second.'
7. **for dear life** – as if one's life were in danger. 'When the two burglars saw Patrick come into the hall, they ran for dear life out of the house and down the garden.'
8. **within an inch of one's life** – very near to losing one's life. Often used as a hyperbole. 'If I catch you stealing again, I will thrash you to within an inch of your life.'
9. **to the life** – an exact likeness, a living likeness. 'The portrait has been very well done; it's you to the life.'
10. to **come to life** – (1) to regain consciousness after a faint; (2) to gain in vigour and excitement. 'The first act of the play was rather dull, but in the second act it really came to life.'
11. a new **lease of life** – an opportunity to enjoy a happier/longer life. 'Robin's change of job has given him a new lease of life. He is his own master now, and looks ten years younger.'
12. to bear/lead a **charmed life** – to escape unscathed from many dangers as if one were protected by a magic power. 'Henry's companions were all injured but he returned without a scratch; he must lead a charmed life.'
13. the **life and soul** of the party – the person who brings the most sparkle and excitement to a party –'Miss Sims is so quiet and demure in the office that you'd never think she was the life and soul of the party last night.'
14. the **high life** – a luxurious, pleasure-loving way of life. 'Donald will find Bromley rather quiet after the high life he has been living in Bermuda.'
15. the **low life** – the life led by riff-raff, vagabonds, tramps and petty criminals.
16. to **see life** – to broaden one's experience by mixing with men and women of all types, including the immoral and dissolute. 'Tom should see life before he marries and settles down.'
17. to lead a **double life** – to lead the life of two distinct and separate people. The classic example is R. L. Stevenson's *Dr Jekyll and Mr Hyde* in which the

same man is depicted as a respectable scientist by day and a monster by night.

1. There's **life in the old dog yet** – I may not be as young as I was, but I am still full of energy. Often said by elderly people to counter suggestions that their powers are failing.

2. I can't do it to **save my life** – it wouldn't be possible, even if my life depended on it. 'I can't play tennis to save my life, but I enjoy watching it.'

LIVE

3. to **live beyond one's means** – to live in a style one cannot afford. 'No wonder the Howards have gone bankrupt; they have been living beyond their means for years.'

4. you **live and learn** – a comment on a new and unexpected fact. 'Who would have thought that Mr Saunders of all people would be arrested for shop-lifting? You live and learn.'

5. to **live up to** – to match someone else's standards. 'I don't want to go to the same school as my brother; I could never live up to him.'

6. to **live up to** one's **reputation** – to behave in a manner that may be expected by one's friends and acquaintances. 'The headmaster is certainly living up to his reputation. He is a real disciplinarian.'

7. to **live on** one's **reputation/name** – to rely on one's past achievements to earn a living. 'It's easy enough to live on one's reputation; the real problem is to win a reputation in the first place.'

8. to **live** something **down** – to repair damage to one's reputation by improving one's behaviour or skill in one's calling. 'The operation was a disaster; I shall never live it down.'

9. to **live a lie** – to be a hypocrite, to mislead people as to one's true nature. 'Mr Holmes had lived a lie for the past five years: by day, he worked as a parson in the parish of St Giles; by night, he frequented the night-clubs in the West End.'

10. **how the other half lives** – how people in a different class from oneself live. 'You should get around and see how the other half lives.'

11. to **live rough** – to live in uncomfortable conditions. 'However long you live rough, you never really get used to the hardship.'

12. to **live with** something – to put up with something unpleasant that one cannot rid oneself of, especially ailments. 'The doctor tells me that it is only a minor inconvenience which I must learn to live with.'

13. **Live and let live** (saying) – to be tolerant and not interfere in other people's lives. 'What does it matter to you who your brother spends his free time with? I believe in live and let live.'

14. to **live in sin** (old-fashioned) – to have a sexual relationship with a person to whom one is not married. 'When are Steven and Pamela going to get married, or are they going to live in sin for ever?'

15. **plain living and high thinking** – moral philosophy and tasteless food. 'After a week's plain living and high thinking at my cousin's, I'm in the mood for a good pub-crawl.'

16. to **live it up** – to spend money recklessly on one's own pleasure. 'I should have thought the Wallaces had better things to spend their money on than living it up in Paris.'

17. **alive and kicking** – very much alive. 'You needn't worry about Robert. He was alive and kicking when I saw him this afternoon.' The phrase derives from the kicking of the baby in the womb.

18. a **live wire** – a person with enormous

energy and initiative who is never inactive. 'If you want to raise money for the orphanage, you should put Bill in charge of the fund-raising; he is a real live wire.' Literally, a live wire is the wire that is charged with electricity.

DEATH

1. **sick to death** – exasperated beyond endurance. 'I am sick to death of his stories. He tells me the same ones every time I meet him.'
2. to be **tickled to death** – to be extremely amused. 'We were tickled to death when we heard Roger had come top in the exams after his terrible school report.'
3. to **bleed to death** (not of a person) – to collapse, in consequence of mounting costs, debts, etc. 'If we don't get fresh orders soon, we shall bleed to death. There is no money to pay the bills.'
4. to hold/hang on **like grim death** – to hold very tightly, as if one's life depended on it. 'The old man was hanging on to his briefcase like grim death. I wonder what he had in it.'
5. to **work** oneself **to death** – to exhaust oneself from overwork. 'We have worked ourselves to death and all for a pittance!' cf. 'to **break one's back**' **101/5**.
6. to **work** something **to death** – to overwork something so much that it can no longer produce useful results, such as when an idea loses its force through constant repetition. 'You've been saying the same thing in your publicity for twenty years. You have worked our idea to death; it's time you thought of something new.'
7. to **catch one's death (of cold)** (colloquial) – to catch a very bad cold. 'You'll catch your death if you go out into the cold night air after that hot bath.' Often used as a warning.
8. the **kiss of death** – an act of betrayal that effectively destroys a project, relationship or life. 'On the pretext of showing concern for her husband's well-being, Mrs Andrews gave him the kiss of death by telephone. Having established his presence at home, she sent two hired assassins to murder him.' The allusion is to the betrayal of Christ by Judas Iscariot by means of a kiss.
9. to be **in at the death/kill** – to be present at the climax, at the final phase. 'Everyone is expecting the chairman to resign this afternoon. Do you want to be in at the death?' The phrase is taken from hunting when the fox is caught by the hounds and killed.

DIE

10. to **die hard** – to resist change, especially changes in tradition, customs and ideas. 'The dogma dies hard that a student should master the grammar of a foreign language before starting to speak it.'
11. to **die in the last ditch** – to resist (something) to the very end, to fight to the death. 'If the government tries to demolish the Health Service, that is the last ditch in which many of us will die' (*Observer*, 8 January 1983).

DEAD

12. to **cut** someone **dead** – to refuse to return someone's greeting, to ignore someone with intentional rudeness. 'Mrs Hammond must be very angry with you to have cut you dead; she is normally so polite.'
13. to make **a dead set** at – (1) to make a vigorous attack on a person (usually verbal). (2) to make a strong bid for a person's affection. 'From the moment I entered the ballroom, Susan made a dead set at me; she ruined my evening.'
14. a **dead loss** – completely unproduc-

tive, useless. 'That course Pietro went on was a dead loss; after three months, he still couldn't speak a word of English.'

1. a **dead letter** – a law (or rule) which has not been repealed but is no longer enforced. 'The punishment for high treason under the Treason Act is death, but it has become a dead letter.'
2. **dead wood** – superfluous material. 'If you cut out all the dead wood, we might consider your book for publication.'
3. **dead-beat** – completely exhausted. 'After a day's shopping in London, I am always dead-beat.' cf. 'to **be whacked' 224/9**.
4. the **dead spit / spit and image of** – exactly alike. 'The twins are the dead spit of each other. How do you tell them apart?'
5. in the **dead hours** of the night/in the **dead of night** – in the middle of the night. 'We'll leave in the dead of night when everyone is asleep; no one will hear us.'
6. to refuse to **be seen dead in** / I wouldn't **be seen dead in** (colloquial) – to have a violent dislike of particular clothes. 'Just look at the price they are asking for that horrible dress in the window. I wouldn't be seen dead in that rag!'
7. **over my dead body** – against my strong opposition. 'If that man wants to marry Joanne, it will be over my dead body.'
8. **dead and buried** – an old quarrel or dispute that was disposed of and forgotten long ago. 'I thought that quarrel you had with Jack over the house was dead and buried.'

SPIRIT

9. to be **with** someone **in spirit** – to be thinking of someone with sympathy, anxiety, etc., without being with him/her in person. 'I wish you every success, Tina; I shall be with you in spirit.'
10. the **moving spirit** – the originator of an idea or project. 'I would like to know who the moving spirit is behind this idea. How stupid of him to put us on shift-work when business is so slack!'
11. to take something **in the right spirit** – to accept advice or criticism without bitterness or resentment. 'We have completed our report on the efficiency of your office staff and are sorry that they have not taken our advice in the right spirit.'
12. to **spirit away** – to remove quickly and secretly. 'I wonder what has happened to the vase Aunt Sheila gave us for Christmas. One of the children must have spirited it away!' The original meaning was to abduct or kidnap, when young Africans were 'spirited away' to the plantations in the West Indies.

HEAVEN

13. **heaven on earth** – perfect conditions in which to live or work. The phrase is often used to draw a comparison. 'Having laboured for three years on his first novel in a Glasgow slum, it seemed like heaven on earth to the young writer to work on his second in Nice.'
14. **in heaven's name!** – an interjection used to express impatience or annoyance. 'What have you done with the plane tickets; in heaven's name, you haven't lost them, have you?'
15. **manna from heaven** – something that arrives unexpectedly to help someone out of his difficulties. 'The spare can of petrol the farmer produced when he found Paul stranded on the moor with his motor-bike, was like manna from heaven to him.' Manna was the

name given by the Israelites to the miraculous food they found on their journey out of Egypt (Exodus XVI. 15).

1. to **stink/smell to high heaven** – to be a public outrage, a scandal. 'The behaviour of these officials stinks to high heaven; there should be a public inquiry.'

GOD

2. a **(little) tin god** – a self-important, dictatorial person. 'Now Sanders has been made manager, he's behaving like a little tin god.'
3. to **put the fear of God into** – to terrify. 'When Ralph takes me out in his racing car, he puts the fear of God into me.'
4. to **tempt God/providence** – to provoke God/providence by taking a needless risk, or by taking the same risk again, especially after a lucky escape. 'To go climbing again today after your lucky escape yesterday would be to tempt providence.' The phrase is almost always used with 'providence'.
5. **There, but for the grace of God, go I** – I have been just as blameworthy but, thanks to good luck, have escaped the consequences. Shakespeare expresses the same idea in *Hamlet*, II, ii, 561: 'Use every man after his desert, and who would 'scape whipping?'
6. to think that one is **God's gift** to – to overestimate one's intelligence, skill or attractiveness. 'Just because Joe is moderately good-looking, he thinks he is God's gift to women!' cf. 'to **fancy oneself' 121/2**.
7. **an act of God** – (1) a legal term for a catastrophe of nature that no one could reasonably have foreseen. (2) In ordinary parlance, what seems like an act of divine mercy. 'It was an act of God that everyone escaped from the aeroplane unhurt.'

ANGEL, ANGELS

8. enough to **make the angels weep** – so foolish that even an angel would despair. 'The way you have treated Helen is enough to make the angels weep.' The allusion is to Shakespeare's *Measure for Measure*, II, ii, 117: 'But man, proud man, / Drest in a little brief authority . . . / His glassy essence, like an angry ape, / Plays such fantastic tricks before high heaven / As make the angels weep.'
9. **like an angel** – with the utmost innocence and purity. 'Thomas sings like an angel in the school choir, but you should see him on the football field!'
10. to be **on the side of the angels** – to be on the right side in the struggle between good and evil; to have the right principles or opinions, from the speaker's point of view. 'We shouldn't be critical of George; with all his faults, he is on the side of the angels.' The phrase has been taken from Disraeli's speech (made at Oxford, 1864): 'Is man an ape or an angel? I, my Lord, I am on the side of the angels.'
11. a **guardian angel** – one who protects another's interests from the purest and most unselfish of motives. 'Margaret has done so much for us without expecting anything in return; she has been a true guardian angel.'

HELL

12. **all hell broke loose** – there was a state of uproar and disorder. 'If you tell the men that they won't be getting the increase in wages you promised them, all hell will break loose.' The derivation is from Milton's *Paradise Lost*, Book IV, 918: 'All hell broke loose.'
13. **come hell or high water** – whatever the obstacles. 'Come hell or high water, I am determined to succeed.'

1. **for the hell of it** – for no particular reason except to give oneself pleasure. 'Asked why he had beaten up a complete stranger, the young man replied that he had done it for the hell of it.'
2. who/what/how (etc.) **the hell** (slang) – an emphatic exclamation expressing anger. 'Who the hell do you think you are, talking to me like that!'
3. **hell for leather** – at a mad speed, recklessly fast. 'Jack was driving his motor-bike hell for leather down the country lane.
4. to **play (merry) hell with** – to aggravate or cause harm. 'This constant damp weather plays hell with my rheumatism.'
5. to **give** someone **hell** – (1) to make someone's life very unpleasant. 'I love my father dearly, but really, he does give me hell sometimes.' (2) to berate someone. 'The manager gave his team hell at half-time when they were losing 3–0.'
6. **to hell with** – to be not in the least concerned with. 'To hell with all your complaints; I shall play the piano all day long if I want to.'
7. **go to hell!** (colloquial and rude) – go away and leave me in peace. Often said in reply to offensive comments or threats.
8. **hellbent on** – absolutely determined, regardless of the consequences. 'I don't know what's the matter with Roger; he seems hellbent on killing himself with those stunts of his!'

DEVIL

9. **the devil's own job** – an immensely difficult task. 'Disentangling all this barbed wire is the devil's own job.'
10. **give the devil his due** – however bad a person may be, give him credit for any good quality he may have. 'Sergeant-Major Andrews used to bully the young recruits without mercy, but, to give the devil his due, he always treated me fairly.'
11. to have the **luck of the devil** – to have a great deal more luck than one deserves. 'Brian always invests his money in rubbish, but instead of going down, his shares always go up; he has the luck of the devil.'
12. to **talk/speak of the devil** – to be talking about someone when he suddenly appears. 'It's bad manners of Dennis always to keep us waiting. Shall we go? Oh, talk of the devil, there he is!'
13. **the very devil** – an appalling nuisance. 'Little Martin is so sweet most of the time but, when he gets cross, he can be the very devil.'
14. **Better the devil you know than the devil you don't** (proverb) – an evil never experienced may be worse than an evil one is already familiar with. 'I can't say I like Dr Knox, but if I change him for another doctor, I may be worse off than I was before. Better the devil you know than the devil you don't.'
15. **The devil looks after his own** (proverb) – a bad character never prevented a person from succeeding. 'That man has been in and out of prison and – would you believe it! – he has just won the football pools! The devil looks after his own.'

6. TREES AND FLOWERS

FLOWERS

1. **flower power** – a social movement of the 1960s, begun in the USA, which believed that love could overcome enmity and hate. Flower power rejects the laws and morality of contemporary society. 'Mr Tebbit, the Trade and Industry Secretary, blamed the end of National Service and the emergence of flower power . . . for the violence in our society' (*Daily Mail*, 25 July 1985).

   flower people – advocates of flower power.

2. the **flower of her youth** – the best of her young men and women. 'England lost the flower of her youth in Flanders in the Great War [1914–18].'
3. as welcome as **flowers in May** – to be welcomed with much joy and happiness.
4. **'Say it with flowers!'** – women often prefer the gift of flowers to protestations of love.

ROSE

5. the **English rose** – the delicate beauty of a young English girl.
6. **roses in her cheeks** – the tender, delicate pink colour in her cheeks. '"We'll get the roses back into her cheeks, Monica," the doctor told her.'
7. it was **roses, roses all the way** – a wonderful success in which everybody co-operated without any difficulty or unpleasantness.
8. a path **strewn with roses** – a career free from obstacles.
9. to **gather life's roses** – to savour the pleasures of life.
10. **'Gather ye rosebuds while ye may!'** – take your pleasures while there is still time. The reference is to Robert Herrick's poem 'To the Virgins to make much of Time'.
11. a **bed of roses** – a pleasant, enjoyable situation without any drawbacks or irritations. 'His job is a bed of roses compared with mine: short hours, a good salary and interesting work.'
12. It isn't a **bed of roses** – it isn't an easy life, the conditions are hard and disagreeable.

    It's not **all roses** – there are difficulties to be overcome, as well as pleasures to be enjoyed.

13. the **white rose** – a symbol of innocence and purity.

OTHER FLOWERS

14. the **primrose path** – the path of self-indulgence that ends in ruin. From Shakespeare's two references: 'the primrose path of dalliance' (*Hamlet*, I, iii, 47), and 'primrose way to the everlasting bonfire' (*Macbeth*, II, iii, 22).
15. **lilies and roses** – a clear, fresh, beautiful complexion.
16. **lily-livered** – cowardly. cf. **'yellow-livered' 114/5**.
17. to **paint/gild the lily** – to flatter.
18. a **shrinking violet** (facetious) – a shy, self-effacing person. 'Adrian expressed his views very freely at the meeting last night; he is not such a shrinking violet as we imagined.'
19. a **wallflower** – a girl who has not been invited to dance, but sits with her back to the wall in the ballroom without a partner.
20. to **lay up in lavender** – to treat something as very precious, carefully preserved for a future occasion.
21. **as fresh as a daisy** – full of energy.
22. the **lotus-eaters** – people who neglect

their friends and families in order to enjoy a life of luxury and idleness. The phrase is taken from Homer's *Odyssey*.

1. an **open sesame** – a means of gaining immediate access to influence and patronage. The word comes from the Greek, sesame, a tropical and subtropical plant that is grown in the East Indies.
2. to **grasp/seize the nettle** – to take drastic action to overcome an unpleasant difficulty. 'It's time you grasped the nettle and told your friend that you can no longer support him.'
3. **'The ivy can grow no higher than its host'** – a remark made by the French philosopher Descartes about critics: No matter how brilliant and learned a critic may be, he can never surpass the writer on whom he is dependent.

THE GARDEN

4. to lead someone **up the garden path** – to deceive, mislead someone. 'We never realized we were being led up the garden path until it was too late.'
5. **Everything in the garden is lovely** – everything is splendid, and there is nothing to worry about. (Often used to express the contrast between appearance and reality.) 'The food was perfect and the management were so friendly; everything in the garden was lovely until the waiter handed us the bill.'
6. in the **bloom of youth** / in her **first bloom** – in the full beauty of youth.

   past her bloom – past her best, when the beauty of her youth is beginning to fade.
7. to **blossom out** into – to develop very well. 'When Lloyd George became Prime Minister in 1916, he blossomed out into a statesman.'
8. the **pick of the bunch** – the best, the outstanding one in a group.
9. to **nip in the bud** – to frustrate a plan, plot, etc., before it has time to gather strength; to destroy at an early stage.
10. a **budding** writer/politician/artist – one who is just beginning to make a name for himself.

THORN

11. a **thorn in the flesh/side** – a constant irritant, a source of continuous annoyance. 'The boy was a thorn in his father's flesh for many years, always contradicting him and criticizing his way of life.'
12. to **sit on thorns** – to be in a painful or embarrassing situation; to be in constant fear of being found out. 'For many years he was sitting on thorns; he had never qualified as a doctor, although he cured many of his patients.'

    a **bed of thorns** – an extremely painful or embarrassing situation.
13. a **crown of thorns** – a legacy of trouble, a source of great tribulation. The phrase suggests that the troubles are pushed on to an innocent and unwilling victim. '"I have inherited a crown of thorns," the young king said sadly.' Taken from Matthew XXVII, 29.

THE FARM

14. to **reap a rich harvest** – to gain a splendid reward for one's efforts.
15. a **corny joke** – a hackneyed joke. cf. **'an old chestnut' 50/5**.
16. to **sow one's wild oats** – to experience youthful pleasures and excesses before settling down. 'What, twenty-two and still living at home! It's time he went abroad and sowed his wild oats.'

HAY

1. to **hit the hay** – to go to bed. 'I think I'll hit the hay now. I have to be up early in the morning.'
2. to **make hay from** – to take advantage of an opponent's mistakes. 'The Republicans may be able to make almost as much hay from the misdeeds of a few Democrats as the Democrats did from the fall of President Nixon' (from *NOW!* magazine). The origin is from the proverb: to make hay while the sun shines.
3. to **make hay of** something, to **make hay with** – to throw into disorder, to confuse, to make a mess of.
4. to **go haywire** – to go crazy, to lose control of oneself. 'When his cat was run over, Michael went completely haywire and wrecked the motorist's car.'
5. **like looking for a needle in a haystack** – to look for something that is impossible to find. 'Robert's office is in such a mess; finding your letter will be like looking for a needle in a haystack.'

STRAW

6. a **man of straw** – a worthless man, one without means or character.
7. a **straw poll / straw vote** – an impromptu, unofficial vote taken to test the direction in which public opinion is moving.
8. a **straw bid** – a worthless bid, one made without any financial backing.
9. to **draw straws** – to draw lots by picking straws of different sizes.
10. to **clutch at a straw** – to employ any means, however useless, to save oneself.

    A drowning man will clutch at a straw (proverb) – a desperate man will resort to any expedient, no matter how impractical or hopeless.
11. **not worth a straw** – worthless. cf. **'not worth a fig' 165/5**.
12. **not to care / give a straw** – a straw stands for something worthless; the expression **'not to give a straw for'**, or **'not to care two straws'**, means to place no value upon a person or object. 'I don't give a straw for his opinion.'
13. the **last straw** – beyond the limit; the breaking point. From the proverb: 'It's the last straw that breaks the camel's back.'
14. a **straw in the wind** – a slight indication of future developments. 'It may only be a straw in the wind, but she left half an hour after the dinner party last night. I don't think she is so keen on doing business with us as she was.'

CUD AND SEED

15. to **chew the cud** – to ponder, consider a problem from every angle, think over carefully and deliberately.
16. to **run/go to seed** – to deteriorate in one's habits and appearance, to become shabby. 'When I called on him this morning, he was unshaven and wearing an old, stained dressing-gown. I am afraid he has run to seed.' The reference is to plants which, instead of developing new shoots, only produce seeds and lose their beauty.
17. to **sow the seeds** of doubt, etc. – to insinuate doubt, often with the idea of starting something without being noticed. 'He set to work sowing the seeds of doubt in their minds by hints and innuendoes.'
18. **seeded** players / **seeds** – players ranked by the organizers of a tournament in order of merit, and drawn so as not to meet one another until the closing rounds.

    an **unseeded** player – one not so ranked who may win, contrary to the opinion of the organizers; an 'outsider'.

1. to **eat the seedcorn** – to spend one's capital, and so destroy the source of one's income. 'Mr Callaghan warned that if we sold our assets in the North Sea, we would be eating the seedcorn.'

CLOVER

2. to be **in clover** – to be in a comfortable situation, enjoying the best things in life without having to make an effort. From cattle feeding in a field of clover.

GRASS, REEDS AND WEEDS

3. to put someone **out to grass** – to retire someone compulsorily on grounds of age. The phrase derives from putting horses that are too old to work out to pasture.
   to **go to grass** – to retire on grounds of age.
4. to **hear the grass grow** – to have very acute hearing.
5. **Keep off the grass!** – don't intrude on someone else's sphere of activity.
6. **grass roots** – the ordinary folk, those with their origins in the soil. In politics, the grass roots of a party are the ordinary membership, as opposed to the leadership.
7. not to **let the grass grow under one's feet** – to waste no time in getting a task done, to set to work quickly, without waiting for other people's agreement.
8. the **turf** – the world of horse-racing.
9. to **turf out** – to oust a person from a position, physically eject.
10. a **broken reed** – a weak, untrustworthy person; someone on whom it would be folly to rely. 'If you ever found yourself in serious trouble, Alex would abandon you without the least hesitation. He is a broken reed.'
11. a **reed shaken by the wind** – someone whose opinions are swayed by the latest fashion.
12. to **grow/spread like weeds** – to proliferate very fast. 'There is a crazy demand for his products. His business will grow like weeds.'
13. to **weed out** – to eliminate the undesirable.

ROOTS

14. to **take root** – to grow, become established. 'The ideas of Karl Marx have never taken root in the United States or Germany.'
    to **have its roots in** – to stem from, to be caused by. 'All crime has its roots in the loveless childhood of the criminal.'
15. to **grow/put down roots** – to develop interests and friendships. 'We have grown too many roots here to emigrate.'
16. to be/stand **rooted to the ground/spot** – to be transfixed or rendered immobile through fear, astonishment or shock.
17. a **deep-rooted** habit – a long-established or chronic habit. 'It won't be easy to rid him quickly of such a deep-rooted habit.'
18. **root and branch** – in its entirety, without any exceptions being made. 'The old customs in China have been destroyed root and branch by the new regime.'

TREES

19. a **family tree** – a genealogical record in the form of a diagram. 'My family tree goes back to the Normans.'
20. **the tree is known by its fruit** – you can judge someone best by his actions; deeds are more eloquent than

words. The origin is from the Bible (Matthew XII, 33).

1. **up a tree / gum tree** – in great difficulty; unable to make any further progress.
2. **at the top of the tree** – at the top of one's profession.
3. to **bark up the wrong tree** – to accuse or blame the wrong person. 'Alison couldn't have stolen your watch. She was out all day. You are barking up the wrong tree.'
4. a **heart of oak** – someone loyal and brave on whom one can rely. 'You can always count on William in a crisis. He has a heart of oak and will stand by you, whatever the consequences.'
5. an **old chestnut** – an old hackneyed joke, one that has been over-used. 'His speech was full of old chestnuts. People in the audience groaned at each one.' cf. 'a **corny joke' 47/15**.
6. to **give the palm to** – to acknowledge as champion.
7. to **bear/carry the palm** – to signal one's triumph.
8. to **carry off the palm** – to win the victor's crown.
9. to **yield the palm** – to admit defeat, to acknowledge the victory of one's opponent.
10. **palmy** days – the days of one's triumphs, past glories.
11. to **look to one's laurels** – to be aware of a new challenge to one's supremacy.
12. to **rest on one's laurels** – to be content with past achievements without making any further effort.

BUSH AND HEDGE

13. to **beat about the bush** – to broach a subject indirectly, to delay coming to the point. 'Stop beating about the bush and tell me what you want.' A shooting idiom: the 'beaters' beat about the undergrowth in order to put the birds up.
14. to **take to the bush** – to withdraw oneself to the wild country, away from civilization. The 'bush' is an Australian term, meaning wild woodland which was originally inhabited by the Aborigines.
15. **bush-telegraph** – the rapid unofficial communication of news or gossip. 'Europe's bush-telegraph spread the news of the abdication crisis long before the British public got to hear of it.' Originally, the spreading of information by the beating of drums, etc.
16. to **hide one's light under a bushel** – to be modest about one's achievements or virtues. The reference is to Christ's parable: 'Neither do men light a candle and put it under a bushel, but in a candlestick' (Matthew V, 15).
17. to **hedge one's bets** – to reduce one's potential betting losses by betting on more than one result.

WOOD

18. **not to see the wood for the trees** – not to be able to make out the essential because of all the detail. 'You have put in so much unnecessary detail that one loses track of the story; one can't see the wood for the trees.'
19. to be **out of the wood** – to be out of trouble or danger. Often used negatively. 'Business is looking up, but there's still a lot of money to repay; we aren't out of the wood yet.'
20. to **touch wood** – a superstitious belief that after congratulating oneself on one's good fortune, one should touch wood in order to avoid supernatural retribution.
21. **against the grain** – against one's instincts, against one's inclinations. 'It

goes against the grain to rebuke a man old enough to be my grandfather.' Wood can be cut more easily if it is cut in the direction of the grain than across the grain.

LOG AND BRANCH

1. to **sleep like a log** – to sleep soundly, without stirring. From the idea of someone in a deep sleep lying absolutely still 'like a log'.
2. **as easy as falling off a log** – something that needs no skill or effort to accomplish. cf. **'as easy as shelling peas' 165/16.**
3. to hold out **the olive branch** – to make a peace offering. 'I thought it was time we held out the olive branch to Angela, so I invited her to dinner tomorrow. This quarrel has gone on long enough.'

STICK

4. a **dry old stick** – a dull, boring man, with very little to say for himself.
5. the policy of the **big stick** – the threat of force. From Theodore Roosevelt's speech on the need for America 'to speak softly and carry a big stick'.
6. to get hold of the **wrong end of the stick** – to misunderstand an explanation. The phrase is often used in reply to an unjust suspicion or accusation. 'You've got the wrong end of the stick; it was your friend, not I, who went through your things.'
7. to be caught **in a cleft stick** – to be forced to choose between two disastrous courses of action. 'Yvonne had promised to pay Susan's fine but then found she hadn't enough money. She would either have to let her friend down or sell her engagement ring; she was caught in a cleft stick.'
8. to **get the dirty/rough end of the stick** – to be treated unfairly, to bear all the blame.
9. to be **as cross as two sticks** – to be in a bad temper.
10. a few **sticks of furniture** – only a few pieces of furniture. 'Everything in the house had been taken except for a few sticks of furniture.'

LEAF

11. to **turn over a new leaf** – to repent one's way of life and make a fresh start; to reform. 'Each time he comes out of prison, Jack promises to turn over a new leaf – but he never does.'
12. to **take a leaf out of** someone's **book** – to follow someone's example. 'I am going to take a leaf out of your book and go into business.' Originally the phrase meant to plagiarize by taking a leaf, i.e. a page, out of someone else's book and making a copy of it.
13. to **leaf through** a book – to turn over the pages of a book without reading it thoroughly, in order to get a general idea of what it is about.
14. to **shake like a leaf** – to tremble with fear.
15. to **read the tea-leaves** – to foretell someone's future by examining the tea-leaves at the bottom of the cup. This refers to an old superstition that the tea-leaves have a hidden meaning for the drinker.

7. ANIMALS

ANIMAL

1. to **behave like an animal / worse than an animal** – a term of abuse for men of great villainy and cruelty, since animals are not credited with a moral sense. 'They have behaved like animals; not even the youngest children were spared.' A common variation of this phrase is **lower than the animals**.
2. a **political animal** – someone with a special talent for politics. 'The ancient Greek was a political animal.'
3. **animal spirits** – the exuberance and cheerfulness of youth that characterize a healthy body. 'He didn't mean any harm; it was only animal spirits.'
4. **animal passions** – what used to be called man's 'lowest instincts'. Often used in reference to lust and lechery.
5. a **rare animal** – an unusual person who may combine two contradictory features or interests. 'He was that rare animal, a scientist turned artist.' cf. **'a rare bird' 65/5**.

CREATURE

6. **creature comforts** – those luxuries which make life pleasant and enjoyable, especially on a material level.

BEAST

7. it's **the nature of the beast** – it's inherent in the character of the man, which will never change.
8. a **beast of burden** – someone on whom an excessive amount of work is imposed. 'I've become just a beast of burden instead of a wife to him.' The allusion is to beasts of burden like donkeys and camels which are used for carrying provisions.
9. **Beauty and the Beast** – a beautiful woman accompanied by a repulsively ugly man. A humorous phrase derived from the old fairy tale of 'Beauty and the Beast'.

PET

10. **pet name** – a special name expressing affection, such as 'Honey', 'Angel', 'Bunny', 'Kitten'.
11. to be **in a pet** – to be in a temper or ill-humour, when the cause of the annoyance is quite trifling. 'When we called on him, he was in a pet because his daughter was late with his breakfast.'

DOG

12. **Every dog has his day** (proverb) – everyone, however humble or unprepossessing, has his moment of glory. We all have our ups and downs; but no life, however bad, is entirely unsuccessful.
13. a **dog in the manger** – one who denies to others the pleasures he can't enjoy himself. From Aesop's Fables, in which the dog prevented the cows from eating the hay in the manger by lying in it and snarling at them, while not wanting the hay himself.
14. to lead a **dog's life** – to lead a thoroughly miserable existence.
15. to treat someone **worse than a dog** – to treat viciously. 'He is a cruel, callous bully; he treats her worse than a dog.'
16. **you can't teach an old dog new tricks** – it is difficult for the elderly to adapt themselves to new conditions, or to start learning again late in life. 'The young girls in the office soon learned how to use the telex, but I just can't

understand it. You can't teach an old dog new tricks.'

1. a **dog's dinner** (slang) – a horrible mess.
2. a **hang-dog air** – a shame-faced, woebegone look.
3. **give a dog a bad name and hang him** – once someone has acquired a bad reputation, it is almost impossible for him to shake it off, and even his most innocent actions will be misunderstood. 'He had a reputation for stealing, so when he handed in a £10 note at the office, he was suspected of having come by the money dishonestly. Give a dog a bad name . . .'
4. to **help a lame dog over a stile** – to help a struggling person. 'He lent me £1,000 to start up my business. It was good of him to help a lame dog over a stile.'
5. **any stick will serve to beat a dog with** – it is easy to find fault with a person if you want to; any excuse will serve your purpose.
6. not to have a **dog's chance** – to have no chance at all. 'He is so much heavier than you, you haven't a dog's chance against him, however cleverly you box.'
7. **love me, love my dog** – if you want to love me, you must put up with my faults, my friends and my relations.
8. **dog doesn't eat dog** – men of the same profession, school, etc., never make trouble for one another. 'It would be useless for you to appeal to the Law Society about your lawyer's behaviour. Dog doesn't eat dog!'
9. to be **top dog** – to dominate, to make oneself the master. By contrast, the **under-dog** – the loser in a fight, the inferior in strength. 'She always sympathizes with the under-dog, right or wrong.'
10. a **dog-fight** – (1) a fight between two people. (2) a battle between two aeroplanes. 'I don't want a dog-fight between the two of you, so behave!'
11. to be **in the dog-house** – to be in disgrace, usually with one's spouse. 'His wife isn't speaking to him. He has been in the dog-house since he came home from a party at four in the morning.'
12. a **dog's-body** – one who does the routine or mechanical work. 'When I was at Bader's, I was only a dog's-body; none of the work I did required any skill.'
13. **dog-eared** – said of the pages of a book which have been turned down or have curled at the corners through excessive use.
14. a **dull dog** – someone who has nothing to say for himself, whose conversation is always uninspired and boring.
15. a **dirty dog** – an evil character; but the phrase is often used humorously for a sly fellow who gets what he wants by dubious methods.
16. a **sly dog** – one who keeps his pleasures to himself, a man who is discreet about his vices.
17. a **gay dog** – a man who enjoys the company of women. 'Gay' has a pejorative meaning and is used today by some people as a synonym for homosexual. 'Gay' can, however, still be used in its original sense as it is here.
18. a **lucky dog** – one who enjoys undeserved luck. 'He isn't in the least good-looking or impressive, but all the girls fall for him – the lucky dog!'
19. to take a **hair of the dog that bit you** – to take more of the alcohol in which one has been over-indulging in order to cure a hangover. It was thought at one time that the hair of the dog that bit one was a cure for rabies.
20. the **tail wagging the dog** – the transfer of power from the leaders of a group to its least valued members. 'Instead

of the doctors giving the porters orders, we were telling the doctors what to do! It was a case of the tail wagging the dog.'

1. to be a **lap-dog** – to be pampered and over-protected. 'She never lets her son play with other children. She has turned him into a lap-dog.'
2. **dog-Latin** – inferior or degenerate Latin used by clerics, lawyers and doctors with an imperfect knowledge of the language. cf. **'pidgin English' 188/11**.
3. **dog-days** – the hottest weather. The phrase is a translation from the Latin 'caniculares dies' meaning the hottest days of the summer (in July and August). According to Roman theory, the hottest weeks of the year were determined by the rising of the dog-star Sirius which they believed contributed to the heat of the sun.
4. **don't keep a dog and bark yourself** – don't do your servants' work for them. There is no point in having servants, if you do their work.
5. to **call off the dogs** – to abandon an investigation when inquiries are leading nowhere. Huntsmen call off their dogs when they follow a wrong scent.
6. **sick as a dog** – horribly sick.
7. **dog-tired** – exhausted after a hard day's work. 'I was dog-tired after working the whole day in the garden.'
8. to **let sleeping dogs lie** – to leave well alone and refrain from stirring up trouble. 'You must have known that mentioning his ex-wife would upset him. You should have let sleeping dogs lie!'
9. **his bark is worse than his bite** – (1) bullies generally prefer bluster to fighting. (2) a person is not so unkind or fierce as he pretends to be.
10. the **dogs of war** – a term of abuse for war-makers, mercenaries and war profiteers. Its original meaning was the horrors of war, e.g. famine, killing and atrocities. Origin: *Julius Caesar*, III, i.
11. to **die like a dog** – to die without honour or dignity, to die in shameful circumstances.
12. to **go to the dogs** – to ruin oneself by licentious or degenerate living.

POODLE

13. **nobody's poodle** – someone with a mind of his own, one who is not easily led or persuaded to act against his better judgement. A poodle is commonly regarded as a foppish breed of dog, due perhaps to its mincing gait. Always used negatively.

PUP

14. to **sell** someone **a pup** – to swindle, to sell something under a false description. 'When we arrived at the hotel, we found we were paying twice as much as the other guests. The travel agent had sold us a pup.'
15. a **puppy / young puppy** – an arrogant or conceited young man. A cocksure young man who corrects his elders.
16. **puppy-fat** – plumpness that the boy or girl will shed on reaching maturity. 'She's a little on the tubby side, but it's only puppy-fat.'
17. **puppy love** – the love of a very young, immature person. cf. **'calf-love' 58/9**.

CAT

18. to **lead a cat and dog life** – used to describe a husband and wife who quarrel furiously with each other most of the time.
19. to **play cat and mouse** – to alternate harshness and leniency in one's treatment of a helpless victim, in the manner of a cat playing with a mouse.

When human beings indulge in this game, there is a strong element of sadism in the character of the dominant party.

1. to **put/set the cat among the pigeons** – to provoke quarrelling and dissension. 'You shouldn't have criticized the vicar in the local newspaper; now you've really put the cat among the pigeons!'
2. to **be catty** – to make spiteful remarks. 'I thought it was catty of her to ask at dinner whether Jim was doing better at school. She knows how sensitive we are about the trouble he has been in.'
3. a **cat-call** – a whistle indicating one's disapproval. 'There were so many catcalls from the gallery that the management were obliged to ring down the curtain.'
4. a **cat burglar** – someone who burgles houses by climbing up the drainpipe and entering by the window.
5. to **let the cat out of the bag** – to blurt out a secret. 'You let the cat out of the bag when you said you were pregnant.'
6. **like a cat on hot bricks** – extremely awkward and uneasy. 'He dropped in by accident at an ante-natal clinic and was like a cat on hot bricks while the exercises were in progress.'
7. a **cat-o'nine-tails** – a whip used for flogging delinquent soldiers, sailors and civilians for crimes of violence up to 1948 in the UK. The instrument consisted of nine thongs of leather which resembled cats' tails.
8. **no room to swing a cat** – a very small, cramped space. The original phrase was probably 'not room to swing a cat-o'nine-tails', and dates from the time when sailors were flogged on board ship. The floggings took place on the deck because the cabins were too small to swing a cat in.
9. **not a cat in hell's chance** – no chance at all. 'You haven't a cat in hell's chance of getting that job. There are half-a-dozen other men after it who are better qualified than you.'
10. **curiosity killed the cat** – excessive curiosity can lead one into trouble. A common rebuke by mothers to their offspring.
11. **there's more than one way to kill/skin a cat** – there is more than one method for achieving an object. If the more conventional method fails, one should try other methods.
12. to **see which way the cat jumps** – to remain uncommitted until it becomes clear which way public opinion is moving before coming to a decision.
13. to **bell the cat** – to attack a common enemy at great personal risk to oneself for the sake of others. The phrase is taken from Piers Plowman's fable of the mice who wanted to hang a bell around the neck of a cat.
14. **'Has the cat got your tongue?'** – 'Have you lost your power of speech?' A question often put jokingly to children who are shy.
15. to **be made a cat's paw of** – to serve as a tool for someone else. From Aesop's fable of the monkey which made use of the paw of his friend, the cat, for pulling hot chestnuts out of a fire.
16. **a cat may look at a king** – spoken by an inferior, meaning 'I have as much right to look at you as you have to look at me. We are both equal'. The remark can also be understood as a snub to the snobbish, viz.: 'However grand you may think you are, you can't stop me looking at you.'
17. to **grin like a Cheshire cat** – to grin widely, from ear to ear. From Lewis Carroll's *Alice in Wonderland*. Nobody knows where Carroll got the idea from.
18. **like the cat that swallowed the cream** –

looking very elated, very pleased with oneself.

1. **the cat's whiskers / the cat's pyjamas** – an American colloquialism for the very best. 'Now that he has beaten the champion, Paul thinks he is the cat's whiskers.'

2. a **wild-cat strike** – an unofficial strike, called without the approval of the trade union, by a number of individuals acting on their own initiative.

3. to **be a copy-cat** – to imitate someone else's behaviour. The expression 'Copy-cat!' is much used by schoolchildren.

KITTEN

4. **as weak as a kitten** – feeble, very weak. 'After her operation, she felt as weak as a kitten.'

PUSSY

5. to **pussy-foot** – to aim soft blows at your opponent which are not intended to hurt him. The blows may be verbal as well as physical. 'Say what you really think about Mark and stop pussy-footing!' The allusion is to the soft paws of the cat.

HORSE

6. a **dark horse** – a person of unknown abilities or one who has kept his abilities to himself and may spring a surprise. This is a racing metaphor indicating an unknown horse which could win the race unexpectedly.

7. a **stalking horse** – a pretext to conceal one's real designs. 'Democracy has been used as a stalking horse for caucus rule.' Hunters would stalk game by hiding themselves behind their horses as they advanced on their prey.

8. an **old war horse** – a veteran of many battles who likes to reminisce over them.

   to **sniff the air like an old war horse** – to anticipate a battle, to sense a war atmosphere.

9. to **back the wrong horse** – to put your reliance on a person who then lets you down. 'If you think Walsh will ever repay you, you are mistaken; I'm afraid you've put your money on the wrong horse.'

10. to **eat like a horse** – to overeat, to eat without restraint.

11. to **work like a horse** – to do a huge quantity of work. 'It's time you had a rest; you've been working like a horse all the afternoon.'

12. a **willing horse** – one who is eager to work and do other people's as well.

13. a **horse-laugh** – a loud guffaw usually expressing derision or incredulity. 'When I told him the government had promised to reduce taxes next year, he gave a horse-laugh and said he had heard that one before.'

14. **horseplay** (school slang) – rough but good-natured games.

15. **horse sense** – rough, earthy common sense.

16. **horse-trading** – hard, shrewd bargaining with no sentiment on either side. 'After a lot of horse-trading we have at last agreed a price for the house.'

17. to **flog a dead horse** – to repeat the same outdated argument over and over again. 'Whatever you think, capital punishment will never come back. Why do you flog a dead horse?'

18. to **ride a hobby horse (to death)** – to introduce one's favourite subject into a conversation at every opportunity.

19. a **horse of another colour** – a completely different matter. '"I don't want the money for myself but for my

brother." "For your brother! That's a horse of another colour."'

1. to be/climb **on one's high horse** – to assume an attitude of moral superiority. Note also the phrase, **'Don't get on your high horse with me,'** meaning, 'Don't set yourself up as my moral superior.'
2. straight from the **horse's mouth** – information received from someone with actual experience whose testimony cannot be questioned. 'I've had it straight from the horse's mouth; he was there when the man was killed.'
3. **Never look a gift horse in the mouth** (proverb) – never find fault with a gift. This phrase is found in almost every language. One looks a horse in the mouth in order to tell its age from the teeth.
4. to **lock the stable door after the horse has bolted** – to take precautions after the event has occurred, instead of before.
5. to **put the cart before the horse** – to mistake the effect for the cause. 'To say that Alex can't take exercise because of his poor health is to put the cart before the horse. Alex is in poor health because he doesn't take any exercise.'
6. to **drive a coach and horses through** a law, rule or regulation – to find a very big loophole in it.
7. **if wishes were horses, beggars would ride** – a wish that cannot possibly be fulfilled. Most wishes are impractical, otherwise the strangest results would arise.
8. to **swap horses in midstream / halfway across the stream** – to make a critical change of plan after a contest has begun. Often used negatively to indicate that a mistake was made. 'It's always a mistake to swap horses halfway across the stream.'
9. **wild horses would not drag it out of me** – I won't give away the secret in any circumstances.
10. to **frighten the horses** – to be indiscreet, to shock public opinion. '. . . capital punishment was not so much as mentioned in the Conservative Manifesto (on the grounds presumably of not unnecessarily frightening the horses)' (*Observer*, 22 May 1983).
11. **hold your horses!** – wait a moment, don't do anything rash. 'Hold your horses! I only broke the window; I didn't burn the hole in the carpet.'
12. **'Horses for courses'** – different jobs require different skills. 'An employer will only offer you a job if you have the particular skill he is looking for. It's horses for courses so far as he is concerned.'

MARE, ASS, MULE AND DONKEY

13. to find a **mare's nest** – to make a discovery that turns out to be worthless.
14. to **make an ass of oneself** – to behave in a ridiculous manner. The ass has always been a symbol of stupidity.
15. **as stubborn as a mule** – one who is unwilling to yield or make any concessions in a dispute.

    as obstinate as a donkey – unwilling to listen to reason or change one's mind. A donkey is proverbial for both its obstinacy and stupidity.
16. to **talk the hind leg off a donkey** – to talk endlessly.
17. **donkey-work** – the hard, boring part of a job; that which requires little or no intelligence. 'It was Joan's idea. I only did the donkey-work.'
18. **like a carrot to a donkey** – a strong inducement or incentive. 'They offered the men a carrot in the shape of a ten per cent rise in wages, and double overtime.'

1. **not for donkey's years** (colloquial) – not for a very long time. 'Wherever have you been all this time? I haven't seen you for donkey's years!' The phrase may have come from a play on the words 'ears' and 'years', which are pronounced the same in some parts of the country.

COW, BULL AND CALF

2. the **sacred cow** – a derogatory term for any institution or custom generally regarded as sacrosanct which, in the opinion of its critics, is useless and should be abolished, such as Parliamentary Sovereignty and the Mixed Economy. The phrase originates in the Hindu belief that cows are sacred and should not be slaughtered, even in times of famine.
3. a **milch cow** – a universal provider, one from whom it is easy to obtain money. 'The boys are old enough to get a job. You are becoming the milch cow of the family.' 'Milch' means 'milk giving' and derives from Anglo-Saxon 'milch' (milk). It is still used in the phrases 'milch cow' and 'milch ewe'.
4. **till the cows come home** – for ever. 'You can argue about that till the cows come home. You won't ever agree.' cf. '. . . **until you are blue in the face' 17/9**.
5. to **take the bull by the horns** – to grapple fearlessly with a problem. 'The young man took the bull by the horns and asked his boss for a rise.'
6. to **score/hit a bull's eye** – to achieve one's exact aim, to make a spectacular success. 'John hit the bull's eye with his invention, and now he is a very rich man.'
7. **like a bull in a china shop** – very clumsy and destructive. This phrase is often used when tact and diplomacy are notably absent. 'In the short time Jack was with us, he upset every member of my family. He was like a bull in a china shop.'
8. to **kill the fatted calf** – to treat a person with special hospitality, usually after a long absence from home. 'We are all longing to see you, Peter. Father is going to kill the fatted calf for you.' The allusion is to 'The Prodigal Son' (Luke XV, 30).
9. **calf-love** – the first adolescent love-affair. cf. **'puppy-love' 54/17**.

SHEEP AND LAMB

10. to **look sheepish** – to look embarrassed, guilty. 'Henry looked sheepish when the doctor told him to take off his clothes.'
11. to **cast/make sheep's eyes** at someone – to look furtively but amorously at someone. 'I saw you casting sheep's eyes at that girl. It was very embarrassing.'
12. **like a flock of sheep** – with mindless obedience. 'As soon as the trade-union leader set off towards the police cordon, the rest of the strikers followed like a flock of sheep.'
13. to **count sheep** – the monotony of counting sheep in one's imagination is a powerful inducement to falling asleep.
14. a **wolf in sheep's clothing** – someone who looks respectable and harmless but whose behaviour is quite the opposite.
15. **as well be hanged for a sheep as a lamb** (proverb) – if you are going to be punished for a small crime, you will have little to lose by committing a serious one.
16. to **separate the sheep from the goats** – to separate the good from the bad, the virtuous from the wicked. The allusion is to the Day of Judgement (Matthew XXV, 32), when the good

are rewarded with a place in heaven and the wicked are sent to hell. Nowadays, the distinction is more often drawn between efficient businesses and those that are inefficient or untrustworthy.

1. **like a lamb / as meek as a lamb** – meekly, without resistance. 'It must have been a terrible shock to Harry when I told him he would have to give up his room, but he took it like a lamb.'

   to go **like a lamb to the slaughter(house)** – to await one's destruction with complete docility.

GOAT

2. to **get one's goat** – to annoy, exasperate. 'It gets my goat the way he lays down the law on every subject under the sun.'
3. to be a **scapegoat** – to be punished for the sins or crimes of others. 'He was made the scapegoat because he had been in trouble before.' From the sacrificial goat that was allowed to escape from the Hebrew temple after the high priest had transferred his sins and those of his people to it. The word would appear to be a contradiction in terms because, in modern speech, the 'scapegoat' does not escape but is wrongly punished in the place of the guilty party.
4. to **show the cloven hoof** – to betray one's evil intentions. The devil is depicted in art and legend as having the cloven hoof of the goat which he can never conceal, thus betraying his evil motives.

PIG AND GUINEA-PIG

5. to look/stare **like a stuck pig** – to be petrified with amazement or fear, to stand with mouth and eyes wide open.
6. **pig-headed** – stubborn, unwilling to listen to advice or change one's mind. cf. 'to **be stiff-necked' 126/14**.
7. a **male chauvinist pig** – a term of abuse coined by the Women's Lib movement for any man who is domineering or aggressive in his attitude to women. 'Chauvinist' derives from Nicolas Chauvin, a French soldier, well known for his exaggerated nationalistic views; 'pig' stands for male greed and insensitivity.
8. to **eat like a pig** – to eat a huge quantity of food noisily and greedily.
9. to **pig it** – to live in squalor.
10. **pigs in clover** – people with more money than manners.
11. a **pig in a poke / to buy a pig in a poke** – something unsatisfactory, bought unseen by the buyer. 'What a pity you didn't get a surveyor to look over the house before you signed the contract. I am afraid you have bought a pig in a poke!' The word 'poke' originally meant 'bag'. Thus an animal in a bag that was taken to market and sold as a pig in a poke might, when the purchaser had time to inspect the bag, turn out to be a cat.
12. a **guinea-pig** – someone who allows himself to be used as a subject for experiments in hospitals and laboratories. (The animal of the same name is in great demand for experimental work on account of its docile nature.)

SOW, SWINE AND HOG

13. **you cannot make a silk purse out of a sow's ear** – it is not possible to make something fine out of inferior material. 'I am afraid you'll never get that lad into the university, however much time you spend on him. You can't make a silk purse out of a sow's ear.' James Howell (1594–1666) wrote of the impossibility of making a 'satin purse out of a sow's ear'.

1. to **cast pearls before swine** – to waste gifts on those who are too uncultured to appreciate them.
2. a **road-hog** – a motorist who monopolizes the road by driving very slowly in the middle, or who drives too fast without any consideration for other road-users.
3. to **hog** (conversation, food, wine, attention, publicity, etc.) – to monopolize, to take more than one's fair share.
4. to **go the whole hog** – to go through with something to the very end. 'I wanted to perfect my knowledge of French so I went the whole hog and spent all my savings on a six months' stay with a family in Paris.' 'Hog' was originally slang for 'shilling'; so to go the whole hog meant to spend the whole shilling at once.

RAT AND LEMMING

5. a **rat** – someone who will betray his cause to further his own interests. A traitor may be motivated by principle, but a rat is only interested in his own advantage.
6. the **rat race** – the frenzied scramble for success in one's job. 'I wish I could opt out of the rat race and just enjoy myself, but I can't afford to.'
7. to **smell a rat** – to suspect that something is not quite right, to have grounds for suspicion. 'I smelt a rat when he kept on postponing the wedding, even though his explanations seemed reasonable enough.'
8. **like a lemming / lemming-like** – self-destructive, suicidal. 'Unity, yes, but not the unity of lemmings!' (Gavin Laird on 'Weekend World', ITV, 9 December 1984). Lemmings are small rats which migrate across Norway to the sea, where they drown in huge numbers.

RABBIT AND HARE

9. to **produce/pull the rabbit out of the hat** – to produce what seems an impossible result with no effort, as if by magic. 'When I told him I had no fancy dress for the party, he produced the costume of a toreador for me just like a rabbit out of a hat.'
10. to **breed like rabbits** – to breed very fast, to multiply at great speed.
11. **as mad as a March Hare** – insane. The March Hare was one of the characters in Lewis Carroll's *Alice in Wonderland*, who vied with the Mad Hatter in making crazy remarks. The month of March is the rutting season when hares go mad.
12. **hare and hounds** – a paper-chase, a trail of paper scattered along the ground by the 'hares' for the 'hounds' to follow.
13. to **run with the hare and hunt with the hounds** – to support both sides in a dispute at the same time.
14. **first catch your hare, then cook him** – make no plans until you have the means to carry them out.
15. to **start a hare, a conversational hare** – to divert a discussion by bringing in an irrelevant topic. 'She was not interested . . . in the dividing line between Journalism and Literature which was started as a conversational hare' (*Howards End* by E. M. Forster). cf. 'to **draw a red herring across the path' 73/2**.

FOX

16. a **sly fox / an old fox** – someone who is very experienced and has acquired much guile. 'You won't take in an old fox like me with such a story.'
17. **as cunning as a fox** – very cunning indeed, as cunning as a fox is reputed to be.

1. to **be foxed** – to be outwitted, baffled or deceived. 'I was completely foxed by the crossword puzzle.'
2. to **shoot someone else's fox** – to demolish or destroy someone else's enemy. 'I was on the point of ordering Stanley's arrest when Scotland Yard did it for me; they shot my fox!'

WOLF

3. to **wolf (food) down** – to swallow one's food without chewing, in the manner of a ravenously hungry wolf.
4. a **lone wolf** – someone who likes to be independent and live alone without having to co-operate with other people. 'Tony will never join your association, however much he sympathizes with your aims. He is too much of a lone wolf.'
5. to **keep the wolf from the door** – to have sufficient funds to pay one's bills and keep the bailiffs out. 'Here's £100. That should be enough to keep the wolf from the door!' The original meaning was to have enough money not to starve.
6. to **cry 'Wolf'** – to sound a false alarm so many times that, when at last you sound a genuine alarm, no one will come to your help. This phrase is taken from 'The Shepherd Boy who cried Wolf' in Aesop's Fables.
7. to **throw to the wolves** – to sacrifice a friend or dependant to appease one's enemies. 'He won't hesitate to throw you to the wolves to protect himself.'
8. a **wolf-whistle** – the whistle of a man at the sight of an attractive girl or woman in the street, made for the purpose of catching her attention.

STAG

9. a **stag party** – a social gathering for men only.

BEAVER, BADGER, FERRET AND WEASEL

10. to **beaver away** – to work hard at a task. 'He has been beavering away at his job for the last three months.' The beaver is renowned for its energy and perseverance.
11. to **badger** someone – to make persistent demands on someone. 'Whenever he sees me, he badgers me to join his club; he won't give me any peace until I do.'
12. to **ferret out** – to find out something after a very diligent search.
13. **weasel words** – words which weaken the force of the words that immediately precede them. They suck the life out of the words, just as a weasel sucks the egg out of its shell. 'We must expand our exports and at the same time protect our home industries' – the first half of the sentence is contradicted by the weasel words in the second half; if we stop countries exporting to us, they will not have enough foreign exchange to import our goods.

OPOSSUM

14. to **play possum** – to avoid trouble by lying low, feigning illness or pretending to be unaware of the facts. The allusion is to the habit of the opossum which feigns death when it is attacked.

HEDGEHOG AND MOLE

15. **as prickly as a hedgehog** – someone who takes offence very easily.
16. a **mole** – a traitor who undermines from the inside the organization in which he is employed.
17. to **make a mountain out of a molehill** – to exaggerate a difficulty. 'Aren't you

making a mountain out of a molehill? There's no need to cancel our holiday just because the airlines are grounded. We can go by boat-train instead.'

BAT

1. **as blind as a bat** – completely blind. 'You must have been as blind as a bat not to have seen me; I was sitting at the next table!'
2. **bats in the belfry** – slightly mad.

FROG

3. to **frogmarch** – to carry an obstinate or unruly person face downwards by holding the arms and legs. 'When I asked Crouch for my money, his servants practically frogmarched me out of his house!'
4. to have **a frog in the throat** – to have an obstruction in the throat which causes hoarseness or loss of voice.

SNAKE

5. a **snake in the grass** – a hidden, treacherous enemy. 'Your friend has been telling your boss tales about you. She's a real snake in the grass!'
6. to cherish **a snake in one's bosom** – to have one's kindness repaid with spite or ingratitude.
7. to **scotch the snake** – to spoil a plan.
8. **Snakes and Ladders** – the ups and downs in life. From the name of a children's game of chance played on a board that contains rewards and penalties.

TURTLE

9. to **turn turtle** – to turn round and run away in the face of danger. The allusion is to the turtle which turns upside down in the water. When the phrase is applied to a boat, it means that the boat capsizes and sinks.
10. to **come out of one's shell** – to overcome one's natural reserve and speak freely. 'Mark was always so shy but, since he has made friends with Nancy, he has come right out of his shell.'

WHALE

11. to have a **whale of a time** – to have a splendid time. The whale stands for something very big, and also something fine or splendid.
    a **whale of a job** – a wonderful job; a **whale of a task** – a huge task.

DRAGON

12. a **dragon** – a formidable, aggressive woman who makes a lot of trouble. 'She's a real dragon. You had better keep away from her.'
13. to **chase the dragon** – to take heroin. 'Two boys crouch in a corner, chasing the dragon. Their shirts are pulled over their heads so they can more easily breathe the smoke from the brown heroin which they bought for £5' (*The Mail on Sunday*, 4 August 1985). In myth and fable, dragons are sometimes represented as breathing out fire and smoke.

CROCODILE

14. a **crocodile** – schoolchildren walking in a procession two by two, usually with a teacher at the back.
15. to **shed crocodile tears** – to shed false, insincere tears. 'Take no notice of her crocodile tears. She's not in the least concerned about your injury.' The crocodile was believed by many

people to shed tears of remorse as it devoured its victim. In fact, the crocodile is getting rid of surplus salt from its nasal glands.

RHINOCEROS AND ELEPHANT

1. to have a **skin like a rhinoceros** – to be insensitive to insults.
2. a **rogue elephant** – someone who flouts authority in order to vent his spite on everyone and everything. 'Your son is making enemies of all our customers; he's a real rogue elephant!' A rogue elephant is a vicious elephant that deserts the herd and runs amok, causing great damage.
3. an **elephant's memory** – a long memory, especially for an ill-turn or an insult. Elephants are proverbial for their long memories.

CAMEL

4. to **swallow a camel and strain at a gnat** – to tolerate a great wrong while protesting at a minor lapse.

KANGAROO

5. to **kangaroo** – to convict and punish unjustly without giving the accused a fair hearing.
6. **a kangaroo court** – a court without any legal authority which tries and punishes people who have endangered the interests of some group or association. The term was originally employed for the illegal trials that were held in jails for offences against the prison community. Today, the same term is used for trade unions when they try members for breaches of union rules and regulations.

MONKEY AND APE

7. to **monkey with** – to interfere, usually with harmful results. 'Dennis has been monkeying with the grandfather clock. Now it won't chime.'
8. **monkey tricks** – spiteful, malicious behaviour.
9. to **make a monkey of** someone – to make someone look ridiculous. 'I don't like being made a monkey of in front of my friends; don't play your jokes on me again when we have guests.'
10. to **get one's monkey up** (slang) – to annoy or irritate someone very much. 'Whenever I turn on my radio, my neighbour knocks on the wall; he really gets my monkey up.'
11. **as clever as a cartload of monkeys** – very artful and sly.
12. **monkey business** – underhanded business, business that is not quite honest or straightforward. 'Paul has been getting up to some of his monkey business again. He needs watching.'
13. to **ape** one's superiors – to imitate people in a higher position than oneself.

LYNX AND LEOPARD

14. to be **lynx-eyed** – to have very sharp eyesight.
15. **the leopard can never change its spots** – one can never change one's character; thus a man with an evil past never changes his ways.

LION

16. **as brave as a lion** – very brave, the lion being a symbol of courage.
17. a **lion-hunter** – hosts or hostesses who seek out celebrities with whom to impress their guests.

1. to **lionize** someone – to make a celebrity of someone by lavishing praise and hospitality on him or her.
2. **the British Lion** – the symbol of Great Britain.
   to **twist the lion's tail** – to humiliate or provoke Great Britain.
3. **the lion's share** – much more than one's fair share, almost everything. 'He took the lion's share, and by the time he had finished there was nothing left for the rest of us except for a few crumbs.' Taken from Aesop's Fables.
4. the **lion's den** – a place of great danger.
5. to **beard the lion in his den** – to challenge a formidable enemy on his own ground.
6. to **put one's head in the lion's mouth** – to put oneself needlessly at the mercy of an enemy.

TIGER

7. he's **a tiger** – an expert, a person of dynamic energy.
   to **fight like a tiger** – to fight with savage, relentless ferocity.
8. **paper tiger** – a sham, a cowardly adversary who is unable to offer any real resistance. The phrase was coined by the Chinese leader Mao-Tse-tung at the height of the Vietnamese Civil War in reference to the capitalist countries who, the Chinese claimed, were too cowardly to defend their interests, although they made a lot of threats against their enemies.
9. to **ride a tiger** – to find that the person you are trying to make use of is your master and is in control of you.
10. to have **a tiger by the tail** – to get involved in unexpected trouble or danger, to find that the person you are hunting is much more formidable than you had supposed. 'You can't shake a tiger by the tail and not expect to get bitten' (from *NOW!* Magazine).

BEAR

11. **like a bear with a sore head** – in a specially bad mood or temper. 'Father is like a bear with a sore head this morning. I wonder what has upset him.' Bears are notoriously bad-tempered; hence the phrase.
12. **bears** and **bulls** on the Stock Exchange – a bull expects a share to rise, and a bear expects it to fall in price. So you can be **'bullish of a share'** and expect its price to rise, or **'bearish of a share'** and expect it to fall.
13. a **bear garden** – a place that is full of noise and contention. The name originated in the bear gardens of Tudor times when bears were baited and attacked by dogs. These 'bear gardens' were well known for the rowdy behaviour of the spectators.

8. BIRDS

BIRD, BIRDS

1. **bird** (cockney) – girlfriend. D. H. Lawrence is known to have used the phrase.
2. an **old bird** – someone who is too experienced and shrewd to be taken in. 'You won't get an old bird like him to believe that tale!' From the proverb: You can't catch an old bird with chaff.
3. an **early bird** – someone who rises early. 'My husband was always an early bird.' From the proverb: It's the early bird that catches the worm.
4. an **odd bird** – an eccentric person.
5. a **rare bird** – an exceptional person who combines two contradictory interests. 'He was that rare bird – a poet and a chemist.' cf. **'a rare animal' 52/5**.
6. a **bird of passage** – someone who never stays long in the same place but is always on the move, a wanderer, like a swallow which migrates according to season.
7. a **jail-bird** – someone who spends his life in and out of prison.
8. to **get the bird** – to suffer a severe rebuff, to be greeted with abuse. 'He offered to give a talk on his travels in India, but he got the bird!'

   to **give** someone **the bird** – to hiss or boo at a person in order to express one's disapproval.
9. the **bird has flown** – the person you want has disappeared. 'The birds have flown' was said by Charles I when he and his henchmen arrived at the House of Commons too late to arrest his political enemies.
10. **free as a bird** – free to come and go as one pleases.
11. **a little bird told me** – someone whose name the speaker prefers not to reveal. Often used when speaking to an inquisitive child, in reference to some gossipy information.
12. a **bird's-eye view** – a general view.
13. a **bird of ill-omen** – someone who brings bad luck, like Jonah (in the Bible), or a messenger who is always bringing bad news. From a bird whose presence signifies misfortune, like the albatross or crow.
14. **A bird in the hand is worth two in the bush** (proverb) – a smaller advantage which can be taken now is better than a greater one at some uncertain time in the future.
15. to **kill two birds with one stone** – to achieve two results with the same means. 'We can kill two birds with one stone by combining our honeymoon with our business trip.'
16. to be **able to charm the birds off a tree** – to have so much charm that one can achieve almost anything with it. 'Richard could charm a bird off a tree if he put his mind to it.'

    to be **unable to charm birds off a tree** – to be lacking in charm.
17. **birds of a feather** – you can judge the character of a person by the company he keeps. The phrase is derogatory and derives from the proverb: Birds of a feather flock together.

FEATHER AND WING

18. **in fine feather** – in splendid condition, lively and cheerful. 'Alan was in fine feather. He has quite recovered from his depression.'
19. **'You could have knocked me down with a feather!'** – I was so overcome with surprise that even an object as light as a feather would have been enough to knock me down.
20. to **smooth** someone's **ruffled feathers**

– to soothe someone's injured pride. 'The Vicar was very upset at the way you spoke to him this morning. You had better do something to smooth his ruffled feathers.'

1. to **make the feathers/fur fly** – to start an angry controversy which leads to quarrelling and fighting. 'Your scheme to convert the local church into a community centre has made the feathers fly.'
2. to **make** someone's **hackles rise** – to make someone very angry, to infuriate him. 'It makes my hackles rise when Len's father takes the credit for getting him into university and ignores the help we gave his son.' The hackles are the long feathers on the neck of the domestic cock which rise when it is angry and preparing for a fight.
3. to **take** someone **under one's wing** – to give a person one's help and protection. 'Since Lady Montague has taken Tim under her wing, the teachers at his school haven't given him any more trouble.'
4. to **clip** someone's **wings** – to tame someone, to curtail his powers. 'Every time I ring my doctor for an appointment, I am cross-examined by his receptionist. It's time her wings were clipped.'

NEST

5. to **feather one's nest** – to make wrongful use of one's position, in order to make or save money for oneself. 'He is not going to feather his nest at our expense!'
6. to **foul one's nest** – to speak ill of one's own family to strangers. 'You shouldn't have fouled your nest like that at Susan's wedding. Your family will never forgive you.' The phrase comes from the proverb: It's an ill bird that fouls its own nest.
7. a **nest-egg** – a small amount of money that is kept in reserve, in case of need.

   to **break into one's nest-egg** – to spend money that has been saved up. 'Prices have gone up so fast in recent years that many people have been obliged to break into their nest-eggs.'
8. to **rule the roost** – to dominate or govern a group. 'In the early part of the century, it was the eldest son, not the widow, who ruled the roost.' The roost is the resting place of the hens where they perch at night.
9. to **come home to roost** – to recoil on the person responsible for a folly or wrong. 'There is always a price to pay for our follies; sooner or later they come home to roost.'

ROBIN, LARK AND SWALLOW

10. a **round robin** – a letter of protest with the signatures in circular form in order to conceal the identity of the ring-leader.
11. **'Who killed Cock Robin?'** – the first line of a nursery rhyme which in modern parlance means 'Who is responsible for the fall of a prominent figure?', a question often posed by political commentators when a Minister is replaced.
12. to **have a lark / lark about** – to play jokes or indulge in horseplay with other children. 'I told the children to stop larking about and go to sleep.'
13. to be **up with the lark** – to be up early in the morning.
14. to be **as happy as a lark** – to be very happy, carefree, jolly. 'Steven is as happy as a lark, playing with his new model railway.'
15. **One swallow doesn't make a summer** (proverb) – one favourable occurrence doesn't prove that the others will be as good. 'That's an encouraging

order you've just had, but it doesn't prove that our business will succeed. One swallow doesn't make a summer.'

JAY, MAGPIE AND CUCKOO

1. a **jay-walker** – a pedestrian who crosses the road without looking.
2. to **chatter like a magpie** – to chatter incessantly, without interruption; often used in reference to children.
3. a **cuckoo in the nest** – an unwelcome intruder. 'Hicks has been a cuckoo in the nest ever since he joined the association. Why join if he doesn't agree with our aims?'

CROW

4. to **crow / crow over** – to gloat, to rejoice at the defeat of an opponent. 'I don't like the way Rolf crows over his opponents when he wins. It is very unsporting of him.'
5. **as the crow flies** – as an imaginary bird would fly; the distance as measured by a straight line from one point to another.
6. **crow's feet** – the little lines or wrinkles which appear under a person's eyes in middle age.
7. a **scarecrow** – the name given to a woman who wears shabby, torn or dowdy clothes. 'I can't possibly wear this at the ball; I shall look a proper scarecrow in it.' Literally, some old tattered clothes put on a stick in a field to frighten the crows away.

PIGEON AND DOVE

8. to **pigeon-hole** – to delay action on a request or complaint indefinitely. A pigeon-hole is one compartment among many reserved for the filing of documents.
9. to **pluck a pigeon** – to swindle a credulous victim.
10. the **dove of peace** – the dove has been a symbol of peace from time immemorial. It was a dove which brought a message from God to Noah in his ark at the height of the flood.
11. to be **as gentle as a dove** – to behave in a peace-loving, tender manner.
12. **'Don't get lovey-dovey with me!'** – 'Don't get amorous with me, don't get the wrong ideas about me.'
13. to **flutter the dovecotes** – to cause a lot of excitement in a peaceful community. 'If you return to the village after all the publicity you've had, you will flutter the dovecotes all right!'

HEN

14. a **hen party** – a party to which only women or girls are invited.
15. a **hen-pecked husband** – a man who is domineered over by his nagging wife.
16. **like a hen with one chicken** – overprotective of one's only child.

COCK

17. to be **all cock-a-hoop** – to be exultant, triumphant. 'Hudson was all cock-a-hoop at the news. He had never expected to get a first-class degree.' The origin is unknown.
18. to **live like fighting cocks** – to be nourished on the best food, like a fighting cock.
19. **this beats cock-fighting** – more exciting, more thrilling than cock-fighting.
20. **that cock won't fight** – that plan won't do; it is impracticable. The phrase is also used when one party to a dispute disappoints his supporters by refusing to fight. 'I was looking forward to taking Peter's headmaster to court, but then Peter refused to testify against him; when the cock won't

fight, there is nothing you can do.' The reference is to cock-fighting.

1. to be **cock of the walk** – to be the champion or victor in one's own particular field, to dominate all one's rivals.
2. a **cock and bull story** – a wildly improbable story, often invented to glorify the speaker or to excuse some wrongful action. 'Harry told me a cock and bull story about a man robbing him of the money he owed me while he was on his way to my house.'
3. to **cock a snook at** – to make a long nose at, by putting one's thumb at the end of the nose and spreading out the fingers as a gesture of contempt. cf. 'to **make a long nose' 84/9**.
4. a **cock sparrow** – a bold, aggressive little fellow, always spoiling for a fight.
5. a **cock-eyed scheme** – a wild, foolish scheme, one that is bound to fail.
   That's cock-eyed – that's all wrong.
6. to **take a cockshot at** – to throw something at an object without taking much care; to make a wild throw at it.
7. at **cock-crow** – at sunrise.

CHICKEN

8. to be **chicken/chicken-hearted** – to be cowardly, easily frightened, to be afraid of a fight. .
9. to **chicken out** – to wriggle out of an obligation through cowardice.
10. **she's no chicken** – she's no longer young. 'No chicken' is often used in reference to a woman who is no longer as young as she would like to appear, and whose behaviour does not become a woman of her age.
11. **as tender as a chicken** – very soft, delicate.
12. **Don't count your chickens** – don't rely on your gains until you have them in your possession. 'Don't count your chickens. Your uncle may not leave you any money at all.' From the proverb: Don't count your chickens before they are hatched; from Aesop's Fables.
13. **that's like asking which came first, the chicken or the egg** – there are some questions to which there is no rational answer.
14. **chicken feed** (slang) – a poor, meagre reward for work done.
15. the **pecking order** – the order of seniority in an organized group of people. 'I am pretty low down in the pecking order, so I don't enjoy my job much.' The phrase is taken from the social order of domestic chickens which ranks chickens according to their strength. Each bird is pecked by the one immediately above it in rank, but pecks the one immediately below it.

DUCK

16. a **sitting duck** – someone who is vulnerable to attack from his enemies. From the idea that it is easy to shoot a duck which is sitting still. cf. **'a sitting target' 205/8**.
17. a **lame duck** – a person who is incompetent and in need of financial assistance. Also a company or industry that is running at a loss and needs public money to survive. Second-term American presidents who have lost their power of patronage, and consequently their influence in the legislature, are known as 'lame ducks'.
18. a **dead duck** – a cause or campaign that no longer has relevance to modern life.
19. **like a dying duck in a thunderstorm** – all forlorn, bedraggled and miserable. 'You do sound sorry for yourself – like a dying duck in a thunderstorm.'
20. an **ugly duckling** – a plain, unprepossessing child who grows into a

beautiful woman. The phrase comes from Hans Andersen's fairy tale *The Ugly Duckling* in which an ugly duckling, after much ridicule, grows into a beautiful swan.

1. **(like) water off a duck's back** – without making the slightest impression. 'She scolded her son again and again for his dishonesty, but her words were water off a duck's back.'
2. to **take to** something **like a duck to water** – to adapt oneself to a new situation without any conscious effort or difficulty. 'Although he had never worked in an office before, he took to the routine like a duck to water.'
3. to **play ducks and drakes** with one's money – to take unjustifiable risks with one's money, to throw it away. The game of ducks and drakes consists in throwing a flat stone along the surface of the water and counting the number of times it bounces on the water.
4. a **duck's egg** (slang) – scoring nought at cricket.

   a pair of ducks – no score in either innings. The term is sometimes used in other connections. The American equivalent for no score is 'a goose's egg'.

   to **break one's duck** – to score a run in cricket, and so avoid making a 'duck' or 'duck's egg'.

GOOSE

5. to be unable to **say boo to a goose** – to be so timid that one cannot make even the mildest protest, however badly one is treated. 'If you were to move your family into his house, he wouldn't try to stop you. He can't say boo to a goose!'
6. to **cook** someone's **goose** – to destroy one's opponent's chances by some dramatic coup. 'That's cooked his goose once and for all. He'll never survive the scandal.'
7. a **wild goose chase** – to go on a profitless journey, to take part in a useless search. Most wild goose chases are unsuccessful because wild geese fly very high and fast and are therefore difficult to shoot.
8. the **goose-step** – a kind of military step with the legs pushed aggressively forward.
9. **goose flesh/skin/pimples** – a rough condition of the skin resembling the skin of a plucked goose, which comes about as the result of cold or fear.
10. to **kill the goose that lays the golden egg** – to destroy the source of one's wealth. 'I know you don't like the way your father paints, but if you discourage him too much, you will be killing the goose that lays the golden egg.' From Aesop's Fables.
11. **What is sauce for the goose is sauce for the gander** (adage) – what is right for one person is also right for all. The same rules should be applied to everybody without exception or favouritism. 'If Roger is allowed the day off, why shouldn't I be? What is sauce for the goose is sauce for the gander.'
12. **all your geese are swans** – you overestimate the value of your possessions or ideas, just because they are yours.
13. **all your swans are geese** – all your hopes have been disappointed.

TURKEY

14. to **talk turkey** – to talk bluntly, usually about business.
15. that's **cold turkey** – (1) the plain truth. (2) withdrawal from drug-taking.

SWAN, STORMY PETREL, COOT AND ALBATROSS

16. **swan-song** – the last achievement of a writer, painter, musician, and so on.

According to legend, the swan only sings when it is about to die.

1. a **stormy petrel** – a turbulent, restless character who stirs up trouble wherever he goes. A stormy petrel is a small sea-bird whose appearance on the surface of the sea foretells a storm. The word 'petrel' is derived from St Peter, the apostle who walked on the water.
2. **as bald as a coot** – completely bald; so called because the coot has a featherless pate on its forehead which resembles the head of a bald man.
3. to have **an albatross round one's neck** – to suffer from some crippling disadvantage. 'We would have made real progress if it hadn't been for this albatross round our necks' (Premier James Callaghan on TV, 1977, referring to the danger of a run on the pound and its devaluation). The albatross has always been regarded as a bird of ill omen.

KINGFISHER

4. **halcyon days** – times of undisturbed happiness and peace. 'Those were the halcyon days of Athens [fifth century BC] when she produced her finest poetry and drama, architecture and sculpture.' The halcyon is Greek for kingfisher, being a compound of Greek 'sea' and 'conceiving'. Thus the halcyon days were the calm days, when the kingfishers were able to breed in peace, undisturbed by wind and storm. cf. **'a hey-day' 36/14**.

PARROT

5. **parrot-fashion / parrot-like / parrot-wise** – learnt by heart without regard to the meaning.
6. **as sick as a parrot** – a cliché often used by football managers, meaning very disappointed.

PEACOCK, PHOENIX AND DODO

7. **as proud as a peacock** – conceited and vain. The comparison is based on the outstandingly beautiful plumage of the peacock's tail, which opens out like a fan to attract the hen.
8. to rise **like a phoenix from the ashes** – a force which has apparently been destroyed, but which emerges once again to triumph over its enemies. According to legend, the phoenix was an eastern bird which set fire to itself and then rose again from the ashes. It is also a symbol of the Resurrection.
9. **as dead as a dodo** – finished, dead, extinct. 'I thought that jazz was as dead as the dodo, but now it seems to have made a comeback.' The dodo was a large bird which died out at the end of the seventeenth century.

OWL

10. **as wise as an owl / a wise old owl** – owls have a solemn look, and solemnity is often associated with wisdom; hence the phrase.
11. a **solemn owl** *(derogatory)* – an excessively solemn person who is lacking in humour.
12. a **night owl** – someone who does not go to bed until the early hours of the morning. 'Since Philip has started work on his book he has become a regular night-owl.'

HAWK AND EAGLE

13. **'hawks and doves'** – in British politics, the 'hawks' are the hardliners of the Conservative right wing, and the 'doves' those on the left wing who favour conciliation and compromise with the other parties. There are also 'hawks' and 'doves' on both wings of the Republican and Democratic

parties in the USA, where the meaning is much the same.

1. an **eagle eye** – a very sharp gaze which takes in the smallest detail; a look from which it is impossible to escape.

VULTURE

2. **like a vulture** – a grabbing, mercenary person. The vulture is a scavenger that feeds on the corpses of rotting animals. Consequently, the word is often used to describe the relations who gather round the rich man's death-bed.

OSTRICH

3. **like an ostrich (with its head in the sand)** – someone who wilfully conceals the truth from himself, who refuses to face reality. Ostriches are generally believed to hide their heads in the sand in the mistaken belief that, if they cannot see the danger, the danger no longer exists. Hence all the phrases connected with ostrich, such as **'ostrich policy'**, **'ostrich belief'**, **'ostrich-like'**, which imply a refusal to face reality. cf. **'to bury one's head in the sand' 78/4**.

9. FISH

FISH

1. a **big fish** – a very important person.
   only a small fish – only an unimportant person.
2. a **big fish in a small pond** – someone whose authority and influence is limited to a small area. 'I'd rather run my own shop in the village, where I'm a big fish in a small pond, than work in a large store, where I'd only be one in two hundred.'
3. a **queer fish** – an odd character.
4. a **cold fish** – a cold, unfeeling person.
5. to **land a fish** – to score a big success like, for example, winning an important contract.
6. to be **like a fish out of water** – to find oneself in an unfamiliar situation, to be ill-adapted to new conditions. 'When he was transferred from the Air Force to the Army, he felt like a fish out of water; the work was so different.'
7. a **pretty kettle of fish** – an awkward predicament with no easy solution. When Queen Mary learned that her son, King Edward VIII, was faced with the choice of giving up Mrs Simpson or of abdicating, she exclaimed: 'This is a pretty kettle of fish!'
8. to **drink like a fish** – to be a hard drinker, a habitual, excessive drinker.
9. to **cry stinking fish** – to disparage one's own wares. 'You shouldn't criticize your father's price rises in front of our customers. You'll lose us business, if you cry stinking fish.'
10. **neither fish, flesh, fowl nor good red herring** – to be neither one thing nor the other, with the result that it doesn't satisfy anyone. 'This is neither a game of chance nor skill. It is neither fish, flesh, fowl nor good red herring.'
11. to **have other fish to fry** – to have other more important things to engage one's attention. 'I tried to interest him in our venture, but he seemed preoccupied with something else. No doubt he has other fish to fry.'
12. **there are as good fish in the sea as ever came out of it** – often said with the object of consoling a person crossed in love. 'There are many other people, besides your boy-friend, who would suit you just as well, so there is no need for you to despair. There are as good fish in the sea as ever came out of it.'
13. to **feed the fishes** (colloquial) – (1) to be seasick. (2) to be drowned.
14. to **fish in troubled/muddy water** – to meddle in matters which may cause one a lot of trouble, to try to make capital out of somebody else's misfortune.
15. to **fish for compliments** – to invite compliments by making disparaging remarks about oneself in the hope that they will be contradicted. '"I'm not nearly as pretty as Isabel." "What are you saying! You are a hundred times prettier! You really are fishing for compliments!"'
16. to **fish for information** – to seek information by asking leading questions. The phrase suggests that the interrogator is relying on the witness to supply the missing evidence. 'The reporters were here all morning fishing for information about your intention to divorce Helen.'
    to **go on a fishing expedition** – this is similar but more explicit. It means to visit someone and interrogate him in the hope that he will incriminate himself.

MACKEREL

1. to throw **a sprat to catch a mackerel** – to invest a small sum in the hope of making a big profit.

HERRING

2. to draw **a red herring** across the path – to introduce an irrelevant issue into a discussion. The 'red herring' may either be introduced intentionally, in order to confuse one's opponent, or accidentally. cf. 'to **start a hare' 60/15**.

EEL

3. **as slippery as an eel** – difficult to pin down, difficult to catch. 'I couldn't get anything in writing out of him; he is as slippery as an eel.'

SARDINES

4. to be packed **like sardines** – to be squashed together among a lot of people. 'We were packed like sardines on the train. I could hardly move my arms.'

FRY

5. **small fry** – unimportant people. 'He was too snobbish to greet the small fry.'

CAVIARE

6. **caviare to the general** – something special that is wasted on the uncultivated. The reference is from Shakespeare's *Hamlet*, II, ii, 465: 'The play, I remember, pleased not the million; 'twas caviare to the general'.

OYSTER

7. **as close as an oyster** – secretive, reluctant to give information.
8. **the world is mine oyster** – to have abundant opportunities, unlimited scope. 'Why, then the world is mine oyster, Which I with sword will open' (Shakespeare, *The Merry Wives of Windsor*, II, ii).

WHELK

9. not to be able even to **run a whelk-stall** – to be hopelessly incompetent. 'Don't give me advice on how to run my business; you couldn't even run a whelk-stall!' A whelk is a small shellfish which is sold as a cheap food, especially at the seaside.

CRAB

10. to **catch a crab** – when rowing, to dip the oar too deep into the water or to miss the water altogether. In either case, the effect is to stop the boat.

SHARK

11. a **shark** – a swindler, a money-grabber, one who charges an extortionate price for his services. The verb 'shark' is derived from the North French 'cherquier' (English – search, but has the added meaning of searching greedily. See *Hamlet*, I, i, 98 – shark up, meaning to snap up. The name has been given to the fish in the same sense.

10. INSECTS

WORM

1. a **worm** (derogatory) – someone lacking in moral fibre, despicable. 'What a worm!'
2. **the worm of conscience** – the nagging voice of conscience.
3. a **worm's eye view** – viewed from underneath.
4. **even a worm will turn** – there is a limit to the extent that even the weakest person can be bullied. The day will come when he will stand up for himself.
5. to **worm out information** – to extract information in a cunning underhand way.
6. to **worm oneself into** another's **favour** or **confidence** – to ingratiate oneself by devious means with another person.

SPIDER

7. **'Come into my parlour, said the spider to the fly'** – an ironic comment on an invitation that, in the opinion of the speaker, could lead a person into a dangerous trap.
8. to **blow the cobwebs away** – to clear one's mind of out-of-date notions. 'Beethoven was a great innovator in his day who blew away the cobwebs in the world of music.'

FLY, BUTTERFLY AND MOTH

9. a **fly in the ointment** – a small blemish that spoils one's pleasure. 'I would like to go to Spain next summer. The only fly in the ointment is we shall have to take our aunt with us.'
10. he **couldn't hurt a fly** – a gentle person who would never hurt anyone.
11. there are **no flies on him** – he is too sharp to be deceived or swindled.
12. to **break a butterfly on a wheel** – to use superfluous strength in order to secure a result.
13. to have **butterflies in one's stomach/ tummy** – to have an attack of nerves before an important event.
14. **like a moth (that flies) round a light** – like someone who is unable to resist temptation.
15. **moth-eaten ideas** – out-of-date ideas. 'He has such moth-eaten ideas that he would be more at home in the Victorian age.'

BEE, DRONE AND WASP

16. to be **as busy as a bee** – to work non-stop.
17. to **make a bee-line for** – to make one's way directly towards. 'Whenever I visit Mr Smith, his sister makes a bee-line for me.'
18. to **drone on** – to talk monotonously and at length on a subject.
19. to **bring a hornets' nest about one's ears / to put one's foot in a wasps' nest** – to bring down an avalanche of retribution on one's head by interference and criticism. 'When the government announced its intention of cutting out the waste in the National Health Service, it put its foot in a wasps' nest.'
20. a **wasp waist** – an exaggeratedly small waist. 'That tailor has given you a wasp waist. You'll have to have the jacket let out.'

BUG

21. a **big bug** – a very important person, often self-important.
22. a **fire-bug** – a compulsive fire-raiser.

1. a **litter bug** – someone who drops litter in the street and doesn't make use of a litter bin.
2. to have a room **bugged** – to install an electronic device in a room for taping conversation.

FLEA, NIT AND LEECH

3. a **(mere) flea bite** – a comparatively small sum of money. 'He was fined £500, but that was only a flea bite for a man of his wealth.'
4. to send someone away **with a flea in his ear** – to snub or rebuke a person. 'When he asked me for a loan, I sent him away with a flea in his ear. He must have felt very humiliated.'
5. **nit-picking** (derogatory) – making small, pettifogging criticisms. 'The critics were all mean, nit-picking people, totally devoid of any artistic sense.' The nit is the egg of a louse, and therefore barely visible.
6. to **stick/cling like a leech** – to act like a parasite whom it is difficult to shake off. 'Whenever we invite Cousin Harry, we can never get rid of him. He sticks like a leech.'

SNAIL

7. **at a snail's pace** – very slowly indeed, unreasonably slowly. 'I'm sorry I'm so late. My train went at a snail's pace all the way.' Often used to express annoyance at someone's excessive slowness.
8. to **draw/pull in one's horns** – (1) to reduce one's spending. 'With the cut in my salary, I've been obliged to draw in my horns, so we won't be taking a holiday this year.' (2) to retract a statement, or withdraw from a position in a debate or controversy. From the snail which retracts its horns when it feels itself threatened.

LIMPET AND CRICKET

9. to **cling like a limpet** – to cling tenaciously. 'I met Tom on the bus yesterday. He clung like a limpet to me the whole afternoon.'
10. **as merry as a cricket** – cheerful, happy. So called because the chirp of a cricket has a merry sound.

LOCUST

11. to **swarm like locusts** – to appear in very great numbers. 'His poor relations swarmed like locusts around the rich man.'

11. BODY

HEAD

1. to **head for** – (1) to go towards. (2) to ask for trouble, danger or disaster, etc. 'I warned you the company was heading for disaster.'
2. a **head start** – an advantage over one's competitors. 'You have a head start over your competitors; your business has been established longer than theirs.'
3. to **come to a head** – (of ill-feeling, disagreements, etc.) to reach a crisis.
   to **bring to a head** – to bring about a crisis. 'The Minister brought matters to a head by resigning from the government.' The reference is to the 'head' which forms on a boil when it is about to burst.
4. **over one's head** – (1) intellectually too difficult to grasp. 'They talked advanced mathematics together. It was completely over my head.' (2) to appeal against the decision of one's immediate superior to someone higher up in the hierarchy. 'The sergeant-major went over the head of his Company Commander and complained direct to the Commandant.'
5. **on one's head** – (1) to deserve blame if anything goes wrong. 'On your head be it if any of the patients suffer.' (2) to do something without the slightest difficulty or effort. 'I could have answered all the history questions on my head' (literally, with my feet in the air, upside-down).
6. to **be off one's head** – to be mad. 'He must have been off his head to try to climb the mountain without a guide!'
   to **go off one's head** – to go mad, to act like a madman. 'When Philip's marriage ended, he went completely off his head.' The idiom may express only a temporary lapse. 'Have you gone off your head? You paid him all that money in advance! You'll never see him again!'
7. **King Charles' head** – a synonym for any quaint or fanciful obsession. The phrase comes from Charles Dickens's novel *David Copperfield*, in which a half-crazy character, Mr Dick, constantly refers in his conversation to King Charles's head. (Charles I was beheaded by Parliament in 1649 after the Great Rebellion, 1642–6.)
8. to **have a head for** – to have a gift or aptitude for. Often used in connection with figures, accounts and business. 'With your head for figures, you should go in for accountancy.'
   to **have a head for heights** – to feel comfortable at great heights. Often used in the negative form. 'I could never be a mountaineer; I have no head for heights.'
9. to **hold one's head high** – to be free from any taint of guilt. 'Now you have been acquitted on all the charges, you can hold your head high.'
10. to **turn someone's head** – to give someone a high opinion of himself, to give him a false idea of his own importance. 'Jack's election to the presidency of our union has turned his head. He has started talking about himself in the third person as if he were royalty!'
11. to **keep one's head / to keep a level head** – to remain calm and sensible.
    to **lose one's head** – to lose one's power of reasoning, to get into a panic. 'When the boat sprang a leak, Susan completely lost her head and began to scream hysterically.'
12. to **keep one's head down** – to avoid drawing attention to oneself. 'All this bad publicity is not doing you any good. You had better keep your head down for the next six months.'

1. to **fling oneself at** someone's **head / at** someone – to pursue someone in a spirit of infatuation. 'The moment she saw the pop star, she flung herself at his head.'
2. to **snap off / bite off** someone's **head** – to speak sharply to someone, to snub or correct curtly. 'You needn't snap my head off. How was I to know?'
3. to **let** someone **have his head / give** someone **his head** – to let someone use his own initiative, his own judgement. Compare 'to **give the horse its head**' – to allow the horse freedom to decide the speed it will gallop at.
4. to **count heads / head-counting** – to accept the view of the majority. 'You are the only person on the committee who understands the subject, so what is the point of counting heads? You must decide.'
5. to **put their heads together** – to enlist someone else's advice in solving a problem, to discuss a problem with someone. From the proverb, 'Two heads are better than one'.
6. to **knock their heads together** – to take drastic action to end a quarrel. 'I wish Ralph and Mike wouldn't quarrel in front of the reporters. Someone should knock their heads together.'
7. to **take it into one's head** – to have a sudden idea, often with the implication that the idea is a mistaken one.
8. to **get into one's head** – to learn, comprehend. 'I can't get this Latin grammar into my head.'
9. to **put ideas into someone's head** – to have a bad influence on someone, to indoctrinate. 'Mark has beem putting ideas into Roger's head, and now he wants a bigger room and more food.'
10. to **put out of one's head** – to dismiss from one's mind some idea, hope or project.
11. to **make headway** against – to make progress, despite strong opposition; to prevail over. 'He made headway against the prejudices of the villagers.'
12. to **knock on the head** – to ruin a plan. 'Jane has broken her leg; that has knocked our skiing holiday on the head.'
13. to **scratch one's head** – to be puzzled, bewildered. 'I've been scratching my head over this game for the last half-hour, but I don't see how I can win; I give up!'
14. **soft in the head** – foolish, dense, mentally retarded; sometimes used as a reproach for some foolish action. 'Tim must be soft in the head to have believed that story.'
15. to be **bone-headed from the neck up** (slang) – to be completely stupid. From the idea of the bone replacing the brain.
16. **hot-headed** – easily aroused to anger. 'I don't know whether they will be happy together; she is mild and gentle, and her husband is quarrelsome and hot-headed, just the opposite of her.'
17. to be **at loggerheads** – to be in constant dispute with. 'He has been at loggerheads with his legal advisers throughout the proceedings.'
18. to **go to one's head** – to be made vain or conceited by success. 'John was much applauded for his speech last night. I only hope his success will not go to his head.'
19. to **have a swelled head** – to be conceited, to have a high opinion of oneself. 'Winning first prize in the song contest has given Jane a swelled head. Now she shows off terribly.'
20. to **go bald-headed at** – to attack with great energy, in total disregard of the consequences. 'Michael went for his enemy bald-headed, although he was unarmed and outmatched by his opponent.'
21. to **rear/raise its ugly head** – to become

a menace. 'The unemployment problem has raised its ugly head once more.'

1. **heads will roll** – those responsible for the blunder will be dismissed. In bygone times, guilty men in high places were sometimes executed. Today, they are removed from office, or transferred to positions of less importance, but the old phraseology has survived.
2. to have something **hanging over one's head** – to have an ordeal in front of one. 'This court case has been hanging over my head for the last six months. I shall be glad when it's over.'
3. to **need one's head examined** – to do something so stupid as to be almost insane. 'You drove at ninety miles an hour on that road! You should have your head examined!'
4. to **bury one's head in the sand** – wilfully to close one's eyes to danger. 'I warned him the company would crash if we didn't economize, but he didn't want to listen to me. For the last three years he has buried his head in the sand.' cf. **'like an ostrich' 71/3**.
5. to **put one's head on the chopping-block** – to take some action which effectively ends one's career. 'For you to vote against the Chairman after all he has done for you would be to put your head on the chopping-block.'
6. to **keep one's head above water** – to earn only just enough money to be able to live or to pay one's debts. 'I'm afraid Philip's business isn't doing at all well; he is barely keeping his head above water.'
7. a **head-on collision** – a violent disagreement with someone whose opinions are completely opposed to one's own.
8. to be **head over heels in love** with – to be madly in love with. Sometimes abbreviated to 'to **be head over heels**'.

   to **fall head over heels in love** – to fall in love very suddenly, very violently. Sometimes abbreviated to 'to **fall head over heels'**.
9. not to know whether one is **on one's head or one's heels** – to be in a state of total confusion. 'After severely reprimanding me for my work, my boss offered me promotion at twice the salary. I didn't know whether I was on my head or my heels.'
10. to **stand logic on its head** – to argue illogically. 'To say that Brian isn't clever enough to benefit from a university education is to stand logic on its head. If Brian weren't clever enough, he wouldn't have passed the entrance examination.'
11. to be **head and shoulders better than** – to be altogether superior to.
12. to **have a head on one's shoulders** – to possess good judgement.

    to have an **old head on young shoulders** – possessing greater wisdom than might be expected of a young person. 'If you are a young man confronted with a difficult problem, you need an old head on young shoulders.'
13. to **put one's head in a noose** – to invite disaster.
14. **Heads or tails?** – the call made when tossing a coin to decide the order of play, especially in a game. 'Heads' refers to the sovereign's head on one side of the coin, and 'tails' the reverse side.
15. **heads I win, tails you lose** – an unequal contest which only one person can possibly win. 'It's not fair. Whatever I decide to do, you will win the lot. It's heads you win, and tails I lose.'
16. to **make neither head nor tail of** something – to be completely baffled.
17. to **hit the headlines** – to achieve notoriety, to be the most important item of news on the front page of the national newspapers. 'What a scandal! If you publish that story, it will hit the headiines.'

HAIR

1. to **have one's hair stand on end** – to be terrified. 'When he saw the ghost, his hair stood on end.'
2. a **hairy story** – an uncouth story.
3. a **hair-raising story** – a horror story, one that shocks you.
4. **don't lose your hair over it / keep your hair on** – keep calm, don't get too excited over it. cf. 'to **keep one's shirt on' 170/5**.
5. **without turning a hair** – without showing any emotion or surprise. 'When she was told her father was dying, she never turned a hair.'
6. to **tear one's hair (out)** – to be desperate, unbearably frustrated. 'He has been tearing his hair over the accounts.'
7. to **let one's hair down** – to speak one's mind, to give vent to one's feelings. 'When I'm with Peter, I can really let my hair down.'
8. enough to **make one's hair curl** – to shock very severely. 'If you could see our electricity bill, it would make your hair curl!'
9. to **have someone by the short hairs** – to have someone at a hopeless disadvantage, to have him in one's power.
10. to **split hairs / hair-splitting** – to make insignificant distinctions, to argue with exaggerated subtlety.
11. to **escape by a hair's breadth** / to **be saved by a hair's breadth** – to escape very narrowly, by a tiny distance. 'She was only saved from falling under the train by a hair's breadth.'
12. **to a hair** – accurate or exact to the last detail.

FACE

13. to **be two-faced** – to support both parties in a dispute at the same time, to agree with a person to his face but disagree with him behind his back. 'Paul praised my painting while sitting for me, but I found out that he had made fun of it behind my back. He is very two-faced!'
14. to **put a bold face on** something – to behave without any embarrassment or shame. 'When Peter was accused of the theft, he put a bold face on it, sat down, and lit a cigar before replying.'
15. **bare-faced** – open, shameless, daring; almost always used in connection with 'insolence', 'impudence', 'cheek' and words with similar meanings. 'He had the bare-faced impudence to ask me for a loan ten minutes after we had been introduced!' cf. **'as bold as brass' 119/5**.
16. to **put the best face on something** – to accept a setback or defeat gracefully. 'Simon put the best face on his dismissal, saying that he had intended to take another job anyway.'
17. to **face a thing out** – to insist that one is in the right, often unreasonably.

    to **look in the face** – to confront bravely. 'After the crash of his business, the future was extremely bleak; nevertheless, he looked it in the face.'
18. to **stare in the face** – to be certain, to be clearly unavoidable. 'Bankruptcy has been staring Tom in the face for a long time, but he won't admit it.'
19. to **make faces** (colloquial) – to grimace. 'The little boy made faces at his aunt when she wasn't looking.'
20. to **pull a face** – to make a grimace which may express disgust, anger, derision or dismay.

    to **pull/make a long face** – to look dismal. 'When I told him that he would have to pay for all the damage out of his own pocket, he made a long face.'
21. to **keep a straight face** – to look as if you really believe a story or are in agreement with the speaker, when in reality you would like to laugh. 'When he told me he was going to photo-

graph the Loch Ness monster, it was all I could do to keep a straight face.'

1. **let's face it** – don't let us deceive ourselves. 'Let's face it, William will never get into College, not in a hundred years.'
2. to **face up to** – to confront a problem realistically without deluding oneself as to the nature of the difficulties. 'You must face up to the fact that we have no money.'
3. **on the face of it** – to all appearances, assuming that the facts have been correctly stated. 'On the face of it, your partner is clearly in the wrong, but have you told me the whole story?'
4. to **have the face to** – to be insolent enough to. 'After I had caught Mark stealing my crystal bowl, he had the face to ask me if he could keep it as a souvenir.'
5. to **show one's face** – to appear, to make one's presence known. 'I wonder she dare show her face here, after the way she has behaved.'
6. **to one's face** – in one's presence instead of behind someone's back. 'Let him make his accusations to my face!'
7. to **set one's face against** – to oppose strongly. 'He has set his face against any change in our plans.'
8. **at face value** – at its nominal or official value. 'The face value of an Elizabeth II sovereign is only £1, but its real value is at least £100.'
9. to **face both ways** – to support both contestants at the same time.
10. to **face about** – to change one's mind, to adopt a contrary opinion.
11. a **slap in the face** – a rebuff or snub. 'It was a slap in the face not inviting her old friend Sandra to her birthday party.'
12. to **lose face** – to be humiliated.
13. to **save face** – not to lose respect, to avoid humiliation.

    a **face-saving formula** – a form of words that seeks to avoid humiliation for the defeated party.
14. to **put a new face on** something – to show something in a different light. 'Higg's presence at the house on the night of the crime has put a new face on the investigation.'
15. to **laugh in** someone's **face** – to mock. 'I told him he was to blame for the accident, but he laughed in my face and told me I must be joking.'
16. to **laugh on the other side of one's face** – to change from exultation to dismay. 'Andrew was looking forward to a few days' freedom, but he'll laugh on the other side of his face when he hears Joyce has gone away for good.'
17. to **wipe the smile off** someone's **face** – to destroy someone's complacency. 'Arnold has been boasting that he is the best heavyweight in our unit, but I'll soon wipe the smile off his face.'
18. to **fly in the face of** – to ignore the facts or logic of an argument, to deny or contradict unreasonably. 'You are flying in the face of all the authorities on this subject.'
19. to **throw in** someone's **face** – to reproach someone for a blunder or fault. 'Alice threw her husband's disgrace in his face.'
20. to **fall flat on one's face** – to make a dismal failure of something. 'A couple of years ago, Steven bought the book shop at the corner but, not having any experience of running a shop, he fell flat on his face.'
21. his/her **face fell** – he/she looked dismayed.
22. **her face is her fortune** – her beauty is her only asset.
23. **faceless men** – anonymous, unfeeling men. This phrase is used with special reference to civil servants who often use their traditional anonymity to escape responsibility for their actions.

EYE

1. to **see eye to eye** – to be in agreement with someone, usually over a wide range of subjects. 'We found it difficult to live together because we don't see eye to eye.'
2. to **be up to the eyes/ears** – to be overwhelmed with, to have an excessive amount. 'I am up to the eyes in work', 'He is up to his eyes in debt.'
3. to **have an eye on the main chance** (derogatory) – to be alert to any opportunity for betterment. 'She was a shrewd woman; she never did a kindness without a good reason, and she always had an eye on the main chance.'
4. to **meet one's eye** – to look straight in the face. 'He could not meet my eyes, but blushed and turned away from me.'
5. there is **more** in something **than meets the eye** – there is some hidden significance. 'Mrs Lewis rang up to say she and her husband couldn't come to dinner today. She said she had a cold, but I think she's offended with us. There is more in this than meets the eye.'
6. to **cast an eye over** – to read through very quickly, to check.
7. **easy on the eye** – attractive, pretty. 'Julie would stand out anywhere with her looks – she is easy on the eye, isn't she?'
8. **beauty is in the eye of the beholder** – there is no objective test for judging beauty; it is only a matter of opinion. Sometimes said to console a girl when she feels dissatisfied with her looks.
9. to be **all eyes** – to be very attentive. 'When she got up to sing, her admirer was all eyes.'
10. **through the eyes of . . .** – from the point of view of . . . 'When you play chess, you should look at the game through the eyes of your opponent.'
11. to **open the eyes to** – to make someone aware of a truth, usually some unpleasant fact. 'I opened his eyes to his wife's unfaithfulness.'
12. to be **an eye-opener** – to be a revelation. The phrase suggests a sudden surprise, which may be good or bad. 'Charles had always had romantic ideas about being a cowboy, so his first day at the ranch was a real eye-opener for him.'
13. **with one's eyes open** – fully aware of the risk one is running. 'He went into it with his eyes open, so he can't complain now if things go wrong.'
14. **with one's eyes shut** – with no difficulty or need for any assistance. 'I know my way to her house so well that I could take you there with my eyes shut.'
15. to **have an eye for** – to have good judgement of something. 'She has an eye for horses; she has bred them all her life.'
16. to **get one's eye in** – to get accustomed to the conditions so that one can display one's skill. 'Once he's got his eye in, he is very difficult to beat.' The reference is to ball games like cricket in which a player has to adjust his sight to the movement of the ball.
17. to **have/keep an eye on** – to watch carefully. 'You must keep an eye on that girl. She is very wild, and is not to be trusted on her own.'
18. to **have a roving eye** – to be always looking for a pretty face. 'It's a pity, Anne's husband has a roving eye and always seems to be with a pretty girl!'
19. to **shut one's eyes to** – to ignore or to pretend ignorance of someone's faults. 'She shut her eyes to all his short-comings, although my brother was always pointing them out to her.'
20. **with an eye to** – with the aim of. 'I studied French with an eye to getting a job in one of the big fashion houses in Paris.'

1. to **see with one's own eyes** – to witness, to experience oneself without having to rely on anyone else's testimony. 'You can take my word for it; I saw it with my own eyes.'
2. **not to believe one's eyes** – to doubt the reality of what one has seen. 'When my sister returned from the beauty parlour, she was so changed that I couldn't believe my eyes.' cf. **'not to believe one's ears' 85/15**.
3. to **cry one's eyes out** – to weep so much that one can't weep any more.
4. to **catch the eye** / to **be eye-catching** – to attract attention. 'With her splendid figure and her elegant gown, she soon caught the eye of the judges.'
5. **an eyeful** – attractive. 'She's an eyeful, isn't she. Really pretty!'
6. that's **one in the eye for** – a snub or rebuff. 'She didn't invite him to her birthday party. That was one in the eye for him!'
7. **my eye!** – rubbish, humbug. 'That's all my eye! Edward isn't ill at all, he is only putting it on.'
   eye-wash – humbug, hypocritical nonsense.
8. **in the twinkling of an eye** – very quickly.
9. to **see out of the corner of one's eye** – to notice, usually for only a second, while one's attention is directed elsewhere. 'As I was entering the restaurant, I saw John out of the corner of my eye, jumping on a bus.'
10. **wide-eyed** – wide-open eyes that express surprise or innocence.
11. a **private eye** – a private detective. 'The police don't like private eyes as a rule, but they had to admit that Hugh was a first-class investigator.'
12. to **clap eyes on** – to see or meet. Nearly always negative. 'I've never clapped eyes on you before!'
13. to **cock the eye** – to look at knowingly. 'As soon as the Vicar began to speak about the drinking in the village, she cocked an eye at me, and I felt myself going red in the face.'
14. to **keep one's eyes skinned** – to be extremely vigilant and alert.
15. to **make eyes at** – to gaze amorously at.
16. to **see with half an eye** – to realize at once. 'You could see with half an eye that Bob and Ruth weren't happy.'
17. the **naked eye** – without the aid of spectacles or a telescope. 'On a fine day, you can see the Bowden Rocks with the naked eye.'
18. to view **with a beady eye** – to look doubtfully or critically at someone. 'When I asked the boss for a day off so that I could nurse my sick mother, he viewed me with a beady eye.'
19. to be **starry-eyed** – to be full of fancies, to have a lot of impracticable ideas.
20. to **give the glad eye** – to give a loving or flirtatious look at someone.
21. the **evil eye** / to **have an evil eye** on someone – a menacing, ominous look. In Voodoo, the evil eye casts its spell over the intended victim, even when they are separated by hundreds of miles.
22. **in the public eye** – very much in the news, much discussed.
23. **in one's mind's eye** – in one's imagination. 'In my mind's eye, I can still see him knocking out his pipe on the mantelpiece, although he's been dead these twenty years.'
24. to **have bigger eyes than one's stomach** – to over-eat, to be a glutton.
25. **an eye for an eye, a tooth for a tooth** – a like punishment, a punishment that is as severe as the crime but not more so, in accordance with both the Muslim and Judaic laws. It has come to be used in the sense of revenge.
26. to **throw dust in** someone's **eyes** –

to mislead or deceive someone wilfully.

1. **the eye of the typhoon** – the centre of the typhoon in the sky.
2. **eye-ball to eye-ball** – direct confrontation between two enemies.

EYELID

3. not to **bat an eyelid** – to show no feeling or concern. 'No matter how outrageously the boy behaved, his father never batted an eyelid but just went on reading his newspaper.'
4. to **hang on by one's eyelids** – to hang by a thread, to maintain only a precarious hold.

EYEBROW

5. a **high-brow** – someone with an intellectual approach to literature and art. The high-brow is interested in style rather than content, and in ideas rather than action.

   a **low-brow** – a person who has no intellectual interests. He likes a story with plenty of action, looks for a pleasant tune in music, and prefers a painting that tells a story.
6. to **raise the eyebrows** – to express surprise, sometimes mild disapproval. 'When her boss ordered flowers for the manageress, the secretary raised her eyebrows.'
7. to **knit one's brows** – to concentrate. 'He knitted his eyebrows as he tried to work out a solution to the puzzle.'
8. to **be steeped to the eyebrows** – to be totally immersed in a subject. 'Since his childhood he had been steeped to the eyebrows in Greek mythology.'
9. **by the sweat of one's brow** – by very hard work, either physical or mental, without anyone's help. 'He reached his present position, not by influence, but by the sweat of his brow.'

NOSE

10. to **nose about** – to pry, to make all sorts of inquiries. 'The inspector has been nosing about among my father's documents all the morning.'
11. to **nose out** – to discover a secret.
12. to **be nosy** – to be inquisitive, to ask too many questions.

    a **nosy parker** – someone who is forever asking questions about one's business and one's private life. A busybody.
13. to **poke one's nose into someone else's business** – to pry, to interfere in another person's private business. 'He has been poking his nose into my affairs again.'
14. to **get up someone's nose** (slang) – to exasperate, irritate. 'Harry gets up my nose with his never-ending complaints.'
15. **under one's nose** – something that happens very close to a person without his knowing. 'He stole my watch from right under my nose.'
16. a **nose for** (trouble, etc.) – a gift for smelling out trouble. 'That journalist has a nose for the latest scandal.'
17. to **follow one's nose** – to go straight ahead or by instinct. 'She couldn't be bothered to explain how to get there. She told me just to follow my nose.'
18. to **be led by the nose** – to be completely dominated by, totally influenced by. 'The secretary led her boss by the nose until she had spent all his money.'
19. to **pay through the nose** – to pay an excessive price. 'I had to pay through the nose for that desk. I could have got it for a fraction of the price anywhere else.'
20. to **rub someone's nose in it** – to draw someone's attention repeatedly to a past blunder. 'It was bad enough for poor Kenneth, losing all that money,

without you rubbing his nose in it all the time.'

1. to **look down one's nose** – to regard with distaste or disdain. 'He looked down his nose at the youth for wearing his hair long.'
2. to **turn up one's nose** at something – to despise. 'She turns up her nose at Frinton and Bournemouth. Nothing but the Riviera is good enough for her.'
3. **with one's nose in the air** – in a snobbish manner. 'Judy never greets me; she always has her nose in the air.'
4. to **see beyond the end of one's nose** – to look beyond one's immediate surroundings, to use one's imagination and intelligence. 'He has no imagination. He can't see beyond the end of his nose.'
5. to **put** someone's **nose out of joint** – to upset or replace a favourite. 'Jenny is to replace Sally as the boss's confidential secretary. That will put Sally's nose out of joint!'
6. to **cut off one's nose to spite one's face** – to injure or deprive oneself while trying to hurt someone else. 'He was determined to punish his son, so he cancelled the cruise he had booked. But it was a case of cutting off his nose to spite his face, because his son went to Cornwall, leaving his father to be miserable at home.'
7. to **keep one's nose clean** (slang) – to keep out of trouble. 'Life in the army can be quite pleasant, provided you obey orders and keep your nose clean.'
8. to **keep/put one's nose to the grindstone** – to work hard and long at the same job without any rest. 'With so many debts to pay off, he'll just have to keep his nose to the grindstone for the next few years.'
9. to **make a long nose at** someone/to **thumb one's nose at** someone – to show contempt for a person or institution. 'When you are making £100,000 a year, you can thumb your nose at convention.' cf. **'to cock a snook at' 68/3**.
10. **hard-nosed** – shrewd, tough, unsentimental.
11. a **nose-dive** – a vertical dive by an aeroplane. 'The aeroplane went into a nose-dive and crashed into the ground.'
12. to **get a bloody nose** – to suffer an unpleasant rebuff.
13. a **Roman nose** – a rather large, bulbous nose.
14. a **Greek nose** – a straight nose that extends down from the forehead in a straight line.

EAR

15. **long ears** – an inquisitive person who is always asking questions.
16. to **have sharp ears for any gossip** – alert to any gossip, not to miss any scandal.
17. a **thick ear** – a swollen ear, the result of being struck hard on the ear. 'The school bully threatened Martin with a thick ear.'
18. to **come to our ears** – to come to our knowledge, to learn of.
19. **coming out at the ears** – having something in superabundance. 'Jack has found so much oil, it's coming out at his ears.'
20. to **gain the ear** – to arouse someone's interest on one's behalf. 'Now that I have gained the chairman's ear, we shouldn't have any more difficulty.'
21. to **lend an ear** – to pay attention, to listen. 'If you will lend me your ear for a minute, I will explain how the burglar alarm works.'
22. to **play it by ear** – to use one's intuition, to improvise. '"I'm new to

this school; so I'll have to play it by ear for the first few lessons," the teacher said.' The phrase derives from playing a piece of music without looking at the musical score.

1. **in one ear and out the other** – heard without making any impression. 'Everything I say to that boy goes in one ear and out the other.'
2. **a word in the ear** – advice given in confidence.
3. to **be all ears** – to listen very attentively. 'What you say is very interesting. I'm all ears.'
4. to **have one's ear to the ground** – to be well-informed on what is going on, to be alert to future developments. 'Paul is always the first to know what's happening in the office. He keeps his ear to the ground.'
5. to be **still wet behind the ears** – to be naïve, inexperienced. 'He will be no match for them; he is still wet behind the ears.' The phrase has its origin in children's neglect to dry themselves behind the ears.
6. **'Are your ears burning?'** – Do you feel embarrassed to hear yourself talked about?
7. to **tickle the ears** – to flatter, to please. 'She said you were very handsome – yes, I thought that would tickle your ears.'
8. to **set** people **by the ears** – to stir up mischief. 'During his short stay, Philip set us all by the ears. We had no peace until he had gone.'
9. to **box the ears** – to strike the ears hard, usually as a punishment.
10. to be **out on one's ear** – to be ejected or sacked, often violently. 'The heckler was soon out on his ear, once he started interrupting the speaker.'
11. to **prick up one's ears** – to listen alertly, become suddenly interested in what is being said. 'He pricked up his ears when they mentioned the salary.' The idea comes from the pricking up of a dog's ears when it hears an unfamiliar sound.
12. to **grate on the ear** – to make a harsh, disagreeable sound. 'The lecturer's voice grated on the ears of his students.'
13. an **ear-splitting noise** – an unbearably loud noise.
14. to be **up to the ears in** work/debt – to have a huge amount of work/debts.
15. to be **unable to believe one's ears** – to be astounded at what one has heard. 'When Anne told me she had been married to my brother two years ago, I couldn't believe my ears.' cf. **'not to believe one's eyes' 82/2**.

MOUTH

16. to look **down in the mouth** – to look depressed, dejected, in low spirits. 'Henry was looking very down in the mouth today; his wife and children had just left for their holiday leaving him to look after the house.'
17. to have a **big mouth** – to speak a lot in a loud voice, to boast.
18. to **shoot off one's mouth** – to talk loudly and indiscreetly. 'Alex was shooting his mouth off in the pub last night about his domestic problems; he should keep all that to himself.'
19. a **mouthful** – a long and difficult name. 'Andrei Andreivitch, that's a mouthful, isn't it?'
20. to **be mealy-mouthed** – to describe something evil with undue mildness. 'If the man is a scoundrel, then say so; why be so mealy-mouthed about it?'
21. a **loose mouth** – an indiscreet person.
22. to **stand convicted out of one's own mouth** – to condemn oneself with one's own words.
23. to **leave a nasty taste in the mouth** – to

leave an unpleasant impression with someone. 'She apologized profusely for making such an accusation against me, and we shook hands at once, but what she had said left a nasty taste in my mouth.'

1. to **put words into** someone's **mouth** – to accuse someone of saying things that he has not said. '"I never said that," the witness protested angrily. "You are putting words into my mouth."'
2. to **take the words out of** someone's **mouth** – to say something before the other person has had time to say it himself. '"This is an appalling play," I said. "You've taken the words out of my mouth. Let's go," Alan replied.'
3. to **open one's mouth too wide** (vulgar) – to ask for too much money. 'My plumber has started opening his mouth too wide. I shall have to find someone else.'
4. to **make one's mouth water** – to tantalize. 'He made my mouth water showing me all his beautiful carpets. I wish I had enough money to buy one!'
5. to **foam at the mouth** – to be overcome with fury, to be so angry as to lose all control over oneself. 'When the football squashed his prize dahlias, the gardener foamed at the mouth with rage.' The foam is the rush of saliva from the mouth.
6. **out of the mouths of babes and sucklings** – the truth is often spoken by children without their being aware of it.
7. **by word of mouth** – through the spoken word, as opposed to the written word. 'Many herbal remedies have been passed down by word of mouth from one generation of gypsies to the next.'
8. the **gift of the gab** – the gift of fluent speech. 'With your gift of the gab you should do well as a lawyer.' Gab derives from Gaelic 'gob' meaning 'mouth', but is only used in this phrase.

JAW

9. a **glass jaw** – a glaring weakness which renders a person extremely vulnerable to attack. Mainly used in boxing. cf. 'to have **feet of clay' 104/10, 'Achilles' heel' 195/8**, 'a **chink in one's armour' 210/7**.
10. to **jaw away** (school slang) – to speak without interruption. 'Jaw, jaw is better than war, war' (Churchill) – to negotiate, even if it takes a long time, is better than making war.
11. out of **the jaws of death** – from the very brink of death. This phrase is often used with the verb 'snatch'. 'He was snatched from the jaws of death by his friend.'

WHISKER

12. **within a whisker** – by a very narrow margin. 'We were within a whisker of being defeated. The result couldn't have been closer.'

LIP

13. to **have one's lips sealed** – to be obliged to keep silent, to keep a confidence or secret.
14. to **bite one's lip** – to regret having said something indiscreet. 'She bit her lip for having made such a clumsy mistake.'
15. **none of your lip!** (colloquial) – don't be cheeky/impudent.
16. to **put a finger to one's lips** – to make a sign to keep quiet.
17. to **curl the lip** – to show contempt.
18. to **keep a stiff upper lip** – to suffer in

silence, to suppress all emotion. 'Lewis suffered dreadfully but he kept a stiff upper lip throughout his ordeal.' From the poem, 'A stiff upper lip', by Phoebe Cary (1824–74).

1. to **pay lip service** – to respect a principle or custom in theory but to ignore it in practice. 'He pays lip service to his wife's wishes but, once she has gone away, he reverts to his old way of life.'
2. to **lick/smack one's lips** – to exult at the prospect of an appetizing meal or other future event to be enjoyed.
3. to be **tight-lipped** – unwilling to say more than is absolutely necessary. 'He was very tight-lipped about his future plans.'
4. to **hang on** someone's **lips** – to listen attentively to every word a person is saying, to give him one's entire attention.

TOOTH

5. to **cut a tooth** – (of a young tooth) to pierce the gum.
6. to have a **sweet tooth** – to have a liking for sweet food, sugar, honey, ice-cream, etc. 'Nicola has such a sweet tooth; it makes it very difficult for her to slim.'
7. to **go over with a fine tooth-comb** – to make a most thorough and painstaking examination.
8. to be **long in the tooth** – old, too old, older than one cares to admit. 'He's a bit long in the tooth for her, isn't he? He must be at least sixty!'
9. the **toothless lion** – a warrior who no longer has the strength to defend himself, someone who has grown feeble and impotent.

TEETH

10. **milk teeth** – the first teeth.
11. to **cut one's wisdom / eye-teeth** – to acquire sense or discretion.
12. to **give one's eye-teeth for** – to wish with all one's heart for, to be prepared to make any sacrifice for. 'I would give my eye-teeth for your job. You have a job in a million!'
13. to **show one's teeth** – to make threats or express hostility. 'Our landlord has always been such a kind, easy-going man, but when I accidentally smashed his window he really showed his teeth.'
14. to **give teeth to** – to give a person or organization special powers and sanctions. 'We must give the Ombudsman teeth so that he can enforce his decisions.'
15. to **get one's teeth into** – to concentrate all one's energy on. 'Short stories are all very well, but I prefer a novel – something I can get my teeth into.'
16. to **get the bit between the teeth** – to throw off all restraint in achieving one's objective. 'Malcolm is determined to buy the house, whatever it costs. Once he gets the bit between his teeth, it is useless to argue with him.' The rider can control his horse by pulling on the bit in the horse's mouth. However, once the horse gets the bit between its teeth, the rider can no longer control it.
17. **in the teeth of** – against the strong resistance of. 'Henry married the girl in the teeth of her parents' disapproval.'
18. to be **fed up to the teeth / back teeth** – to be exasperated beyond endurance. 'I'm fed up to the back teeth with all his complaints.' cf. **'to have a bellyful' 99/13**.
19. to **be kicked in the teeth** – to suffer a severe blow from someone from whom you least expect it. 'After I had given her son all those private lessons for nothing, she cut me dead at the

party last night. It was a real kick in the teeth.'

1. to **set one's teeth on edge** – to grate or jar on the nerves. 'Her voice sets my teeth on edge, like scraping a plate with a knife.'
2. to **grind one's teeth** – to express one's fury. 'Herbert ground his teeth when he heard his daughter was going to marry his junior clerk.'
3. to **cast in the teeth** – to reproach a person to his face for some blunder or fault. 'She cast his drunkenness in his teeth.'
4. to **gnash one's teeth** – to regret bitterly, either one's own mistakes or the success of somebody of whom one is jealous. 'He gnashed his teeth at the idea of Michael marrying his old girl-friend.' A biblical phrase, '. . . there shall be weeping and gnashing of teeth' (Matthew VIII, 12).
5. to **grit one's teeth** – to suppress one's feelings when suffering a painful or frightening experience. 'He gritted his teeth and dived into the cold water.'
6. to **lie through one's teeth** – to lie shamelessly. 'If Richard told you that he was a rich man, he was lying through his teeth. Why, only yesterday he asked me to lend him £50!'
7. to **draw someone's teeth** – to render a dangerous person harmless. 'The Prime Minister drew the teeth of the Opposition by announcing that there had been a drop of a quarter of a million in the number of the unemployed.'

TONGUE

8. to have a **sharp tongue** – to have a pointed, barbed way of speaking.
9. to be **loose-tongued** – to be garrulous, indiscreet.
10. to **give tongue to** – to express in words, cry out. (From the sound made by hounds when hunting.)
11. to **keep a civil tongue in one's head** – to speak respectfully to one's superiors. 'The director ordered his manager to keep a civil tongue in his head.' A little old-fashioned.
12. **with the tongue in one's cheek** – words spoken insincerely. 'When he congratulated Martin on his twenty years' public service, he must have had his tongue in his cheek, because he is always talking about Martin's bad work in the office.'
13. to **wag one's tongue** – to talk behind someone's back, to gossip.

    to **set tongues wagging** – to give cause for gossip through one's indiscretions.
14. to **get one's tongue round** – to have difficulty in saying a word. 'Hypothesize? I can hardly get my tongue round it.'
15. to have a **tongue that runs away with one** – to talk too much, to be indiscreet. 'How your tongue ran away with you last night, Roy! You shouldn't have talked about your father like that to a stranger.'
16. to **hold one's tongue** – to say nothing, to be discreet. 'If I tell him something in confidence, do you think he can be trusted to hold his tongue?'
17. a **slip of the tongue** – a mistake in one's speech, through carelessness or, more often, a conflict of wishes. An example: a chairman in his welcoming speech to his co-directors declared the meeting closed instead of open because he didn't want to see them (*Psychopathology of Everyday Life* by Sigmund Freud).
18. **I could have bitten my tongue off** – I was angry with myself for having said something (usually something tactless or stupid). 'I thought my joke

would amuse our guests but, instead, there was an embarrassed silence. I could have bitten my tongue off.'

1. to give someone **the rough edge of one's tongue** – to reprimand someone harshly. 'If he doesn't mend his ways, I shall give him the rough edge of my tongue, and he'll be sorry he was so impertinent.'
2. to have a **dirty tongue** to use bad language.
3. **on the tip of one's tongue** – (1) to be on the point of saying something. 'It was on the tip of my tongue to tell Mervyn that I had already read the book he had given me, but I stopped myself just in time.' (2) very nearly remembered. 'Her name was on the tip of my tongue just now; it will come back to me.' This use is almost always confined to the names of people or places.
4. **tongue-tied** – unable to speak through shyness or fear. 'The student stood tongue-tied in front of the examiners.'
5. **Have you lost your tongue?** – Why can't you speak? Addressed to someone who is speechless, silent.
6. to **find one's tongue** – to regain one's speech. 'Oh, you've found your tongue again, have you?'

THROAT

7. to have a **lump in one's throat** – to feel sad, to be on the verge of tears. 'When I waved good-bye to Angela, I had a lump in my throat. I had grown very fond of her.'
8. to have **the words stick in one's throat** – to find it impossible to say the words, owing to dislike, pride or prejudice. 'I wanted to congratulate him, but I disliked him so much that the words stuck in my throat.'
9. to **force/ram down one's throat** – to force a belief or idea upon someone. 'It's a mistake to force your own ideas down his throat. He is old enough to think for himself.'
10. to **jump down one's throat** – to criticize someone for some trifling mistake, to speak sharply to. 'However carefully the student spoke, the teacher jumped down his throat.'
11. **at each other's throats** – deadly enemies, constantly fighting each other. 'The two brothers will never make peace; they have been at each other's throats for the last twenty years.'
12. to **slit one's throat** – to damage one's own interests. 'You would be slitting your throat if you reduced your prices still further.' It can also be used to express a strong negative attitude. 'I would rather slit my throat than work together with that rogue Maynard.'
13. **cut-throat competition** – ruthless competition by any method, fair or foul. 'You will find it difficult to open a shop in the High Street. There is a lot of cut-throat competition in this town.'

CHEEK

14. **to give** someone **cheek / to cheek** someone – to show disrespect to anyone in authority, or senior. 'The girl gave cheek to the teacher.'

    to **have a cheek** – to be extremely disrespectful towards someone. 'He has a cheek. The minute we were introduced, he asked me for a loan.'
15. **the cheek of the devil** – uninhibited insolence. 'She has the cheek of the devil, asking her boss to post her letter for her.'
16. **none of your cheek** – don't be impertinent to me. 'Don't give me any of your cheek.'
17. to **turn the other cheek** – to submit to violence, not to resist the blows of one's oppressor. The charity of the

Christian ethic, which distinguishes it from many other religions. 'Resist not evil. Whoever shall smite thee on thy right cheek, turn to him the other also' (Matthew V.39).

1. **cheek by jowl with** – very close to one another.

CHIN

2. **'Chin up!'** – take courage, don't despair.
3. to **stick one's chin out** – to persist in one's own opinion, to defy other people's wishes. 'It was a stupid idea of the boss's, but I'm not going to stick my chin out.'
4. to **lead with one's chin** – to lay oneself open to a dangerous counter-attack when attacking an opponent. 'You were leading with your chin when you accused Williams of lying. You might have known he would say the same to you.' A boxer leads with the chin when he drops his guard as he moves forward.
5. to **take (it) on the chin** – to undergo a painful experience or punishment with courage. 'Rolf had a hard time when he was a recruit in the army but he took it all on the chin.'
6. to **have a chin-wag** – to have a talk or chat.

NECK

7. **neck and neck** – absolutely level. The phrase is taken from horse-racing.
8. **on the neck of** – immediately following.
9. to **get it in the neck** – to be severely punished.
10. **it's neck or nothing** – one must risk everything, one must gamble all on one throw.
11. to **stick one's neck out** – to make predictions which may be falsified by events.
12. to **chance one's neck** – to risk one's reputation by accepting responsibility, often when there is no need to. cf. 'to **chance one's arm' 91/17**.
13. to **break one's neck** – to be in a tremendous hurry. Used with such adverbs as almost, nearly, practically. 'You might have told me you weren't coming. I nearly broke my neck getting to the station in time to meet your train.'

    at breakneck speed – recklessly, dangerously fast.
14. to **save** someone's **neck** – to help someone out of a very unpleasant situation. 'If I hadn't taken the blame, you would have got the sack. This isn't the first time I have saved your neck.'
15. to **rubber-neck** – to listen to somebody else's conversation or read his newspaper over his shoulder.
16. to **breathe down someone's neck** (slang) – to supervise someone very closely. 'I would like the job much better if the boss wasn't breathing down my neck all the time.'
17. to be **up to one's neck in** something – to be deeply implicated in a crime or trouble. 'You knew very well what we were doing. You are in this up to your neck.'
18. **neck and crop** – entirely, the whole body. Nearly always used in connection with 'throwing out'. 'The man was ejected from the building, neck and crop.' cf. **'bag and baggage' 176/7**.
19. to **carry a millstone round one's neck** – to be burdened with a responsibility from which it is impossible to free oneself. 'My brother-in-law, who depends on us financially, has been a millstone round my neck ever since we married.'

1. to **come a cropper** – to fail disastrously. 'Even the most experienced businessman can come a cropper.' A hunting phrase meaning to fall heavily from a horse. The crop is the head.

SHOULDER

2. to **carry/have on one's shoulders** – to bear responsibility for, to have to answer for. 'He had on his shoulders the whole burden of his father's debts.'
3. to **shoulder out** – to grab someone else's job.
4. to **shoulder the blame** – to accept full responsibility.
5. **straight from the shoulder** – frank, outspoken.
   to **give it** to someone **straight from the shoulder** – to tell someone the plain truth without sparing his feelings.
6. to **give** someone **the cold shoulder** – to treat someone with marked coldness, to ignore him in a noticeable manner. 'When I greeted Lucy this morning, she pretended not to see me. I wonder why she is giving me the cold shoulder.'
7. to **rub shoulders with** – to meet frequently, or to come into frequent contact with, a person.
8. to **have broad shoulders** – to be able to bear the full weight of one's responsibilities.
9. a **chip on the shoulder** – a grievance on one's mind which colours one's attitude to life. 'Steven has had a chip on the shoulder ever since he was thrown out of the army.'
10. to **put one's shoulder to the wheel** – to throw all one's energy into a task.
11. **a shoulder to cry on** – someone you can rely upon to offer sympathy and comfort in a time of sorrow or depression, a good friend. 'If you ever want a shoulder to cry on, you know where to come.'

ARM

12. to receive/welcome **with open arms** – to accept/greet with great willingness, without any hesitation.
13. **at arm's length** – at a distance. 'Alan wanted to get to know Helen better, but she kept him at arm's length.'
14. to stand **with arms akimbo** – to stand with each fist on the hip bones, with the elbows pushed forward, a posture which may express shock or anger. The word 'akimbo' is derived from the Icelandic, 'Keng' ('into a crook') with the English doublet 'bow' unnecessarily added to it.
15. a **right arm** – the main supporter to whom one first turns for help when there is difficulty or trouble. 'Since Mother's death, Susan has been Father's right arm.'
16. **one would give one's right arm to . . .** – one would make a great sacrifice in order to . . . 'I would give my right arm to see Janet again.'
17. to **chance one's arm** – to take a big risk. cf. **'to chance one's neck'** which has much the same meaning **90/12**.
18. **with one arm tied behind one's back** – without the slightest difficulty, in spite of a huge disadvantage. 'Why, my man could beat yours with one arm tied behind his back!' Originally used of boxers. Now used to indicate a decisive superiority in any competitive situation.
19. **arm-twisting** – threatening, putting pressure on someone. 'After some arm-twisting by the management, the men withdrew their claim for a massive increase, for fear of the factory closing down.'

ELBOW

1. **at one's elbow** – within very easy reach. 'I have all the books I want at my elbow.'
2. **elbow-room** – space in which to move. 'I haven't got any elbow-room in this tiny office.'
3. to **elbow one's way through** – to push opposition to one side.
4. to **give someone the elbow** – to get rid of someone. 'Hughes isn't worth his wages; it's time we gave him the elbow.'
5. **More power to your elbow!** – to wish someone success in what he is trying to do. 'Alan deserves a lot more money for the job he's doing. More power to his elbow.'
6. **elbow-grease** (colloquial) – energy, industry and sweat.
7. to be **out at elbows** – shabby, poorly dressed; sometimes used with 'down at heel', to describe someone whose clothes are patched or torn.
8. to **lift the elbow** – to be a habitual drinker. 'Have you noticed? Peter lifts the elbow!'

WRIST

9. a **slap on the wrist** – a mild, ineffective punishment.

   wrist-slap diplomacy – a punishment inflicted by one government on another, which is too small and ineffective to serve any useful purpose. Diplomatic illnesses and cancellations of state visits both come into this category.

HAND

10. to be **a great hand at** something – skilful; generally used in an ironic sense. 'He is a great hand at giving advice, but when it comes to doing some work, he is not so good.'
11. a **dab hand** – to be clever at doing something, often something of a practical nature. 'Why don't you let me decorate your sitting-room for you; I'm a dab hand at decorating.'
12. a **free hand** – complete freedom, without any interference or restriction. 'My husband has given me a free hand as to how I bring the children up.'
13. an **old hand** – experienced, skilful. 'He'll finish the fence for you very quickly. He is an old hand at that kind of work.'
14. to be **even-handed** – to be fair, unbiased, equally critical of both parties to a dispute.
15. to be **high-handed** – to be tyrannical, unwilling to listen to reason.
16. to **give** someone **the glad hand** – to give a warm and friendly welcome to someone. An Americanism.
17. to be **under-handed** – to be unfair, dishonourable. 'That was an underhanded trick he played on you, telling you your friends were at the airport waiting for you, when they were not.'
18. to **come away empty-handed** – to return with nothing to show for one's efforts. 'He went on a business trip to Rome and came back empty-handed.'
19. to be **short-handed** – to be short of assistance. 'We are very short-handed just now. Three of our staff are ill.'
20. a **handful** – a person who is always up to some mischief, in need of strict supervision. 'Their small son was quite a handful while they were on holiday.'
21. to **have one's hands full** – to be fully occupied, to be unable to accept any fresh work. 'I have my hands full running the business, so I've had to resign from the village council.'
22. to **have only one pair of hands** – to be incapable of working any faster. 'I can't look after the children and cook

the dinner at the same time; I've only got one pair of hands.'

1. to be **tied/bound hand and foot** – to have obligations which severely restrict one's freedom. 'I'd love to take a holiday with you but I'm tied hand and foot to my business.'

   to **have one's hands tied** – similar in meaning to the above, but a little less emphatic. 'I'm not allowed to advance you any money without your father's permission. I'm sorry I can't oblige you, but my hands are tied.'

2. **hands off** – do not interfere.

3. a **cool hand** – someone with good nerves, calm, not easily flustered. 'When the staff walked out, the boss sat down and lit a cigar. He's a cool hand all right.'

4. **with an open hand** – generously. 'Whenever we asked Mr Jones for money for the charity, he responded with an open hand.'

5. **with a heavy hand** – severely, oppressively. 'We were brought up with a heavy hand. None of us dared contradict our parents.'

6. to **hold a good hand / a bad hand** – to hold good cards / bad cards. 'You dealt me a good hand, but Martin has had one bad hand after another.'

7. one's **right-hand man** – someone's principal support and adviser.

8. a **left-handed compliment** – an apparent compliment which is really just the opposite. '"Your sister is very well preserved, isn't she? She doesn't look a day over forty." "My sister is thirty-five!"'

9. **close at hand** – within easy reach. 'If you need help, we are always close at hand.'

10. **at first hand** – direct from the person concerned and not from someone else. 'I got the news at first hand, so I know it's true.'

11. **at second hand** – indirectly, from somebody not immediately concerned. 'I have only received the news second hand, so it may not be reliable.'

12. **second hand** – sold for the second time, no longer new, having been used already.

13. to **have/hold the whip hand** – to have someone in one's power.

14. to have **clean hands** – to be above reproach. 'He who seeks equity must come to court with clean hands' (a legal maxim).

15. **when the left hand doesn't know what the right hand is doing** – when the activities of an organization are not properly co-ordinated and, as a result, there is confusion. 'My offer was accepted by the director but refused by the manager. The left hand of Vernon's doesn't know what the right hand is doing.'

16. to **soil/dirty one's hands** – to do something dishonest or shameful. 'I wouldn't soil my hands doing business with that firm; they are cheating the public.'

17. to **give a slow handclap to** – to show one's disapproval of a public speaker.

18. a **backhander** – (1) a sudden surprise blow given with the back of the hand; which can also be used metaphorically; (2) a bribe.

19. to **hand it to someone** – to give someone credit for something he has done. 'I'm sorry Philip has failed his examination again, but you've got to hand it to him for trying.'

    'I've got to hand it to you' – I must congratulate you.

20. to **work hand in hand** – to work together in close agreement.

21. to **make a poor hand at** – to work unskilfully at something. 'I should make a poor hand at doing your job. Book-keeping is not in my line.'

1. **with a strong hand** – firmly, vigorously, severely. 'The officer dealt with the man's insubordination with a strong hand.'
2. to **gain the upper hand** – to obtain a decisive advantage over someone, to master him. 'He was much stronger than his opponent and soon gained the upper hand.'
3. to **accept with both hands** – to accept most eagerly. 'If I'd been in your place, I'd have accepted his offer with both hands. You won't get a better one.'
4. to **join hands** – to unite with, work together with. 'We must join hands with our friends in Europe.'
5. to **go down on one's hands and knees** – to beg most humbly. 'I won't go down on my hands and knees to him, no matter how important he is.'
6. a **hand-out** (colloquial) – a free distribution of money, goods, etc., which may amount to bribery. 'When Lewis was leader of the local Council, there were plenty of hand-outs to his friends.'
7. to **hand down** – to bequeath, as a rule from one generation to the next. 'That gold watch has been handed down to us from our great-grandfather.'
8. to **have in hand** – (1) to put money on one side, or in reserve, usually for a special purpose. 'I have £300 in hand, in case the job works out dearer than they estimated.' (2) to attend to a job. 'We have the matter in hand and will inform you as soon as the work has been completed.'
9. to **get** something **in hand** – to have under control. 'I am making the holiday arrangements now, so you needn't worry. I have got everything in hand.'
10. to be **out of hand** – (1) to be undisciplined, out of control, ill-behaved. 'When his son was in Paris, the boy got out of hand and ran up big gambling debts.' (2) without any discussion. 'He refused the offer out of hand, and broke off negotiations.'
11. to **take in hand** – to take control of someone, usually for some particular purpose. 'He is ten kilos overweight. The dietician is taking him in hand.'
12. to **get one's hand in** – to regain one's skill. 'After a couple of games, you'll soon get your hand in.'
13. **off-hand** – (1) without referring to one's notes or records. 'I can't tell you off-hand, but, as soon as I get back to the office, I'll telephone you.' (2) casual, lacking in respect. 'She was off-hand with me, and went on with her housework while I was speaking.'
14. to be **in one's hands** – to be under one's control, to be one's own responsibility. 'It is in your hands now whether or not you succeed. I can't help you any more.'
15. to **have on one's hands** – to have a responsibility to attend to, often an irksome one. 'I shall have their boy on my hands all through his summer holidays.'
16. to have something **taken off one's hands** – to be relieved of an irksome responsibility. 'I am grateful to you for taking Judy off my hands. She was getting too much for me.'
17. to **raise/lift one's hand to** – to strike. 'I've never raised my hand to him, but one day I shall if he goes on like this!' cf. **'to lay hands on' 95/10**.
18. **hand-to-hand fighting** – fighting at close quarters with the enemy, with bayonets, knives or even fists.
19. to be **behindhand** – to be late in paying a debt or in completing a task. '"You've got badly behindhand with the work!" "Yes, we've had a lot of orders this month, and we can't keep up with the work."'

1. to **keep one's hand in** – to retain one's skill by practising. 'Mike keeps his hand in during the winter on the indoor tennis courts.'
2. to **have a hand in** something – to play a part in something, bear some of the responsibility for. This is often used in reference to something illicit. 'I suspect he has had a hand in the robbery, although I can't prove it.'
3. to **show one's hand** – to make one's intentions clear. 'When I asked Digby if he was planning to take over our company, he pretended to be very surprised. He doesn't want to show his hand yet.' The idiom comes from card-playing, e.g. from bridge in which it is important for the players not to show their cards during the bidding.
4. to **try one's hand** – to see how well one can do in an activity, instead of just watching others. 'Why don't you try your hand at weaving? You might do just as well as us.'
5. to **shake hands on it** – to signify one's assent to an agreement.
6. to **wash one's hands of** something – to absolve oneself from responsibility. 'That boy is quite impossible. From now on I wash my hands of him!' The allusion is to Pontius Pilate who washed his hands in a bowl of water in order to show that they were innocent of the blood of Jesus Christ (Matthew XXVII, 24).
7. to have **blood on one's hands** – to be responsible for the injury or death of a person. 'I don't think we should stop the surgeon operating; we don't want the patient's blood on our hands.'
8. to **sit on one's hands** – to wait passively, without doing anything.
9. to **win hands down** – to win very easily, by a large margin.
10. to **lay hands on** – to strike. 'If you lay hands on me, I will charge you with assault.' cf. 'to **raise/lift one's hand to' 94/17.**

    to **lay hands on** also has two negative meanings: (1) to seize, arrest. 'The police have not yet laid hands on the wanted man.' (2) to find an object that has been mislaid. 'I know it's somewhere in the office, but I can't lay my hands on it.'
11. to **give a hand** with – to help, usually for only a short time. 'Please give me a hand with the suitcase. It's rather heavy.'
12. to **hold one's hand** – to refrain from taking any action, on receiving certain assurances. 'If you undertake to pay us by Tuesday, we will hold our hand.'
13. to **throw in one's hand** – to yield, to stop trying. 'When he was told that his men had called a strike, Fison threw in his hand and closed the factory.' From card-playing, when a player who had been dealt a bad hand threw his cards on the table and stopped playing.
14. to be **on one's hands** (commercial) – to be lying in the shop unsold. 'The antique furniture is still on our hands, we just cannot get rid of it.'
15. to **play into** someone's **hands** – to use the tactics which most benefit one's opponent/enemy. 'You should never have confided your business troubles to your competitors. Now they can make matters worse for you. You have played into their hands.'
16. to **overplay one's hand** – to press one's advantage too far. The phrase is derived from games of cards where a player with good cards bids or calls higher than the hand justifies.
17. to **turn one's hand to** – to turn one's attention to, to apply oneself to, to attempt. 'Everything your father turns his hand to, he does well.'
18. to **force** someone's **hand** – to bring pressure to bear on someone. 'I didn't

want to mention your name but, by going to the police, they forced my hand.'

1. to **stir a hand** – to help, make an effort. 'It's time you stirred a hand!'
2. to **be caught with one's hand/fingers in the till** – to be caught stealing from one's employer. 'You would think I had been caught with my hand in the till from the way my boss talks to me.'
3. **Hand on heart / Cross my heart and let me die** – I promise you, I am telling you the truth. 'I didn't smoke one cigarette while you were out. Hand on heart!'
4. **hand over fist** – (1) very rapidly. 'My son is very bright. He is making progress hand over fist.' (2) to make money very fast. 'Since Andrew started his own business, he has been making money hand over fist.' The phrase has probably been taken from rope-climbing, when the free hand is passed over and above the fist that is holding the rope.
5. to **wait on** someone **hand and foot** – to serve somebody with complete dedication. 'I was waited on hand and foot; I only had to ring a bell and a servant came to my room in a few seconds.'
6. to live **from hand to mouth** – to make only enough money to supply one's immediate needs, not to know where one's future income is coming from. 'I'm sick of this hand-to-mouth existence; I think I'll look for a regular job.'
7. to **bite the hand that feeds you** – to injure the person on whom you depend for your living. 'You shouldn't have criticized your father in front of his guests. You were biting the hand that feeds you!' (Edmund Burke, *Thought and Details on Scarcity*, 1800).
8. to **eat out of** someone's **hand** – to submit willingly to someone's wishes, to do anything to please someone. 'After our talk, Mary was eating out of my hands.' A tame animal will eat from its keeper's hand.
9. a **show of hands** – the taking of a vote by asking all those present who are in favour of a proposal to raise their hands.
10. **sleight of hand** – skilful trickery (often used humorously). 'With a sleight of hand, the Prime Minister was able to persuade the workers that they had won a victory over the employers, and the employers that they had got the better of the workers.' Literally, the clever use of the hands in conjuring and juggling.
11. to **know a place like the back/palm of one's hand** – to know a place intimately. 'I know London like the back of my hand.'
12. **all hands to the pumps** – Please help, everyone. It's urgent!
13. to be **man-handled** – to be moved by physical force. 'When I called for the money at Pearson's home, I was man-handled by his servants and thrown out of the house.'
14. to have **time hanging on one's hands** – to be in a state of boredom, when time passes slowly. 'Time hung heavy on the hotelier's hands in the winter when the tourists went home and her children were at boarding school.'
15. to **take one's life in one's hands** – to risk losing one's life. 'If you let him drive you there, you will be taking your life in your hands. He is the worst driver I've ever met.'
16. **with an iron hand** – with great severity. 'The leader crushed the rebellion with an iron hand.' cf. 'an **iron hand in a velvet glove' 172/10.**
17. to be **in good hands** – to be well looked after. 'If your mother goes to the Lavington Sanatorium, she will be in

good hands; the doctors and nurses there are really good.'

PALM

1. to **palm** someone **off with / be palmed off with** – to be offered something inferior. Usually used in a negative sense. 'They made me a much better offer to start with, so I'm not going to be palmed off with such a rotten job now.'
2. to **have** someone **in the palm of one's hand** – to have someone completely in one's power. A somewhat melodramatic expression.
3. to **grease** someone's **palm** – to bribe. Often used in connection with the bribing of minor officials.

   palm oil (colloquial) – money used for bribery, on the analogy of greasing the palms.

   to have an **itching palm** – to accept bribes eagerly. 'In that country the officials all have itching palms; they are only too anxious to take bribes.'

FIST

4. to **make a good fist of** – to write well about. 'Graham made a good fist of his Life of Henry VIII.'
5. to **be close-fisted** – to be miserly, stingy, mean. The term expresses a person's reluctance to open his fist and let go of the money he is holding.

THUMB

6. to have someone **under one's thumb** – to dominate, or domineer over. 'She has her son completely under her thumb. He would never dare contradict or disobey her.'
7. **rule of thumb** – a rough, practical calculation made without the benefit of theoretical knowledge or scientific measuring instruments. 'Although his methods are more or less rule of thumb, he gets excellent results.'
8. to **give the thumbs down** – to veto a plan or course of action. 'After consulting together for an hour, the Committee gave the thumbs down to the young architect's proposals.' The 'thumbs down' derives from the Roman Emperor Nero who gave the 'thumbs down' signal at the Colosseum when he wanted a defeated gladiator slain.
9. to **give the thumbs up** – a sign indicating a positive answer, good news or approval of a person or scheme. 'When I asked the young man whether he had enjoyed his evening with Jenny, he smiled and gave me the thumbs-up sign.'
10. to **thumb a lift / thumb one's way** – to ask for a lift from a vehicle driver.
11. to **twiddle one's thumbs** – to be idle, to have nothing to do. 'We had to twiddle our thumbs for an hour while Helen was getting dressed.'
12. to **stick out like a sore thumb** – to be conspicuous on account of some odd or peculiar feature. 'Why did you have to paint your house that colour? It sticks out from the others like a sore thumb.' cf. 'an **eye-sore**' **128/6**.
13. to **thumb through** (the pages of a book) – to turn the pages of a book, usually without reading properly, but out of curiosity.
14. a **thumb-nail sketch** – a very abbreviated or miniature sketch – so small that it can be done on a thumb nail. 'The novelist only gave a thumb-nail sketch of his characters, as he thought their actions were more revealing than mere description of their appearance.'
15. to be **all thumbs / all fingers and**

thumbs – to be clumsy, as if each finger were a thumb, which would result in a loss of dexterity. 'I can't thread this needle; I am all thumbs today.'

FINGER

1. to be **light-fingered** – to have a strong inclination to steal whenever the opportunity arises.
2. to **have money stick to one's fingers** – to wrongly keep money that belongs to someone else.
3. to **burn one's fingers** – to suffer the consequences of some error of judgement. 'I burned my fingers badly by investing money in your friend's company. I shan't make that mistake again.'
4. to **twist** someone **round one's little finger** – to know how to impose one's will over someone, or to have a strong influence on someone.
5. to have **at one's fingertips** – to be an expert in a subject, to know a subject to perfection. 'He has parliamentary procedure and the rules and traditions of the House of Commons at his fingertips.'
6. **to one's fingertips** – in every respect, completely. 'Evans never made a decision without consulting his book of rules first; he was a bureaucrat to his fingertips.'
7. to **keep one's fingers crossed** – to hope and pray for success. 'Good luck with your driving test; I'll keep my fingers crossed for you.' Making the sign of the cross – in this case with the fingers – was believed to preserve one from bad luck. Today, the phrase is only used light-heartedly.
8. **'I can't put my finger on it but . . .'** – I have a feeling that something is wrong, without knowing exactly what it is.
9. to **work one's fingers to the bone** – to work until one is exhausted.
10. to **slip through one's fingers** – to miss a good opportunity. 'I took too long making up my mind, and let the house slip through my fingers.'
11. to **snap one's fingers at** – to show contempt for a person or institution.
12. to **point the finger at** – to blame a person/organization for a blunder or crime. 'The finger has been pointed at the Government for the high level of unemployment.'
13. to **be able to count on the fingers / on the fingers of one hand** – to emphasize the smallness of a number by counting it on the fingers / fingers of one hand. 'You could count on the fingers of one hand the number of times old Westwood arrived late at the office during the thirty years he worked for the firm.'
14. to **lay a finger on** – to hurt or harm. 'If you lay a finger on the child, you will regret it.'
15. a **two-fingered gesture** – a rude gesture indicating contempt. The gesture is made with the palm of the hand facing inwards. Contrast the V-sign, which is made with two fingers but with the palm facing outwards.
16. to **put the finger on** – to determine or diagnose the cause. 'You've put your finger on it: too many late nights and parties. That's no way to prepare for an examination!'
17. **not to lift a finger** – to refuse to do the least thing to help. 'All the time we were staying there, the girl didn't lift a finger to help her mother.'
18. **pull/take your finger out** – get on with the job. 'Prince Philip appealed to British industry to pull its finger out.' The complete phrase is 'pull/take your finger out and get stuck in' (a naval phrase).

1. to **have more** (of something) **in one's little finger than someone else has in his whole body** – to be greatly superior in one quality (such as intelligence, knowledge, skill, ability, talent) to another person. 'Mary has more talent in her little finger than you have in your whole body, which isn't saying much!' Often said in the heat of an argument.

QUICK

2. to **cut to the quick** – to hurt someone's feelings very deeply. 'Robert was cut to the quick when his wife told him that she didn't want to go abroad with him.' The quick is the sensitive part of the flesh beneath the fingernail.

KNUCKLE

3. **too close to the knuckle** – too realistic for comfort, embarrassing. 'Genet's plays are too close to the knuckle to be entertaining.'
4. to **knuckle down** – to accept discipline.
5. to **knuckle under** – to submit to authority. The phrase suggests that the submission is unwilling.
6. to give someone a **rap on the knuckles** – to reprimand someone severely. 'He was given a rap on the knuckles for his bad work.' The person who gives the rap is always in a position or rank of superiority. This phrase is often abbreviated to **'take the rap'**, with the same meaning: 'Why should I take the rap for you?'

CHEST

7. to **play one's hand/cards close to one's chest** – to be secretive about one's plans. 'I know he is up to something, but he is playing his cards very close to his chest.' cf. 'to **keep one's own counsel' 230/15.**
8. to **get something off one's chest** – to talk freely about something one has concealed. 'It's been on my conscience for a long time but, now I've got it off my chest, I feel a lot better.'

BREAST

9. to **make a clean breast of** the matter – to make a full and complete confession. 'If you have stolen the money, you had better make a clean breast of it to your boss at once.'
10. to **beat one's breast** – to show remorse for one's mistakes. 'No wonder Peter is beating his breast; if he had remembered to post his coupon, he would have won the football pools.'

BOSOM

11. **bosom friends** – very close friends who confide all their secrets to each other (applicable to either sex). 'The two girls were bosom friends and kept nothing back from each other.'
12. to be **in the bosom of one's family** – to live with one's family, surrounded by one's parents and brothers and sisters.

BELLY

13. to **have a bellyful** – to be exasperated beyond endurance. cf. 'to **be fed up to the teeth / back teeth' 87/18**, and 'to **have a basinful' 155/13**.
14. a **pot-belly** – a large, protruding stomach. 'If you drink so much beer every day, you will get a pot-belly.'
15. a **belly-dance** – a dance in which the dancers rotate their hips in the manner of Hawaiian dancing girls.

LAP

1. to **drop into someone's lap** – to acquire something easily, without the least effort. 'All the best things in life must be worked for – love, friendship, success . . . they won't drop into your lap.'
2. to live **in the lap of luxury** – to live in a state of great comfort and ease, having all one's material needs supplied without having to make any effort.
3. **in the lap of the gods** – completely unpredictable. 'I have no idea whether we shall win or not. It's in the lap of the gods.'

BACK

4. to **back** – to support, morally, politically or financially; to show confidence in, to put one's money on. 'Peter is stronger than Alex and moves faster in the ring. I am backing him to win.'

   to **back a horse** – to wager money on a horse.
5. to **back up** – to give one's support to a person under attack or involved in a quarrel. 'Why didn't you back me up when they insulted me?'
6. to **back out of** – to withdraw from a promise or undertaking. Backing out is not so abrupt or decisive as the synonym 'breaking a promise'. Backing out often suggests a reluctant change of mind, accompanied by excuses and explanations. 'When he heard how much the scheme was going to cost, he backed out rather than pay the extra money.'
7. to **back down** – to yield, withdraw a demand. 'When I told him he could sue me if he wasn't satisfied, he backed down at once, pretending he hadn't been serious.'
8. a **back-up service** (commercial) – visiting a customer to check that the equipment sold him is working properly. 'This firm provided a back-up service free of charge.'
9. to **hold back** – to suppress or withhold news or information, to withhold support.
10. to **hang back** – to hesitate, remain passive when action is called for. 'When she was mugged in the street, her companions hung back because they were afraid of the robbers.'
11. to **give one's (full) backing** – to give one's (full) support to a person or a plan of action.
12. to **backfire** – to injure the author of a scheme instead of its intended victim. 'Your plan could backfire if the authorities get to hear of it.'
13. a **backlash** – a strong reaction to excessive provocation. 'If the judges continue handing out these ridiculously light sentences, there could be a nasty backlash from the public and people will take the law into their own hands.'
14. **Get off my back!** – Leave me alone! Stop making demands on me!
15. **behind one's back / when one's back is turned** – in a person's absence, without his knowledge. 'Christine has been saying some very nasty things about you behind your back, George.'
16. to **get one's own back** on someone – to revenge oneself on someone. 'I mean to get my own back for the injury he has done me, even if it takes me ten years.'
17. to **get** someone's **back up** – to provoke someone to anger. 'You really got his back up with your criticisms of his house.' From the idea of a cat being threatened by a dog, when the cat arches its back to show its anger.
18. the **backbone** – the main support. 'He has been the backbone of the team for the whole of the season.'

1. to **have no backbone** – to lack strength of purpose, to be morally submissive. 'That boy has no backbone. He gives in to the slightest opposition.'
2. **to the backbone** – completely, absolutely, without any question. 'She was a Tory to the backbone.'
3. **broken-backed** – damaged, lacking the ability or means to survive. 'It's been a broken-backed business ever since it lost its major customer.'
4. to **break the back of** a task – to finish the hardest part of a task. 'By the time his brother arrived, they had broken the back of the work, and there was little left for him to do.'
5. to **break one's back** – to exhaust oneself with overwork. 'I have broken my back trying to keep this business going, but I couldn't go on any longer.' cf. **'to work oneself to death' 42/5**.
6. to **stab in the back** – a forceful phrase for betrayal, indicating the indignation of the victim. 'He has been my best friend for the last twenty years. I would never have dreamed he would stab me in the back like that.'
7. **with one's back to the wall** – in a desperately dangerous situation from which there is no escape. On 18 April 1918, Field Marshal Haig gave this famous order to the Allied forces: 'With our backs to the wall and believing in the justice of our cause, each one must fight on to the end.'
8. to **make a rod for one's own back** – to create difficulties for oneself. 'Why did the silly man argue with the magistrate? He made a rod for his own back.'
9. to be **glad to see the back of** someone – to be glad to see the last of someone.
10. to have **a good background** / to have **no background** – to be from a good/poor family. 'I don't want her to marry Steven. He has no background.'
11. to **have a broad back** – to be willing to accept responsibility for other people's mistakes. 'Put all the blame on me if it makes you feel better. I have a broad back.'
12. **backscratching / you scratch my back and I'll scratch yours** – you praise me and I'll praise you; you help me and I'll help you.
13. to give someone a **pat on the back** – to praise or applaud, to congratulate, often in a mild manner. 'Although his plan had not completely succeeded, she gave him a pat on the back for having tried so hard.'
14. to **put one's back into** – to put all one's energy into a task.
15. to **back the field** – a betting phrase for wagering one's money against one particular horse – usually the favourite.
16. **the back of beyond** – a remote, inaccessible place. 'I wish you didn't live in the back of beyond.'
17. to **be backward** – (1) a slow learner, a slow developer. Often used in the phrase 'dull and backward'. 'He is thirteen years old, and they have put him in a class with ten-year-olds. His teacher tells me he is very backward for his age.' (2) the term can also be applied to a country or race. 'The villagers live in abject poverty and are very backward in their ways. Few of them can read or write.'

BOTTOM

18. to **knock the bottom out of** an argument – to prove the falsity of an argument, to refute an argument. 'Pauline knocked the bottom out of our argument in a short but effective speech.'

HIP

19. to have **one on the hip** – to gain a decisive advantage over one's opponent. A wrestling term.

1. to **smite hip and thigh** – a biblical phrase, meaning to make a merciless attack on the enemy.

LEG

2. **not a leg to stand on** – without any reasonable justification in a dispute, without the semblance of a case. 'Mark accused the doctor of negligence, but when he admitted he hadn't taken the medicine prescribed, he hadn't a leg to stand on.'
3. to be **on one's/its last legs** – to be on the point of collapse, worn out. 'Mr Jones hasn't enough money left to renew his stock; his business is on its last legs.'
4. a **leg-up** – a helping hand. 'He gave me a leg-up when I was starting work by introducing me to some new customers.'
5. to **stretch one's legs** – to take exercise by walking about after a period of inactivity. 'We've been sitting here all the morning. It's time we stretched our legs.'
6. to **pull someone's leg** – to play a joke on someone, to tell him some misleading story that momentarily shocks or frightens him but which amuses everybody else.

   a **leg-pull** – a joke or untrue story with the same meaning as above.
7. to **leg it** – (1) to run away, (2) to walk when other means of transport have failed.
8. to **shake a leg** – to take part in a dance.
9. to **show a leg** – to get up and be quick about it. 'If you want to catch your coach, you had better show a leg.' 'Show a leg!' is a naval order which dates from the days when sailors were allowed to have their wives on board ship with them. The order was given in order to distinguish between the sailors who had to get up and the women who were allowed to lie in.
10. to **be bow-legged** – to have one's legs bent outwards so that there is a big space between them. The opposite of 'knock-knees'.

KNEE

11. **on one's knees** – in a position of submission.
12. to **bend the knee** – to submit to a stronger force, to obey submissively.

    on one's bended knees – in a position of abject submission. 'My husband treated me so badly during our marriage that I wouldn't have him back if he came to me on his bended knees.'
13. to **bring to his/its knees** – to defeat or force to submit. 'The recession has brought our company to its knees.'
14. a **knee-jerk reaction** – an unthinking, automatic response. 'We got the usual knee-jerk reaction to our request for a rise in our salaries.' When the knee is tapped below the joint, it kicks involuntarily; this is known as the knee-jerk reflex.
15. **weak-kneed** – someone who is unable to resist pressure. 'He was so weak-kneed that he allowed the man to ransack his flat, although he was twice as big as the burglar.'

FOOT

16. **My foot!** – a comment expressing disbelief. 'Paul's too weak to carry his suitcase upstairs! Too weak, my foot! He's twice as strong as I was at his age.'
17. to **put one's foot in it** – to cause embarrassment with a tactless remark. 'You put your foot in it when you told her how much you admired her husband. They were divorced last year!'

1. to **put one's foot down** – to impose one's authority, to call a halt to some action of which one disapproves. 'When his eighteen-year-old son wanted to start a business with his girl-friend, his father put his foot down and told him he wouldn't allow it.'
2. to have **a foot in both camps** – to have an interest in supporting both parties in a contest. 'Sooner or later, you'll have to choose between Labour and the Conservatives; you can't have a foot in both camps indefinitely.'

   to **have/get a foot in the door** – to have/gain access to a business, market, occupation, etc., in spite of opposition. 'Now we've got a foot in the door, we are hoping to open up a big market in China.' The commercial traveller puts his foot in the door to prevent the housewife from shutting it in his face, so that he can persuade her to buy his merchandise.
3. to **set on foot** – to initiate, to get things moving. 'The mothers of the district intend to set on foot plans for opening a kindergarten.'
4. to **start on the wrong foot** – to make a mistake at the very beginning (of a relationship). 'You started on the wrong foot, asking the boss for a week's leave only a few days after you had joined.' The reference is to starting to march with the right foot instead of the left.
5. to **put a foot wrong** – to make a mistake, to break the rules. 'Since Alan came out of prison, he hasn't put a foot wrong.'
6. to **wrong-foot** someone – to put someone at a disadvantage in a contest, to surprise him. 'Mr Jukes wrong-footed us by calling our manager as a witness. We hadn't expected him to do that.'

   to **catch** someone **on the wrong foot** – to take advantage of an opponent's mistake.
7. to be **on a friendly / good footing** – to enjoy a friendly relationship with someone.

   on a firm footing – on a solid foundation. 'We have put our business with Phillips on a firm footing.'
8. to be **light-footed** – to be nimble, light on one's toes. 'Although he is such a fat man, he is light-footed when he dances.'
9. **footloose and fancy free** – unattached, free of romantic ties.
10. to put one's **best foot forward** – to walk briskly, to walk faster, to hurry. Usually with the meaning of reaching a place by a particular time. 'If you want to catch your train, you'll have to put your best foot forward.'
11. to **follow in** someone's **footsteps** – to do the same as he. 'So, young man, you are going to follow in your father's footsteps and be a doctor!'
12. to **foot the bill** – to pay someone else's bill. 'Mr Brown had to foot the bill for his son's drunken escapades.' So called because the person called upon to pay was required to sign his name at the foot of the bill.
13. to **trample/tread underfoot** – to beat down all opposition, to crush the body and the spirit of one's enemy.
14. **with one foot in the grave** – so old or ill that one is on the point of dying. 'With one foot in the grave, I am afraid he is in no position to help you.'

FEET

15. to **be on one's feet** – to stand, to be standing. The phrase is often used to emphasize the length of time the subject has been standing. 'The medical students have been on their feet all day long in the operating theatre.'
16. to **set** someone **on his feet** – to give someone a fresh start, to help him over his difficulties.

1. to **fall/land on one's feet** – to adjust oneself to new conditions (after a set-back) with unexpected success. 'No sooner had he lost his job than he obtained another at twice the salary. He always falls on his feet.'
2. to **find one's feet** – to get adjusted, to settle down. 'The boy soon found his feet at his new school.'
3. to **drag one's feet** – to show reluctance. 'It's over a month since Hughes had the contract, but he hasn't signed it yet. I wonder why he is dragging his feet.'
4. to **walk someone off his feet/legs** – to walk a long way with a companion until he is exhausted. 'Whenever we go out together, Alan walks me off my feet.'
5. to be **rushed off one's feet** – to have so many claims on one's time that everything has to be done in a great hurry.
6. to **sweep off one's feet** – to make a swift conquest. 'She was so captivated with his good looks that he swept her off her feet within a few minutes of meeting her.'
7. to **get back on one's feet** – to make a full recovery, to become adjusted again. 'Once you've got back on your feet, you will feel quite differently about your work.' The idiom is often used in the sense of recovering from the effects of an illness.
8. to cast oneself **at** someone's **feet** – to throw oneself on the mercy of another, to submit to another person's will.
9. to have/get **cold feet** – to feel afraid to commit oneself to a decision or action which may prove risky or dangerous. 'Simon is getting cold feet about advancing you the money, now that your firm is in difficulties.'
10. to have **feet of clay** – to have an insecure base. The phrase is often used in reference to men or governments of seemingly great power which conceals some fatal weakness. Origin: biblical, Daniel II, 31–45. cf. **'Achilles' heel' 195/8**, 'a **glass jaw' 86/9**, 'a **chink in one's armour' 210/7**.
11. **under someone's feet** – in the way, obstructing one's movements. 'I can't cook the lunch with you under my feet all the time.'
12. to **have one's feet under the table** – to have a friend in whose home one is made welcome. cf. **'to hang up one's hat in a house' 173/12**.
13. to **cut the ground from under one's feet** – to take an opponent by surprise by suddenly depriving him of his advantage. 'When Nancy's father complained about the teaching at the school, the headmaster cut the ground from under his feet by announcing that Nancy had won a scholarship at Marlborough College.' cf. 'to **pull the rug from under one's feet' 152/5**, 'to **take the wind out of** someone's **sails' 30/13**.
14. to **stand on one's own (two) feet** – to be independent, self-reliant, in an economic or emotional sense. 'My son must get a job and learn to stand on his own two feet.'
15. to **put one's feet up / take the weight off one's feet** – to sit down and rest. Often said to a guest who has arrived after a tiring journey.
16. to **sit at a person's feet** – to listen with respect to an intellectual authority. 'We all admired Professor Stanton for his original thinking and sat at his feet when we were at the university.'
17. to **vote with one's feet** – to show one's dissatisfaction with one's country by leaving it instead of voting for better conditions. 'In the last twenty years, tens of thousands of people have voted with their feet in the hope of finding a better life elsewhere.'

1. to **think on one's feet** – the ability to speak in public, and to respond quickly to unexpected questions.
2. to **keep one's feet** – to avoid falling. 'After three glasses of whisky, he found it difficult to keep his feet.'
3. **with both feet on the ground** / to **have one's feet planted firmly on the ground** – free from fanciful, impractical ideas; sensible and practical. 'Margaret won't get carried away by a lot of silly notions; she has both feet on the ground.'

HEEL

4. to be **down-at-heel** – to be shabbily dressed. Sometimes the phrase is combined with **'out at elbows'**. 'I found my friend sadly changed for the worse; he was down-at-heel and out-at-elbows.'
5. **well heeled** (derisive) – well paid. 'His henchmen were all well heeled.' The original meaning was 'well-armed'. The phrase is taken from cock-fighting, when cocks were fitted with metal spurs or 'heels'.
6. to **dig one's heels in** – to resist a request by all the means at one's disposal. 'When the parents told the headmaster they had decided to send their daughter to another school and demanded a refund of the fees, he dug his heels in and refused point blank.'
7. to **kick up one's heels** – to enjoy one's newly gained freedom. 'When the teachers at our school went on strike and walked out of the class-rooms, we kicked up our heels with joy.'
8. to **lay by the heel** – to arrest and subdue. The reference is to 'laying by the ankles' of petty criminals in the stocks in the Middle Ages.
9. to **come to heel** – to obey, to submit after being disciplined. 'Once I have talked to them, they will come to heel quickly enough. They will soon learn who is the master here!' From the command given to a dog to rejoin his master.
10. to **tread on the heels of / follow upon the heels of** – to follow close behind. 'The recession trod on the heels of the oil crisis.'

    to be hard on someone's **heels** – to walk close behind someone.
11. to **show a clean pair of heels** – to remove oneself from the scene as quickly as possible. 'As soon as I asked them for money, they showed a clean pair of heels!'

    to **take to one's heels** – to run away.
12. to **turn on one's heel** – to turn round abruptly.
13. to **kick/cool one's heels** – to be kept waiting a long time. 'I had to kick my heels outside his office for an hour.'

TOE

14. a **toe-hold** – a small and precarious entry, often used in a business sense. 'He gained a toe-hold in Japan, but it will take him some time to consolidate his position.'
15. to **toe the line** – to obey the rules and regulations. The phrase implies that the person 'toeing the line' is being pressured, against his will. 'Unless he toes the line, he will be expelled from the party.'
16. to **tread on** someone's **toes** – to offend someone with a tactless remark. 'You trod on his toes when you told him his novel was very promising. He has been five years writing it!'
17. to **keep** someone **on his toes** – to keep someone alert and attentive. 'The sergeant-major kept the recruits on their toes by continually firing orders at them.'
18. to **go/walk on tip-toe / to tip-toe** – to

walk on the tips of the toes. 'When their mother was ill, the children tiptoed up and down the stairs so as not to wake her.'

BRAIN

1. to have the **brain of a pigeon** (colloquial) – to be quite brainless. Pigeons are supposed to have a very small brain.
2. **hare-brained** – wild, mad.
   a **hare-brained scheme** – a wild, mad scheme.
3. to **be scatterbrained** – to be careless and disorganized. 'I hope he won't forget the theatre tickets. He is so scatterbrained.'
4. a **brainwave** – a sudden insight into a problem, a flash of inspiration. 'She didn't know what to wear at the fancy-dress ball. Then she had a brainwave; she put on her oldest clothes, smeared some soot on her face and went as Cinderella.'
5. **a brainstorm** – a violent reaction with loss of emotional control. 'When he was told that all his possessions had been destroyed in the fire, he had a brainstorm.'
   a **brainstorming session** – a meeting at which all the members are encouraged to contribute suggestions and solutions, however far-fetched, to a problem.
6. **brain-washing** – to control a person's thinking and ideas by psychological and physical torture, disorientation and other forms of coercion.
7. **Brains Trust** – a panel of intelligent people who express their views on questions of current interest put to them by television or radio audiences.
8. the **Brain Drain** – the emigration from Britain to America of many college and university graduates who were tempted by the higher salaries and better facilities in the USA.
9. to **have something on the brain** – to have an obsession, to be preoccupied with an idea that won't give one any rest. 'Our plumber has fishing on the brain. He talks about it all day long.'
10. to **pick** someone's **brains** – to enlist the aid of someone more clever or expert in a given subject. 'This is much too difficult for me. Do you mind if I pick your brains?'
11. to **rack/cudgel one's brains** – to make a great intellectual effort by, for example, working for a long time on a problem, or trying to recollect some forgotten experience, name, etc.
12. to **turn** someone's **brain** – to madden or drive insane. 'The news that his daughter had married a criminal turned his brain.'

NERVE

13. to **have the nerve to . . .** – to have the impudence to . . . 'When I caught him helping himself to the things in my larder, he had the nerve to ask me where the mayonnaise was.' cf. 'to **have the gall to' 113/17**.
14. to **nerve oneself to / nerve oneself for . . .** – to brace oneself mentally to . . . 'He nerved himself to ask his boss for a rise.'
15. to **get on** someone's **nerves** – to exasperate someone by the repetition of some irritating action. 'Her never-ending complaints got on my nerves.'
16. a **bag of nerves** – someone who is unable to control his anxiety or irritability. 'Since her divorce, Pamela has been a bag of nerves.'
17. to be a **strain on one's nerves** – to be a source of intense irritation or anxiety. 'Living with two other men in one cell was a great strain on all our nerves.'

1. **not to know what nerves are** – to be fearless, to be free from fear. 'He goes at tremendous speeds on the race-track without any fear. He doesn't know what nerves are!'
2. to have **nerves of steel** – to have very strong nerves, to have nerves that are strong enough to withstand any fear.
3. to have a **fit of nerves** – to have an uncontrollable bout of anxiety.
4. to **live on one's nerves** – to be in such a nervous state that one's whole life is affected. 'Since the car accident when she was badly injured, she has been living on her nerves.'
5. to **strain every nerve** – to exert oneself to the utmost. 'He strained every nerve to remain cool and collected and not to let his fingers shake when he opened the telegram.'
6. to **lose one's nerve** – to be reduced by fear to a state of helplessness. 'After hitting an air shot on the first tee in front of a big crowd, Henry lost his nerve and bolted.'

VEIN

7. **in the same vein** – in the same style or mood. 'He wrote many stories in the same vein, humorous and light-hearted.'

FLESH

8. **in the flesh** – in bodily form. 'I knew him better than any of you. In fact, I saw him in the flesh just before he died.'
9. **flesh and blood** – human, with all the weaknesses of human nature.
10. **one's own flesh and blood** – one's parents, brothers and sisters and one's children. 'You can't cut yourself off from your son; after all, he is your own flesh and blood.'
11. to **flesh out** – to add weight to, to make more substantial. 'You can flesh your article out by adding a descriptive passage.'
12. to **put on flesh** – to put on weight. 'Harold has put on a lot of flesh since he was here last. He'll have to cut down on cakes and sugar.'
13. **more than flesh can stand** – more than human nature can endure. 'To expect him to work six weeks on end without a break was asking too much. It was more than flesh could stand.'
14. to **make one's flesh creep** – to frighten or horrify with some dreadful tale. The allusion is to 'the fat boy' in Charles Dickens's *Pickwick Papers*.
15. to **have one's pound of flesh** – to exact what is due, to the very last ounce. 'All right, if you are going to insist on your pound of flesh, I'll work for you all next weekend, although you've paid me little enough for the work.' From Shakespeare's *The Merchant of Venice*.
16. to **press the flesh** – to canvass support in an election campaign by mixing with the voters, shaking hands, kissing babies and so on. 'I've done my share of pressing the flesh for the last six months; now I want a rest.' An American phrase.
17. **flesh-pots / the flesh-pots of Egypt** – great luxury, the finest food and drink. A biblical allusion to the captivity of the Israelites in Egypt (Exodus XVI, 3).
18. the **sins of the flesh** – love of physical pleasure like eating, drinking, fornication. 'The priest told his parishioners to resist temptation and fight against the sins of the flesh.'
19. **the spirit is willing but the flesh is weak** – because of our human frailties, we are not always able to resist the demands made on us by our bodies, even when we want to. Often used

facetiously: 'I wanted to get up at six o'clock this morning and study, but I just couldn't. The spirit was willing but the flesh was weak!'

1. to go **the way of all flesh** – to die. 'However rich and important they are, they will go the way of all flesh like the rest of us.'

SKIN

2. to **save one's skin** – to escape from a disagreeable predicament. 'She saved his skin by telling the police he had spent the evening with her.'
3. to **escape with a whole skin** – to escape without injury.
4. to escape **by the skin of one's teeth** – to have a very narrow escape. 'That was a near thing! I only escaped being conscripted into the army by the skin of my teeth.'
5. to **jump out of one's skin** – to receive a tremendous shock. 'She nearly jumped out of her skin when she unlocked her front door and found a burglar standing in her hall.'
6. to **be in someone else's skin** – often used negatively to indicate some kind of trouble. 'I wouldn't be in his skin if he paid me £1,000.' cf. 'to **be in another's shoes' 168/5**.
7. to **get under one's skin** – to exasperate, to irritate. 'I can't stand the way he patronizes us. He gets under my skin.'
8. to be **all skin and bones** – to be undernourished, very thin. 'We must give that stray cat some food. It's all skin and bones.'
9. **skin-deep** – superficial, shallow. 'Her emotions were only skin-deep. She was incapable of any deep feeling.'
10. to **be thick-skinned / have a thick skin** – to be insensitive to criticism, insults, or the broadest of hints. 'Don't worry, you won't hurt his feelings. He is very thick-skinned.'
11. to **be thin-skinned** – to be over-sensitive to criticism, to take offence at the slightest provocation. 'I didn't mean him to take my remarks personally. He is very thin-skinned!'
12. to be a **skin-flint** – to be mean, miserly. 'You won't get a penny out of him. He's a real skin-flint.'
13. to **skin alive** – to punish very severely. 'If Paul finds out that you've been using his movie camera, he'll skin you alive.' cf. 'to **come down on** someone **like a ton of bricks' 144/12.**

BONE

14. a **lazy bones** / to be **bone idle** – slothful, idle. 'His son is a lazy bones. He never gets up before lunch!'
15. a **bone of contention** – an unresolved quarrel or dispute. 'The ownership of the ancestral home has been a bone of contention between the two brothers for the last twenty years.' The phrase derives from two dogs fighting over a bone.
16. to **feel it in one's bones** – to have a premonition that something (probably unpleasant) is about to happen, although one cannot give a reason for it. 'I am certain that something terrible will happen to Barbara very soon. I can't explain why, I just feel it in my bones.'
17. to **have a bone to pick with someone** – to have cause for making a complaint to someone. 'I have a bone to pick with you. My sister saw you take a £5 note out of my handbag this morning.'
18. to **make no bones of/about** – to speak very frankly, without holding anything back. 'I'll make no bones about it: my father was from a working-class family.'

1. the **bare bones** – just the essentials but no more. 'Those are the bare bones of the system. I'll fill you in on the details later.'
2. to **cut to the bone** – to reduce to an absolute minimum, to eliminate all inessentials. 'We have cut our housekeeping to the bone, but we still have a struggle to pay the bills.'
3. to be **bone dry / as dry as a bone** – to lack moisture. 'I can't grow anything in my garden. The soil is bone dry.' The same idiom can be used humorously for wanting a drink very badly. 'Let's stop at the pub; I'm as dry as a bone.'
4. to **bone up on** (slang) – to work hard on. 'If you are going to get a job in Italy, you had better bone up on the language.'

SKELETON

5. a **skeleton in the cupboard** – a source of embarrassment and shame to a family, which is kept secret from strangers. 'I'm sure there is a skeleton in the Wellards' cupboard. Don't they have a relative who has been in prison?'
6. a **skeleton at the feast** – a reminder of sorrow or trouble on even the merriest occasions.
7. a **skeleton key** – a special key that will unlock many doors, a master key. 'Don't worry if you have lost your bedroom key. Reception has a skeleton key.'
8. **skeleton staff/crew**, etc. – a much-reduced staff, crew, etc., which is capable of maintaining the minimum service required for the organization to function.

MARROW

9. **chilled to the marrow** – freezing cold, frozen through and through. 'We had better turn up the heating. Jack was chilled to the marrow, watching that football match.'

SINEW

10. **the sinews of war** – the means to wage a war: money, arms, etc. 'Without the sinews of war, we have no power to defend our rights.'

LIMB

11. to be **out on a limb** – having taken the initiative, to find oneself without effective support. 'As soon as the organizers saw they were out on a limb, they cancelled their campaign.'
12. to **escape with life and limb** – to escape without any broken bones.
13. a **danger to life and limb** – anything which threatens the health and security of other people. 'The way you drive your car is a danger to life and limb.'

MUSCLE

14. **not to move a muscle** – to be immobile, motionless. 'All the time we were watching the sentry, he didn't move a muscle.'
15. to **use one's muscle** – to use superior strength. 'The printers have used their muscle to obtain far higher wages than they deserve.'

    to **carry a lot of muscle** – to make one's influence felt. 'The money you earn today depends on the muscle your union carries, nothing else.'
16. to **muscle in** – to take away the business of a competitor by force, or by the use of unethical methods. 'It's a good idea, but Philpot's will muscle in on you if they can. They are quite ruthless.'
17. to be **muscle-bound** – to have stiff,

unwieldy muscles, as a result of excessive exercise and training. 'The crew practised too hard at the beginning of the season, with the result that they were muscle-bound on the day of the race.'

BLOOD

1. a **man of blood** – a man of violence.
2. to **make bad blood** between – to cause two people to quarrel with one another. 'He made bad blood between the two brothers.'
3. to be **after/out for one's blood** – to seek revenge. The idiom can be used humorously: 'Now that you have beaten him in the finals, Tom is after your blood.'
4. to **get one's blood up** – to become enraged. 'He is furious with the way they behaved to the old woman. They have got his blood up.'
5. **it makes one's blood boil** – it exasperates one beyond endurance. 'It made my blood boil to see him stealing our roses and then presenting them to his girl-friend.'
6. to **shed blood** – to kill or wound.
   to **shed one's blood** – to be wounded or killed in a war. 'They shed their blood that we might live.'
7. to **sweat blood** (slang) – to work until one is exhausted. 'I've sweated blood to make a success of your company and you haven't given me a word of thanks!'
8. to act **in cold blood** – to act coldly and deliberately, with premeditation. 'The jury found that the man had murdered his wife in cold blood, not in the heat of the moment.'
9. to **make the blood run cold / to chill the blood** – to terrify someone. 'The sight of the masked man climbing through her bedroom window was enough to make Julie's blood run cold.'
10. to act **in hot blood** – to act in anger, to be motivated by passion, not reason.
11. to be **hot-blooded** – passionate, easily aroused to either anger or amorousness.
12. a **full-blooded attack / to make a full-blooded attack** – to attack with one's whole strength, keeping nothing in reserve. 'He has made a full-blooded attack upon your policy, your character and your motives.'
13. to **draw blood** – to make a damaging attack on a person's pride or reputation. 'The Minister has been forced to write an angry letter to the *Daily Telegraph* in reply to our article. We have drawn blood!'
14. to **give** someone/something **a blood transfusion** – to give fresh life to, to reinvigorate. 'North Sea Oil has given Britain a blood transfusion, and only just in time.'
15. to **bring in new/young blood** – to employ people with fresh ideas. 'Now that they have brought in new blood, the marketing should be more energetic.'
16. a **blood-sucker** – a person who obtains money by blackmail or extortion.
17. **you can't get blood out of a stone** – you won't get pity or sympathy from someone who is completely unfeeling. 'It's no good appealing to Uncle Joe. You can't get blood out of a stone.'
18. **blood money** – the reward paid for information that secures the death or betrayal of a person.
19. a **blood-bath** – murder and bloodshed on a large scale. 'The revolutionaries are demanding a blood-bath.'
20. **blood and iron policies** – the attainment of political objectives by the use of brute force. 'Blood and iron was at the core of Bismarck's *Realpolitik*.'

1. **blood will tell** – one's innate qualities will come to the surface sooner or later. 'The adopted child was given the same opportunities as the other children, but he turned out completely different from them. Blood will tell.'
2. **it runs in the blood** – it is an inherited quality. 'The Mayers have been distinguished doctors for generations. It runs in the blood.'
3. **blood is thicker than water** – the ties between relations are closer than those between friends.

HEART

4. **be of good heart** – take courage, don't lose hope!
5. **in good heart** – in good spirits, cheerful.
6. to **do one's heart good** – to cheer up, make one happy. 'It does my heart good to watch the children opening their Christmas presents.'
7. **after one's own heart** – with one's full approval and admiration. 'Saving the baby seals from the fishermen was an action after my own heart.'

   a man/woman **after my own heart** – the kind of man/woman whom I most admire. 'Peter is a man after my own heart. He fights for what he believes in and never gives up.'
8. to **steel one's heart against** – to suppress one's natural pity. 'He steeled his heart against the cries for help of the sick children.'
9. a **heart of stone** – pitiless, unfeeling. 'To turn away your own son! You must have a heart of stone!'
10. **with a light heart** – cheerfully, happily, in a carefree manner. 'I came home with a light heart. I had paid off all my debts at last.'
11. **with a sinking heart** – with growing dismay. 'The schoolboy listened to his examination results with a sinking heart. He realized that he would never get into university.'
12. to be **sick at heart** – to feel very miserable about something. 'When we saw our champion being knocked about in the boxing ring, we all felt sick at heart.'
13. to **break one's heart** – to suffer a personal loss from which it is impossible to recover, to be reduced to a state of complete despair.
14. a **heart-throb** – a charismatic personality, one who captivates members of the opposite sex.
15. a **hearty** – a low-brow, someone lacking in intellectual tastes, loud-mouthed and vulgar.
16. to **be hearty** – to be noisy and boisterous.
17. **the heart of the matter** – the essential problem.
18. **heart and soul** – passionately, in a totally committed way. 'Charles worked heart and soul for the cause.'
19. to **put one's heart (and soul) into** something – to work at something with energy and enthusiasm. 'Research is tiring and laborious work. If you can't put your heart into it, you should try something else.'
20. **one's heart is not in it** – to be not interested in or to feel unenthusiastic about something. 'In the last few weeks your heart hasn't been in your work. Would you like to talk to me about it?'
21. **from the bottom of one's heart** – with the utmost sincerity, most deeply. 'I wish you every success from the bottom of my heart.'
22. **at heart** – fundamentally. 'He has many faults, but at heart he is a very decent young man.'

    to **have at heart** – to feel deeply about; to be extremely concerned about. 'I am sure your mother has your best interests at heart.' The phrase can be used with 'health', 'happiness', 'safety', etc.

1. a **heart-to-heart talk** – a confidential and serious discussion between two people about some personal problem. 'I had a heart-to-heart talk with Lucy's father about our plans to marry, and my prospects.'
2. to **take heart** – to be encouraged. 'You can take heart from Robert's success. If he can pass the exam, so can you!'
3. to **take to heart** – (1) to take something badly, to be very much hurt by. 'When Martin forgot his date with Susan, she took it very much to heart.' (2) to take a warning very seriously. 'I hope you will take to heart what I have told you.'
4. to **take to one's heart** – to accept someone with love and joy. 'The people have taken Your Royal Highness to their hearts.'
5. to **give one heart** – to encourage, make one bold. 'You have given me heart. I'll try again.'
6. to **put (fresh) heart into** – to encourage, to give someone confidence. 'After so many failures, I was going to give up, but you have put fresh heart into me.'
7. **have a heart!** – the phrase is used as a plea in reply to some unreasonable demand. 'I've already typed thirty letters for you today, and now you want me to do another thirteen. Have a heart!'
8. to **have no heart** – to be unfeeling, inhumane. 'A man who shoots dumb animals can't have any heart at all.'
9. to **find it in one's heart to** – to be generous enough to . . . 'If you can find it in your heart to forgive Jenny, you will never regret it.'

   not to have the heart to – not to be able to . . . 'I didn't have the heart to tell Peter the bad news on his birthday and spoil his fun.'
10. to **lose heart** – to lose courage, to despair. 'When the skating champion tumbled on the ice, he lost heart and did not complete his programme.'
11. to **lose one's heart to** – to fall in love with. 'She lost her heart to the new arts teacher.'
12. **in one's heart of hearts** – if one is absolutely honest with oneself. 'In his heart of hearts, he knew that he wasn't cut out to be a lawyer, despite his academic success.'
13. **with all my heart** – with the utmost sincerity, with all best wishes. 'I hope with all my heart that your marriage will be a happy one.'
14. **close to one's heart** – especially valued by someone. 'The work you are doing for the sick children has always been close to his heart.'
15. to **learn (off) by heart** – to know a piece so well that one can recite it from memory. 'Our teacher makes us learn everything off by heart.'
16. to **set one's heart upon** – to want above all else, to have an intense longing to . . . 'His grandfather has set his heart on sending the boy to his old school.'
17. to **allow the heart to rule the head** – to be influenced by one's emotions and not by one's reason. 'In business, it is a mistake to allow the heart to rule the head.'
18. **to one's heart's content** – to one's complete satisfaction. 'There's a piano in your room, and you can play it to your heart's content. No one will disturb you.'
19. a **change of heart** – a change of mind or decision, prompted by a change in one's feelings. 'His father was against the marriage at first, but, after getting to know the girl better, he had a change of heart.'

1. **my heart goes out to** – I feel intense pity and sympathy for. 'My heart goes out to the victims of the bomb explosion.'
2. **one's heart bleeds for** someone – to feel extremely sorry for someone. Often used ironically: 'I'm sorry you won't be taking your usual holiday in the Bahamas this year. My heart bleeds for you.'
3. to **eat one's heart out** – to suffer intense grief, often resulting from failure or disappointment, especially over the loss of a person's love. 'Elizabeth has been eating her heart out ever since Dennis broke off their engagement.'
4. **with one's heart in one's mouth** – in a state of great fear. 'When the postman handed me the telegram, my heart was in my mouth.'
5. to **have one's heart in the right place** – to be kind and well-meaning. This idiom is almost always used when appearances are to the contrary. 'He may be a bit of a show-off sometimes, but his heart is in the right place.'
6. to **warm the cockles of one's heart** – to raise someone's spirits, to gratify. 'It warmed the cockles of her heart to have all the children and grandchildren seated at her dining-table at Christmas time.'
7. to **pour out one's heart** – to confide all one's sorrows, fears, anxieties, hopes and joys to another person. 'When we were alone, she poured out her heart to me about her broken marriage.'
8. to **have heart failure** (colloquial) – to suffer a great shock, to be demoralized. 'It was the audacity of its contents which gave them heart failure and persuaded them to surrender . . .' (*New Statesman*).
9. **one heartbeat from the Presidency** – on the death of the American President the immediate assumption of office by the Vice-President without any action by the legislature or judiciary.

STOMACH

10. to have a **strong stomach** – to be not easily shocked or disgusted. 'You'll need a strong stomach if you are going to be a surgeon.'
11. to **have no stomach for** – to have no courage for, no desire for. 'He hated quarrelling and had no stomach for a fight.'
12. to **turn the stomach** – to disgust, to nauseate. 'Your hypocrisy turns my stomach.'
13. to **stomach** (an insult, etc.) – to accept, to submit to. 'If you want to be his friend, you'll have to stomach his insults.'
14. **on an empty stomach** – a stomach that lacks food. 'You must take these pills on an empty stomach.'
15. to have a **sinking feeling in the pit of one's stomach** – to have a great fear, a premonition of disaster.

GALL

16. **as bitter as gall** – extreme bitterness. Gall is the old synonym of bile, the bitter liquid secreted into the stomach by the liver.
17. to **have the gall to . . .** (colloquial) – to have the impudence to . . . 'Sandra had the gall to ask for her job back two days after we had sacked her for dishonesty.' cf. 'to **have the nerve to**' **106/13**.
18. to **dip one's pen in gall** – to write with venom and bitter sarcasm.
19. **gall and wormwood** – that which arouses the most bitter resentment. Both words stand as symbols of extreme bitterness. 'It was gall and

wormwood for him to have to make a public withdrawal of his accusations.'

BILE

1. to be **full of bile** – to be full of resentment and bitterness. 'His speeches were full of bile.' 'His opponents aroused his bile.'

SPLEEN

2. to be **filled with spleen** – to be filled with anger and vexation. 'In his autobiography, he vented his spleen on all his enemies.'

GUT

3. to **have the guts to . . .** – to have the courage to . . . 'He didn't have the guts to stand by his friend when he was in trouble.'

KIDNEY

4. **of the same kidney** – of the same character, of the same type. It usually has a bad meaning. 'Have nothing to do with those two prisoners; they both have violent characters and long records. They are men of the same kidney.'

   of another kidney – of a different character, of a different type. 'Roberts has nothing in common with Taylor. Roberts enjoys classical music, while Taylor listens to pop. Roberts is a man of another kidney.'

LIVER

5. **yellow-livered** (a term of abuse) – cowardly. There was a superstition that a coward's liver contained no blood; hence the phrases **yellow-livered, white-livered, lily-livered,** etc. cf. 'to **be yellow' 18/10**.

BODY

6. to **have body** – to have weight or substance. 'That wine has body, as well as bouquet and clarity.'

   to **have no body** – to be lacking in substance. 'Richard's novel was quite amusing but very light; it had no body.'
7. to **be a nobody** – to be a person of no significance, no importance. 'I won't take orders from a nobody like Smith.'
8. a **busybody** – someone who meddles, or pries into other people's affairs. 'My neighbour has been asking me a lot of questions about my girl-friend. He is an appalling busybody.'
9. to **keep body and soul together** – to support life. 'When I left home, work was difficult to find, and I earned hardly enough to keep body and soul together.'
10. a **body-blow** to all one's hopes – a very severe blow, a disastrous blow. 'Failing to qualify after so many years' study dealt a body-blow to all her hopes.'

FIGURE

11. to **cut a poor figure** – to look foolish. 'I must have cut a poor figure in front of the guests. I had quite forgotten how to dance.'
12. **a figure of fun** – an object of ridicule. 'When he was younger, the boys treated the master with respect, but now he's only a figure of fun.'

12. MIND

MIND

1. **mind over matter** – the triumph of willpower and courage over physical pain or infirmity. 'Whether a patient recovers from a dangerous illness often depends on his own willpower. It's a case of mind over matter as a rule.'

2. to **make up one's mind** – to come to a decision. 'I have made up my mind to sell my house and go abroad.'

3. to **have a good mind** to do something – to have a strong inclination. The phrase usually expresses irritation. 'He has behaved so badly, I've a good mind not to go to his party.' More often than not, the inclination is suppressed.

4. to **be in one's right mind** – to be sane. 'No one in his right mind would do a thing like that!'

5. to be **out of one's mind/senses** – to be extremely stupid or insane. 'You must have been out of your mind to talk like that to your boss.'

   to **be driven out of one's mind** – to be driven insane with worry, fear, suspicion, anxiety, etc. The phrase is often used with the adverbs 'nearly', and 'almost'.

6. to **have in mind** – to consider or propose. 'Yes, we have a number of four-bedroom houses on our books. What price did you have in mind?'

7. **an open mind** – an unprejudiced mind, one that is receptive to new ideas. 'I have an open mind whether to take him on. I will decide after I have seen him.'

   a closed mind – a mind that is prejudiced, one that is not receptive to new ideas. 'Rupert has a closed mind on the subject of politics, so you are wasting your time arguing with him about it.'

8. the **master-mind** – the person in charge of an operation, the originator of the plan on which the success of the operation depends. 'The police believe they know the master-mind behind the bank robbery.'

9. to **call to mind** – to recall, remember. Usually used negatively. 'I can't call to mind his ever having mentioned it, but he may have done so.'

10. to **cast one's mind back** – to make a conscious effort to recall an incident. 'Can you cast your mind back to the day you first visited him?'

11. to **know one's (own) mind** – to have a clear and firm conviction, usually as to what should be done. 'He never had any doubts about being a doctor; he always knew his own mind.'

    not to know one's own mind – to be undecided, usually as to what should be done. 'It would be a mistake putting Jim in charge; he never knows his own mind.'

12. to **have a mind of one's own** – to be capable of making decisions without depending on other people's opinions. 'Why do you always ask your father what to do? Surely you are old enough to have a mind of your own.'

13. to **be in two minds** (over a matter) – to be undecided. 'I could see the advantages and disadvantages of living in New Zealand. I was in two minds about moving there.'

14. to **change one's mind** – to change one's decision or opinion.

15. **mind you** – even so, all the same. 'Paul did wrong. Mind you, many people would have done the same in his place.' (An interjection used to qualify a statement.)

16. to **set one's mind on** – to be absolutely determined on a course of action. 'I

can see you have set your mind on taking the job, so I won't try to dissuade you.'

1. to be **of one mind** – to be unanimous, to be of the same opinion.
2. **to my mind** – in my opinion. The phrase is often used to indicate a difference of opinion. 'I know you won't agree with me but, to my mind, the whole idea was a mistake.'
3. to **put/give one's mind** to – to concentrate on. 'If he would only put his mind to his studies, he could be a brilliant scholar.'
4. to **bear/keep in mind** – to pay heed to, to take into consideration. 'You must bear in mind that Alan is very young.'
5. to **cross one's mind** – to occur to one, to have a momentary thought. 'It did cross my mind that the maid might have stolen the money.'
6. to **slip one's mind** – to forget, usually as a result of carelessness rather than a defective memory. 'It quite slipped my mind that Maureen was coming to tea today.'
7. to **prey/weigh on one's mind** – to worry, preoccupy or make one feel guilty. 'My unkindness to the old woman weighed on my mind for a long time.'

   to **have** something **on one's mind** – to be worried, preoccupied or feel guilty about something. 'I can see you have something on your mind; would you like to tell me about it?'
8. **a weight off one's mind** – relief from an anxiety or feeling of guilt. 'It was a weight off my mind to know that he was being well looked after.'
9. to **put** someone's **mind at rest** – to dispel someone's anxiety. 'I can put your mind at rest – your wife is out of danger.'
10. to be **easy in mind** – to be calm, to be free from anxiety.
11. to **put to the back of one's mind** – to dismiss (an idea) from one's mind for the time being.
12. to **get** something **out of one's mind** – to free oneself from an idea. 'I have made a terrible mistake and now I can't get it out of my mind.'
13. to **take one's mind off** something – to seek distraction from one's troubles. 'There is nothing like a good book to take one's mind off one's troubles.'
14. to **speak one's mind** – to speak very frankly. 'He said exactly what he thought; he spoke his mind.'
15. to **give** someone **a piece of one's mind** – to scold someone severely, to tell someone what one thinks of him. 'When James didn't trouble to see the girl home after the party, I gave him a piece of my mind.'
16. **presence of mind** – a quick response in an emergency. 'When the child fell out of the moving train, she had the presence of mind to pull the emergency cord.'
17. to **make the mind boggle** – to astonish. The alternative phrase is 'the mind boggles'. 'The mind boggles at the bills he ran up in such a short time.'
18. to **broaden the mind** – to develop new interests. 'Why don't you learn a foreign language and travel? That will broaden your mind.'

MENTAL

19. **mental** (colloquial) – mad or idiotic.
20. a **mental block** – a psychological obstruction to the free flow of ideas. 'Whenever the psychiatrist asks me questions about my childhood, I have a mental block.'
21. **quick/slow in the uptake** – quick or slow to understand. 'I kept looking at my watch, but he made no move to leave; he must be a little slow in the uptake.'

WIT, WITS

1. to have **quick wits / to be quick-witted** – to have a quick understanding, to be quick with an answer.
   to be **slow-witted** – to be slow in understanding.
2. to be **half-witted** – to be mentally sub-normal, or idiotic. 'It's a half-witted idea emigrating with no money or contacts.'
3. to **addle the wits** – to make someone incapable of using his brain, to make him stupid. 'I think George's two years at the Foreign Office must have addled his wits.' The verb 'addle, addled', means rotten, muddle, confuse, from the Anglo-Saxon word 'Adela' meaning mud.
4. to **have/keep one's wits about one** – to be alert and resourceful 'If he hadn't had his wits about him, he might have been drowned.'
5. to **live by/on one's wits** – to resort to expedients from day to day for a living rather than take a regular job.
6. **out of one's wits** – mentally disturbed, mentally disabled or senile.
   to **frighten** someone **out of his wits** – to terrify someone so much that he is unable to think properly. 'That alsatian of the Masons frightens me out of my wits whenever I pass their house; they should keep it chained up.'
7. **at one's wits' end** – in despair of finding a solution to one's problems.
   to **drive** someone **to his wits' end** – to drive someone to despair. 'The boy was so slow that he drove his teacher to his wits' end.'

SENSE, SENSES

8. **out of one's senses** – mad.
   to **take leave of one's senses** – to go mad. 'Have you taken leave of your senses? The wedding is tomorrow; you can't possibly cancel it now!'
9. to **come to one's senses** – to start behaving sensibly again. 'You should warn John that you will stop his allowance unless he behaves himself; then he will come to his senses.'
   to **bring** someone **to his senses** – to persuade someone to stop behaving foolishly.
10. a **sense of loss** – a feeling of sadness that a person or thing is irretrievably lost. 'When Lucy saw her younger brother off to India, she felt a strong sense of loss and wondered whether she would ever see him again.'
11. a **sense of proportion** – the ability to see things in their proper perspective. 'So you have failed your examination, but there are worse things in life than failing exams; you mustn't lose your sense of proportion.'

REASON

12. to **listen to reason** – to adopt a sensible approach to a question without being influenced by one's emotions. 'I warned you that the idea would never work; what a pity you wouldn't listen to reason.'
13. **it stands to reason** – there is only one conclusion to be drawn. 'It stands to reason that if the railway is losing money, fares should be reduced to attract more passengers.'
14. **without rhyme or reason** – nonsensical, illogical. 'At first, I could see no rhyme or reason in Gertrude Stein's writing, but later I changed my mind about her.'

CONSCIENCE

15. **in all conscience** – taking a fair and reasonable view. The phrase is often used to emphasize one's doubts about the reasonableness of a demand. 'I should have thought that his charges were high enough in all conscience

without his asking for any extra money.'

1. to **make** something **a matter of conscience** – to be guided by one's sense of right and wrong. 'I agree with you that many laws are unjust, but if you make every law a matter of conscience you will end up in gaol!'
2. **conscience money** – money paid anonymously to ease one's conscience, for example when income tax has been evaded.

MORAL, ERR AND FAULT

3. a **moral certainty** – such a strong probability as to exclude almost any doubt. 'This time next year, it is a moral certainty that we shall be living in America.'
4. **moral support** – encouragement which stops short of physical or financial help. 'I am making my first speech at our local debating society. I hope you'll be there to give me moral support.'
5. a **moral victory** – a defeat that should by rights have been a victory. 'We played better football than Honiton and would have won easily if two of our men hadn't been injured. Honiton agreed with us that it was a moral victory for our side.'
6. to **err on the right side** – to make a mistake which benefits someone else. 'You are not late; in fact you are erring on the right side coming in at half past eight instead of nine.'

   a **fault on the right side** – a mistake which benefits someone else. 'Molly got the account wrong. We owe her £80, not £60. At least, it's a fault on the right side.'

CHARACTER

7. **in character** – in accordance with a person's usual behaviour; in a way anyone knowing him would expect.

   out of character – not in accordance with a person's usual behaviour; in a way anyone knowing him would not expect. 'I was surprised Francis was so rude to you; it was completely out of character.'
8. **(quite) a character** – peculiar, eccentric. 'Mr Fraser goes out in long flowing yellow and scarlet robes. Yesterday, he stopped the traffic in the Strand. He is quite a character.'

PURPOSE, DESIRE, WILLING, WILL

9. **to all intents and purposes** – in essence, effectively. 'To all intents and purposes, the property was a complete loss; only the kitchen remained, the rest of the house having been burned to the ground.'
10. to be **at cross-purposes** – to have a misunderstanding because of conflicting intentions. 'I am afraid we are at cross-purposes; I am offering you a job, not asking you for one.'
11. to **leave a lot to be desired** – to be unsatisfactory in many respects. 'Although the hotel charges were very high, the cuisine and service left a lot to be desired.'
12. to **show willing** – to show that one is ready to co-operate even if one has no desire to. 'You may not want to strike, but you should show willing to protect your rights.'
13. **with a will** – with strength and determination. 'When the old man was attacked by the mugger, he defended himself with a will.'
14. **willy-nilly** (literary) – whether one wishes it or not. 'Paul wanted to keep aloof from his companions but, willy-nilly, he was drawn into their revels.' Willy-nilly is a corruption of 'will he,

nill he', 'nill he' deriving from Anglo-Saxon 'nillan', short for 'ne willan', not to wish.

WISE, WISER

1. to **be wise to** – to be fully aware of, to be alert to. 'He is wise to all their tricks; he won't let them make use of him.'

   to **put** someone **wise to** – to make someone aware of the facts, to warn him as to the true position. 'I thought I had better put you wise as to what's going on here. Your conduct is being criticized in the officers' mess.'

2. to be **wise after the event** – to know what should have been done to prevent something happening when it has already taken place. 'Aren't you being wise after the event? How could we have known that the burglar would get in by the window on the second floor?' cf. 'to **second-guess' 216/20**.

3. **none the wiser** – knowing no more than one did before. 'I have spent six hours interrogating witnesses and I am none the wiser.'

COURAGE, BOLD AND VIRTUE

4. to **have the courage of one's convictions**–to declare one's principles openly, regardless of the danger to oneself or to one's reputation. 'I don't agree with you, but I admire you for having the courage of your convictions.' cf. 'to **stand up and be counted**' **222/5**.

5. **as bold as brass** – impertinent, shameless. 'Harry asked me what my income was the first time we met. The man is as bold as brass.' cf. **'barefaced' 79/15**.

6. to **make a virtue of necessity** – to turn an unwanted obligation into a positive advantage. 'I am being sent to North Europe. I didn't want to move but they are going to teach me skiing free of charge; so I'll be making a virtue of necessity.'

KINDNESS, KINDLY, GENEROUS

7. to **kill with kindness** – to spoil someone's character, especially a child's, by indulging all his wishes and not correcting his faults. 'They've sent their daughter to a modern school where she can do exactly as she likes, and where punishments are forbidden. The teachers are killing her with kindness.'

8. **not to take kindly to** – not to welcome or approve (only used in the negative). 'These men and women are experienced teachers; I am afraid they won't take kindly to being told how to do their job by your inspector.'

9. **generous to a fault** – excessively generous, so generous as to cause difficulties or embarrassment. 'Matthew is generous to a fault; people are always taking advantage of him.'

PROUD, PRIDE

10. to **do** someone **proud** – to treat someone with great generosity. 'Meg's parents did us proud; they treated us to a box at Wyndham's Theatre followed by dinner at Claridge's.'

11. to **swallow one's pride** – to submit humbly, to accept a humiliation. 'You made a mistake resigning in a temper like that. You had better swallow your pride and ask the boss to take you back.'

CRUEL, MERCIES, PITY

12. to be **cruel to be kind** – to inflict pain on or punish a person in order to rid him of a distressing habit or fault. 'Mrs Fry warned her daughter that if

she continued taking drugs, she would turn her out of the house. She explained she had to be cruel to be kind.'

1. to **leave a person to** someone's **tender mercies** – to abandon a person to rough, brutal treatment. 'I could see at once that Harry's new guardian was a bully, and I was sorry to leave the boy to his tender mercies.'
2. **more's the pity** – so much the worse, that only makes it worse; generally used as a rejoinder to an excuse or explanation. '"I didn't send you a Christmas card this year. I haven't sent one to any of my friends." "More's the pity", replied Joan.'

GRACE

3. a **saving grace** – one good quality which redeems many faults. 'Anne is lazy, untidy and disrespectful; her one saving grace is that she is good with the children.'
4. **with a good/bad grace** – in a good-humoured/ill-humoured manner. 'Rose paid me back the money, but with a bad grace as if I had done her a wrong.'
5. to **fall from grace** – to lose favour. 'Since smashing up Lady Robinson's car, I have fallen from grace, and expect very soon to lose my job.'

PATIENCE, FAITH AND CHARITY

6. to **try the patience of a saint** – to be so tiresome or stupid that even the most tolerant and easy-going of people would get annoyed. 'If I've explained it to you once, I've explained it a hundred times. You would try the patience of a saint!' cf. 'to **try the patience of Job' 194/7**.
7. **in (all) good faith** – honestly and sincerely. 'I acted in good faith when I sold you that washing-machine. So far as I knew, it was in perfect condition.'
   in bad faith – dishonestly.
8. an **article of faith** – a crucial element in someone's philosophy. 'It is an article of faith among Conservatives that competition should be encouraged and state monopolies should be abolished.'
9. **as cold as charity** – hard and unfeeling. A reference to the cold, unsympathetic way charity is sometimes dispensed to the poor and needy.

HAPPY, HUMOUR, BORED

10. a **happy event** – the birth of a child. 'Will your daughter be back in England for the happy event, or are you going to look after her in Germany?'
11. a **happy medium** – a middle way which avoids extremes. 'You should take plenty of exercise but avoid anything too strenuous like tennis or squash. Golf would be a happy medium for a man of your age.'
12. a **happy hunting-ground** – a place which offers good chances of success for hunters, collectors and other people with special interests. 'The International Club was always considered a happy hunting-ground for young men who were looking for a girl-friend.' 'The happy hunting-grounds' was the name given by the American Indians to their life after death.
13. to be **out of humour** – to be in an ill-humour, in a bad mood. 'William is out of humour this morning because he didn't get a letter from his daughter.'
14. **bored stiff / bored to tears** – very much bored, uninterested. 'I am bored stiff by many of the television programmes.'

FANCY AND DREAM

1. to **take a fancy to** someone/something – to take a sudden liking to someone/something. 'You do take a fancy to the most extraordinary things. Where are we going to put a palm tree in this tiny flat?'

   to **take** someone's **fancy** – to attract. 'I don't really know why I bought it; it just took my fancy.'

2. to **fancy oneself** – to have a high opinion of one's looks or of one's abilities, to be conceited. 'Derek fancies himself as a ladies' man, but he spends too much time admiring himself in the mirror for my liking.' cf. 'to **think that one is God's gift to' 44/6**.

3. **a flight of fancy** – a free, unrestricted use of the imagination. 'Jack's play has nothing to say about our social or political problems. It is a flight of fancy, nothing else.'

4. **not dream of** – not think of, not consider. The phrase is used in order to make an emphatic denial. 'I wouldn't dream of charging you a fee for doing your portrait; please accept it as a gift.'

5. to **go like a dream** – to move with power and smoothness. The phrase is usually applied to cars, yachts or aeroplanes.

LOVE

6. **a labour of love** – a work done without payment, either for its own sake or for the sake of a loved one. 'Miss Watts had worked for three years on the tapestry; it was a labour of love done for the church.'

7. **love in a cottage** – a love match or marriage which is not supported by sufficient means to keep a couple in comfort.

8. **love-birds** – two people who are very much in love with each other. 'Mr and Mrs Sanders still walk hand in hand, although they are over sixty; they are still love-birds.'

9. there's **no love lost** between them – two people who dislike each other very much. The original meaning was the exact opposite. Goldsmith writes in *She Stoops to Conquer* (I, v): 'As for mumures, Mother, we grumble a little now and then, to be sure. But there's no love lost between us' (meaning that none of the love between them was wasted).

10. **not for love or money** – not at any price. 'The London hotels are booked out at this time of the year; you can't get a room for love or money.'

11. to **play for love** – to play a game without gambling on it. 'I never gamble, but I'll play you for love if you like.'

HATE AND FURY

12. a **pet hate/aversion** – a special dislike. 'My pet hate is the shift-workers who march past our house singing at the top of their voices at three o'clock in the morning on their way to work.'

13. **fast and furious** – excited, wild, noisy. 'Bill and Alison danced the waltz fast and furious round the room until they became too giddy to go on.'

14. **like fury** – with demonic energy and determination. 'After being a goal down, we played like fury and beat the champions 2–0.'

15. **all the rage** – in great demand, the height of fashion. 'Please, Mother, let's have a video. All our friends have one; it's all the rage.'

16. **with a vengeance** – in far greater measure than one expected or wanted. 'When the weather finally broke, it rained with a vengeance every day and all day for the next two weeks.'

SHAME, CRYING, DOUBT

1. **Shame on you!** – you should be ashamed of yourself. 'Do you mean to say you let Doris carry all her luggage down the stairs without helping her? Shame on you!'
2. a **crying shame** – a great wrong that calls for action. 'It's a crying shame that the children should be separated from one another because of their parents' divorce.'
   a **crying need** – an urgent need that demands action.
3. to **put** someone **to shame** – to make someone feel inferior by showing up his faults. 'While you were sunning yourselves in Tenerife, Vivien worked over Christmas without once complaining. She has put you all to shame.'
4. a **nagging doubt** – a doubt that continually troubles the conscience. 'I had a nagging doubt whether we had been right to send William abroad with no one to accompany him when he was only thirteen.'
5. to **give** someone **the benefit of the doubt** – to accept the most charitable explanation of someone's actions. 'Very well, Mrs Brown, we will give you the benefit of the doubt this time, but in future please make sure you have paid for everything in your bag before you leave the shop.'

FEAR, AFRAID, SCARE

6. **without fear or favour** – completely fair, without prejudice or fear of threats. 'It's expensive going to law, but one thing you can be certain of: your case will be heard without fear or favour.'
7. there's **not much fear of . . .** – it's not very likely that . . . (used in reference to future events). 'The only way to save our jobs would be for all of us to accept a ten per cent cut in our wages, but there's not much fear of that happening, worse luck.'
8. **in fear and trembling** – in a state of great fear, shaking with fear. 'When the boss sent for me, I went to his office in fear and trembling, but he only wanted to praise my work.'
9. to be **afraid of one's own shadow** – to be afraid to meet people, to be shy and timid. 'It's no good inviting Pam to your party. She never goes anywhere; I do believe the poor girl would be afraid of her own shadow.'
10. **scared stiff** – terrified, overcome with fear. 'When the alsatian leapt at me, I was scared stiff and couldn't move.'
11. to **scare the pants off** someone – to give someone a terrible fright. 'Spending the night in the haunted room of that castle would scare the pants off me.'

SORROW, GRIEF AND MISERY

12. **more in sorrow than in anger** – with feelings of sadness and disappointment rather than anger (at someone's wrongdoing). 'When Kenneth told his wife that he had gambled away her money, she looked at him more in sorrow than in anger.'
13. to **drown one's sorrows** – to drink heavily to console oneself for a setback or misfortune. 'Margaret has just told me she won't be seeing me again, so I am drowning my sorrows.'
14. **in a sorry state** – in a pitiful condition. 'When I called on Oliver, I found him in a sorry state; he was lying in great pain on the floor.'
15. to **come to grief** – to fail disastrously. 'Owing to his lack of experience, all Gerald's ventures came to grief.'
16. to **put** someone **out of his misery** – to put an end to someone's suspense by giving him the information he

was hoping for. 'The doctor has put me out of my misery; there's nothing wrong with my lungs.' The original meaning was to kill a sick or injured animal that was suffering unnecessarily.

SUFFER AND WOE

1. to **suffer fools gladly** (almost always used in the negative) – to tolerate stupidity in others. 'Alan is too impatient to suffer fools gladly.'
2. **woe betide you** – you will be sorry . . . 'Woe betide you if you miss your interview. You won't get another chance.' The phrase is sometimes used humorously. 'Betide' means 'happen to' and derives from Anglo-Saxon 'tide', 'time', 'hour'. It is only used in this phrase.

DUMPS AND DAMPER

3. **in the dumps / down in the dumps** – depressed, miserable. 'Yvonne has been in the dumps ever since her brother went to Canada.' 'Dump' is a cognate of Dutch 'dompen' to quench, extinguish, and English 'damp'. Cf. 'a **wet blanket' 149/9**.
4. to **put a damper on** someone – to discourage or depress someone cf. **'in the dumps' 123/3**, 'a **wet blanket' 149/9**.

   to **put a damper on** an idea, enthusiasm, hope – to discourage someone's idea, enthusiasm or hope. 'I wish John weren't so negative; he puts a damper on all my ideas.' cf. 'to **pour cold water on' 25/9**.

JOY AND HOPE

5. to be someone's **pride and joy** – to be the special object of someone's love and pride. 'The bird sanctuary which the old man had built himself was the pride and joy of his life.'
6. to **wish** someone **joy of** a person/thing – to express pleasure at being rid of a person/thing one doesn't like. An ironic comment on the person/thing one has been parted from. 'So Mrs Anderson has deserted us for Dr Boyd; I wish him joy of her!' 'I'm not sorry to have lost my new brooch; it was always pricking me. I wish the finder joy of it!'
7. to **get no joy from** – to get no help from. 'I've been looking everywhere for a room; I tried the information bureau, but got no joy from them.' cf. 'to **get no change out of' 243/1**.
8. to **hope against hope** – to keep on hoping even though there are no longer any grounds for hope. 'We were hoping against hope that Grandfather would get better, although the doctor had given him up.'
9. a **fond hope** – a foolish hope. 'The old man nourished the fond hope that his grandson would qualify as a doctor, although the boy had no interest in medicine.' 'Fond' derives from East Friesian 'fone', 'fon' meaning a girl, weakling, simpleton; hence foolish, whose meaning it has retained to the present day but only in this phrase,
10. to **pin one's hopes on** – to rely on a single thing or person for the fulfilment of one's hopes. 'We are pinning our hopes on a new German drug to cure our son.'

FEELINGS

11. to **feel small** – to feel humiliated or ashamed. 'When Martin found he hadn't enough money to pay the bill, he felt very small.'
12. to **get the feel of** – to become accustomed to. 'After hammering away all day on the manual typewriter, it took me a little time to get the feel of the electric one.'
13. to **feel out of it** – to feel as if one

doesn't belong. 'All the guests at the party were teenagers. I was much too old and felt quite out of it.'

1. to **get the feeling that** – to suspect without understanding the reason. 'I get the feeling, Marion, that you don't want to come out with me.'
2. to acquire a **feeling for** something – to develop a sympathy for something. 'If you want to speak a foreign language well, you must acquire a feeling for it.'
3. to **feel the draught/pinch** – to suffer discomfort through lack of money. 'Now that people are short of money, the shops in the High Street are feeling the draught/pinch.'
4. **no hard feelings** – no ill-feelings or resentment. 'Since we don't agree, wouldn't it be better for us to part, with no hard feelings on either side?'
5. to **have mixed feelings** about – to be undecided, to feel regret as well as pleasure about a certain course of action. 'When my parents decided to emigrate to Australia, I had mixed feelings about going.'
6. to **vent one's feelings on** – to find an outlet for one's anger in; to divert one's anger on to. 'Just because you didn't get an increase in your salary, you needn't vent your feelings on me!'
7. **not to feel oneself** – to feel slightly unwell or depressed. 'I am sorry if I was a little short with you just now; I don't feel myself today.'

13. ILLNESSES AND AILMENTS

BLIND

1. to be **blinded by hatred** – to hate to such an extent that one's judgement of a person is distorted.
2. to **turn a blind eye to** – deliberately to overlook a fault in another person, which one does not wish to acknowledge, even to oneself. 'The old man adored his grandson and always turned a blind eye to his misbehaviour.'
3. to **have a blind spot for** – to have uncritical enthusiasm for. 'Most parents have a blind spot for their children, and ignore their faults.'
4. a **blind date** – an introduction to an unknown person arranged by an agency or a third party.
5. a **blind-alley occupation / job** – one that offers no chance of promotion. It is always unskilled and therefore badly paid in the long run.
6. **the blind leading the blind** – an ironic comment on leaders who are as ignorant and incompetent as the people they are leading. From the Bible (Matthew XV, 14) 'And if the blind lead the blind, both shall fall into the ditch.'

DEAF

7. to **turn a deaf ear to** – to refuse to listen, usually to some request for help.
8. to **fall on deaf ears** – to meet with no response, to be ignored.
9. a **dialogue of the deaf** – a fruitless discussion, one in which all the participants have closed minds and are unreceptive to any rational argument.
10. to be **as deaf as a door-post** – completely deaf. Sometimes said of a person who is not conscious of his deafness. 'He's as deaf as a door-post but he gets very angry if you shout at him.'
11. a **deafening silence** – a silence which expresses more embarrassment than any words could do. 'When Jack asked the bride at the wedding reception whether she had been married before, there was a deafening silence.' One can also say: **the silence was deafening**.
12. **hard of hearing** – having difficulty in hearing.

DUMB

13. to **strike dumb** – to render someone speechless with surprise.
    to **be struck dumb** – to be made speechless with astonishment.
14. **dumb insolence** (a military phrase) – an insolent attitude conveyed by a subordinate towards a superior in rank without any words being uttered.
15. **the dumb millions** – the masses who have no say in the way they are governed.
16. **our dumb friends** – our animal friends.
17. **dumb animals** – a phrase used in pity because animals are unable to complain of ill-treatment.
18. a **dumb blonde** – (Americanism) – a girl who is good-looking but lacking in intelligence. The Americans use the word 'dumb' in the sense of 'stupid' in the same way as the Germans use the cognate 'dumm'.
19. a **dumb-waiter** – an arrangement of revolving shelves introduced in the eighteenth century for replacing servants in the drawing-room. The object of the device was to ensure

greater privacy rather than save labour.

LAMENESS

1. a **lame excuse** – an excuse that is weak and unconvincing.
2. to **tread on** someone's **corns** – to mention a very delicate or sensitive subject, to speak tactlessly. 'You trod on his corns last night when you asked about his wife. Didn't you know, she has run off with his junior partner?'
3. **crippling taxes** – a tax that is so high that it discourages businessmen from expanding their enterprises or taking risks.
4. a **fractured sentence** – a sentence in which the subject and the object have been separated by one or more subordinate clauses, e.g. 'I wanted, when I was staying with my friends in Massachusetts, in the spring of 1983, to pay a visit to the Niagara Falls' instead of: 'When I was staying with my friends in Massachusetts in the spring of 1983, I wanted to pay a visit to the Niagara Falls.'

FEVER AND COLDS

5. **at fever heat/pitch** – with the utmost exertion and excitement. 'The children worked at fever heat to get their play ready in time for Christmas.'
6. **not to be sneezed at** – not to be despised, considerable. 'An income of £30,000 a year is not to be sneezed at, even today.'
7. to **cough up** (vulgar) – to pay up.

INFECTIONS

8. an **infectious laugh** – a laugh that is quickly echoed by the other people present. 'His laugh was so infectious that we all joined in, even though we didn't understand the joke.'
9. to **plague** someone – to pester someone with constant requests.
10. to **avoid like the plague** – to keep something you consider harmful or dangerous at as great a distance from you as possible. 'If you want to write well, you must avoid jargon like the plague.'
11. **a plague on both your houses** – a phrase of disgust with both parties in a contest. It is often said by Liberals and Social Democrats about the two major parties in British politics, the Conservative and Labour parties. The reference is to Shakespeare's *Romeo and Juliet* (III, i, 96).

OTHER AFFLICTIONS

12. **intellectual myopia** – a phrase recently coined for stupidity.

    a myopic view of a problem – a short-sighted or narrow-minded conception of a problem.
13. to have **teething trouble** – to have initial difficulties that stem from inexperience or novelty of design. 'When we bought our new television set, the salesman warned us that we might have teething trouble with it, since the design of the model was a new and complicated one.' The reference is to the pain associated with the cutting of a tooth. cf. 'to **have growing pains**' **128/2**.
14. to be **stiff-necked** – to be very obstinate, impossible to argue with; unwilling to listen to reason. cf. **'pig-headed' 59/6**.
15. to **cramp** someone's **style** – to hinder or spoil what someone is trying to do. 'My husband loves to entertain our guests with his funny stories but, when Father comes to dinner, Alan always forgets what he wants to say. I don't know why, but Father seems to cramp his style.'
16. to **work in spasms** – to work irregu-

larly, some days many hours on end and some days not at all.

1. **with a jaundiced eye** – with a sour, disapproving look. 'Having already lost a lot of his money on his wife's wild schemes, Philip viewed her new project with a jaundiced eye.'
2. a **measly reward** – a mean, miserly reward.
3. a **rash** of new ideas, etc. – one (idea) very quickly following another.
4. to **have itching fingers** – to have a strong impulse to hit someone. 'My fingers were itching to smack Peter's face.'
5. **warts and all** – with all its faults and imperfections, a realistic portrayal. The modern artist tries to render a true likeness, 'warts and all', and avoid flattering his subject. The phrase comes from Oliver Cromwell's statement that he wanted his portrait to show him accurately, 'warts and all'.
6. an **anaemic character** – a weak, subdued character.
7. to get **dizzy with success** – success has often been compared with climbing to the top of a pole, when it would be natural to feel dizzy on looking down.
8. to **play the giddy goat** – to behave wildly, irresponsibly. Goats have always been associated with wildness and lack of control.
9. **verbal diarrhoea** (colloquial) – compulsive talkativeness. 'Hewitt spoke to the conference for three hours, scarcely pausing to draw breath; a bad case of verbal diarrhoea.'
10. **with a sting in its tail** – a speech or article that reserves its venom until the end.
11. **only a hiccup / a mere hiccup** – only a small, temporary setback in one's progress, or in a relationship with someone. 'We look forward to doing a lot of business with you; your dispute with our director was only a hiccup.'
12. a **barren harvest** – a worthless reward.
13. **cancerous growth** – a pathological tendency to grow and spread. 'In the last few years there has been a cancerous growth in drug-taking which has affected all sections of society.'
14. **sick humour / a sick joke** – humour that is morbid or sadistic; for example, when an armless person is given a tennis racquet for his birthday.
15. to **pile on the agony** – to aggravate the pain. 'There was no need to tell Dennis he would have to get a job now that he has failed his exams and can't go to university. That was piling on the agony.'
16. to **add insult to injury** – to aggravate a wrong that one has done someone by adding another. 'Having failed to pay the doctor's bill, the patient then complained about his treatment to the medical association. He added insult to injury.'
17. to **lick one's wounds** – to console oneself after a severe blow.

ACHES

18. to **be a headache** – to be a great trial to other people, due to one's misbehaviour and bad temper.
19. to **belly-ache** (Australian) – to complain continually. The phrase is now becoming fashionable in Great Britain.

PAINS

20. to be **a fool for one's pains** – to work hard, or try to help someone else without proper reward or acknowledgement. 'Only £10 for all that work! You were a fool for your pains!'
21. to be **at pains / to take pains to** – to

exert oneself to, to make a great effort to. 'The teacher took pains to correct the girl's pronunciation.' 'They were all at pains to make me feel at home, and I soon forgot I was homesick.'

1. a **pain in the neck** (slang) – a pest, a real nuisance, a source of continuous annoyance. 'That man has been a pain in the neck ever since we took him on. He quarrels with all our customers and staff.'
2. to have **growing pains** – just as a child has 'growing pains' in its limbs, so an industry may have 'growing pains' when it has difficulties in getting itself established on a profitable basis. cf. **'teething trouble' 126/13**.

SORES

3. to **be sore about** – to feel aggrieved about. 'He is still sore about Vivien going out with Norman.'
4. a **sore spot** – a subject about which someone is particularly sensitive. 'You shouldn't have mentioned his father's bankruptcy. You touched a sore spot with him.'
5. a **sight for sore eyes** – an object of outstanding beauty, capable of inspiring the most jaded observer.
6. an **eye-sore** – hideous, offensive to the eye. 'The new building was an eye-sore, quite out of place in its surroundings.' cf. 'to **stick out like a sore thumb' 97/12**.
7. to **open old sores** – to revive old quarrels. 'Why did you talk to Martin about Father's will? What was the point of opening old sores?'

MADNESS

8. **midsummer madness** – madness has always been associated with the full moon, so that the midsummer heat, combined with the full moon, was the time when madness was at its fullest intensity.
9. there is **method in his madness** – although he seems to be acting illogically, he has, in fact, a purpose in everything he does. 'Our approach to our clients may surprise you at first, but you will soon see there is method in our madness.' (See Shakespeare's *Hamlet*, II, ii, 211.)
10. **hopping mad** – absolutely furious. 'When the bus went all the way at walking pace, the passengers were hopping mad with the driver.'
11. to **throw a fit** – to experience an attack of nerves, brought on by shock, anxiety, rage, etc. 'Your father would throw a fit if he knew what you were up to!'
12. **by fits and starts** – irregularly, spasmodically. 'Mary works by fits and starts. One day she will work for ten hours; the next two days she won't work at all.'
13. a **mania for** (fresh air, fast driving, stamp-collecting, etc.) – an overwhelming desire for or interest in some object or activity.
14. a **schizoid attitude to** – mixed or contradictory feelings and views about a particular topic. Schizoid is a psychiatric term meaning a dissociation between the reason and the emotions.
15. the **lunatic fringe** – the fanatics in a political party who seek to impose their extremist policies on the country by force.

ILLNESS

16. to be **ill at ease with** – to feel awkward in the presence of someone. 'Bernard always felt ill at ease when he was with his father; he never understood why.'
17. a **diplomatic illness** – a sham illness to provide an excuse for non-

attendance at a party or function. Diplomatic illnesses are sometimes pleaded in order to extricate someone from an embarrassing situation; at other times, to express annoyance or resentment.

MEDICINE AND HEALTH

1. to give someone **a dose/taste of his own medicine** – to treat a wrongdoer in the same way as he has his victims. 'While Johnson was breaking into the vicarage, his own flat was burgled. He was given a taste of his own medicine!'
2. a **bitter pill to swallow** – to be obliged to accept a great disappointment or humiliation. 'It was a bitter pill for him to swallow when he discovered that after twenty years of marriage his wife did not love him.'
3. to **give a clean bill of health** – after a medical check-up, to inform someone that he is in good physical condition. 'Now that the doctor has given me a clean bill of health, I can start training for the European Championship.'

14. RELATIONS

RELATIONS

1. **poor relations** – relatives who are despised for their lack of money. The phrase is often applied to people who beg from their richer relations; but it can also be used ironically. 'My sister-in-law is a terrible snob. She always makes me feel like a poor relation when I visit her.'
2. **relations are rather strained** – a change for the worse in the feelings of two persons or parties towards one another, e.g. between the USA and Soviet Russia; a cooling-off of a friendship, usually brought about by some unresolved problem or dispute. 'Since I told my fiancée that I wanted to take a job in America, our relations have been rather strained.'

FAMILY

3. a **family man** – a man whose interests are in his home, rather than outside it, e.g. in his career, or in sport, socializing, etc.
4. to **be family** – someone who is entitled to special consideration because he is one of the family. 'We always keep a room free for Pamela; she is family.'
5. **in the family way** (vulgar) – pregnant.
6. a **person of family** – born into a good family.
7. a **family doctor** – a doctor who attends the family when they are ill.
8. the **head of the family** – usually the father or, in his absence, the eldest son.
9. to **run in the family** – (of a characteristic or talent) to pass from one generation to the next. 'Jack's three children are all musical, just like their father; it must run in the family.'

MARRIAGE

10. **marriage lines** – a marriage certificate.
11. a **shot-gun marriage** – one that the couple are forced into by circumstances beyond their control (for example, the pregnancy of the bride). It has come to mean any partnership that is forced on the parties. 'There may well be a shot-gun marriage between the trade unions and small business if the economic depression continues.' This is an American idiom which owes its origin to the old days when a young man who had seduced a girl would be forced by her angry parents to marry her at the point of a shot-gun.

KINDRED

12. **kindred spirits** – two people who share the same ideas and interests. 'Anne and I must be kindred spirits; we have the same views on everything.'

WIFE

13. a **fish-wife** – a woman who is vulgar and uses bad language.
14. an **old wives' tale** – an old story or belief that has no foundation in fact, a myth. Here are a few examples of old wives' tales: that a drowning man rises to the surface twice before sinking for the last time; that children suffer from 'growing pains'; that you will catch a cold if you sit about in wet socks; and that musical people learn a foreign language quicker than unmusical people.
15. **like Caesar's wife** – above suspicion (of any crime or immoral behaviour). Only used of important public figures.

'Ministers of the Crown must be like Caesar's wife. If their private lives give rise to scandal, they are expected to resign.' When asked why Caesar divorced his wife, he replied: 'I wished my wife to be not so much as suspected' (Caesar, Roman *Apothegms*).

FATHER

1. a **father figure** – a man who takes the place of a father. He may play the part of a father to a young man, as Dr Johnson did to Boswell, or to a whole nation, as President Tito did to Yugoslavia.
2. **the father of** literature, history, modern psychology, etc. – the originator or the first example of. Chaucer is the father of English literature. Freud is the father of psycho-analysis.
3. **the wish is father to the thought** – we believe what we wish to believe – a common human failing.
4. **when Father turns, we all turn** – an ironic comment on the type of leader who, as he changes his views, expects his followers to do the same. The phrase is based on the idea of a man sleeping in one bed with his wife and children, who expects them all to turn over when he does so.
5. to be **gathered to one's fathers** (biblical) – to die.
6. **the sins of the fathers are visited on the sons** (biblical) – later generations suffer the consequences of their ancestors' vices.
7. **like father, like son** – resemblance of the son to the father from the intellectual or emotional point of view.
8. **the child is father of the man** – the child's behaviour indicates how the character of the man will develop. 'The childhood shows the man / As morning shows the day' (Milton, *Paradise Regained*, Book IV, l.220). 'The child is father of the man' (Wordsworth, 'My heart leaps up when I behold . . .').
9. **on the father's/mother's side** – a relative of the father, for example the father's parents, or his brother, sister or cousin, etc. The same applies to the mother.
10. to **stand godfather** – to pay the bills, godfathers being people from whom one expects generous gifts.

DADDY

11. a **sugar daddy** – a rich old man who keeps a girl young enough to be his daughter.
12. **Big Daddy** – a father who is very protective of his daughter.

MOTHER

13. **'Like motherhood, we are all for it'** – to declare one's support for a policy which has the support of everybody; like saying: 'I'm in favour of a fair and just society.'
14. **mother tongue** – the first language one learns to speak.
15. a **mother-complex** – an unhealthy or abnormal emotional tie between the son and his mother, resulting in the son's emotional dependence on the mother and coolness towards other women.
16. a **mother's boy/darling** – a boy who is indulged or spoilt by his mother.
17. the **wicked step-mother** – step-mothers are often regarded as wicked by the step-children who look upon them as intruders.
18. a **fairy god-mother** – a person who provides one with every possible blessing. 'You've been a real fairy god-mother to me.' A figure of speech taken from fairy stories in which a woman with supernatural powers pro-

tects the interests of the young heroine.

1. **the mother and father of** – the biggest and the worst. 'I'm sorry I can't go out with you tonight. I've got the mother and father of a toothache.'

CHILD

2. **child's play** – a simple task for anyone who has the gift or experience to accomplish it. 'It was child's play to teach the boy English, he was so quick and intelligent.'
3. **Spare the rod and spoil the child** – without strict discipline, a child's character will be ruined by his parents' indulgence. A Victorian adage which has been rejected by later generations of parents.
4. **child of nature** – someone who is innately good, even if unpolished.
5. a **child wife** – a wife who is too young to carry out her duties, for example David Copperfield's first wife (in *David Copperfield* by Charles Dickens).
6. a **brain-child** (colloquial) – one's original idea. It can be used in a derogatory way when the speaker disclaims responsibility for an idea that has failed in practice. 'The new shift system at the office was the manager's brain-child, not mine. He is to blame for its failure.'
7. **second childhood** – the simple-mindedness of old age which resembles in some ways the mind of a child.

BABY

8. a **cry-baby** – someone who cries or complains at the smallest provocation. 'That boy cries out whenever he is touched. He's a real cry-baby.'
9. **baby-face** – round cheeks, innocent air and adolescent appearance, though advanced in years.
10. to **baby-sit** – to look after a baby or small children while the parents are out. This is done by a **baby-sitter**.
11. to **throw out the baby with the bath water** – to destroy the good while trying to eliminate the bad. 'When the new director dismissed a large number of his staff to make the company more profitable, he also got rid of some of his best engineers. He had thrown out the baby with the bath water.'
12. to **be left holding the baby** – to be forced to take over someone else's responsibility. 'When the firm started to lose money, Harry resigned, and I was left holding the baby.'
13. a **baby-snatcher** (derogatory) – a woman who has a boy-friend much younger than herself.
14. **the babes in the wood** – innocent, naïve people lacking in experience and over-trustful. 'We've been doing this work for many years; we aren't exactly babes in the wood.'
15. a **babe-in-arms** – someone who is completely naïve and inexperienced in the ways of the world. 'How can John think of starting a business at his age! He is only a babe-in-arms.'

SON

16. he is **his father's son** – he resembles his father in character.
17. the **prodigal son** – someone who returns home after a long absence, and is received with great joy by his family despite his past behaviour. Today, the phrase is used in a humorous sense. 'Are you going to kill the fatted calf for the prodigal son, Tom?' The allusion is to the parable of the prodigal son in Luke XV, 30.
18. **son of the soil** – a person who has been

brought up on the land, e.g. a farm labourer.

1. a **son of a bitch** (vulgar) – an Americanism meaning a mean, nasty man who will take unfair advantage of you to further his own ends.
2. a **natural son/daughter** – an illegitimate son/daughter.

DAUGHTER

3. a **daughter language** – a language which has been derived from an older one; for example the Romance languages, French, Italian, Spanish, etc., from Latin.

BROTHER

4. the **brotherhood of man** – human society considered as one big family.
5. **Big Brother** – in George Orwell's novel *1984*, Big Brother is the dictator of an imaginary country who dominates the lives of all its citizens. Big Brother is able to observe each citizen through an electronic eye, so that there is no escaping him, however cautiously his opponents conspire against him. Big Brother has become a symbol of power and tyranny against whom it is useless to struggle.
6. **'Am I my brother's keeper?'** – often used as a disclaimer of responsibility for the actions of one's close associates. From Genesis IV, 9: 'And the Lord said unto Cain, Where is Abel thy brother; and he said I know not. Am I my brother's keeper?'
7. **brothers in arms** – originally fellow soldiers, but used metaphorically in the sense of participants in the same struggle.

TWIN

8. a **twin-set** – matching jumper and cardigan.

COUSIN

9. **country cousins** – people from the country rather than the town, who are presumed to be ignorant and unsophisticated.

GRANDMOTHER

10. **don't teach your grandmother to suck eggs** – don't try to instruct someone who is more experienced than you.

AUNT

11. an **Aunt Sally** – an object of ridicule whose policies have failed or become unpopular. 'The Prime Minister, Mrs Thatcher, has no intention of allowing the Home Secretary to be made an Aunt Sally for the increase in crime this year.' An Aunt Sally was originally a female effigy stuck on the end of a pole at which sticks and stones were thrown with the object of knocking the pipe out of its mouth; hence an object of derision.

UNCLE

12. **Uncle Sam** – a nickname for the typical American. cf. **'John Bull of England' 192/12**.
13. **Uncle Tom** – a derisive term used by black nationalists for black people who collaborate with the white authorities. Uncle Tom was the black hero of *Uncle Tom's Cabin*, a story by Harriet Beecher Stowe.
14. **Uncle Tom Cobbleigh and all** – all and sundry, including the most ordinary people you can think of.

BACHELOR

15. a **bachelor girl** – an unmarried girl.
16. a **bachelor's wife** – the perfect wife in the mind of the unmarried man.

WIDOW

1. a **grass widow** – a woman whose husband is away temporarily. Originally, an unmarried woman who has lived with one or more men. The phrase suggests illicit relations out of doors rather than in the marriage bed.

   a **golf widow** – a woman whose husband spends much of his time on the golf course, so that she is alone for most of the day.
2. **not for widows and orphans** – not for investors of limited means who cannot afford to take risks with their money.
3. a **merry widow** – merry because she is now free to make new friends and have a merry time. The reference is to Franz Lehár's operetta 'The Merry Widow'.
4. **the widow's mite** – although the gift was very small, it had more moral worth coming from a poor woman than a bigger gift from a rich one. From Christ's parable, Mark XII, 42.
5. **widow's weeds** – a widow's mourning dress. 'Her widow's weeds become her.'

15. TOWN AND AROUND

TOWN

1. to **go to town** – to spend one's money recklessly. 'The Howards have really gone to town on a house for their daughter. They have bought her an absolute beauty.' **'Go to town'** is an American colloquialism referring to the people who come into town from the countryside to spend their money. It was originally used about cowboys and ranch hands.
2. a **man about town** – a sociable man who attends many fashionable parties and has a wide circle of wealthy friends. 'My brother has become quite a man about town; when he was young, he hated going to parties.
3. a **lady of the town** – a woman of loose morals.
4. the **talk of the town** – someone whose behaviour and wild way of life give rise to gossip and scandal-mongering. 'You had better behave yourself, Pauline. You are becoming the talk of the town.'

   it's the talk of the town – it's the most talked-about or fashionable place or thing.
5. a **ghost town** – a town that is no longer inhabited.

STREET

6. to **take to the streets** – to demonstrate against authority, to make a show of force. 'The students took to the streets in support of the health workers' claim for higher wages.'
7. to **go on the streets** – to work as a prostitute.
8. **streets ahead of** – far superior to, very much in advance of. 'You are streets ahead of us in technology.'
9. **not in the same street** – far inferior to, in no way comparable. 'All right, I'll have a game with you, but you know very well I'm not in the same street as you.'
10. the **man in the street** – the ordinary, typical man and woman. 'We are doing market research work, and we want the reaction of the man in the street to our suggestions.'
11. to **go back to Civvy Street** – to return to civilian life after serving in the armed forces. 'What are you going to do when you go back to Civvy Street?'
12. **in Queer Street** – in financial trouble, in debt. 'If we go on spending money like this, we shall soon be in queer street.' 'Queer Street' may be a corruption of Carey Street where the Courts in Bankruptcy are situated.
13. **grub street** – an inferior writer, inferior writing. '. . . any mean production is called grubstreet' (Dr Johnson, *Dictionary*). Grub Street near Moorfields in the East End of London (now Milton Street) was inhabited in the seventeenth century by a group of inferior writers and literary hacks.
14. **right up my street** – that's a subject I'm very familiar with. 'I'll be glad to advise Brian about his advertising. Advertising and publicity are right up my street.'

ROAD

15. **one for the road** – a final drink before one leaves a social gathering.
16. to **take to the road** – to become a tramp. 'I would rather take to the road than work in an office from 9 till 5 each day. I want to be free.'
17. **at the end of the road** – (1) towards the end of one's life. 'I have come to the

end of the road, my dear; the doctor has given me only another six months.' (2) finally, last of all.

1. **at the cross-roads** – at a point in one's life when important decisions have to be made. 'Peter and Sue are at the cross-roads; they will have to decide very soon whether to make their home in England or emigrate.'

DEAD END

2. a **dead end** – leading nowhere.

   a **dead end job** – a job with no prospects or advancement, similar in meaning to a **'blind alley job' 125/5**.

WAY

3. to **pave the way for** – to create the necessary conditions for . . . , usually followed by some event. 'World War II paved the way for the independence of India.'
4. to **go all the way** with – to be in complete agreement with. 'I'm not sure whether I would go all the way with you, but I certainly sympathize with your aims.'
5. **way out** – (1) quite wrong, totally mistaken. 'You are way out in your calculations. The holiday will cost £300, not £200.' (2) out of the ordinary, bizarre. 'Some of the costumes at the party were way out, especially the exotic pyjamas which would have been more suitable for the bedroom.'
6. to **rub someone up the wrong way** – to be tactless, to say the very thing that is certain to annoy someone. 'You certainly rubbed Mrs Parker up the wrong way, telling her you don't like Sussex. She has lived there all her life and adores the county.'
7. to **go about something the wrong way** – to use the wrong method or approach to achieve an object. 'If you wanted Howard to back your project you went about it the wrong way contradicting him at dinner.'
8. **at the parting of the ways** – a time when it is best to separate. 'I am so sorry, Tim, but I'm afraid we've come to a parting of the ways. We are only making each other unhappy.' From the Bible, Ezekiel XXI, 21: 'For the king of Babylon stood at the parting of the way, at the head of the two ways . . .'
9. to **go one's own way** – to follow one's inclinations, to rely on one's own judgement and ignore other people's. 'All right, Tom, go your own way, if that's how you feel about it, but I wish you would listen to us just once.'
10. to **have a way with one** – to have a natural charm, which is very persuasive. 'Jenny certainly has a way with her. I found myself agreeing with everything she said.'
11. to **have come a long way** – to have accomplished a great deal. 'You've come a long way since we last met. You were a clerk then, and now you own your own factory.'
12. **in a big way** – on a large scale. 'Ian is very ambitious, he does everything in a big way.'

    in a small way – on a small scale, only to a small extent. 'If you could help me, even in a small way, I should be most grateful.'
13. to **find out the hard way** – to learn the truth from one's own painful experience. 'We warned you that you wouldn't like boarding school but you wouldn't listen. Now you've found out the hard way.'
14. to **make way for** – to surrender one's position to someone else. 'You've done a wonderful job for the Company, but we think, Sir, that at the age of seventy it is only fair you should make way for a younger man.'

1. to **have it one's own way** – to insist on doing what one wants despite arguments to the contrary. 'Have it your own way, Hugh, but if things go wrong, don't blame us.'
2. to **have it both ways** – to support two incompatible arguments or courses of action at the same time. 'If you want an absolutely safe investment, then you can't expect a high rate of interest. You can't have it both ways.'
3. to **cut both ways** – to have advantages and disadvantages at the same time. 'This new drug will relieve your arthritis, but you must put up with the side-effects; it cuts both ways.'
4. **set in one's ways** – having fixed ideas and habits. 'Turner is too set in his ways to adopt your ideas; you had better look for a younger man.'
5. to **look the other way** – to pretend not to see, to overlook a breach of the rules or some irregularity. 'Even a disciplinarian like the sergeant-major has to look the other way sometimes.'
6. **on its way out** – becoming unfashionable. 'The mini-skirt was already on its way out by 1969.'
7. to **pay one's way** – to support oneself without having to borrow money. 'Many American students pay their way through college by taking a part-time job.'
8. to **mend one's ways** – to change one's behaviour or habits, for the better. 'If you want your uncle to help you, you'll have to mend your ways. That will mean cutting out night clubs and starting to study seriously.'
9. a **way of life** – a set of principles according to which one lives one's life. 'Alan soon got used to the Muslim way of life, but his sister found it more difficult.'
10. to **see one's way to** – to feel justified in. 'After Peter's ingratitude to her, his cousin didn't see her way to giving him any more help.'
11. to **go out of one's way** to – to put oneself to some trouble to . . . , to make a special effort to . . . 'When we visited London, our hosts went out of their way to make our stay enjoyable.'
12. **no way** (colloquial American English) – out of the question, impossible. '"Could you please lend me £50?" "No way, I haven't got that much myself."'
13. **by the way** – incidentally, which reminds me. 'I'm sorry your cousin is ill. By the way, have you got his new address? I have some letters for him.'
14. **there are no two ways about it** – there is no other possibility or explanation. 'When you are in the army, you have to obey orders, no matter how unreasonable or stupid they may be. There are no two ways about it.'
15. to **stand in someone's way** – to obstruct or hinder someone in his aims. 'If you want to take a job abroad, don't let me stand in your way.'
16. **in a bad way** – physically or mentally in a serious condition. 'Your brother has had an accident. Will you go to the hospital at once; he's in a bad way.'
17. **not to know which way to turn** – to be in desperate difficulties. 'I was stranded in New York one winter without money or friends; I didn't know which way to turn until the British Consulate helped me out.'
18. to **put business** someone's **way** – to be the means of placing custom or orders with someone. 'If you are interested, I can put some business your way.'
19. to **fall by the wayside** – to fail to achieve one's aim, because of laziness, lack of strength or distractions. This phrase is generally used humorously. 'My father put me into accountancy, but I am sorry to say I was one of

those who fell by the wayside.' The allusion is to Luke VIII, 5: 'A Sower went out to sow his seed, and as he sowed, some fell by the wayside; and it was trodden down and the fowls of the air devoured it'.

LANE

1. to **go down memory lane** – to revive old memories. 'Let's be sentimental, Joan, and go down memory lane this afternoon.'

RIVER

2. to **sell down the river** – to betray, to act deceitfully towards. 'When we went back to the bookie's office to collect our winnings, he had already run off with the stakes; he had sold us down the river.' The phrase was first used by the black slaves who were sold by their owners to plantation owners further down the Mississippi, where conditions were usually much harsher.

BRIDGE

3. to **cross one's bridges before one comes to them** – to worry unnecessarily about something that may never happen. 'I don't know why you are worrying about Father catching one of those tropical diseases in Africa. His company hasn't decided yet whether to send him to Africa. Don't cross your bridges before you come to them.'
4. **that's (all) water under the bridge** – that is all past now, and there is nothing that can be done about it. 'Yes, it's a pity you didn't accept Fred's offer, but it's useless to reproach yourself now. It's all water under the bridge.'
5. to **pull up the drawbridge** – to keep visitors out in order to ensure privacy for oneself and one's family. 'We enjoy entertaining, but at Christmas we like to pull up the drawbridge and be on our own.'

AVENUE

6. to **explore every avenue** – to make the most thorough inquiry. 'We are exploring every avenue to obtain the information you are asking for.'

TOWER

7. an **ivory tower** – a haven from the harsh realities of life. 'Living in your ivory tower at Oxford, you can't imagine, can you, what it's like to go hungry?' The term 'tour d'ivoire' (ivory tower) was first used by Sainte-Beuve (1837) to describe the retreat of the French poet, Vigny.
8. a **tower of strength** – a person one can always turn to for sympathy and support in times of trouble. 'When my parents' marriage broke up, my eldest sister was a tower of strength to the children. We couldn't have managed without her.'

EXHIBITION

9. to **make an exhibition of oneself** – to invite public ridicule or contempt by one's behaviour. 'I wish Henry wouldn't make an exhibition of himself shouting at the waiter like that. It is so embarrassing.'

MUSEUM

10. a **museum piece** – something antiquated or worn-out. 'We can't go to Scotland in that museum piece. Surely the car-hire company can do better than that!' The literal meaning is a specimen of an earlier civilization exhibited in a museum.

PUBLIC HOUSE

1. to have someone **over a barrel** – to have a person in one's power, so that he can be forced to do whatever is asked of him. 'The boss has got you over a barrel. If you don't withdraw your accusations, he will take you to court, and if you do withdraw, you will lose the respect of the staff.'
2. to **scrape the bottom of the barrel** – to content oneself with poor quality when all other possibilities have been exhausted. 'Dorothy must have scraped the bottom of the barrel to have married a man like that!'

MARKET

3. a **captive market** – a monopoly of an essential product or service which the consumer is obliged to accept without exercising his normal freedom of choice. 'We can ask any price we like for our water supply; we have a captive market.'
4. to be a **drug on the market** – to find no customers, something for which there is no demand. 'Gramophone records have become a drug on the market since cassettes were introduced.'
5. to be **in the market for** – to be interested in obtaining or buying something. 'We are not in the market for diamonds at present.'
6. to **play the market** – to speculate in the buying and selling of stocks and shares or commodities. 'Herbert calls it playing the market; I call it gambling.'
7. to **put something on the market** – to offer something for sale. 'We have decided to leave London, so we are putting our house on the market.'
   to **come on the market** – to be offered for sale.
8. to **corner the market** – to obtain a monopoly of the supply of particular goods or services. 'Once a government has cornered the market, as for instance in gas or electricity, there is always a huge rise in prices.'
9. a **rising/falling market** – a rising/falling demand for goods or services which will be reflected in their prices.
10. to **price oneself out of the market** – to ask so much more money for one's services or products that customers go elsewhere. 'The school fees you are charging are so high that you are in danger of pricing yourself out of the market.'
11. to **spoil the market for** – to reduce the demand for services or products by lowering their quality or putting too many on offer. 'The dishonest advertising agencies will spoil the market for the good ones.'
12. to **flood the market** – to offer services or goods far in excess of the demand for them.
13. to **drive a hard bargain** – to come to an agreement on one's own terms without making any worthwhile concessions. 'You drive a hard bargain, but I suppose I'll have to accept your offer.'
14. **under the counter** – of goods illegally sold in shops, secretly, without the knowledge of the authorities. 'Johnson always sold the stolen jewellery under the counter to clients who could be trusted not to go to the police.'
15. to **have no truck with** – to have no dealings with, not to tolerate. 'I'll have no truck with their demands for a higher wage.' 'Truck' originally meant to exchange goods for services, to barter, to have dishonest dealings with someone.

HILL

16. **up hill and down dale** – everywhere. Idiomatically, this phrase is only used with verbs like look for, search for,

hunt for. 'Wherever have you been all this time? We have been looking for you up hill and down dale.'

1. **as old as the hills** – very old indeed. 'That car of yours is as old as the hills. Don't you think you ought to buy a new one?'
2. to **go downhill** – to suffer a decline in one's health or fortunes. 'Poor Bill, he has gone steadily downhill since he lost his job.'

   to **go down** – to suffer a decline in its reputation, quality or appearance. This is only used of things, not people, especially of neighbourhoods and districts. 'This was one of the most fashionable districts in London, but it has gone right down in the last ten years.'

TRACK

3. to be **on the right/wrong track** – to make / not to make progress in one's search for . . . 'The police believe that they are at last on the right track in their hunt for the murderers.' 'If you think I had anything to do with it, you're on the wrong track.'
4. to **keep track of** – to keep oneself informed of someone's movements, activities, etc. 'I try to keep track of all my old school friends, but it isn't easy.'

   to **lose track of** – not to be informed of the movements, etc., of someone. 'Joyce has been married so many times that I've quite lost track.'

   to **lose (all) track of time** – not to be aware of the passage of time.
5. to **make tracks for** – to leave quickly for. 'It's getting late. We had better make tracks for home.'
6. a **track record** – a record of one's successes/failures. 'I think we should consider Holmes for the headmastership. His track record for getting his pupils into the universities is very good.'
7. **in one's tracks** – in the very place where one is standing at a particular moment. 'Hugh was on the point of hitting his son when his wife entered the room; that stopped him in his tracks!'
8. to **cover one's tracks** – to conceal traces of one's movements. 'The bank robbers have covered their tracks very cleverly.'

PATH

9. to **keep to the straight and narrow (path)** – to resist temptation and lead a virtuous life. 'As a clergyman, I am naturally expected to keep to the straight and narrow path, but it hasn't always been easy.' The phrase comes from the Bible (Matthew VII, 14): 'Because strait is the gate, and narrow is the way which leadeth into life, and few there be that find it!'
10. to **beat a path to** a place – to visit in large numbers. 'Now that Vivien has become famous, all sorts of people will be beating a path to her door.' The path to a place is beaten flat by the feet of so many people.
11. to **cross** someone's **path** – (1) to meet someone accidentally. 'Since I left school, I haven't crossed Smith's path, and I can't say I have any wish to.' (2) to thwart someone. 'If Jones crosses your path again, let me know and I'll put a stop to his interference.'

PITCH

12. to **queer someone's pitch** – to thwart or spoil someone's plans. 'The War Office queered our pitch by posting me overseas twenty-four hours before our wedding day.' 'Queer' is used as a verb only in this phrase. The pitch

refers to the pitching of a tent in which a street vendor could carry on his business or a circus performer could entertain the public. Sometimes the police would order these tented structures to be taken down, thus 'queering someone's pitch'.

TRANSPORT AND TRAFFIC

1. to be **a slow coach** – to be very slow in one's actions, to keep one's companions waiting impatiently. 'What a slow coach you are! Do hurry up; everyone is waiting for you!'
2. to **jump the queue** – to try to seize an advantage without waiting one's turn. 'Everyone queues up in England. You'd make yourself very unpopular if you jumped the queue.'
3. to **miss the bus** – to lose an opportunity. 'I am fifty years old but I still haven't been promoted. Now it's too late; I've missed the bus.' cf. 'to **miss the boat' 180/1**.
4. to **tell** someone **where to get off** – to give someone a stern rebuke. 'When Joe started lecturing me on how to paint, I soon told him where to get off. He seemed to forget that I've had years of experience at it and he is only a beginner.' The phrase refers to the bus-conductor's right to order any passenger off a bus if he makes trouble.
5. to **fall off the back of a lorry** – a euphemism for 'to be stolen'. 'I wonder where Philip got that crate of very expensive wine. Did it fall off the back of a lorry?'
6. a **backseat driver** – someone who offers unwanted advice to the person in charge, while having no responsibility himself for the way a task is performed. 'We'd manage much better without the help of backseat drivers like Williams.' The phrase refers to the passenger in the back of a car, who is always telling the driver what to do.

16. THE HOUSE

HOUSE

1. to **keep open house** – to be at home to visitors at all times; to offer them hospitality regardless of who they are.
2. a **rough house** – a fight, a violent disturbance. 'The soldiers are getting very aggressive. We had better leave before there is a rough house.'
3. a **full house** – a theatre that is fully attended.
   an **empty house** – an empty theatre. 'The ageing actress refused to retire, even though she was playing to empty houses.'
4. **The House of God** – a church or chapel.
5. to be **houseproud** – to take pride in keeping one's house clean and tidy. 'Anne is so houseproud, her drawing-room is like a shop window.'
6. a **household word** – something that is familiar to every household in the country.
7. a **drink on the house** – a drink that is paid for by the landlord of the public house. 'Have another; it's on the house.'
8. **in the best houses** – in the best society. The phrase suggests a country house with a retinue of servants to which the most distinguished people are invited.
9. a **house of cards** – an idea that has no foundation in fact, a wildly impracticable idea. 'His schemes for the future are no more than a house of cards that may topple over any moment.'
10. a **house of ill-fame** – a brothel.
11. a **madhouse** – one in which there is great commotion and disorder. 'I'll never visit my friend again. There was so much noise all through the night that it was impossible to sleep. It was a madhouse!'
12. **house arrest** – confinement to one's own home by order of the authorities.
13. to **bring the house down** – to receive resounding applause. 'The Prime Minister made a powerful speech which brought the house down.' The reference is to the applause of a theatre audience.
14. to **shout the house down / don't shout the house down** – to make a terrible commotion. 'I can't study while our brother is shouting the house down.'
15. to **cry/shout something from the housetops** – to tell everyone. 'If I'd known you were going to shout it from the housetops, I wouldn't have said anything.' The phrase derives from the East where the roofs are normally flat and are used as meeting places for the family.
16. a **house-warming party** – a party given in celebration of the new owners taking possession of their house.
17. to get on **like a house on fire** – to be in whole-hearted agreement with someone. The idiom suggests that the relationship of the two people grows in warmth. 'We have a great deal in common and work very well together. We are getting on like a house on fire.'
18. to be **as safe as houses** – to be absolutely safe. 'Your money will be quite safe in that company. It's well managed and it has huge assets. It's as safe as houses.'
19. to **have the run of the house** – to have free access to every room in the house. 'You can have the run of the house while we are on holiday.'
20. to **eat** someone **out of house and home** – to eat an excessive amount of one's host's food. 'My son William has a terrible appetite. At the rate he is going, he will eat us all out of house and home.'

1. to **set/put one's house in order** – to correct one's own mismanagement, often used with reference to business. 'Before we criticize others, we ought to put our own house in order.'

HOME

2. to **be/feel at home with** – to be on familiar ground, to be well informed on a given subject.
3. to **be 'at home' to people** – to be willing and prepared to receive friends in one's home.
   an **'at home'** – a meeting in one's own house of selected guests.
4. **not at home** – a euphemism for not wishing to receive an unwelcome guest. 'The maid was instructed to tell John Lane that her mistress was not at home.'
5. a **home from home** – a place or situation where one feels completely happy and at ease, where one is treated like one of the family.
6. to be **homesick** – to have a painful longing for one's own home and family.
7. the **last home** – the last resting-place, i.e. the grave.
8. to be **home and dry** – to have succeeded in one's aim. '"If the accused can prove he was at his mother's between 2 p.m. and 4 p.m., then he is home and dry", said the judge to defending counsel.'
9. to **do one's homework** – to be properly prepared, to master the facts before presenting one's case. 'Counsel paused for a few minutes to look at his papers before resuming his speech. It was obvious he hadn't done his homework.'
10. to **bring** something **home** to a person – to make someone aware of the truth, often painfully. 'His wife's nervous breakdown brought it home to Donald how cruel he had been to her.' This idiom is often connected with the idea of punishment.
11. a **home truth** – a statement that hurts someone because it tells him of a fault or weakness of which he is ashamed.
12. **nothing to write home about** – nothing special or out of the ordinary. 'Mary plays the piano quite competently but she's nothing to write home about. We were expecting much more.' The phrase suggests that a person's expectations have been disappointed.
13. to **romp home** – to leave all the others in the race far behind.
14. to **home in on** – (of a missile) to seek out and destroy a moving target after it has been launched.

WALL

15. to **go to the wall** – to fail, go bankrupt or collapse.
    the weakest go to the wall – the weakest are forced out of business by their more powerful competitors.
16. to drive someone **up the wall** – to irritate someone unbearably. 'When Alec talks about all the illnesses he has had, he drives me up the wall.'
17. **walls have ears** – you must be very careful what you say because someone may be eavesdropping. There is always a danger of being overheard, however private the conversation may be.
18. **within these four walls** – in confidence.
19. the **writing on the wall** – a warning of impending doom. 'Sanders & Duke are dismissing their staff. I am afraid the writing is on the wall for them.' From the Bible, Daniel V. 31.

STONE

20. to **stonewall** – to defend oneself with great caution in order to avoid mis-

takes and thus deny one's opponent any advantage. Originally, cricket slang for playing purely defensively, by blocking every ball and making no attempt to score.

1. to **leave no stone unturned** – to spare no effort to attain one's ends.
2. **only a stone's throw from** here – within easy calling distance, a very short walk.
3. to **break stones** – to do useless, unrewarding work.
4. a **stony stare** – to stare without any recognition or feeling.
5. to be **stony-broke** (slang) – to have no money.
6. to be **stone deaf** – to be completely deaf.
7. the water was **stone cold** – the water was devoid of any warmth.
8. to **lay the corner-stone** – to complete the most essential part of a work. The corner-stone is the most important part of the building.
9. to **cast the first stone** – to make the first accusation. From the New Testament, John VIII. 7: 'Let those among you who are without sin cast the first stone.'

BRICK

10. a **brick** / a **regular brick** (slang) – a kind-hearted, unselfish person. 'Jean looked after the children all the time I was in hospital. She is a regular brick.'
11. to **drop a brick** – to make a tactless remark unintentionally. 'Have you ever seen such a horrible colour for a car? It's your car! Oh dear, I have dropped a brick, haven't I?'
12. to come down on someone **like a ton of bricks** – to punish someone with great severity. 'If Brian catches you reading his diary, he'll come down on you like a ton of bricks.' cf. 'to **skin alive' 108/13**.
13. **like talking to a brick wall** – to waste one's breath trying to persuade someone who is too obstinate to listen to reason. 'He is so dogmatic; it's like talking to a brick wall arguing with him.'
14. to **knock one's head against a brick wall** – to waste time and energy attempting the impossible. 'I told you that you would never get Alan to change his mind. You have been knocking your head against a brick wall!'
15. to **see through a brick wall** – to understand a truth which is beyond the grasp of ordinary people.
16. to **make bricks without straw** – to try to achieve some result with inadequate means. 'We were unable to give you an opinion because you didn't give us the information we needed. We can't make bricks without straw.' The reference is to the captivity of the Israelites in biblical times when they were commanded by the Egyptians to make bricks without straw: 'There is no straw given unto thy servants and they say to us make brick . . .' Exodus V. 16.
17. **'redbrick'** – a modern or recently built university, as distinct from the traditional universities like Oxford, Cambridge and St Andrews whose colleges were built of stone. The term is sometimes used in a derogatory sense.

ROOF

18. to **raise the roof** – to arouse tremendous applause.
19. to **hit the roof / to go through the roof** – to be furiously angry, to explode with rage. 'When I told my father I had crashed his car, he went through the roof.'

TILE

1. to **have a tile loose** – to be mentally deficient. 'If Sheila believes that, she must have a tile loose!'
2. to be **(out) on the tiles** – to be out all hours of the night, drinking and having a good time. 'I'll give George a piece of my mind when he gets home. He's been on the tiles again.'

CHIMNEY, GUTTER, DRAIN AND PIPE

3. to **smoke like a chimney** – to smoke cigarettes incessantly.
4. **out of the gutter** – from the lowest and poorest family; without any education or breeding; with nothing to commend one socially.
5. a **guttersnipe** – a hooligan, someone of very bad character. The snipe is a bird that lives on the refuse in the gutters.
6. to **go down the drain** – to be irretrievably lost, usually as a result of waste or extravagance. 'He gambled away all his inheritance; every penny went down the drain.'
7. **in the pipe-line** – in preparation, not yet complete. 'John has two more novels in the pipe-line.'

PILLAR AND PEDESTAL

8. to be driven **from pillar to post** – to be driven all over the place; to find it impossible to settle down.
9. a **pillar of society** – a prominent, important member of the community who can be relied upon to give it his support.
10. to **put on a pedestal** – to credit someone with qualities that he/she does not possess, to consider someone to be above criticism. 'It is a pity that Helen puts all her friends on a pedestal. Sooner or later she is disillusioned, and all her friendships end in disappointment and bitterness.'

CORNER

11. to **drive** someone **into a corner** – to deprive an opponent of any possibility of retreat. The phrase is often used in boxing.
12. **in a tight corner** – in a dangerous position from which it is difficult to escape.
13. to **fight one's corner** – to fight hard for one's own interests. 'A minister will always resist cuts in public money for his own department. I don't blame a minister for fighting his corner' (former Premier James Callaghan on TV, 1981).
14. a **hole-and-corner affair** – a love affair between two people that is kept secret to avoid shocking public opinion.
15. to **turn the corner** – to make a recovery, often said with reference to health or finance. 'The doctor says that Mary has turned the corner and is out of danger.'
16. to **cut (off) a corner** – to achieve one's objective by breaking or stretching a rule to one's own advantage.
17. to **knock the corners off** someone – to make someone conform in his behaviour to the accepted pattern. 'I wouldn't worry about Peter being a problem child; once he gets to boarding school, they will soon knock the corners off him.'
18. to **stand** someone **in a corner** – to rebuke a subordinate publicly. 'The Prime Minister stood the young Under Secretary in the corner for attacking government policies in a newspaper article.' It used to be the custom in primary schools to stand children in the corner for misbehaving in class.

1. **all the corners of the earth** – every part of the earth.

DOOR

2. to **shut the door in** someone's **face** – to terminate any further negotiations. **to slam the door in** someone's **face** is the same as above, but more violent.
3. to **show** someone **the door** – to request someone to leave.
4. to let someone/something **in through the back door** – to introduce a measure in a way which one's opponents will not notice. 'The private motor-car has not been abolished yet, but there has been a great deal of back-door legislation making its use more expensive and less enjoyable – by increasing road tax, restricting parking facilities, making driving tests more difficult and so on.'
5. to **lay at** someone's **door** – to blame a person for something that has gone badly wrong. 'The delay in bringing relief to the victims of the earthquake was laid at the door of the government.'
6. to **leave a door open** – to offer an opportunity for further discussion.
7. to **open the door to** – to create an opportunity for some abuse. 'When a government acts as an agent for private business, it opens the door to bribery.'
8. **behind closed doors** – in complete privacy. Often used in the sense of denying a hearing to an interested party. 'The decision was reached behind closed doors and so was contrary to natural justice.'
9. to be **next door to** something – so close as to be almost identical. 'To suppress the truth about dry-rot in the house was next door to fraud.'

HINGE

10. to **hinge on** – to depend on. 'His future career will hinge on his success in the June examinations.'

KEY

11. to have **the key of the door** – to have free access to the house. A privilege granted to the children when their parents think that they are old enough to be trusted.
12. a **latch-key child** – a child who has been given a key to let himself into his home after school while his parents are still out at work. 'Most of the pupils who get into trouble at our school are latch-key children.'
13. **keyed up** – in a state of nervous expectation, as one would feel before making an important speech. 'He was all keyed up, knowing that his big moment had arrived.'
14. **the key to the problem** – the essential means of solving a problem.
15. the **key position** – a position of vital strategic importance.
16. the **key word** – the word that is needed for breaking a code.
17. a **key industry** – an essential industry without which other industries cannot function properly.

BELL

18. to be **as sound as a bell** – to be in the best of health; in this context 'sound' is a cognate of the German 'gesund', meaning healthy. cf. **'as fit as a fiddle' 238/11**.
19. **that rings a bell** – that sounds familiar, I've heard that before.

WINDOW AND SHUTTER

20. **window shopping** – looking at articles in a shop-window without buying anything.

1. **window-dressing** – to display things of little or no value so that their deficiencies are concealed. 'The Chairman manipulated the figures very cleverly to conceal the company's heavy losses. It was all window-dressing.' One dresses a window by arranging the merchandise to the best advantage so that it will attract the attention of the passers-by.
2. to **put all one's goods in the window** – to show off all one's good qualities without holding anything in reserve. To be immodest.
3. to **put up the shutters** – to close a house or business; to go into liquidation.

FLOOR

4. to **cross the floor of the House** – to change political parties, to take one's seat on the opposite side of the House. The reference is to the House of Commons. 'Winston Churchill crossed the floor of the House twice during his parliamentary career.'
5. to **wipe the floor with** – to defeat decisively, to humiliate one's opponent.
6. to **have/take the floor** – (1) to be the centre of attention, when everyone is listening to you. (2) to start dancing.
7. to **fall through the floor** – to collapse. 'The dollar has fallen through the floor.'

   to **sink through the floor** – to feel extremely embarrassed. 'When she asked me in front of all the guests why I had been expelled from school, I was so embarrassed I could have sunk through the floor.' By sinking through the floor, the subject would no longer be visible and would thus avoid any further embarrassment.
8. to **get in on the ground floor** – to join forces with an enterprise that is still in an early stage of development with a view to profiting later.
9. **floor show** – a cabaret which is performed on the floor of a club or restaurant as opposed to the stage of a theatre.

CORRIDOR AND STAIRS

10. the **corridors of power** – that part of Whitehall where the Civil Service Establishment wields power. From a novel of the same name, by C. P. Snow.
11. **backstairs** – something underhanded, e.g. backstairs intrigue/gossip/influence, etc. 'As a result of a backstairs intrigue, he got a well-paid job in one of the Ministries.' Originally, in a large house, one staircase was for the family and their guests, and a second staircase was for their servants.

GATE AND FENCE

12. a **gate-crasher** – an uninvited guest.

    to **gate-crash** – to gain admittance to a party without having been invited.
13. **between you, me and the gate-post** – what I am telling you must not go any further, it is a secret.
14. to **sit on the fence** – to be unwilling to commit oneself to either party in a dispute.
15. to **come down on the right/wrong side of the fence** – to ally oneself with the successful/unsuccessful party in a dispute.
16. to **rush one's fences** – to take premature action, to take action without proper preparation. 'Aren't you rushing your fences proposing to Christine? You've only known her a week.' The phrase is taken from show jumping.
17. to **mend one's fences** – to improve relations with someone by removing the cause of the annoyance or dispute.

'If we want to trade with that country, we had better mend our fences with it without delay.' When fences are broken, disputes between neighbours often arise over their rights to the land.

ROOMS

1. to **prefer** someone's **room to his company** – to like someone for his money rather than for his own sake.

HALL

2. to **have the hallmarks of** – to show a person's characteristics. 'The article wasn't signed but it had all the hallmarks of S. Smith.' Literally, to bear the stamp of the Goldsmith's Company which certifies the standard of the gold or silver article tested.
3. **Liberty Hall** – a state of chaos, a place where people may do just as they please. 'I would never send my son to that school – no discipline there at all – pure Liberty Hall!' From Goldsmith's *She Stoops to Conquer*, Act II.
4. **in the hall of fame** – the imaginary hall in which all the famous characters in history are placed.

KITCHEN

5. **kitchen talk** – uneducated talk, consisting for the most part of gossip and idle chatter. 'That is only kitchen talk.'
6. **'If the kitchen is too hot, you should get out of it'** – if you find the responsibilities of office too nerve-racking, you should relinquish your post. Quoted by Harry S. Truman during his presidency of the United States.
7. **kitchen cabinet** – a group of advisers at the disposal of the Prime Minister, whose salaries are financed privately. These advisers are not civil servants but have access in some cases to Cabinet Minutes and other confidential documents. The term was first used in 1829 when Andrew Jackson, the American President, dismissed large numbers of civil servants and installed his own friends at the White House as his personal advisers.

CELLAR

8. to **have a good cellar** – to possess a cellar that is stocked with plenty of good wine.

17. FURNITURE AND HOUSEHOLD ARTICLES

FURNITURE

1. **part of the furniture** – a person whose presence is ignored because he no longer plays any part in the life of a family or enjoys their respect. 'I've been a servant here for fifty years, but no one thought of telling me that we are moving. But then, I'm only a part of the furniture.'

BED

2. a **good bedside manner** – a manner that inspires a patient with confidence in the doctor; a willingness to listen to the patient's complaints, and to reassure him whenever it is possible.
3. to **get out of bed on the wrong side** – to get up in a bad temper. 'What's the matter with you this morning, Paul? You got out of bed on the wrong side, didn't you?'
4. to **featherbed** – to cushion an industry from the effects of rising costs or competition from abroad by means of government grants and subsidies.
5. a **bed of nails** – a duty or situation which brings much annoyance or pain to a person. 'With my boss changing his instructions from one day to the next, my job has become a bed of nails.'
6. a **hotbed** (of vice, sedition, reaction) – a place where the tendency in question is nourished and developed. 'In biblical times, Sodom and Gomorrah were hotbeds of vice.'

PILLOW AND BOLSTER

7. **pillow talk** – confidences exchanged between husbands and wives or between lovers when they are in bed.
8. to **bolster up** – to give one's support to a weak or unconvincing theory, argument, etc. 'Although Reed bolstered up his theory with many new arguments, he got no support from the experts.' The bolster is used as an under-pillow for supporting the sleeper's head.

BLANKET

9. a **wet blanket** – one who spoils other people's fun by ill-humour or excessive seriousness, a depressing influence. The idiom has its origin in the seventeenth century when farmers used wet blankets for extinguishing fires in their cornfields. Later, by association of ideas, spoilsports and killjoys were dubbed 'wet blankets'. cf. **'in the dumps / down in the dumps' 123/3**, 'to **put a damper on someone' 123/4.**
10. to be **born the wrong side of the blanket** – to be illegitimate.
11. a **blanket regulation** – one that is applied to all alike, regardless of differences in size, quality and so on. 'If the Minister applies this blanket regulation to every school, he will destroy many of the best.'

TABLE

12. **table talk** – light conversation, talk that avoids any serious or gloomy topic.
13. to **keep the table laughing** – to keep one's guests at table entertained.

    to **set the table in a roar** – to set the guests at table laughing uproariously at a joke or story.
14. to **keep a good table** – to provide a good cuisine and excellent wine.
15. **table manners** – polite, considerate

behaviour at meals. George Mikas remarked that the French have a good table, and that the English have good table manners.

1. to **turn the tables** – to reverse the position, to seize the advantage from one's opponent. 'The Rangers were three goals down at half-time, but in the second half they turned the tables on Wandsworth and won by 5–3.' The idiom originates in the one-time custom of turning the table round in the middle of a game of chess or draughts, so that the player who had the inferior position could then take advantage of the stronger position of his opponent.
2. to put a proposal **on the table** – to make a definite offer in the course of negotiations.
3. to **table a motion** – to put forward a proposal for debate.
4. a **round-table conference** – a conference at which the participants can confer on equal terms, the shape of the table ensuring that none of the seats take precedence.
5. **High table** – the table in a college that is reserved for the President, the Fellows and the most distinguished guests.
6. to **drink** someone **under the table** – to defeat one's companion in a drinking contest.

CHAIR AND ARMCHAIR

7. to **take the chair** – to act as chairman at a meeting, to take charge of the meeting.
8. to **address the Chair** – to direct one's remarks to the Chairman.
9. to **appeal to the Chair** – to ask for the protection of the Chairman.
10. **playing musical chairs** – a children's game. Idiomatically, it means the shuffling of portfolios among the same ministers in a government to avoid the unpleasantness of making dismissals.
11. an **armchair strategist** – one who plans a military operation from the security of his own home without having to fight.
12. an **armchair critic** – one who is in a position to criticize the way a job is done, without being involved in the work himself. His criticism therefore tends to be vague and unrealistic.
13. an **armchair traveller** – someone who looks at travel films on television or reads books on travelling from the comfort of his armchair instead of visiting the countries himself. 'It's much safer to be an armchair traveller – and cheaper, too.'

SEAT

14. a **hot seat** – a position of responsibility carrying great risks. 'The President of the United States is in the hot seat of world power.'
15. to **keep a seat warm for** someone – to keep a job until another person is ready to take it. 'Martin should have resigned his office this year, but he is staying on an extra year to keep the seat warm for you.'
16. to **take a back seat** – to retire from the active conduct of a concern and let someone else take control. 'I've been managing this company for the last twenty years; it's time I took a back seat.'
17. to **lose one's seat** – to lose a position of influence. The phrase often refers to a seat on a committee, local council or in Parliament.
18. a **seat of learning** – a retreat for scholars where learning is an end in itself, like the universities.
19. **the seat of the trouble** – the source of the difficulty or pain.

STOOL

1. to **fall between two stools** – to fail through hesitation between two different courses of action, or through trying to combine both. 'Holmes fell between the stools of philosophy and mathematics. Having divided his time equally between both subjects, he left university without a degree in either.'
2. a **stool-pigeon** – someone employed to inform on his companions.
3. the **stool of repentance** – a low seat in Scottish churches on which sinners were set in full view of the congregation. The phrase may be used to indicate that someone has fallen into disfavour with the authorities.

BENCH

4. to be **on the bench** – to be a judge or magistrate.

   to **be raised to the bench** – to be appointed to a judgeship either in the High Court or the County Court.

DESK

5. a **desk general** – a general whose experience has been limited to administration, and who has had no battle experience. In World War II General Eisenhower was dismissed by his critics as a 'desk general' before the invasion of Europe in June 1944.

CUPBOARD

6. **cupboard love** – a display of affection motivated by selfish interest. 'Jane's dog always gives me a wonderful welcome but I'm afraid it's only cupboard love.'

SHELF

7. to be **on the shelf** – to have reached an age when a woman is unlikely to receive a proposal of marriage.
8. to **shelve** (a plan or proposal) – to postpone (a plan or proposal) indefinitely, often with the idea of putting it out of one's mind for good.

DRAWER

9. **not out of the top drawer** (almost always used negatively) – not a lady or a gentleman.

CURTAIN

10. **it's curtains for . . .** (slang) – it's the end of, or the finish of . . . 'It will be curtains for Norman if he doesn't find the money by next Wednesday.'
11. to **draw a curtain over** – to pass discreetly over an incident, to suppress it. This is done when the scene is too painful or embarrassing to relate. cf. 'to **draw a veil over' 174/12**.
12. to **suffer a curtain lecture** – to be scolded in bed by an irate wife.
13. **the iron curtain** – the military and political barrier which separates the Western democracies from the Warsaw Pact countries. The phrase first appeared in Dr Goebbels' diaries but was made famous by Winston Churchill in numerous speeches made after World War II.

CARPET

14. to **sweep** something **under the carpet** – to banish from one's mind a subject that is unpleasant or embarrassing, to discourage its discussion. 'Sooner or later, you'll have to discuss Jane's marriage; it's no good sweeping the whole thing under the carpet.'
15. to be **carpeted** – to be rebuked by

one's employer. Origin: in the old days when there was a carpet only in the boss's office, an employee stood on the carpet to hear complaints about his work, or to be dismissed.

1. to **roll out the red carpet** – to treat a new arrival as a very important person. 'He had a wonderful tour of the United States. Everywhere he went, they rolled out the red carpet for him.'
2. to **bite the carpet** – to be very angry. 'He was so angry at the news that he almost bit the carpet.'
3. a **carpet-bagger** – a candidate for election who has no roots or interest in the constituency he wishes to represent. The original meaning was a Unionist financier or adventurer who exploited the cheap labour in the American South after the Civil War. The carpet bags carried by these adventurers were bags made of carpet material.
4. **like a magic carpet** – as if one could be transported by magic to any place one wanted to visit. The phrase is often used in a sarcastic sense. 'I'm sorry we can't deliver the furniture before next week. We haven't got a magic carpet.'

RUG

5. to **pull the rug from under one's feet / under one** – to take one's opponent by surprise by suddenly depriving him of his advantage. 'Thomas got fifty customers to sign a complaint against the manager, but when he presented the petition to the company, they pulled the rug from under his feet by announcing the manager had already retired.' cf. 'to **cut the ground from under one's feet' 104/13** 'to **take the wind out of** someone's **sails' 30/13**.

PICTURE AND FRAME

6. to **put** someone **in the picture** – to bring someone up to date with the latest developments. 'As you are new to this particular project, I had better put you in the picture before we go any further.'
7. a **perfect picture** – (1) a full and accurate description. 'The author has given us a perfect picture of Tasmania.' (2) lovely to look at. 'The bride was a perfect picture.'
8. to be **the picture of health** – to exhibit all the qualities of a healthy person: rosy cheeks, glistening skin, shining eyes, etc.
9. a **frame-up** – the fabrication of evidence with the object of incriminating an innocent party. 'Can you help me? I've been framed.'

CANDLE

10. **not fit to hold a candle to / cannot hold a candle to** – not fit to compare with someone, to be in every way inferior. 'He paints quite well but he isn't fit to hold a candle to his brother.' The literal meaning was not fit to hold a light for the person doing the work to see by.
11. **the game is not worth the candle** – not worth the effort or money. 'I have tried to reorganize the company, but it's hopeless. It isn't worth the candle.'
12. to **burn the candle at both ends** – to exhaust one's energy recklessly, to allow oneself insufficient rest or sleep. Often said of students who prepare hastily for an examination by working late into the night and getting up early in the morning to resume their studies. The night is thus shortened at both ends like the candle.
13. **candle-end economies** – small paltry economies that serve no purpose. 'The government should stop making candle-end economies which only annoy the public.'

CUP AND MUG

1. **my cup was full** – my happiness/bitterness was complete.
2. **in one's cups** – getting drunk. 'Matthew can be quite aggressive when he's in his cups.'
3. to **mug up** (slang) – to learn as fast as one possibly can, almost always in preparation for an examination.

BOTTLE AND CRYSTAL

4. to **hit the bottle** – to drink too much (alcohol). 'Whenever my husband has a bad day at the office, he hits the bottle.'
5. to be **on the bottle** – to be a habitual drinker. 'She's been on the bottle ever since her husband died.'
6. to **bottle up** one's feelings, anger, etc. – to suppress one's feelings, to prevent them coming to the surface.
7. a **bottle-neck** – (1) an accumulation of unfinished goods in a factory whose production is interrupted owing to shortages of labour or materials. (2) the narrow part of a street in which the passage of traffic is constricted and delays consequently occur.
8. **crystal clear** – transparently clear, so that there is no room for misunderstanding. 'I thought I had made it crystal clear that I was very much opposed to your idea.'

PLATE, DISH AND SAUCER

9. to have **enough on one's plate** – to have enough work or responsibility. 'I should have thought she had enough on her plate without playing nursemaid to her niece.'
10. to **be handed** something **on a plate** – to obtain an important advantage without having had to work for it in the usual way. 'Peter was handed the directorship on a plate; his uncle is the chairman of the company!'
11. **What a dish!** – what an attractive, beautiful person.
12. to **dish out** (slang) – to supply in plentiful measure. 'They enjoy dishing out advice.'
13. **a flying saucer** – possibly an unidentified object from another planet, but its existence has never been proved.

KNIFE AND FORK

14. an **accent you could cut with a knife** – a very strong accent, one that is immediately noticeable. 'As soon as he opened his mouth, I knew he was a Yorkshireman. You could have cut his accent with a knife.'
15. to be/walk **on a knife-edge** – to be in the uncomfortable position of having to please both parties in a dispute. 'My two best friends are having a fierce quarrel. I have to walk on a knife-edge between them.'
16. **under the knife** – on the operating table.

    to **have a horror of the knife** – to be in great fear of an operation.
17. a **fork in the road** – the junction of two divergent roads.
18. to **fork out** – to pay out money on behalf of another person who has accumulated a big bill.

SPOON

19. to be **spoon-fed** – to be given so much assistance that the subject has no need to make any effort on his own behalf. 'The nationalized industries have been spoon-fed for so long that they no longer care whether they give value for money, or make a profit or loss.'
20. to be awarded **the wooden spoon**

(ironical) – to get a bad mark for doing something wrong, in contrast with winning the gold or silver spoon. 'Richard got the wooden spoon for failing to stand up for his members.' The wooden spoon is similar to the booby prize, wood being material of very small value. Formerly, a custom at Cambridge University when a wooden spoon was awarded to the student who did worst in the examinations.

1. to **need a long spoon** – to need extreme caution in one's dealings with an evil person. 'If you do business with Roberts, you will need a long spoon; he is a terrible liar.' The phrase is derived from the proverb: 'He needs a long spoon who sups with the devil'.
2. to **count one's spoons** – to make sure one's guest hasn't stolen any valuables, the suggestion being that the guest is a bad character. 'The more he talked of his honour, the faster we counted the spoons' (Emerson in *Conduct of Life*, 1860).

SIEVE

3. to have **a memory like a sieve** – to have a very bad memory. 'When it comes to people's names, I have a memory like a sieve.' The sieve, being full of holes, is unable to retain liquid poured into it. Similarly a bad memory is incapable of retaining information, impressions, etc.

POT

4. to **go to pot** – to ruin oneself or one's prospects. 'Harry has let his business go to pot.'
5. to **take pot luck** – to eat whatever has been cooked just for the family. This is often said to an unexpected guest.
6. to **keep the pot boiling** – (1) to keep things moving at a lively pace, to maintain the momentum. 'If you want to keep the pot boiling, you'd better think of a new game or the children will get bored.' (2) to maintain one's living standards. 'While Father is looking for a new job, Mother is working part-time to keep the pot boiling.'
7. a **pot-boiler** – work that is well below the level of the writer's ability, done for the sake of making money quickly. Pot-boilers are often produced quickly by well-known writers to capitalize on their reputation.
8. **in the melting pot** – in a fluid condition when the outcome is still uncertain. 'In mid-term, with more than three million unemployed, the fortunes of the government were in the melting pot.' From the title of a novel by Israel Zangwill.
9. a case of **the pot calling the kettle black** – to blame someone for a fault that one has oneself in equal or greater degree.
10. a **pot of money** – a large sum of money obtained all at once from speculation or gambling.

    to have **pots of money** (slang) – to be in possession of a fortune. 'He spends every winter at St Moritz. His father has got pots of money.'
11. a **pot shot** – a shot taken at a sitting target, considered unsporting.
12. a **pot hunter** – someone who takes part in sporting events for the sake of the prizes and not for the fun of it.
13. a **tin-pot** (army slang) – a self-important official who inspects an active unit in the army and expects a lot of ceremony and fuss.
14. **pot** (slang) – soft drugs, like marijuana.

PAN

15. a **flash in the pan** – a chance success which is unlikely to be repeated.

'Robin's book was a great success, but he hasn't written one since; I'm afraid it was only a flash in the pan.'

1. **out of the frying-pan into the fire / to jump out of the frying-pan into the fire** – to exchange a bad situation for one that is even worse. 'Rolf changed his job because he wanted more freedom, but in his new job he couldn't leave the office without the manager's permission. It was a case of out of the frying-pan into the fire.'

GRILL

2. to **grill** someone – to interrogate someone very intensively, with the object of breaking a person's resistance and extracting a full confession.

POKER

3. **as stiff as a poker** – unyielding, unresponsive.

BUCKET

4. to **kick the bucket** (slang) – to die. One explanation of the phrase is that the suicide kicks away the bucket on which he is standing after he has tied the rope round his neck.

BROOM AND BRUSH

5. **new brooms sweep cleaner** – a new manager will often make many reforms to justify his appointment and impress the staff with his importance.

6. to **have a brush with** – to come into conflict with someone else. 'He had a brush with the law yesterday.'

7. a **brush-off** – the dropping or rejection of a friend. 'After I had waited an hour for her, she rang up to say she didn't want to see me again. It was a real brush-off.'

8. to **brush to one side/aside** – to ignore or make little of.

   to **brush over** – to disregard. 'When I told him I hadn't enough money to repay him, he brushed over the incident with a wave of his hand.'

9. to be **tarred with the same brush** – to be suspected of having the same faults as one's relations or associates. 'Just because Dennis has been in prison, no one will have anything to do with his brothers and sister. They have all been tarred with the same brush.'

10. to **brush up** one's French, Spanish, etc. – to renew one's knowledge of a subject; often used in connection with a foreign language that has been neglected. 'I'll be staying in Hamburg for the next four weeks to brush up my German.'

11. a **toothbrush moustache** – a short, bristly moustache.

SINK AND BASIN

12. a **sink of iniquity** – a place of vice and corruption. 'The Vicar denounced the village as a sink of iniquity.'

13. to **have a basinful** (vulgar) – to suffer from an excess of a thing or person. 'Tom has spent the whole day telling me his travelling stories. I've had a basinful of them.' cf. 'to **have a bellyful' 99/13**, 'to **be fed up to the teeth/back teeth' 87/18**.

TAP

14. **on tap** – always available, like water from a tap.

SPONGE AND SOAP

15. to **throw up the sponge** – to admit defeat, to be guilty of cowardice. The phrase is taken from boxing, when the second throws the sponge into the

ring to indicate that his man is unable to go on with the fight.

1. to **sponge on** someone – to squeeze money out of another person without giving him anything in return.
2. to **soft soap** (slang) – to conciliate a person one has wronged with false reassurances and compliments. cf. **'soothing syrup' 159/15**.
3. **soap opera** – an inferior play in serial form on radio or television.
4. **soap-box oratory** – speaking in public on a make-shift platform or soap-box. 'If you want to enjoy soap-box oratory, you should go next Sunday to Speaker's Corner in Hyde Park.'

PEG

5. **square pegs in round holes** – people who are not suitable for their work or surroundings. 'That man should never have become a lawyer. He's a square peg in a round hole.'
6. to **take down a peg** – to reduce someone's self-importance, deflate his pride. The idiom suggests corrective action which falls short of total humiliation. 'The office-boy has been taking too much on himself lately. He was beginning to forget his position. I had to take him down a peg this morning.'
7. a **peg to hang** something **on** – an opportunity or excuse for discussion. 'The inspector said that he only used grammar in his English language classes as a peg for conversation, and that grammar had no value in itself.'

HANDLE

8. to **fly off the handle** – to lose one's temper, speak violently, to lose one's self-control. 'When I told Harry that I would have to charge him for the work I had done for him, he flew off the handle and started to shout at me.' cf. 'to **go up in the air' 24/15**.
9. to **have a handle to one's name** – to have a title of rank or honour, such as Viscount, Lord, Professor, or of courtesy, such as Mr or Mrs. 'Please remember I have a handle to my name. I am Mr Chapman to you.'
10. to **give a handle to** – to provide evidence for rumour-mongers and gossips.
11. to **be good at handling people** – to know how to deal with people. The phrase has a commercial sense, and often suggests the idea of making use of people to suit one's own interests.

18. FOOD

MILK

1. to **milk** – to swindle or cheat. 'The tourists were milked by the souvenir sellers.'
2. **the milk of human kindness** – compassion, sympathy. 'Pamela is clever and hard-working but she lacks the milk of human kindness.'
3. it's **no use crying over spilt milk** – it is useless to regret one's past mistakes. We cannot undo the past.
4. **milk and water** – insipid, feeble. 'These milk and water policies won't help the country. We need something more drastic.'
5. a **land of milk and honey** – a land overflowing with the good things of life, a land abounding in riches.
6. **mother's milk** – that which supplies an essential need. 'The professor's revolutionary ideas were mother's milk to his students.'

   to **imbibe with one's mother's milk** – to adopt instinctively. 'He imbibed a hatred of the old order with his mother's milk.'

CREAM

7. to **cream off / to skim the cream** – to take the best. 'Oxford and Cambridge are still creaming off the most brilliant scholars, despite all the social changes that have taken place since the end of the war.'
8. **the cream** of society, etc. – the aristocracy, the most highly favoured class. The phrase is often used ironically. From the French: 'la crème de la crème.'

CHEESE

9. to be **as different as chalk and cheese** – to be completely different, to have nothing in common. 'You'd never think that Paul and Sue were brother and sister. They are as different as chalk and cheese.'
10. **cheese-parings** – objects of no more value than cheese-parings, junk or trash. 'When the old man died, they found only cheese-parings in his house.'

    to **be cheese-paring** – to be extremely mean, to give grudgingly. 'The father was so cheese-paring with his son's pocket money that the boy hadn't enough money to buy a table-tennis bat.'
11. to be **cheesed off** (slang) – to be fed-up, bored, disgruntled.
12. **hard cheese!** – bad luck! 'That was hard cheese spraining your ankle just at the start of your holiday.' The phrase usually indicates a lack of sympathy for the victim.

EGGS

13. to have **egg on one's face** – to be humiliated. 'Paul couldn't understand Marie-Louise when she asked him a simple question in French, although he has always boasted that he can speak French fluently. When he left, he had egg all over his face.'
14. a **bad egg** – a bad character, a rascal. 'We are so worried; our daughter has made friends with a very bad egg.'
15. an **egg-head** (American English) – an intellectual, probably from the belief that a long head with a high forehead, i.e. an egg-shaped head, is a sign of superior intelligence.

1. to **tread upon eggs** – to broach a subject with the utmost delicacy, as if treading on eggs.
2. **as sure as eggs is eggs** – absolutely certain, as certain as night follows day.
3. **don't put all your eggs in one basket** – don't invest all your money in one thing, but spread your risks.
4. **you can't make an omelette without breaking eggs** – you can't achieve anything in this life without causing somebody pain.
5. to **over-egg the cake** – to exaggerate very badly. 'When Jones told the Chairman that it was a privilege to work for him, and then called for a vote of thanks for him from his workmates, we all felt that he was over-egging the cake.'
6. to **unscramble** – to undo, to change back. 'Now that so much money has been spent on the plans, it will be difficult to unscramble them.' The reference is to scrambling eggs; once they have been scrambled, they cannot be cooked in any other way.

BUTTER

7. to **butter up** – to flatter, to pay insincere compliments to someone. 'The boys buttered up the new master in the hope of getting less homework.'
8. to **spread the butter too thick** – to flatter, to exaggerate one's praise.
9. **butter-fingers** – someone who lets something slip between his fingers as if they were made of butter. 'That's the third time you've dropped the ball. What a butter-fingers you are!'
10. to look **as if butter wouldn't melt in one's mouth** – to look very innocent, although one is not innocent at all. 'He looked as if butter wouldn't melt in his mouth, but he didn't take me in. I knew he had done it.'
11. a **butter mountain** – the name given to the huge reserve of butter maintained by the EEC in order to ensure that the butter brought to market is not sold too cheaply. Note the similarity to the term **'wine lake'** which serves to maintain the prices of wine in the EEC.

FAT

12. **the fat will be in the fire** – there will be an explosion of anger. This happens when news of someone's misbehaviour gets out. 'If Father hears you've been gambling on the Stock Exchange with his money, the fat will be in the fire.' The derivation is from the spitting and spluttering of a fire when fat is thrown into it.
13. **to live on/off the fat of the land** – to live in the most luxurious conditions.
14. **a fat lot** (ironical) – nothing at all, none at all. 'A fat lot they care whether you get well or not.' 'A fat lot of good that will do you.'

BREAD

15. the **bread-winner** – the wage-earner who supports the family. 'With Father ill, our eldest brother has become the bread-winner of the family.'
16. **on the bread-line** – in a state of great poverty, when one is obliged to queue up for one's ration of food. It has come to mean poverty in general.
17. to **take the bread out of** someone's **mouth** – to deprive someone of his living. 'If you open your shop next door to Harry's, you will be taking the bread out of his mouth.'
18. one's **bread and butter** – one's living. 'I can't afford to give it up. It's my bread and butter.'

1. **the bread and butter of a business** – the main source of a business's income. 'The business they are doing with Japan is coming along nicely, but the bread and butter is with Europe.'
2. to **quarrel with one's bread and butter** – to find fault with one's livelihood. 'I wouldn't quarrel with your husband's bread and butter if I were you. If he gives up his job, you will have nothing to live on!'
3. to **know which side one's bread is buttered** – to know where one's interest lies. 'However much he sympathizes with you, he won't say anything to offend his boss. He knows which side his bread is buttered.'
4. to **have one's bread buttered on both sides** – to have a very easy life, to obtain an easy comfortable living.
5. a **bread and butter letter** – a thank-you letter for hospitality from a departed guest.

LOAF

6. **'Use your loaf!'** (vulgar) – 'Use your brain', 'Think'.

SANDWICH

7. to **sandwich between / in between** – to squash between, insert between. 'On the flight, I was sandwiched in between two very fat passengers so that I scarcely had room to raise my fork to my mouth.'
8. a **sandwich course** – a course which provides practical instruction as well as lectures on theory, the practical being 'sandwiched' between the theoretical.
9. a **sandwich man** – a man who carries advertising boards both in front and behind; so called because the man is sandwiched between the two boards.

TOAST

10. to be **as warm as toast** – to be comfortably warm, very warm.
11. to **have** someone **on toast** – to have someone in one's power, to enjoy a decisive advantage over someone, usually in consequence of some mistake he has made. 'Now, I've got you on toast. You must do as I say.'

CRUMB

12. a **crumb of comfort** – a small consolation, a small mercy. 'One crumb of comfort is that, although he will be bedridden, he can continue with his writings.'

HONEY AND SYRUP

13. to be **as sweet as honey** – to be unnaturally sweet, perhaps from some ulterior motive. 'The girls were as sweet as honey as long as I did what they wanted.' cf. 'to **be as sweet as pie**' **161/2**.
14. **the honeymoon is over** – criticism which was muted for the first few weeks (of a new government's term of office, a new appointment, and so on) now becomes unrestrained. The allusion is to the change in attitude of the newly married couple which often occurs when the honeymoon is over.
4. **soothing syrup** – words designed to comfort rather than tell the truth. cf. **'soft soap' 156/2.**

JAM

16. to be **in a jam** – to be in great difficulties, to be in a mess, like a fly caught in a jar of jam from which it is unable to extricate itself.
17. **money for jam** – money that is made with no effort. 'All I had to do was to walk up and down the room and smile

at the customers. It was money for jam.'

1. **'It's jam tomorrow, jam yesterday, but never jam today!'** – You are always boasting about what you have given us in the past and what you are going to give us in the future. Unfortunately, nothing ever comes of your promises, and we are still as badly off as ever.

SUGAR AND SWEETS

2. to **sugar the pill** – to make something which is unpleasant seem less so. 'I shall sugar the pill by sending Owen on a week's paid holiday before I make him redundant.'
3. a **toffee-nosed** person (mildly derogatory) – an upper-class person. A 'toffee-nose' is one that points upwards in a snobbish, disdainful manner.
4. 'I can't jump **for toffee**' – 'I jump very badly', the idea behind the phrase being 'I couldn't jump well, even if you offered me a toffee to do it'.
5. a **lollipop man**, **lollipop lady** – nickname for a traffic warden who escorts children across the road.
6. **chocolate box** – a face which possesses pretty features but is lacking in individuality or distinction, the kind of 'pretty' face one sees on the lid of a chocolate box. 'She was a nice chocolate box – nothing more.'

CAKE, PANCAKE, BUN AND BISCUIT

7. **you can't have your cake and eat it** – you have a choice, meaning either/or, not both. 'You must make up your mind whether you want to buy a house with Uncle Tom's legacy, or invest the money. You can't have your cake and eat it.'
8. **a piece of cake** – something very easy to do, requiring little or no effort. 'The General Knowledge examination was terribly easy. It was a piece of cake.'
9. **icing on the cake** – an extra incentive which is not necessary, but gives a great deal of pleasure. 'If they send me to Saudi Arabia, I shall get a salary increase of 25% with my promotion, but the icing on the cake will be a two months' paid holiday every two years.'
10. a **slice of the cake** – a share of the profits. 'After such a wonderful year, your workers will want a slice of the cake.'
11. to **go like hot cakes** – to sell very quickly, to be snapped up. 'The new line in sports cars is going like hot cakes; there is a crazy demand for them.'
12. to **fall as flat as a pancake** – to have no effect at all. Sometimes abbreviated to **'fall flat'**. 'The joke fell flat; nobody laughed.'
13. hair done **in a bun** – with the hair piled up in the shape of a bun.
14. **That takes the biscuit!** – used ironically for something scarcely credible because it is so absurd. 'That takes the cake. The teacher has proposed to his granddaughter's schoolfriend.'

PIE

15. **pie in the sky** – hopes and dreams that will never be realized. 'Universal brotherhood and peace is a wonderful ideal but, I am afraid, it is all pie in the sky.' cf. **'castles in the air' 24/13**, and **'castles in Spain' 186/8**.
16. to **eat humble pie** – to submit or apologize humbly. 'After boasting that he would win the boxing tournament, he had to eat humble pie when he was knocked out in the first round.' 'Humble pie' was made from the offal

of deer and offered to the footmen at a banquet.

1. to have **a finger in every pie** – to take a meddlesome interest in many affairs. 'When Mark heard there was to be a jumble sale, he was soon busy organizing the stalls. He has a finger in every pie.'

2. to be **as sweet as pie** – very charming, often used sarcastically. 'She could be as sweet as pie if she wanted to get something out of me'. cf. 'to **be as sweet as honey' 159/13.**

3. **promises are like pie-crust** – promises are made to be broken (a cynical view). From the fairy story 'The Beauty and the Beast'.

PUDDING

4. **the proof of the pudding is in the eating** – the test is whether it works or not. 'The yacht has elegant lines all right, but how will she sail? The proof of the pudding will be in the eating.'

PORRIDGE

5. **save your breath to cool your porridge** – the words used to scold someone who has given unwanted advice. 'Well, Friar, spare your breath to cool your porridge; come let us talk with deliberation, fairly and softly' (Rabelais: *Works* (1552), Book V, Chapter 28).

SPAGHETTI

6. **spaghetti junction** – the centre of a whole network of roads near Birmingham – so called because the pattern of the roads resembles spaghetti.

MEAT

7. **easy meat** – something easily and quickly accomplished or someone easily vanquished. 'The "A" level mathematics examination was easy meat for Ruth; she got full marks in every paper.'

8. **there's a lot of meat in it** – something which gives one plenty to think about. 'I like a novel with plenty of meat in it, for instance Tolstoy's *War and Peace*.'

9. **strong meat** – material that is difficult to accept or appreciate. 'He took his son to a play by Aristophanes – strong meat for a boy of twelve.'

10. **It must have been meat and drink to you** – it must have given you enormous satisfaction. Often used when a person's critics acknowledge they have been in the wrong. 'The apologies of her old rival were meat and drink to her.' cf. **'music to one's ears' 238/4.**

11. **one man's meat is another man's poison** – what favours one person, injures another. 'The epidemic kept the young doctor busy all day. One man's meat is another man's poison.'

12. to **make mincemeat of** someone (colloquial) – to win a devastating victory over an opponent. 'She made mincemeat of his arguments. Under her cross-examination, his case collapsed.' The idea comes from chopping meat up into tiny pieces and serving it as mince.

13. to **beef about** (Australian colloquialism) – to complain about.

14. **as dead as mutton** – completely dead. Similar to **'as dead as Queen Anne' 193/15**, and **'as dead as a door-nail' 211/10.**

15. **mutton dressed as lamb** – an older woman who dresses up to look like a young one. The phrase can be extended to ideas. 'Their ideas are exactly the same as twenty years ago; only the jargon has changed. Mutton dressed as lamb.'

16. to **talk tripe** – to talk utter nonsense. As well as being slang, the phrase can

be very rude. 'I don't agree with a word you are saying. You are talking tripe.' Tripe is the lining of a cow's stomach, and is considered a delicacy in the north of England.

1. **salami tactics** – achieving one's objective in small steps, like cutting salami up into slices.
2. to **stew in one's own juice** – to take the consequences of one's own actions. 'How many times have I told you not to borrow money? This time I am not going to help you out. You can stew in your own juice.'
3. to **bring home the bacon** – to succeed, achieve one's aim, to supply the needs of one's family. 'With all his faults, her husband certainly brings home the bacon. She can't complain on that score.'
4. to **save** someone's **bacon** – to get someone out of a difficulty. 'If you hadn't hidden me in your cupboard, I should have been terribly embarrassed. You really saved my bacon.'
5. **ham-fisted/ham-handed** – clumsy with one's hands. 'That girl is too ham-fisted to wait at table. She drops everything.'

SOUP, SAUCE AND GRAVY

6. to be **in the soup** – to be in trouble. 'If you lose our passports, we shall be in the soup!'
7. to **soup up** (slang) – to make an engine more powerful by tuning it up. A souped-up version of an engine is one that has been developed into a racing model.
8. **a mess of potage** – something of little or no value. 'They have sold their comrades for a mess of potage' (Arthur Scargill, President of the National Union of Miners, referring to the working miners in the coal strike, December 1984). The allusion is to Esau's birthright which he sold to his brother Jacob for a mess of potage, Genesis XXV, 33.
9. **don't give me any of your sauce!** – don't give me any impertinence, insolence, cheek.
10. **to join/get on the gravy train** – to take one's share of the rewards. 'When a new party comes to power, there is always a scramble to join the gravy-train.'

SALT

11. to be **above/below the salt** (humorous) – to be in favour/out of favour with one's host or hostess. 'Since his rudeness to his sister-in-law, Donald no longer sits above the salt when he visits his brother at Maybrick Hall.' In the old days when the family and the servants ate at the same table, the salt was placed half-way up the table to mark the dividing line between them. The master of the house sat with his family and guests 'above the salt', and their servants, including the governess and tutor, sat 'below the salt'.
12. to **eat salt with** – to enjoy a person's hospitality. There is a tradition among the Arabic people that you may not accept someone's hospitality and abuse him afterwards. 'If you eat salt with your Arab host, he will provide you with his benevolent protection.'
13. to **salt away** – to hide away, used in reference to money secretly hoarded. 'He must have salted away the best part of a fortune in the last ten years of his life.'
14. to **take with a pinch of salt** – to believe only a part of what you have been told, to allow for considerable exaggeration. This phrase is a translation from the Latin 'cum grano salis' which has the same meaning.

1. to **rub salt in a wound** – to add deliberately to someone's misery, to make an injury even worse. 'As you have just given your tenant a week's notice, I wouldn't ask him to clean up the flat before he leaves. You will only be rubbing salt in the wound.'
2. **worth one's salt** – worth one's pay, worth having. 'Any boy worth his salt wants to get into the school football team.'

   not worth one's salt – not worth one's pay. The phrase is taken from the Latin word 'salarium', which meant the salt money that was paid to Roman soldiers instead of their salt. A man not worth his salt was considered worthless.
3. the **salt of the earth** – God's elect, God's own people. The phrase comes from Matthew V.13, in reference to Our Lord's disciples: 'You are the salt of the earth.' The distinction has been claimed by many people since the time those words were spoken.
4. an **old salt** – an old sailor, one whose skin has absorbed a lot of salt from the sea.

PEPPER AND MUSTARD

5. to **pepper** someone with questions – to put many questions quickly to someone. The questioning is similar to sprinkling pepper on one's food; the holes in the pepper-pot determine the way the pepper comes out.
6. **as keen as mustard** – very keen, full of enthusiasm.

PICKLE

7. to be **in a pickle** – to be in chaotic disorder, to be in a mess. 'Your bedroom is in such a pickle, I wonder you can find anything in it.'

   to be **in a nice/fine pickle** – to be in trouble; used ironically for an awkward situation. 'We'd have been in a fine pickle if we had missed the last bus home.'

GINGER

8. to **ginger up** – to put life into, to stir up. 'The new manager was determined to ginger up his staff if they didn't work harder.'
9. a **ginger group** – a group within a political party that tries to prod it into bolder and more energetic action. The '92 Group' is the ginger group of the Conservative Party.
10. to **take the gilt off the gingerbread** – to spoil or rob something of its main attractiveness. 'I spent a pleasant holiday with my aunt, but on the last day I overheard her saying to her housekeeper: "What a strain the visit has been." That took the gilt off the gingerbread.'

FRUIT

11. to **bear fruit** – to produce results.
12. **stolen fruit / forbidden fruit** – a sin which is regarded as a pleasure. 'Forbidden fruit is always the most desirable.' The phrase is connected with the forbidden fruit in the Garden of Eden, taken by Adam in disobedience of God's commandment.
13. **Dead Sea fruit** – a thing of great promise which turns out to be worthless. 'Poor Andrew, he never got his invention to work; after five years of ceaseless effort, he had only produced Dead Sea fruit.' The reference is to the legendary apples of Sodom, which grew on the shores of the Dead Sea. The apples were very beautiful but would dissolve into ashes as soon as they were touched or tasted.

ORANGE AND LEMON

1. to **squeeze the orange until the pips squeak** – to extract information by questioning someone until he is exhausted.
2. a **sucked orange** – someone who has served his purpose and is no longer wanted. 'After working twenty years for the company, Alex was discarded like a sucked orange.'
3. **the answer's a lemon** – a joking retort to a long, complicated problem which is not worth the time and effort needed to solve it.

APPLE

4. **as sure as God made little apples** – with absolute certainty, as sure as night follows day.
5. the **rotten apple** – the one bad person among a number of good ones. 'His youngest son was the rotten apple.'
6. to **upset the apple cart** – to spoil a carefully laid plan. 'That has upset the apple cart! We can't go away while the men are on strike.'
7. to be **the apple of one's eye** – to be the one for whom a person has the tenderest affection. 'He loved his sons, but his daughter was the apple of his eye.'
8. to be **in apple-pie order** – to be clean, tidy, well organized. 'The room is in apple-pie order for our guest.'

BANANA

9. a **banana skin** – a pitfall for the unwary which makes the victim look ridiculous. 'The government has slipped on too many banana skins for its own good.'
10. a **banana republic** – a republic whose governments are repeatedly overthrown and replaced by new ones, equally unstable.
11. to **go bananas** – to get into a rage, to lose all control over oneself.

GOOSEBERRY

12. to **play gooseberry** – to accompany a pair of lovers, to be a chaperone to them. 'I am not playing gooseberry to you two. You will be perfectly all right without me.'

RASPBERRY

13. to **give a raspberry** – to give someone a rebuke (slightly dated).

GRAPE

14. **sour grapes** – to disparage something because it is unattainable. 'It is sour grapes to say you wouldn't accept the car, even if it were given you. Of course you would!' From Aesop's fable of the Fox and Grapes.
15. I heard it **through the grapevine** – the grapevine is a source of information, rumours, gossip, which is forever churning out new items. 'I heard it through the grapevine that the boss and his secretary are getting married at the end of the month.'
16. to **wither on the vine** – to die through neglect (with special reference to ideas or proposals). 'Our new manager had lots of ideas about reorganizing the business. Instead of arguing with him, we allowed his proposals to wither on the vine.'

PLUM, CHERRY AND PEACH

17. a **plum** role/job, etc. – the most desired, the very best.

    to **land a plum job** – to obtain, by good luck or good management, the most sought-after job.
18. a **plummy voice** – an upper-class voice which is either affected by the

speaker, or which sounds affected to the listener.

1. to take **two bites at a cherry** – to make a second attempt, having failed the first time.
2. a **peach / she's a peach** (slang) – an outstandingly beautiful girl, stunningly attractive.

PRUNE

3. to **prune** a book, thesis or story – to eliminate all unnecessary words and passages.
4. **prunes and prisms** – a mincing way of speaking (from *Little Dorrit* by Charles Dickens).

FIG

5. **not worth a fig** – worth nothing at all. cf. **'not worth a straw' 48/11**.
6. **not to care a fig / not to give a fig for** – to care nothing for. 'I don't care a fig (I don't give a fig) for his opinions.'

VEGETABLES

7. to be a **vegetable** – to be alive but without the proper use of one's faculties. 'If he had survived the head injuries he got in the crash, he would have been a vegetable for the rest of his life.'

BEAN

8. to be **full of beans** – to be bursting with energy and health, to be in high spirits.
9. to **give someone beans** – to rebuke someone, to give someone a good thrashing.
10. to **spill the beans** – to talk indiscreetly, to let information slip out. 'She has spilt the beans about your engagement. It will be all over the town by now.'
11. **not to have a bean** – to have no money, to be penniless.
12. **not worth a bean / a row of beans** – worthless.
13. to **know how many beans make five** – to be alert, shrewd. From the custom of teaching small children to count with beans.

PEA

14. a **pea-souper** – a thick yellow fog. 'I can't see my hand in front of me. It's a real pea-souper!'
15. to be **as like as two peas** – to be indistinguishable from one another. 'The twin boys are as like as two peas.'
16. **as easy as shelling peas** – something so easy that it requires no skill or effort. cf. **'as easy as falling off a log' 51/2**.

OTHER VEGETABLES

17. the **stick and carrot policy** – rewarding success and punishing failure, just as one rewards a donkey for obedience and punishes it for disobedience. 'In every school, no matter how progressive, the stick and carrot policy is employed. The good children are rewarded and the bad children are punished.'
18. to drop something **like a hot potato** – to withdraw quickly from a commitment as soon as one discovers how embarrassing it could become. 'When he heard that his brother-in-law was an alcoholic, he dropped his temperance campaign like a hot potato.'
19. to **know one's onions** – to know one's job, to be extremely capable. 'If you want any information, ask Mrs Jones to give you a demonstration. She knows her onions.'

1. to **mushroom** – to multiply very fast. Almost always used in a bad sense. 'The number of travel agencies has mushroomed in the last ten years.' The mushroom is a vegetable that is well known for its phenomenal rate of growth.
2. **as red as a beetroot** – red with embarrassment, or from excessive heat.
3. a **cauliflower ear** – an ear that has been permanently swollen and disfigured as a result of having been repeatedly struck. Often a feature of veteran boxers.
4. **fine words butter no parsnips** – actions are more important than words; speeches are no substitute for hard work. 'When I was dismissed, the boss gave me a marvellous reference, but what's the good of that, now I can't get a job! Fine words butter no parsnips.'
5. **as cool as a cucumber** – serene, calm, undisturbed when under stress. 'While the rest of us were getting tremendously excited, she remained as cool as a cucumber and went on with her sewing as if nothing special had happened.'
6. **salad days** – inexperienced youth. 'My salad days / When I was green in judgement' (Shakespeare, *Antony and Cleopatra*, I. v).
7. **the pumpkin has not turned into a coach** – the early promise has not been fulfilled, and disenchantment has followed. In the fairy story of Cinderella, the fairy godmother turned Cinderella's pumpkin into a golden coach to convey her to the palace ball.

NUT AND PEANUT

8. to be **nuts about** someone – to be madly enthusiastic, infatuated with. 'You know, don't you, that he is nuts about you.'
9. to be **off one's nut / to be nuts** – to be mad, insane. 'You mean to tell me you left all our money on the bus. You must be off your nut!' Nut is slang for head, so the phrase has the same meaning as 'off one's head'.
10. a **nut-case** (colloquial) – a mad person. 'Don't waste your time explaining it to her. She's a nut-case.'
11. **a hard nut to crack** – a tough, intractable problem or person to overcome. 'He is a difficult man to convince. You will find him a hard nut to crack.'
12. to **put in a nutshell** – to explain in a few words, to give a bare summary. 'That's right – we are broke. You've put it in a nutshell.'
13. to **pay peanuts** – to pay a ridiculously small sum of money. 'They pay him a salary of £6,000 a year; that's peanuts for a man of his experience and qualifications!'

TEA

14. **not one's cup of tea** – not to one's taste. 'I was offered quite a well-paid job in the City, but the work wouldn't have been my cup of tea.'
15. **that's another cup of tea** – that's another matter, that puts a different complexion on it.
16. **I wouldn't do it for all the tea in China** – I wouldn't do it whatever you offered me. 'I wouldn't live with them for all the tea in China.'

WINE

17. to **wine and dine** – to entertain on a lavish scale.
18. **good wine needs no bush** – if your products are good, they will speak for themselves without needing to be advertised. The bush was the bunch of ivy hung outside which advertised the vintner's business.

1. to put **new wine in old bottles** – to put new ideas into an old framework which cannot accommodate them. 'Some physicists tried to put Einstein's theory of relativity into a Newtonian framework – like putting new wine into old bottles.'

BEER

2. **small beer** – people or things of trifling importance. 'He didn't trouble to acknowledge our greeting. Now that he has become famous, we are only small beer!'
3. **'Life isn't all beer and skittles'** – Life is not just a game; it has a serious side to it as well.' From *Tom Brown's School-days* by Thomas Hughes (1822–96).

MEAL AND PICNIC

4. a **square meal** – a substantial meal. 'Kenneth is terribly thin, isn't he? He looks as if he could do with a square meal.'
5. to **make a meal of** it (colloquial) – to make an unnecessary fuss about someone's mistake. 'All right, we should have warned you earlier, but there's no need for you to make a meal of it.'
6. it's **a picnic** – something very pleasant which costs no effort. 'Last year's play was a picnic to produce compared with this year's.'

   no picnic – something that is both difficult and disagreeable. '"You must put up with a lot of hardship and discomfort. War is no picnic," the Major told his soldiers.'

BITE AND EAT

7. to **bite off more than one can chew** – to undertake more than one can fulfil. 'I shall have to cancel some of my orders; I've bitten off more than I can chew.'
8. to **eat one's words** – to suffer a humiliation by having to withdraw a statement that has been proved wrong. 'Our critics said that we would never make a success of our magazine; now that we have proved them wrong, they will have to eat their words.'
9. to be **eaten up with jealousy** – to be consumed with jealousy, obsessed with jealousy. 'Maureen told me that if I bought a large car, she would drop me. The poor woman is eaten up with jealousy.'

TASTE

10. **in good taste** – in a pleasing, agreeable manner.

    in bad taste – in a vulgar, offensive manner. 'All his jokes were in bad taste.'

19. CLOTHES

SHOE

1. **where the shoe pinches** – the source of the discomfort. 'Helen is bringing up four children on £30 a week with no help from her husband, so she knows where the shoe pinches.'
2. to work **on a shoe-string** – to run a business with practically no capital. 'We had to work on a shoe-string, with hardly any staff.'
3. to **step into another person's shoes** – to replace a person, taking over his responsibilities (often someone who is occupying an important position). 'I hope that, by the time you retire, your son will be old enough to step into your shoes.'
4. to step into a **dead man's shoes** – to benefit from the death of a person by inheritance or by taking over his job.
5. to be **in another's shoes** – to be in someone else's situation. 'Betty told me you smashed up the car last night. I shouldn't like to be in your shoes when Father hears about it.' cf. 'to **be in someone else's skin' 108/6**.
6. to **shake in one's shoes** – to tremble with fear. 'He shook in his shoes when he heard he was wanted by the police.'

BOOT

7. **the boot is on the other foot** – the circumstances are the other way round. 'The boot is on the other foot. It was your son who stole the money from the beggar, and not the beggar who stole from your son.'
8. to **boot out of a job** – to dismiss someone on the spot, without ceremony.
9. to **pull oneself up by one's own bootstraps** – to make one's way by one's own exertions without help from anyone.
10. to **lick** someone's **boots** – to flatter someone in a servile manner to obtain an advantage, to fawn on someone. 'It's nauseating the way he licks his boss's boots all the time.'

    a **bootlicker** – a person who does this.
11. **too big for one's boots** (slang) – conceited, pleased with oneself. 'Ever since that boy won the tennis tournament, he has been too big for his boots. He needs putting in his place.'
12. **Smarty-boots** – a know-all, someone who knows all the answers.
13. to **have one's heart in one's boots / to have one's heart sink into one's boots** – to be dismayed, to be in despair. 'When I saw the nurse's face, my heart sank into my boots.'
14. **as tough as old boots** – to be extremely tough, strong and unaffected by severe conditions. 'I wouldn't worry about Stephen if I were you. He's as tough as old boots and can look after himself.'
15. to be **booted and spurred** (humorous) – to be ready for action.
16. to **hang up one's boots** – to retire. 'I'll be hanging up my boots next year. I think I deserve a rest after running the business for thirty years.' The allusion is to the football player who hangs up his boots after the match.
17. to **die with one's boots on** – to die while still at work. Originally a military phrase, meaning to die in battle.
18. to **put the boot in** – to make a brutal attack on someone when he is at a serious disadvantage. 'After ransacking the widow's house, the burglars put the boot in by smashing up the place.'

SOCK

1. to **pull up one's socks** (slang) – to work harder, to reform. 'You've had another bad school report. If you don't pull up your socks, you will have to work in the holidays.'
2. to **sock** a person / **to sock on the jaw** (slang) – to hit someone hard.
3. to **put a sock in it** (slang) – to keep quiet, to hold one's tongue.

STOCKING

4. a **Christmas stocking** – it is the custom in England for children to hang their stockings at the end of their beds on Christmas Eve for Father Christmas to fill with Christmas presents. The custom is based on the belief that Father Christmas comes down the chimney of the child's bedroom.

DRESS

5. to **dress up** – (1) to dress with the greatest possible care, usually for a special occasion (2) to wear fancy-dress costume.
6. a **fancy-dress ball/dinner** – a ball or dance at which the guests are dressed in the costumes of historic or fictional characters or anything else that takes their fancy.
7. to **dress down / to give** someone **a dressing-down** – to reprimand severely. 'The Colonel dressed the regiment down for their untidy appearance.'
8. **dressed to kill** – to be sumptuously dressed with the object of arousing interest or making a seduction. cf. **'dressed up to the nines' 218/13.**
9. **the dress circle** – the seats on the first floor of the theatre overlooking the stalls – so called because it was the custom for the audience in the dress circle to wear evening dress.
10. to **dress the soil / ground** – to make the soil ready for sowing and planting. 'The gardener has been dressing the soil – hoeing and raking in compost in time for the spring sowing.'
11. to **dress a fowl**, etc. – to pluck a fowl, clean and prepare it for cooking.

    to **dress a lobster** – to prepare a lobster for the dining-table.

SKIRT

12. to **hide behind a woman's skirts** – to try to avoid the consequences of one's actions by putting the blame on a woman. 'Mary was acting on your instructions, and now that things have gone wrong you are hiding behind her skirts.'
13. a **skirt / a piece of skirt** (slang) – any young woman.
14. to like a **bit of skirt** – to enjoy the companionship of women. The phrase always has a sexual significance.

    to **run after anyone in skirts** – to chase women, to womanize. Neither of these phrases is in good taste.
15. to **skirt round** – to talk round a subject, to avoid the main issue.
16. to **skirt the coast** – to sail close to the coast to avoid squalls.
17. to live **on the outskirts** – to live on or near the boundary of a town.

FROCK

18. to **unfrock a priest** – to expel a priest from the church for misconduct, neglect of duties, immorality and so on.

PETTICOAT

19. to be under **petticoat government** – to be ruled by a woman domestically, socially, economically or politically.

'We haven't had a petticoat government since Queen Victoria.'

FRILLS

1. **without frills** – the essence, without adornment. 'I would like a simple, straightforward account of what happened, without the frills, please.'

APRON

2. to be **tied to a woman's apron-strings** – to be emotionally dependent on a woman, often used in reference to boys and young men. 'It's time that young man left home; he is tied too much to his mother's apron-strings.'

PANTS

3. to **bore the pants off** someone – to bore someone very much. 'For goodness sake, don't invite Major Williams; he will bore the pants off our guests.'

TROUSERS

4. to **wear the trousers** – to be the dominant party in the marriage, to command or rule. The idiom is more often used when the wife dominates her husband. 'From her wedding day until her death, she wore the trousers.'

SHIRT

5. to **keep one's shirt** on – keep calm, don't get excited or angry. cf. 'to **keep one's hair on' 79/4**.
6. to **put one's shirt on** something – to wager or bet on. 'I am putting my shirt on that horse. It is certain to win.' The idea behind the idiom is that it is such a strong runner that you can put your last remaining possession on it in complete safety.
7. **without a shirt to one's back** – in dire poverty, with practically no possessions.
8. to **put on a hair-shirt** – to punish oneself for some sin. Politically, to sacrifice one's present comforts in order to strengthen the economy of the country. 'Mrs Thatcher is preparing to gamble her political life on the present hair-shirt policy to get through the next two to three years' (*Daily Mail*, 6 October 1982). Some monks put on hair-shirts to do penance.
9. a **stuffed shirt** – someone who is always on his dignity, a pompous bore.
10. to be **shirty** – to be in a bad temper. A word which usually implies that the person in question is being unreasonable. 'Don't get shirty with me; I didn't take your book.'

SUIT

11. to be in one's **birthday suit** – to be naked, just as one was born.

JACKET

12. an **Eton jacket** – a short jacket reaching only as far as the waist, similar to the jacket worn by junior boys at Eton College.
13. to put someone **in a strait-jacket** – to restrict someone's freedom. 'I feel as though I were in a strait-jacket; I can't do anything at that school without asking permission first.' A strait-jacket is a tight-fitting waistcoat that is put on violent patients to restrict their movements.
14. **strait-laced** – strict, puritanical, keeping one's feelings under strict control. 'You had better be careful what you say to Julian. He is strait-laced and easily shocked.' Literally, having the laces in the corset pulled very tight,

so that the wearer has a stiff rigid posture.

TIE

1. the **old school tie** – the badge of former public school pupils. In the eyes of many people, the old school tie has become a symbol of class privilege which provides an elite with important social and business advantages. This charge is hotly denied by advocates of the public school system.

COLLAR

2. a **dog-collar** – the name given to the collar worn by the clergy; so called because of its resemblance to a dog's collar.
3. to be **hot under the collar** – to be angry, excited. 'There's no reason for you to get hot under the collar. No one has stolen your room key; there it is on the hook.'
4. to **collar someone** – (1) to tackle, grab someone by his collar. (2) (school slang) – to help yourself to something without the permission of the owner.

CUFF

5. **off the cuff** – without prior thought. 'In a case like this, off-the-cuff advice is useless. You must make a careful study of the problem before deciding what to do.'
6. to **cuff / give** someone **a cuff** – to slap or strike a light blow.

BRACE

7. **'Brace up!'** – a command often used in the army, meaning: 'Stand up straight, and pay attention!'
8. **brace yourself for a shock** – prepare yourself for a shock so that, when it comes, you won't be overwhelmed.

BELT

9. to hit **below the belt** – to make a mean or unfair attack. 'When he made fun of his opponent's deafness, he was roundly condemned for hitting him below the belt.' The idiom originates in boxing, hitting below the belt being expressly forbidden by the Queensberry Rules.
10. to have **under one's belt** – to have an achievement already to one's credit. 'Gerald already has two novels under his belt.'
11. to **tighten the belt / to pull in one's belt** – to make economies, eat less when food or money is scarce. Applicable to nations as well as individuals. 'The Chancellor warned the nation it would have to pull in its belt if the balance of trade figures showed no improvement.'
12. to **belt away / to belt along** (colloquial) – to drive very fast.
13. to **belt up** (slang) – to keep quiet or stop talking (rude).
14. to **belt** someone (slang) – to hit someone hard.

CLOAK

15. **under the cloak of** – under the guise or pretence of. 'Under the cloak of assisting the Vicar, he did a lot of business with the parishioners.'
16. a **cloak and dagger play** – a Victorian melodrama of mystery and intrigue.
17. a **cloak and dagger operation** – an operation in espionage, involving secrecy, danger and often undercover violence and assassination.

GOWN

1. **Town and Gown** – the age-old feud between the undergraduates at Oxford and Cambridge, and the townspeople.

COAT

2. to **cut one's coat according to one's cloth** – to live within the limits of one's income. Often said of someone who has suffered a big drop in his earnings and who will be obliged to accept a lower standard of living. 'Now her husband has lost his job, she will be obliged to cut her coat according to her cloth.'
3. to **ride on / hang on** someone's **coat-tails** – to advance one's own career by associating with someone who is currently achieving quick promotion. 'If you want promotion, all you have to do is to ride on Crane's coat-tails; he's the favourite of the boss.'
4. to **be dragged by one's coat-tails** – to be forced against one's will into taking a particular action. 'But Britain is being dragged by its coat-tails into lining up with France and Germany . . .' (Gordon Greig, Political Editor, reporting on the GATT negotiations from Geneva, *Daily Mail*, 25 November 1982).
5. to **trail one's coat** – to provoke a fight. Trailing one's coat-tails, in the hope that someone would tread on them and thus give one the excuse to start a fight, used to be popular, especially in Ireland.
6. to **be a turncoat / to turn one's coat** – to change sides in a dispute, to betray one's principles.

GLOVE

7. to be **hand in glove with** – to be in very close co-operation with someone else, almost always in a bad sense. 'The two of them were working hand in glove, and were arrested by the police together.'
8. to **fit like a glove** – (1) to fit perfectly, to follow the contours of the body exactly. 'She looks very elegant in her ski-suit. It fits her like a glove.' (2) to describe exactly. 'The description in the *Police Gazette* fitted the suspect like a glove.'
9. to treat someone **with kid gloves** – to treat someone with the utmost gentleness and tact, so as not to cause offence. The significance of the phrase lies in the fact that leather made from kid skin is of the softest texture.
10. **an iron hand in a velvet glove** – forceful action concealed in mild, restrained words. cf. **'with an iron hand' 96/16**.
11. to fight **with the gloves off** – to fight ruthlessly, without showing mercy. Boxing is normally conducted with the gloves on.

GAUNTLET

12. to **throw down the gauntlet** – to challenge someone to a contest. 'Gauntlet' is derived from the French word 'gant', meaning a glove. In medieval times, one knight would challenge another by throwing down his gauntlet (glove). cf. 'to **throw one's hat into the ring' 173/6**.

    to **take up the gauntlet** – to accept the challenge by picking up the gauntlet (glove).
13. to **run the gauntlet** – to submit to a punishing ordeal. The phrase has been taken from the custom in the army and public schools of making an offender run between two lines of soldiers or schoolboys who would beat him with straps, sticks, etc., in order to demonstrate their disapproval of his misconduct.

HAT

1. a **bad hat** – a bad character.
2. to pass **round the hat** – to ask for money.
3. to **talk through one's hat** – to talk nonsense.
4. **I'll eat my hat if I'm wrong!** – a promise to do something impossible if one is wrong – in other words, a declaration of absolute confidence in the correctness of one's judgement. 'I'll eat my hat if he hasn't passed his exam this time.'
5. to **take off one's hat to** someone – to show one's admiration for someone by (figuratively) taking off one's hat. 'I take off my hat to him for having the courage of his convictions, even if I don't always agree with him.' Removing one's hat has always been the traditional way of showing respect.
6. to **throw one's hat into the ring** – to challenge one's rivals to a contest for office. It is similar in meaning to the medieval custom of **throwing down the gauntlet**, see **172/12**.
7. **that's old hat** – that is old-fashioned, out of date. 'Everything he told me was old hat. I've heard it all a hundred times before.'
8. **at the drop of a hat** – without warning, without any special reason. 'She is quite capable of deserting you whenever she feels like it – at the drop of a hat.'
9. to **keep** something **under one's hat** – to keep something secret, confidential. 'I was told this in confidence, so I'd be grateful if you would keep it under your hat.' The allusion is to the art of the magician who conceals a number of articles under his hat in the performance of his act.
10. to **wear different hats**, e.g. Judge's hat, director's hat, politician's hat, etc. – the role played by a person at any particular time. 'When he speaks from the pulpit, he is wearing his clergyman's hat. When he writes a newspaper article, he is wearing his journalist's hat.'
11. to **get one's bowler-hat / to be bowler-hatted** – to be dismissed from the armed services. The phrase is much used in the army, despite the virtual disappearance of the bowler-hat, except in the City.
12. to **hang up one's hat in a house** – to be accepted as one of the family. cf. 'to **have one's feet under the table**' **104/12**.
13. to **knock into a cocked hat** – to defeat decisively, to smash. 'I don't fancy taking him on in a fight. He would knock me into a cocked hat.'
14. a **hat trick** – to score three victories in succession. 'Bjorn Borg did the hat trick in 1978 by winning the Men's Singles Championship at Wimbledon for the third time in succession!' From taking three wickets in successive balls in cricket.
15. **as mad as a hatter** – completely insane. Taken from *Alice's Adventures in Wonderland* by Lewis Carroll.

CAP

16. **that caps it all! / to cap it all** – (1) to give something the finishing touch, to crown a person's achievements. 'He capped a wonderful year by winning a scholarship at Balliol.' (2) that is the limit! 'You were expelled from school, you lost your job, and now you are in trouble with the police. That caps it all!'
17. to **put on one's thinking cap** – to give something the most careful thought. 'I don't know what the answer is to your problem. I shall have to put on my thinking cap.'
18. to **wear a dunce's cap** – to be scoffed at for one's stupidity. It used to be the custom in schools to put a big conical hat on the head of the most stupid

pupil or 'dunce' and hold him up to the mockery of the class.

1. a **mad-cap** – a crazy, reckless person. 'He took that corner at over a hundred miles an hour. He is a real mad-cap!'
2. a **night-cap** – a drink taken last thing at night before going to bed.
3. a **feather in one's cap** – something one can be proud of, that does one credit. 'That's a feather in his cap, being asked to perform for them twice in one year!'
4. **If the cap fits, wear it** – no one is making any accusations against you, but if you are to blame, then by all means say so! Often used in reply to someone who claims he is being falsely accused, and is becoming aggressive.
5. to **throw up one's cap / to throw one's cap in the air** – to rejoice, to exult.
6. to **go cap in hand** – to beg humbly for favours or money. 'Why should I go cap in hand to him? I have a right to the money.'
7. to **set one's cap at** – to flirt with a man with the object of friendship or marriage. 'That girl sets her cap at all the tradesmen who call at our house. She is mad keen to marry, and not particular whom she does.'
8. to **cap a story** – (1) to finish off someone else's story for him. (2) to go one better with a story of one's own. 'Whenever I try to tell a story, he interrupts and caps it before I have finished.'
9. **cap and bells** – the badge of the professional clown or jester. 'Evelyn Waugh's immodest proposals, though they masquerade in cap and bells, are totally in earnest. He is an ironic writer only in the lightest social sense' (taken from Jonathan Raban's review of Gallacher's book on Evelyn Waugh, *New Statesman*, 23 December 1977).

BONNET

10. to have a **bee in one's bonnet** – to be obsessed with a strange idea. 'Joan has a bee in her bonnet about illnesses; she thinks they only exist in the mind, so that it's a waste of time calling in the doctor.'

VEIL

11. to **take the veil** – to become a nun.
12. to **draw a veil over** – to hide the facts, maintain a complete silence over. 'I will draw a veil over the events that followed, in order to spare the lady's feelings.' cf. 'to **draw a curtain over**' **151/11**.

WIG

13. a **big-wig** – a very important, influential person. 'She must have invited a big-wig or she wouldn't have spent so much on the dinner.'

BLOOMER

14. to **make a bloomer** – to make a very bad mistake that arouses merriment. A bloomer was originally a garment for ladies which covered the hips and thighs. Introduced into the USA by Mrs Amelia Bloomer in 1849, it never caught on as a fashion. To make a bloomer may therefore have originated in the idea of doing anything which exposed one to public ridicule like, for instance, being seen in one's underwear, i.e. one's bloomers!

SLEEVE

15. to **laugh up one's sleeve** – to conceal one's amusement at the discomfiture of someone. 'Martin pretended to be so sympathetic when you lost the game, but I am sure he was laughing up his sleeve at you.' When wide,

loose sleeves were worn, one could 'laugh up one's sleeve' without being detected.

1. **nothing up my sleeve** – in an open, frank manner with nothing hidden or secret. 'You can trust me. I have told you the whole truth and I promise you I have nothing up my sleeve.' Conjurors conceal cards, birds, small animals, etc., up their sleeves when performing their tricks.
2. to **wear one's heart on one's sleeve** – to show one's feelings too obviously, to lack self-control in concealing them. 'I always know when Anne has quarrelled with her boy-friend. She wears her heart on her sleeve.' From Shakespeare's *Othello*, I, i: 'But I will wear my heart upon my sleeve / For daws to peck at'.

BUTTON

3. **as bright as a button** – intelligent, lively; often used in reference to small children.

   as cute as a button – an American colloquialism with the same meaning.
4. to **button-hole** someone – to delay someone on his way in order to talk to him. The phrase comes from the habit of grasping a man by his button-hole so as to gain his attention.
5. to **press the button** – (1) to press the fatal button which would unleash a nuclear war. (2) to set in motion various kinds of machinery (administrative or otherwise). 'When you press buttons in Whitehall, things really do start to move' (said by Harold Wilson in November 1964, soon after being elected to power).
6. to have something **buttoned up** – an idiom much used in the army, meaning that all the necessary preparations have been made. 'Our unit is being sent overseas at the end of the week. Everything has been buttoned up.'

POCKET

7. to be **in pocket** – to show a gain after deduction of all expenses.

   to be **out of pocket** – to show a loss after deduction of all expenses. 'The money he paid me for looking after his children wasn't enough. At the end of the school holidays I was £100 out of pocket.'

   out-of-pocket expenses – expenses incurred in doing a job, which may or may not have been foreseen.
8. to **line one's pocket** – to make an unlawful profit. 'The government officials lined their pockets with bribes and commissions.'
9. to **pick** someone's **pocket** – to steal money from someone's pocket without being noticed.
10. to **put one's hand in one's pocket** – to pay out of one's own resources. 'The soldiers were given a splendid welcome by the people in the pub and didn't have to put their hands in their pockets once during the whole evening.'
11. to **pocket** something – to take possession of something one is usually not entitled to. 'The beggar saw a £5 note in the road and, after looking round, he pocketed the money.'
12. to **pocket an insult** – to accept an insult without protest. 'I am not going to pocket his insults any longer.'
13. to **pocket one's pride** – to submit to a humiliation. 'The agent walked about my house giving orders to my staff as if he owned the place; but although I felt very offended, I pocketed my pride in order not to lose the contract.'
14. to **have** someone **in one's pocket** – to have someone under one's control. The phrase derives from the days of the 'pocket borough' when some constituencies contained only a handful of voters, under the control of one

man who was able to decide the outcome of the election and send his own Member to Parliament. The owner of the borough was said to 'have it in his pocket'. Pocket boroughs were abolished by the Reform Act of 1832.

PURSE

1. **purse-proud** – proud of one's wealth.
2. to **hold the purse-strings** – to keep the finances under one's control. 'She let her husband do the talking, but she held the purse-strings.'
3. to **loosen one's purse-strings** – to give one's money, make money available. The idiom often suggests that the donor is mean and has been persuaded against his inclination to spend his money.
4. to **dig (deep) into one's purse** – to pay out more money when one hasn't very much left. 'A ski-ing holiday in Switzerland! I don't like to ask Father to dig into his purse again just after he's paid all those bills.'
5. to **put up a purse** – to collect a sum of money for the giving of a prize.
6. **out of the public purse** – out of the taxpayers' money. 'Money from the public purse is soon spent, with nothing to show for it.'

BAG

7. **bag and baggage** – completely, without anything left behind. 'The angry landlady threw her student-lodger out of her house, bag and baggage.' First used in this sense by Gladstone when he called for the expulsion of the Turkish army from Bulgarian soil, 'bag and baggage'. cf. **'neck and crop' 90/18.**
8. to be a **bag of bones** – to be reduced to almost a skeleton through illness or undernourishment. 'When I saw the dog last, he was a bag of bones. I hope he'll put some flesh on in his new home.'
9. **it's in the bag** – we have as good as accomplished our objective. 'After three hours with the director, I was offered a position in the firm. It's in the bag!'
10. to **pack one's bags** – to leave as the result of a quarrel, usually with one's employer. 'When I told Martina that she would have to pay for all the broken china, she packed her bags and left.'
11. a **mixed bag** – a collection of people / objects of very uneven quality. 'The passengers on the cruise were a mixed bag. We were disappointed.'

SUITCASE

12. a **suitcase economy** – an economy that suffers from raging inflation. The phrase comes from the inflation in Germany after World War I, when prices were so high that people were obliged to carry huge quantities of banknotes in their suitcases to do their shopping.

RAG

13. the **local rag** – the local newspaper. Local newspapers, especially in London, are rightly or wrongly looked down on. Hence the phrase.
14. the **rag-tag and bob-tail** – the poorest of the poor. People dressed in rags and tatters.
15. to feel **like a wet rag** (colloquial) – to feel completely exhausted.
16. **glad rags** – a woman's best clothes, usually worn for a special occasion. 'You'd better put your glad rags on, Mary. I've invited the Admiral and his wife to dinner.'
17. **from rags to riches** – from extreme

poverty to great affluence. 'It was like a fairy story. After a few months in America, he had gone from rags to riches.' The opposite of this, **from riches to rags**, is sometimes used humorously.

CLOTH

1. to **respect the cloth** – to show the respect that is due to a clergyman, 'the cloth' being the traditional name for the clergy.
2. **in sackcloth and ashes** (facetious) – showing extreme remorse and penitence for one's wrongdoing. 'I must have been in a bad mood when I reviewed Anne's book. I shall have to go to her in sackcloth and ashes and beg her forgiveness.' In biblical times, it was the custom for sinners to wear sackcloth and sprinkle ashes over their hair to make a public show of their penitence. Sackcloth is made from flax or hemp – the coarsest of material.
3. to **steal** someone's **clothes** – to adopt someone else's ideas and pass them off as your own. A favourite phrase in politics when one party is said to steal the clothes of the other.

SILK

4. to **take silk** – to become a Queen's Counsel at the British Bar and wear a silk robe in Court in place of a Junior Counsel's stuff gown.

LINEN

5. to **wash one's dirty linen in public** – to advertise in public the moral lapses and difficulties of one's private life. 'Of course, your brother has behaved very badly to you, but you will only make matters worse by washing your dirty linen in public.'

COTTON AND WOOL

6. to **cotton on to** (colloquial) – to grasp, understand. 'When the tourist forgot to tip the chambermaid, she went back to his room and said good-bye to him a second time. He cottoned on to her meaning at once, and handed her a £5 note.'
7. to **wrap** someone **up in cotton wool** – to pamper, to be over-protective, generally used in reference to a child. 'It's time you stopped wrapping Ronald up in cotton wool and let him play with other children.'
8. to **pull the wool over** someone's **eyes** – to deceive, mislead, cheat. 'You certainly pulled the wool over our eyes with that sob-story of yours!'
9. to be **woolly-headed** – to be unclear or muddled in one's thinking.
10. to be **wool-gathering** – to let one's mind wander. 'Henry must have been wool-gathering or he would never have crashed the car. He always drives very carefully.'
11. **dyed-in-the-wool** – holding fixed and unalterable opinions. 'It's no good arguing with my uncle; he is a dyed-in-the-wool Conservative.' The literal meaning is that the wool has been dyed in its raw condition so that the dye is indelible.

PATCH AND SEW

12. to **patch up a quarrel** – to put an end to a quarrel without going into the rights and wrongs of the dispute. 'It's time we patched up our quarrel with Johnson, otherwise we shall lose a lot of business.'
13. **not a patch on . . .** – nothing like as good as . . . 'I play tennis reasonably well but I'm not a patch on my brother.' A patch is a piece of cloth sewn on to a garment to cover a hole. The patch is of minor

importance compared with the garment itself.

1. to **sew up** – to come to an agreement on all the details of a plan. 'Now that the agreement has been sewn up, we can begin to work.'

THREAD

2. to **lose the thread** – to be unable to follow an argument, either because it is too hard to understand or because the listener's concentration has failed.
3. to **pick up the threads** – to resume one's work after a period of inactivity. 'It will be difficult for Alex to pick up the threads after neglecting his book for so long.'
4. to **hang by a thread** – to be in a precarious position. 'After the collision with the lorry, Oliver's life hung by a thread.'
5. to **wear** someone's **patience thread-bare/thin** – to exhaust someone's patience. 'I'm sorry I can't continue with the lessons. After three months, Toby has worn my patience thread-bare.' When an article of clothing is worn out, the threads of the material show.

20. SHIPS

SHIP

1. **all shipshape** – everything in good order, all neat and clean. 'The rooms are all shipshape for our guests.' The phrase was originally 'all shipshape and Bristol fashion', meaning that the ship was properly prepared for sea. The port of Bristol was well known for its efficiency in preparing ships for sea.
2. **when my ship comes home** – when I get rich, when I make my fortune. 'When my ship comes home, we'll buy that house by the sea.'
3. **ships in the night / ships that pass in the night** – casual acquaintances and friendships that last only a very short time. 'A pity you've been posted overseas just when we've met. Ships in the night!'
4. to **spoil a ship for a ha'porth of tar** – to lose a great deal for the sake of a small economy. 'What a pity you didn't use some good wood-preserver on that cedarwood of yours; then it wouldn't have warped. It was a case of spoiling the ship for a ha'porth of tar.' The 'ship' in the idiom is actually 'sheep', the two words being pronounced the same in some parts of England. In former times, sheep were smeared with tar to protect them from disease. cf. **'penny wise pound foolish' 244/2**.
5. **like rats leaving the sinking ship** – like traitors who desert the losing side in a contest. Rats are said to have a premonition when a ship is about to sink, and to leave it.
6. to **go down with the ship** – to stay at one's post until the bitter end. There was a tradition that the captain should go down with his ship. When the *Titanic* sank (1912), both the captain and the designer went down with the ship, although they were offered places in the life-boats. In modern times, the rule has been relaxed, and the captain is expected to be the last to leave the ship.
7. **the ship of the desert** – the camel. The journey of the camel across the desert has been compared with the voyage of a ship. Both are dependent on their own resources during the journey.
8. **spick and span** – clean, neat, tidy. 'Everything is spick and span now for our visitor. It has taken me all the morning to get his room ready.' A nautical phrase meaning that, on a new ship, every spick (nail) and span (chip) is new.
9. **in the wake of** – immediately after, in consequence of. 'In the wake of their electoral defeat in 1983, the divisions in the Labour Party came out into the open.' The wake is the track of smooth water left by a moving ship.

BOAT

10. **in the same boat** – to suffer the same predicament as somebody else. 'We are affected by rising prices just as much as you; we are all in the same boat.'
11. to **push the boat out** (somewhat dated) – to join one's friends in a celebration. It used to be the custom to have a celebration before starting on a voyage.
12. to **rock the boat** – to hinder the success of a concern in which one is involved. 'For goodness sake, don't criticize the management in front of our customers; you won't help us by rocking the boat.'
13. to **burn one's boats** – to commit oneself to a course of action that cannot possibly be changed. 'Now you have resigned your position in the com-

pany, you can't ask them for it back; you have burned your boats.'

1. to **miss the boat** – to miss an important opportunity. 'I'm afraid my husband is too old at sixty to be promoted; he has missed the boat.' cf. 'to **miss the bus**' **141/3**.

SAIL

2. to **sail through** – to succeed without any difficulty. 'Philip simply sailed through his exams – no trouble at all.'
3. **plain sailing** – an easy, uncomplicated plan of action. 'Nobody is opposing your application; it should be plain sailing for you from now on.' The term was originally 'plane sailing', meaning that the sailing was as simple as if you were sailing on a flat instead of a spherical plane.
4. to **sail into** someone – to scold or attack someone. 'Without more ado, Geoffrey sailed into the man with his fists.'
5. to **trim one's sails** – to change one's views, to withdraw them in the face of opposition. The full phrase was 'to trim the sails before the wind', meaning to adjust one's sails when the direction of the wind changed. In politics, a **'trimmer'** is someone who will change his principles under pressure of circumstances.
6. to **sail against the wind** – to oppose the prevailing view. 'Andrew never minded how much opposition he provoked; he liked sailing against the wind.'
7. to **strike one's sails** – to submit to a more powerful opponent, to accept humiliation. From the custom in the days of sail of a smaller ship lowering its sails as a sign of defeat by another ship.
8. **the cut of** someone's **jib** – someone's appearance. 'Since you ask me, I don't like the cut of his jib. I think Margaret has made a most unfortunate choice.' The jib is the foremost sail of a ship and derives from Dutch 'gijpen', (of sails) 'to turn suddenly'.

BEAM

9. **broad in the beam** – broad-hipped.
10. **on one's beam ends** – in extreme financial difficulties, very short of money. 'Can you lend me some money, I'm on my beam ends.' A ship is on its beam ends just before it goes under.

BOARD

11. to **go overboard** – to be extravagant. 'A Chippendale dining-suite and a Chinese carpet; you have gone overboard with your dining-room, haven't you?'
12. to **go by the board** – to manage without, often used in the sense of sacrificing everything to one purpose. 'Everything went by the board – holidays, new clothes, entertaining, lunches out – in order to get Vivien into college.' The original meaning was to throw unwanted articles overboard, i.e. over the side of the ship.
13. to **take on board** – to tolerate or acknowledge the truth of an idea. 'Today, people are taking on board the view that unemployment is a worldwide phenomenon and not the fault of any particular government.'

OTHER PARTS OF THE SHIP

14. a **shot across the bows** – a warning signal. 'We've had a shot across the bows from the solicitor, warning us not to repeat our accusations.' A shot across the bows was a cannon-ball warning a ship either to surrender or to turn about.

1. to **clear the decks** – to get ready for action. 'We are clearing the decks for the launching of our new campaign.' The derivation is from naval warfare when the decks are cleared of any unnecessary objects which could obstruct the free movement of personnel and weapons during the action.
2. to **batten down the hatches** – to take every possible precaution to preserve one's money. A phrase that is much used by financial correspondents, meaning that when there has been a bad fall on the Stock Exchange, the only thing to do is to wait for the market to recover. When there is a storm at sea, the hatches, i.e. the openings in the ship's deck, are closed and secured to prevent the water getting in and sinking the ship.
3. **Davy Jones' locker** – the sea bed which receives the bodies of drowned sailors. 'Jones' is thought to be a corruption of 'Jonah', who was swallowed by a whale.
4. the **sheet anchor** – the basis of someone's livelihood, what he relies upon when everything else fails. 'I earn some money from my compositions, but the music lessons are my sheet anchor.'
5. to **throw a life-line** – to help somebody who is in trouble. The life-line is thrown from a ship to a person in danger of drowning.
6. to **show** someone / **know the ropes** – to be familiar with the way a business is organized. 'You'll find everything strange at first, but Carter will show you the ropes.' From the ropes used for sailing a ship.

BERTH, TACK AND LEEWAY

7. to **give** someone **a wide berth** – to avoid someone's company, to keep a good distance away from someone. 'If you quarrel with Jakes, he can get very nasty; I would give him a wide berth if I were you.' The berth is the space in which a ship rides at anchor.
8. to be **on the right/wrong tack** – to take the line that leads to the right/wrong conclusion. If one took the wrong line in sailing, one went in the wrong direction.
9. to **make up leeway** – to compensate for time that has been wasted. 'You have a lot of leeway to make up, if you want to pass your examinations in June.' The leeway is the distance that the ship has deviated from its proper course.

COAST AND SEA

10. **the coast is clear** – there is no danger of interference from the authorities. Much in use at schools when the pupils are on the look-out for a teacher. This was a smuggling term which meant that the coast was free from coastguards.
11. a **sea change** – a fundamental change, a transformation. 'The Prime Minister is convinced that there will soon be a sea change in the relations between East and West.'
12. **at sea / all at sea** – bewildered, confused. 'After listening a few minutes to their conversation, I was all at sea. Botany is not my subject.'
13. to **find one's sea-legs** – to adjust oneself to the roll and pitch of the ship. 'Once you've been on board a day or two, you'll soon find your sea-legs.' cf. 'to **be a good sailor' 232/12**.

CANOE, BARGE AND ARK

14. to **paddle one's own canoe** – to use one's own ability and efforts to make one's way without anyone's help. 'In future I will paddle my own canoe

without asking for my parents' support.'

1. **not to touch with a barge-pole** – to dislike somebody or something intensely, to avoid. 'That man is a thoroughly disreputable character. I wouldn't touch him with a barge-pole.' cf. **'not to touch** someone **with a pair of tongs' 212/3**.
2. **out of the ark** – excessively old, ancient. 'Wherever did you get that wardrobe from? It looks as if it had come out of the ark!' The reference is to Noah's ark which Noah and his family built to escape from the Great Flood (described in Genesis).

WRECK

3. a **nervous wreck** – mentally and physically exhausted. 'I feel a nervous wreck after looking after Jenny's children.'

21. THE WORLD AND ITS PLACES

WORLD

1. **it's a small world** – to be surprised at meeting a person one knows in an unexpected place. 'Fancy meeting you here, in the middle of a highland moor! It's a small world!'
2. to **make/get the best of both worlds** – to enjoy the advantages of two different situations or ways of life. 'As a day-pupil at a nearby boarding-school, Peter has the benefit of a good education, while enjoying the advantages of living at home with his parents. He gets the best of both worlds.'
3. to **carry the world before one** – to enjoy a resounding success. 'Stephen carried the world before him with his new invention.'
4. to **set the world on fire** – to achieve fame. 'I see you've set the world on fire with your latest symphony, Jack!' cf. **'not to set the Thames on fire' 185/3.**

   to **make a noise in the world** – to be talked about, to become famous.
5. to **come up in the world** – to improve one's professional and social standing. 'You've come up in the world since we last met.'

   to **come down in the world** – to lose one's professional and social standing.
6. to **make one's way in the world / to make one's way** – to advance in one's job. 'My three sons are all making their way in the world without any help from me.'
7. a **man of the world** – a man with a good understanding of men and women, and experienced in the ways of the world. 'If you are in trouble, Valerie, would you like to talk to my father; he is a man of the world and very understanding.'
8. to **take the world as one finds it** – to adapt oneself to the ways of the world without trying to change it, to respect social convention. 'It's best to take the world as you find it, then you won't be disappointed.'
9. **for all the world like** somebody/something – exactly like . . . 'Angela stood there in her mother's long white dress, for all the world like her mother when she was Angela's age.'

   for all the world as if – just like; e.g. 'When I visited my old university, I felt for all the world as if I were back in my student days.'
10. **not for all the world** – in no circumstances. 'I wouldn't leave London for all the world.'
11. **it's not the end of the world** – things could be worse. 'It's disappointing not getting into university but it's not the end of the world. You have a good job waiting for you.'
12. to **do** someone **a world of good** – to make a huge improvement to someone. 'You don't look well, Susan. Three weeks at the sea-side will do you the world of good.'
13. **on top of the world** – elated by one's own success. 'No one thought Tony would win the by-election; he is on top of the world.'
14. **out of this world** (slang) – fantastically beautiful, marvellous. 'Just wait until you have seen the house. We must buy it; it is out of this world.'
15. **with the best will in the world** – no matter how much one tries. 'With the best will in the world, we can't help you if you won't co-operate with us.'
16. **the old world** – Europe, Asia and Africa, as distinct from North and South America.
17. **in a world of one's own** – in a make-

believe world of one's own, in a world of fantasy. 'I don't think my sister recognizes me any more. She is living in a world of her own.'

1. **dead to the world** – in a deep sleep, very difficult to awaken. 'Alec must have drunk an awful lot. He is lying on his bed, dead to the world.'
2. **the world to come** – the life after death.

PLACE, PLACES

3. **in place** – suitable, appropriate.
   out of place – unsuitable, inappropriate. 'The elegantly dressed woman felt out of place at the party where all the other women were wearing jeans.'
4. **all over the place** – in disorder, untidy. '"Keep to your positions," the football manager shouted angrily at the players. "You are all over the place!"'
5. to **keep** someone **in his place** – to keep in order, to keep under control. 'The teacher only had to look at the children to keep them in their place.'
6. to **put** someone **in his place** – to discourage familiarity. 'When the young lad took the lady by the hand, she promptly took her hand away from his, intending to put him in his place.'
7. **there's a time and place for everything** – a good thing can be spoilt by bad timing or an unsuitable setting. 'I love the Moonlight Sonata, but I should hate to hear it at breakfast! There's a time and place for everything.'
8. **not to be one's place to** (always used in the negative) – not to be right or proper to . . . '"It's not my place to give you advice," the clerk said to the manager.'
9. to **know one's place** – to accept the limits of one's position in society. In England up to the beginning of World War II, there was a deferential society in which everyone had a certain place or station in life, and respected their social superiors. This has now been largely replaced by an egalitarian society, with people claiming the same rights and privileges as the upper classes.
10. **a place in the sun** – a share of the good things in life. 'No one can dispute with us the place in the sun which is rightly ours' (said by Kaiser Wilhelm II, the German emperor, in 1911 during the Agadir crisis).
11. **pride of place** – the best position, often the most central or conspicuous, for the honoured guest, the most valuable objet d'art, and so on. 'He had a number of interesting ornaments on his mantelpiece, but pride of place was given to a silver snuff-box he had inherited from his father.'
12. to **fall into place** – to make sense, to follow a logical order. 'The work was difficult at first but, after a few weeks, everything fell into place.'
13. **in high places** – having power and influence. 'You had better be careful how you talk to me; I have friends in high places.'
14. to **come to the right place** – (1) to approach the best person for advice or help. (2) (vulgar) to sound a warning. 'If you are looking for trouble, you have come to the right place!' meaning: 'If you don't behave yourself, you'll be sorry.'

IN LONDON

15. to **put** someone **in Chancery** – (1) to hold a person's head under one arm, leaving you free to punch him. (2) to put someone into an awkward position from which it is difficult to extricate himself. The reference is to the Court of Chancery which at one time had a reputation for delaying lawsuits and ruining the parties in dispute.

1. **the old lady of Threadneedle Street** – a nickname for the Bank of England.
2. to **talk Billingsgate** – to talk like fishmongers at Billingsgate. Billingsgate was formerly the principal fish market in London, and notorious for its bad language.
3. **not to set the Thames on fire** – not to distinguish oneself in any way, to be quite ordinary. 'Martin gets a lot of pleasure from his painting but I'm afraid he'll never set the Thames on fire.' cf. 'to **set the world on fire' 183/4**.
4. to **be/end up in Carey Street** – to go bankrupt. 'We shall end up in Carey Street at the rate we are spending money.' The Courts in Bankruptcy are situated in Carey Street, off the Strand.
5. **bedlam** – a mad commotion. 'The chairman was quite unable to keep order. Everyone was on his feet shouting and swearing. Absolute bedlam!' Bedlam, a corruption of 'Bethlehem', was the name of a mad house in the Middle Ages. (Today it would be called a mental hospital.)
6. **You are not at the Ritz!** – the Ritz is a hotel in Piccadilly (London) which has made a name for the excellence of its cooking and accommodation. When servicemen complained about the bad cooking in the army during World War II, they were often told that there was a war on and that they were not 'at the Ritz'.

IN ENGLAND

7. to **send to Coventry** – to punish someone for disloyalty to his companions or workmates by refusing to speak to him. 'Sending to Coventry' is a common practice in schools and trade unions. The idiom has its origin in the Civil War between King Charles I and Parliament (1642–6). In his *History of the Great Rebellion*, Volume 2, VI, 83, Clarendon says that Royalist prisoners captured at Birmingham were sent to Coventry, a Parliamentary stronghold, where some of them were beheaded; whence the association of 'sending to Coventry' with the punishment of disloyalty, which later took the form of not speaking to the offender.
8. to **carry coals to Newcastle** – to bring a thing to a place which is famous for its production, like trying to sell wine to the French, or kimonos to the Japanese, and so on.
9. a **Norfolk dumpling** – a person who is dull and stupid. The inhabitants of East Anglia have this reputation, for reasons which are not apparent.

IN SCOTLAND

10. **off to Gretna Green** – couples who were under age (in English law) would run away together to get married at Gretna Green, a small town on the English–Scottish border. The conditions for marrying under Scottish law being less strict than under English, this was a favourite device for couples who had not obtained the consent of their parents.

IN IRELAND

11. to be **full of Blarney / to talk Blarney** – to make wild promises, to flatter and deceive. The Irish have a reputation for making wild promises. From kissing the Blarney Stone in Killarney.
12. **beyond the Pale** – socially unacceptable; any form of serious misbehaviour. 'I won't invite those boys; I saw them throwing stones at Jane yesterday. They are beyond the Pale.' The word 'Pale' is derived from the Latin 'palus', a stake, stakes having been used, in the fourteenth century, to mark out the boundary between

the land settled by the British colonists in Ireland and the rest of the country. The people living beyond the Pale were regarded by the colonists as uncivilized. The same phrase was adopted by the English in their own country to indicate people of 'inferior class', who were not received in polite society. There was also a Pale of Settlement for the Jews in Czarist Russia from 1792.

IN BELGIUM

1. to **meet your Waterloo** – to suffer a final, decisive defeat. The phrase has been taken from Napoleon's defeat by Wellington and Blücher at the Battle of Waterloo. It is usually applied to an unexpected defeat after a string of successes.

IN ITALY

2. **Rome was not built in a day** – nothing of value has ever been achieved without great effort.
3. to **fiddle while Rome burns** – to occupy oneself with trifles during a crisis. Legend has it that the Emperor Nero fiddled while Rome burned.
4. **all roads lead to Rome** – Rome has always possessed a special importance – as capital of the ancient world, then as capital of Christendom. As the seat of the papacy, Rome commands the allegiance of six hundred million Catholics.
5. **See Naples and die** – Naples is the most beautiful city in the world and, when you have seen Naples, you may die happy. There is a small town near Naples called Mori, the Italian for 'die', where thousands once died of typhoid and cholera, so this is a joke phrase.
6. **the Venice of the North** – there are three cities in the north of Europe which boast that they are comparable with Venice: Bruges, Amsterdam and Stockholm.
7. to **cross the Rubicon** – to do something irrevocable. In ancient Rome, generals were guilty of treason if they failed to disband their armies before crossing the Rubicon. Caesar took the decision to cross the Rubicon with his army to seize power.

OTHER COUNTRIES IN EUROPE

8. **castles in Spain** – unreal wealth and splendour which only exists in the mind of the dreamer. cf. **'castles in the air' 24/13, 'pie in the sky' 160/15**.
9. **the gnomes of Zurich** – Swiss bankers, so called because they were the guardians of huge treasures under the earth, i.e. in the vaults of their banks. The name was intended humorously.
10. an **Olympian detachment** – an impersonal, unemotional view of human conflict. From Olympus, the home of the Greek gods where Zeus reigned. The gods of ancient Greece were endowed with all the human passions and weaknesses – love, jealousy, vindictiveness and anger; so the modern meaning of the idiom has changed.
11. a **Marathon** – a long-drawn-out contest, an event which calls for great endurance. 'The conference began at eight this morning and went on all day until eleven o'clock at night. It was a real Marathon!' The name has been taken from the Battle of Marathon between the Greeks and the Persians, fought in 490 BC. The messenger, who announced the result of the battle, fell dead on his arrival in Athens after running nearly 23 miles.

IN THE EAST

12. **Sodom and Gomorrah** – synonym for a centre of vice (Genesis XVII, 19).

1. the **Gadarene Swine** – to stampede with the herd (or crowd) to destruction. From the Bible, when Jesus told the people how the evil spirit that had been cast out entered the Gadarene swine, causing them to hurl themselves in a fit of madness over the edge of the cliff to their destruction (Matthew VIII, 28–34).
2. a **perfect Babel / a Babel of sounds** – an uproar in many different languages.
3. **the walls of Jericho didn't fall down in a day** – if you want to defeat your enemy, you will have to fight very hard.
4. **like the walls of Jericho** – any sudden unexpected collapse. 'To Ferdy, they [the English hostesses] fell like the walls of Jericho!' (from Somerset Maugham's Short Stories, Volume 2, 'The Alien Corn'). The allusion is to the collapse of the walls of Jericho when the Israelites blew their horns outside the city.
5. **'His road to Damascus', 'Her road to Damascus'** – a dramatic change of mind on some burning issue. When Saul of Tarsus, who had for a long time been a vigorous persecutor of the Christians, was on the road to Damascus, he heard the voice of God and immediately became an ardent disciple of Christ, adopting the name of Paul.
6. **Mecca** – a place which has a strong appeal for the enthusiast. 'Between the wars, Paris was the Mecca of painters and artists.' Mecca is the birthplace of the prophet Mohammed, and a holy place for Muslims.

IMAGINARY PLACES

7. an **El Dorado** – an imaginary country where the traveller can make a fortune without any effort.
8. to **live in Eden** – a place of sheer bliss and delight. The place where Adam and Eve were created.
9. to **consign to Limbo** – to put out of one's mind once and for all. Limbo was a place adjoining hell which accommodated unbaptized infants.
10. **in the land of Nod** – asleep. Note the related phrase 'to **nod off**', meaning to fall asleep.
11. **Shangri-la / like Shangri-la** – a state of mind lacking in drive or interest, dull placidity. Shangri-la is the paradise described in James Hilton's *Lost Horizon* (1933) up in the mountains of a Buddhist country. In Hilton's city, the people lived in perfect peace and serenity, with no quarrelling or strife, but also with an absence of emotion or ambition.
12. a **fool's paradise** – a comfortable but false illusion which could have deceived only a fool. 'I knew all along that the business would never recover. You have been living in a fool's paradise all these years!'

22. LANGUAGES AND NATIONALITIES

LANGUAGE

1. to **pick up a language** – to learn a language by listening to native speakers talking together, without taking lessons or studying the grammar.
2. a **second language** – the first foreign language that one learns. Hundreds of millions of people have learned English as a second language. Usually the English learn French as their second language.
3. **bad/strong language** – language that is full of swear-words and obscene expressions.
4. to **talk the same language** – to share a common background with the person one is speaking to, to share the same problems and difficulties. 'We have both been running English language schools for the last twenty years. We talk the same language.'
5. to **use the language of violence** – to resort to intimidation and force instead of common sense or the Courts. 'I know you have been treated disgracefully, but to write threatening letters is to use the language of violence.'
6. to **murder a language** – to make every conceivable mistake in the course of learning a foreign language. One school of thought holds that in order to learn a language one must 'murder' it first, because practice is more important than theory.
7. a **dead language** – a language that is no longer spoken today, except by scholars, theologians and experts. The classical languages of ancient Greek, Latin and Sanskrit are dead languages. Cornish is a dead language; the last person known to have spoken it was Dolly Pentreath (1685–1778).

ENGLISH

8. **broken English**/French/Spanish, etc. – badly spoken English/French/Spanish, etc., containing many mistakes in grammar and pronunciation.
9. **Queen's English** – correct, grammatical English. It may be spoken in any accent, provided it is clear and intelligible.
10. **received English** – a phrase coined by Professor Daniel Jones for the socially most acceptable accent. It is the only accent that is not tied to any particular region but is local to the whole country. Jones called it 'received' because at one time this pronunciation was an essential condition for being received in the best society.
11. **pidgin English** – a corrupt, simplified form of English used by many people in Papua New Guinea and the Far East for trading. cf. **'dog-Latin' 54/2**.
12. **plain English** – (1) blunt, outspoken English. 'I told him in plain English what I thought of his idea', meaning I expressed my disapproval frankly and forcefully. (2) good, clear, easily understood English as opposed to the jargon that is sometimes employed by civil servants. We give below an example of bureaucratic English which we have rendered into plain English.

    Bureaucratic English: A distinction should be made at an age appropriate to the background and nationality of the student, below which the concept of the course should be for juveniles and above it for young adults (British Tourist Authority, 1979 BLE/1980).

    Plain English: The courses should take into account the ages, background and nationality of the students.
13. **the English disease** – the calling of

strikes, both official and unofficial, without reasonable justification.

WELSH

1. to **welsh on** someone – to trick or swindle someone, to break a promise, often in connection with some business. At one time, Welsh bookies had a reputation for running off with the punters' stakes. (That is how the English explain the phrase. It reflects the hostility in former times between the Welsh and the English.)

DUTCH

2. to **go Dutch** – each person pays his own bill in a restaurant. A practice favoured by students or young people who are working.
3. a **Dutch party** – a party to which each guest contributes some food or drink.
4. **double Dutch** – nonsense, meaningless words. 'I didn't understand a single word. It was all double Dutch to me.'
5. to **talk to someone like a Dutch uncle** – to lecture with excessive seriousness.
6. **Dutch courage** – false courage acquired by drinking. 'I ordered myself a double whisky to give myself some Dutch courage.'
7. **I'm a Dutchman if . . .** – a way of denying a supposition. 'If you're right, I'm a Dutchman', means I am quite sure you are wrong.
8. a **Dutch auction** – an auction at which the starting price is pitched high and then slowly reduced until a bid is made.

OTHER NATIONALITIES

9. **Prussian efficiency** – a general term for all the qualities associated with the history of Prussia: energy, thoroughness, industry, patience and discipline.
10. **Teutonic thoroughness** – especially characteristic of Prussia. The Germans have always had a reputation for studiousness, theoretical analysis and research in depth, in contrast with Anglo-Saxon empiricism.
11. to **take French leave** – to leave without first obtaining permission. The French have a similar saying to the English: 'filer à l'anglaise'.
12. **French letter** – a contraceptive.
13. **Gallic humour** – humour that is logical and intellectual, wit rather than humour.
14. to **make a Roman holiday** – to organize a gruesome spectacle for the public. The words are from a quotation from Byron's *Childe Harolde's Pilgrimage*, IV cxli: '. . . butchered to make a Roman holiday'. Public executions and whippings would both come into this category.
15. **When in Rome, do as the Romans do** – you should adopt the manners and customs of the people you are living with. First said in a slightly different form by St Ambrose (Epistle 36, II Kings VI 18): 'When I am in Milan, I do as they do in Milan. But when I go to Rome, I do as Rome does!'
16. **when Greek meets Greek** – when two men of formidable strength engage in combat, the contest will be hard fought and severe.
17. a **Greek gift** – a gift which brings only trouble and sorrow. The reference is to Vergil's *Aeneid* II, 'I fear the Greeks, even when they bring gifts'.
18. **It's all Greek to me** – I can't understand a word of it, it's like listening to a foreign language (from Shakespeare's *Julius Caesar*, I, ii: 'But for my own part, it was Greek to me').
19. **'Young Turks'** – young agitators, young militants who are in a hurry to

make changes in the established order.

1. a **Bohemian life** – in some countries, the name 'Bohemian' was a synonym for 'gypsy' in the mistaken belief that gypsies came from Bohemia. It means an irregular, unconvential way of life, and is often applied to writers and artists.
2. **Bohemian tastes/dress** – bright, colourful, unconventional tastes or dress.
3. the **Russian soul** – a vague, unfulfilled yearning for a better, spiritual life which would bring consolation and relief to the suffering masses. Copiously described and dramatized in the works of Dostoyevsky and other Russian novelists of the nineteenth century.
4. **Russian roulette** – gamblers would stake their lives by putting a bullet in one of the six chambers of a revolver, spinning the chamber then holding it to their head and pressing the trigger.
5. a **Tartar** (term of abuse) – a grim, uncivilized, bad-tempered person who makes a lot of trouble. The Tartars are Asiatics of Turkish origin, and are said to be notorious for their savagery in war.
6. to **catch a Tartar** – to take prisoner a man who makes so much trouble that one regrets ever having captured him.
7. the **Amazons** – active, assertive women in different walks of life. The Amazons were a legendary tribe of women who fought on horseback against the ancient Greeks. They were renowned for their bravery in battle.
8. **Spartan simplicity** – absolute simplicity in one's way of life, the simplest diet and the avoidance of luxury or comfort in any form. The phrase has been taken from the Spartans, who were the most disciplined and austere people in ancient Greece.
9. **Spartan endurance** – great fortitude and discipline – a characteristic of the Spartan way of life.
10. **like the laws of the Medes and the Persians** – unchangeable.
11. a **Trojan horse** – an enemy concealed within. 'I think it would be dangerous to elect that man to the board; he could be a Trojan horse.'
12. a **Parthian shot** – a cutting remark made by someone on leaving, which gives the victim no opportunity of retaliating. It often means one final insult in addition to many others, with the idea of getting in the last word. The Parthian horsemen used to shoot at their enemy while retreating at full speed from them.
13. a **Philistine / to have Philistine tastes** – someone without cultural interests. The phrase was coined by Matthew Arnold but is really a misnomer because the Philistines who lived around 1200 BC were highly cultured, combining discipline and efficiency with a taste for luxury.
14. a **good Samaritan** – someone who goes out of his way to help a stranger in distress, although the stranger has no claim on him. The phrase has been taken from Christ's parable of the Good Samaritan, Luke X, 29.
15. **there are too many chiefs and not enough Indians** – there are too many highly paid directors and managers, and not enough men to carry out the orders.
16. the **Mandarin mentality** – Mandarin was the name given to the officials in the Chinese Civil Service who had ruled China for centuries before the Communist Revolution. The Mandarin mentality means the mentality of the ruling class, self-satisfied, domineering and very conscious of its superiority to the rest of the country.

23. NAMES

NAME

1. **one's good name** – one's reputation. 'He had a good name for honest dealing.'
2. a **bad name** – a bad reputation. 'That hotel has a bad name for its accommodation and food.'

   to **give** someone **a bad name** – to do harm to someone's reputation. 'You'll give us a bad name if you talk to our customers like that!'
3. to **have a name for** – to be well known for. 'He has a name for his wit.'
4. to **make a name for oneself** – to distinguish oneself, usually used in a good sense. 'Arthur has made a name for himself in physics.'
5. to **know by name** – to know a person's name, but not to know him to speak to.
6. to **call** someone **names** – to address someone insultingly.
7. to **clear one's name** – to be acquitted of a serious accusation. 'The inquiry cleared Peter's name of all blame for the death of his patient.'
8. to **win a name for** – to be well known for. 'He has won a name for his rowdiness and bad manners.'
9. to pass **by the name of** – to assume the name of. 'He used to pass by the name of Thorn. His real name is Jones.'
10. to **lend one's name to** – to allow the use of one's name in support of a campaign or crusade.
11. **in the name of** – at the command of. 'In the name of the law, let me pass!'
12. **what's in a name?** – a name by itself has no significance. It is the associations which give it meaning. Shakespeare makes the same point: 'What's in a name? That which we call a rose / By any other name would smell as sweet' (*Romeo and Juliet*, II, ii).
13. to **name names** – to make accusations against certain people. 'I don't want to name names, but I will if the stealing doesn't stop.'
14. **maiden name** – a wife's family name prior to her marriage.
15. **nickname** – an extra name often coined by friends or school fellows to describe some physical characteristic, such as 'Tubby', 'Fatty', 'Ginger', 'Sandy', 'Tiny'. The word is derived from Middle English 'ekename', eke meaning other or additional.
16. a **household name** – a name familiar to every household in the country.
17. to **drag** someone's **name through the mud** – to damage someone's reputation by denigrating him in public.
18. to **drop names / name-dropping** – mentioning the names (especially the Christian names) of important people in one's conversation to give the impression that one is friendly with them.
19. **no names, no packdrill** – it's better not to mention the people involved because one doesn't wish to make trouble for them. 'Just as I was locking up the office, I overheard someone telephoning a friend in Tokyo. No names, no packdrill.' Packdrill was a punishment used in the British Army which obliged offenders to march up and down with heavy packs on their backs.

BOYS' NAMES: JACK

20. **I'm all right, Jack!** – the slogan of the self-seeking opportunist who will forget his friends for the sake of his own interests.
21. a **jack in office** – a self-assertive official who misuses his authority.
22. to be a **cheap jack** – to sell shoddy

goods; to indulge in mean, dishonest tricks to sell one's goods.

1. **every man jack of them** – every single one. 'All the men on the building site went on strike, including the foreman, every man jack of them.'
2. to **climb like a steeplejack** – to be agile in climbing and sure-footed.
3. **Jack is as good as his master** – there is no difference between the boss and the worker. We are all equal and we should all have equal rights.
4. a **Jack of all trades** – a man who knows a little of many jobs but none properly. The phrase derives from 'A Jack of all trades is a master of none'.
5. **Jack Sprat** – a small, undersized boy or man. The sprat is a very small fish. From the nursery rhyme: 'Jack Sprat could eat no fat and his wife could eat no lean, but 'twixt them both they licked the platter clean.'
6. **every Jack has his Jill** – every man can find the right woman if he looks for her. (From the nursery rhyme, 'Jack and Jill went up the hill . . .')
7. **before one could say Jack Robinson** – in a moment, before one could turn round. The phrase was used, probably for the first time, by Fanny Burney, in her novel *Evelina* (1778), Letter 82, 'I'd do it as soon as say Jack Robinson.'
8. **Jack/Jack Tar** (nickname) – an ordinary sailor.
9. a **jack-in-the-box** – a toy man who springs out of a box as soon as the lid is lifted. Sometimes used as an idiomatic comparison. 'They were jumping to their feet like jacks in the box on points or order.'
10. to **hit the jackpot** – to get a huge return on one's money all at once; to make a lucky gamble. The phrase is taken from the card game Poker when one scoops the pool.
11. to **jack up** – to increase suddenly. 'By installing new machinery, they were able to jack up production by more than half.' One jacks up a car by raising up one end of it to change a wheel.

JOHN, ROGER, PETER, PAUL AND OTHER BOYS' NAMES

12. **John Bull** – he is supposed to personify the typical Englishman, having been described by Arbuthnot in his *History of John Bull* in 1727: 'The Englishman is honest, straightforward, irascible, bold and quarrelsome, plain-dealing and independent.' cf. **'Uncle Sam' 133/12.**
13. to hoist **the Jolly Roger** – to challenge the authority of the state. The Jolly Roger is the black flag of piracy.
14. to **rob Peter to pay Paul** – to give to one person what rightfully belongs to another. 'To reduce income tax by doubling VAT is to rob Peter to pay Paul.'
15. to be a **Peter Pan** – to be a male adult who mentally remains fixated on his childhood. Peter Pan was the boy in Barrie's play of the same name who never wanted to grow up.
16. to be a **Paul Pry** – someone who is always interfering in other people's affairs, an objectionable busybody.
17. a **doubting Thomas** – a sceptic, someone who will believe only the evidence of his own eyes. Thomas, a disciple of Christ, was unwilling to believe in His resurrection until he had seen the marks left by the nails on the hands of Christ.
18. **Tommy / Tommy Atkins** – a generic name given to the English infantry soldiers in World War I.
19. a **peeping Tom** – a voyeur, a man who takes pleasure in looking secretly at nude women.

1. **tommy-rot** (slang) – the most utter nonsense. 'He's talking tommy-rot as usual.'
2. a **tomboy** – a young girl, below the age of adolescence, who behaves like a boy, preferring the company of boys and their games.
3. **Tom, Dick and Harry** – any nonentity. 'I'm not going out with any Tom, Dick or Harry. If Ronald doesn't invite me, I won't go out at all.'
4. a **simple Simon** – someone who is easily taken in. From the nursery rhyme: 'Simple Simon met a pieman going to the fair . . .'
5. a **proper Charlie** – a fool. The name refers to the pensioners who were employed by King Charles I. These men had a reputation for stupidity.
   to **make a Charlie of** someone – to make a fool of someone.
6. to **take the micky out of** – to make fun of someone.
7. a **smart Alec** – a disagreeable know-all.
8. **And Bob's your uncle!** – now you have what you want. When the young Balfour was given a ministerial post by his uncle, Lord Robert Salisbury, the Prime Minister, members of the opposition said 'Bob's your uncle', meaning that with such an uncle he could have whatever he wanted.
9. a **silly Billy** – a foolish fellow. The nickname for William IV who was considered none too bright. This phrase is often used in the plural form. 'The silly Billies in the Ministry!'
10. **jerry-built** – a badly built house without a foundation.
11. to **gerrymander** – to manipulate the boundaries of a parliamentary constituency so as to gain an unfair advantage, e.g. by transferring a large number of one's opponents to another constituency. Gerry was a governor of Massachusetts.
12. to give **a Roland for an Oliver** – to give as good as one gets, to retaliate effectively.
13. a **Valentine** – a letter or card sent anonymously by a man to a girl on St Valentine's day expressing love and admiration.

GIRLS' NAMES

14. **plain Jane** – a plain girl.
15. **as dead as Queen Anne / 'Queen Anne is dead'** – said in reply to news that is no longer new. 'Did you say your brother is engaged to Judy? Yes and Queen Anne is dead. I knew about their engagement weeks ago.' cf. **'as dead as mutton' 161/14, 'as dead as a door-nail' 211/10.**
16. **not on your Nelly** – a derisive refusal. 'Not on your Nelly, you won't catch me doing that.'
17. **Lady Bountiful** – a country lady who gave half her money to charity. '"I am not going to play Lady Bountiful with tax-payers' money," was said by Mrs Thatcher soon after becoming Prime Minister.'

BIBLICAL NAMES

18. the **old Adam** – the primitive, sinful nature of a man which is concealed under a veneer of good breeding and education.
19. **not to know** someone **from Adam** – to have no knowledge or recollection of someone. 'I can't think why the man by the window keeps waving at me; I don't know him from Adam!'
20. **the mark of Cain** – the stain of a crime or misdeed on one's reputation. 'You will bear the mark of Cain for the rest of your life for your cruelty to her children.' The allusion is to the murder of Abel by his brother, Cain. 'And

the Lord set a mark upon Cain lest any finding him should kill him' (Genesis IV. 9).

1. to **raise Cain** – to create a terrible row, to explode with anger. 'He will raise Cain when he hears his son has been expelled from school.' So called because the name of Cain is associated with the most violent temper.
2. to be a **Daniel come to judgement** – to show judgement and wisdom beyond one's years. 'A Daniel come to judgement, yea, a Daniel! O wise young judge, how I do honour thee!' (Shakespeare, *The Merchant of Venice*, IV, i).
3. they are **like David and Jonathan** – inseparable friends. A perfect friendship (2 Samuel I, 26).
4. a **David and Goliath situation** – a situation in which one adversary is hopelessly outmatched by the other. 'How can you possibly compete with the shop across the road. They have a hundred times more capital than you. It's a David and Goliath situation.'
5. a **Jeremiah** – one who always sees everything in the gloomiest light. 'What a Jeremiah you are. You are always prophesying disaster!' Jeremiah was a prophet of gloom of the Old Testament.
6. the **worship of Mammon** – an excessive love of wealth which is pursued at the cost of one's duty to family and friends. Mammon is a synonym of avarice and the worship of money. 'You cannot serve God and Mammon' (Luke XVI, 13).
7. to **try the patience of Job** – to provoke even the most patient person. 'I've explained it to you a hundred times and you still don't understand! You would try the patience of Job!' Job was afflicted with every possible calamity but learned from God to bear his misfortunes with courage and patience. From the Old Testament. cf. 'to **try the patience of a saint**' **120/6**.
8. a **Job's comforter** – someone who calls to offer sympathy but makes matters worse by blaming the bereaved person for what has happened. 'I was so sorry to learn of your little boy's death. What a pity he was never inoculated.' In the Book of Job (Old Testament), Job is reproached by his friends for bringing calamity on himself by his disobedience to God.
9. to **out-herod Herod** – to exceed Herod in cruelty and wickedness. It was King Herod who had the babes of Bethlehem put to death (Matthew II, 16). The phrase comes from Shakespeare: 'I would have such a fellow shipped for o'erdoing Termagant; it out-herods Herod' (*Hamlet*, III, 2, 1).
10. to **play Judas** – to be a traitor. Judas Iscariot betrayed Jesus for thirty pieces of silver.
11. **the kiss of Judas** – any display of affection whose purpose is to conceal an act of treachery. It was the kiss of Judas that betrayed Jesus to the Roman soldiers (Matthew XXVI, 49).
12. a **piece of Jesuitry** – a very subtle argument, full of sophistry and logic carried to extremes.

CLASSICAL AND MYTHICAL NAMES

13. an **Adonis** – any young man of striking beauty. The phrase is sometimes used as a light-hearted compliment. 'With an Adonis like Mark at your side, you had better watch out. Half the girls in Tonbridge will be after him!'
14. **beyond the dreams of Croesus** – unimaginable riches. Croesus, King of Lydia 560–546 BC, was reputed to be the richest man of all time.
15. a **Janus** – having two faces, front and back, with contradictory expressions.

The phrase comes from the Roman god who guarded doors and gates. 'Descartes (the French philosopher, 1596–1660) was a Janus with one face smiling at the conventional wisdom, and the other sceptical of it' (from Frederic Raphael's review of Bernard Williams's *Descartes: The Project of Pure Inquiry*).

1. to **play Cupid** – to play the matchmaker. Cupid (Greek: Eros), son of Venus (Aphrodite), was the god of love. He is represented in fable as a boy of great beauty, with wings, carrying a bow and arrows.
2. **opening Pandora's box** – accepting a dangerous present which will bring every conceivable ill upon one's head. From the Greek myth which relates how Pandora, the first woman ever made, was given a box by the gods whose contents when released would afflict the human race ever after.
3. to be **as old as Methuselah** – the name is a symbol of longevity and the phrase is often used humorously; for example, 'That joke is as old as Methuselah.' Methuselah is a mythical figure who was reputed to have lived for 969 years.
4. **Homer sometimes nods** – even the greatest of mortals errs from time to time. Horace excuses Homer's occasional drowsiness in view of the great length of his poem.
5. **platonic love** – pure love between men and women in which there is no sexuality. The phrase occurs at the end of the *Symposium* when Plato refers to the non-sexual love that Socrates felt for young men.
6. **socratic method** – the rigorous logical analysis that the Greek philosopher, Socrates, applied to every problem.
7. a **caesarean operation / a caesarean** – the cutting of the abdomen to effect delivery of the child, as with Julius Caesar. Caesarean is derived from the Latin 'caesus', the past participle of 'caedere', meaning to cut.
8. **Achilles' heel** – the one and only weakness, but a fatal one. 'Brian could have been a rich man today had it not been for his gambling, his Achilles' heel.' From the legend of Achilles whose body, when a baby, was immersed by his nurse in the river Styx to make him invulnerable (the *Iliad* of Homer). cf. 'a **chink in one's armour' 210/7**, 'to **have feet of clay' 104/10**.
9. **Herculean efforts** – immense, almost superhuman efforts. Hercules earned immortality for himself by accomplishing twelve enormously difficult tasks set him by the Argive king. 'It will need Herculean efforts to master French in six months.'
10. the **sword of Damocles / like the sword of Damocles hanging over one** – the danger that looms ahead and threatens our well-being. 'The danger of war hangs over humanity like the sword of Damocles.' From the legend of King Dionysius, who made his courtier Damocles sit under a sword that hung from the ceiling by a single hair, in order to demonstrate to him the precariousness of a king's life which he so much envied.
11. the **Midas touch** – a person is said to have 'the Midas touch' when all his business ventures prosper spectacularly. The phrase comes from the legend of Midas, King of Phrygia, whose prayer that anything he touched might turn to gold was granted by the gods as a reward for his hospitality to Dionysius's tutor.
12. to **cut the Gordian knot** – to take decisive action in order to gain one's ends. There was an ancient legend that the first person to untie the Gordian knot would gain the empire of Asia. Many travellers had failed to unravel the knot, but Alexander of Macedonia solved the problem by

cutting the knot with his sword, and then went on to win all Asia in accordance with the legend.

1. a **Procrustean bed** – a harsh, inhumane system into which the individual is fitted by force, regardless of his own needs or wishes. The phrase is taken from the name of the Greek robber who forced his victims to lie on a couch. If they were too long, he chopped off their feet, and if they were too short, he stretched their bodies to the required length. The phrase is often used in political debate.
2. **like a Sphinx** – an expressionless face which conceals a secret.
3. the **Oedipus complex** – the association of patricidal fantasies and feelings of guilt in the mind of the young boy; a concept of the Freudian school of psycho-analysis based on the ancient Greek myth of Oedipus, who unwittingly slew his father and married his mother.

NAMES FROM LITERATURE

4. an **Aladdin's cave** – a place full of riches and good things. 'It was like an Aladdin's cave for a poor country boy.'
5. like a **Rip van Winkle** – a man who lives in the past, and is out of touch with modern life. 'You might have got the house for that price twenty years ago but not today. Where have you been living all this time? You are a real Rip van Winkle!' In Washington Irving's fable, Rip van Winkle falls asleep for twenty years, and when he awakes, he finds his house deserted; he is bewildered and lost.
6. **Lilliputian** – fussy, small-minded people. Taken from Dean Swift's *Gulliver's Travels*, whose purpose was to show how small-minded we all are by portraying mankind as a race of pygmies preoccupied with the pettiest pursuits.
7. to be a **Shylock** – to be a ruthless, pitiless money-lender who will extract the last penny from his debtor. Taken from Shakespeare's *Merchant of Venice*.
8. a **Don Juan** – a man who is always falling in and out of love, one who has an insatiable love for women. 'He's a real Don Juan.' A notorious rake of the fourteenth century, Don Juan is the legendary hero of many stories, plays and poems. He is the central figure in Mozart's *Don Giovanni* and Byron's *Don Juan*.
9. a **Jekyll and Hyde personality** – someone who alternates great kindness and nobility of character with extreme brutality and barbarism. The phrase is taken from Robert Louis Stevenson's novel which depicts the good Dr Jekyll changing into the evil Mr Hyde. The character created by Stevenson was intended as a symbol of the struggle between good and evil in each one of us.
10. **like a Micawber/Micawberish** – someone who makes no provision for the future and hopes something will turn up. Taken from a character in Dickens's *David Copperfield*.
11. **Pipsqueak** – a small unimportant man who irritates people with his bossy manner. 'I'm not going to be pushed around by that Pipsqueak!' From the name Pip.
12. **Robin Hood policies** – the policy of taking money from the rich and giving it to the poor. Robin Hood was the name of the legendary outlaw who lived with his men in Sherwood Forest in the thirteenth century and was reputed to rob the king's officers in order to help the peasants.
13. **the Cinderella of** – the least admired. 'Woodwork has always been the

Cinderella of the Arts.' The phrase is taken from the fairy tale in which Cinderella was forced to drudge all day at home while her step-mother and two step-sisters enjoyed themselves at palatial balls.

1. **like Alice in Wonderland** – an imaginary world where the inhabitants are all insane, and the laws of logic and reason have been suspended. 'First, I am blamed for taking the girl out, then the next day, I am blamed for not taking her out. It's like Alice in Wonderland.' From *Alice's Adventures in Wonderland* by Lewis Carroll.

2. to be **as pleased as Punch** – absolutely delighted, usually with oneself over some achievement. 'My daughter is as pleased as Punch. She has just had an article published in the *Daily Mail*.' Punch is always portrayed as laughing or singing with pleasure at his own escapades.

3. a **Frankenstein monster** – the product of an inventor's imagination which destroys his creator. The phrase is taken from the famous horror story by Mary Shelley about a young student, Frankenstein, which describes how he made a monster which became so powerful that it eventually destroyed him. Parallels have been drawn with modern scientific discoveries, particularly in the biogenetic field.

4. a **Heath Robinson affair** – any machine that has been made amateurishly. 'Who ever installed your water-heater? It's a Heath Robinson affair!' W. Heath Robinson (1872–1944) illustrated the most complicated contraptions in the humorous magazine *Punch* and elsewhere.

5. **waiting for Godot** – waiting for ever because Godot never comes. From the play *Waiting for Godot* by Samuel Beckett.

POLITICAL AND HISTORICAL NAMES

6. **Rabelaisian wit** – the earthy humour characteristic of the great French writer François Rabelais (1494–1553).

7. **Machiavellian cunning** – the most subtle, unprincipled cunning. In his treatise on state-craft, *The Prince*, Machiavelli tried to establish the principles of political power which he maintained were based on realism rather than conventional morality. Machiavelli's book foreshadowed Bismarck's 'Realpolitik' in the nineteenth century.

8. like the **Luddites** – a term of abuse for anybody who opposes the introduction of labour-saving machinery which may threaten his livelihood. The phrase comes from the 'Luddite' mechanics who attempted to destroy the new machinery in the Midlands and North of England which had been installed to replace their handicrafts, 1811–16.

9. **on a Napoleonic scale** – on a huge, ambitious scale.

10. a **maverick** – someone who is wild, reckless, out of control. Originally, an unbranded calf, named after a Texan ranger of that name who did not brand his cattle. Later, the name was given to politicians who refused to give allegiance to the party leadership.

11. to **boycott** – to coerce a person by forbidding any social or commercial relations with him. In 1880, the Irish Land League resolved that anyone buying the farm of an evicted tenant should be treated like a leper. The first victim of this policy was Captain Boycott who had defied the League and was consequently 'boycotted'. The term 'boycott' was later extended to similar action taken against organ-

izations or countries, and has been used in this way ever since.

1. **Custer's last stand** – any man who goes down to defeat in a spectacular manner. Custer was an American general whose troops were wiped out in an Indian ambush.
2. a **Blimpish point of view** – any reactionary or unprogressive point of view that harks back to the pre-war period in Britain. Colonel Blimp, a red-faced elderly colonel, invented by David Low, the celebrated cartoonist, was a familiar figure of fun in the 1930s.
3. to have **Hobson's choice** – to have no choice at all. 'You advertise a wide choice of holidays but you are only offering me one! It is Hobson's choice!' Tobias Hobson, a seventeenth-century Cambridge carrier, who hired out horses to the undergraduates of the university, never allowed his customers to choose a horse but insisted on their taking the horse nearest the stable door, so that they had no choice at all.
4. **Occam's razor** – the ruthless analysis of a problem which eliminates all superfluous factors. Occam of Ockham, Surrey (died 1349), held that entities must not be needlessly multiplied and that we were only entitled to generalize from experience.
5. **Parkinson's Law** – the title of a book by C. Northcote Parkinson in which he makes fun of the civil service. Parkinson's Law states: (1) the work done is in inverse proportion to the number of civil servants employed, and (2) public expenditure rises to accommodate the growth in bureaucracy. In other words, the more civil servants the state employs, the more work they will make in order to justify their existence and their salaries.

JONES

6. **keeping up with the Joneses** – trying to maintain the same standards of material comfort as one's neighbours, who are represented by the very ordinary name of Jones. 'Just because our neighbours have bought a Daimler, that's no reason why we should buy one. I have no intention of keeping up with the Joneses.'

24. MONARCHY AND PARLIAMENT

KING

1. **fit for a king** – suitable for a king's use. 'That was a wonderful dinner you gave me – fit for a king.'
2. a **king-pin** – the most important person in any organization. 'You'd better not quarrel with Johnson; he's the king pin on the local Council.' In the game of skittles, the king-pin is the most important piece.
3. the **king of the castle** – the most important person in the locality. From the children's game of the same name; one child stands on top of a sandcastle while the other children try to knock him off.
4. a **king's ransom** – a huge, excessively large sum of money. 'You'd have to pay a king's ransom for a house that size looking on to the sea.' Originally, the money that had to be paid for the release of a captured king.

KINGDOM

5. to **send/blow to kingdom come** – to send/blow to the next world, to kill. The kingdom is the Kingdom of God. 'If the bomb explodes, we shall all be sent to kingdom come.'

QUEEN

6. to **queen/lord it** – to domineer over, to take advantage of one's rank to humiliate someone. 'I don't like the way your friend Doris queens it over the other girls in the office. Who does she think she is!'

PRINCE

7. **the prince of liars** – the biggest liar of all, the worst of liars. 'Peter is an awful liar but he is nothing compared with your brother, who must be the prince of liars.' The reference is to the Devil.
8. **like *Hamlet* without the Prince** – said when the most important person at an event is absent. 'To have the last day of the party conference without the leader would be like *Hamlet* without the Prince.'
9. **put not your trust in princes** – men of power and influence can be just as fickle and unreliable as the rest of us. 'I am not in the least surprised that the boss has forgotten about your promotion. Put not your trust in princes.' The reference is to Psalms CXLVI, 3.

LORD

10. to **live like a lord** – to live in great luxury with the best food and wine, and be waited upon by many servants. 'I don't know where he gets the money from, but he seems to be living like a lord.'
11. **as drunk as a lord** – very drunk indeed. 'When I arrived at the party last night, your boy-friend was already as drunk as a lord.' Lords had a reputation for drunkenness, because they had so much money and nothing to spend it on except their own pleasure.

ROYAL

12. a **battle royal** – a tremendous battle worthy of a contest between two kings. 'There was a battle royal going on between the two grandmothers who each wanted to look after the baby during the mother's absence.'
13. the **royal road to** – the easiest and quickest way to. 'There is no royal

road to freedom; you have to fight for it.'

1. a **royal welcome** – a splendid welcome, one that is fit for a king. 'When we arrived at a small village in Lapland, we were surprised at the royal welcome the villagers gave us.'
2. **right royal** – splendid, marvellous. 'Right royal' can also be used ironically in the sense of terrible or appalling. 'You made a right royal mess of the business while I was away; it will take months to put it right.'

KNIGHT

3. a **knight in shining armour** – a man of great nobility and gallantry who will defend our rights without asking anything in return. 'If you want my advice, I'm afraid you'll have to pay for it; I'm a solicitor, not a knight in shining armour.'

THRONE

4. **the power behind the throne** – someone with real, as opposed to nominal or symbolic, power. 'If you want a job in that company, you'd better apply to the secretary, not to the chairman. The secretary is the power behind the throne.'

CROWN

5. to **crown it all** – on top of everything else. 'Harry left his briefcase in the train, was told off by his boss for arriving late at the office, and, to crown it all, found that his house had been burgled when he got home.'

COURT

6. **a friend at court** – someone in an influential position, who is able to help you. 'I'm not worried about the consequences; I have a friend at court.'

CEREMONY

7. to **stand on ceremony** – to do something in the manner prescribed by custom or etiquette. 'Don't wait to be asked but help yourselves to the cakes. There's no need to stand on ceremony.'

THE UPPER CLASS

8. **'U' and 'Non-U'** – upper class and non upper class, based on Nancy Mitford's system of distinguishing social classes according to the words they use. For example: it is 'U' to say lavatory, and 'Non-U' to say toilet; 'U' to say napkin, 'Non-U' serviette; 'U' to have a bath, 'Non U' to take a bath.
9. the **upper crust** (humorous) – the aristocracy. 'Joan is from the upper crust; you can tell by the way she walks and talks.'

PARLIAMENT

10. **the Mother of Parliaments** – the oldest Parliament in the world, a distinction that is claimed by the Parliaments in Westminster, the Isle of Man and the Swiss cantons; but, in England, the phrase is a synonym for Westminster.
11. a **hung parliament** – one in which no single party commands a clear majority, and government can only be carried on by a coalition.
12. a **maiden speech** – the first speech a member makes in Parliament.
13. to **lobby an MP** – to canvass an MP for support of one's case by going to Parliament and requesting to speak to him.
14. to **make a U-turn** – to pursue a policy in government that is directly

opposed to one's party's election promises. **'There will be no U-turn'** means that there will be no change in policy. At the Conservative Party Conference in October 1981 Margaret Thatcher declared: 'The lady's not for turning', meaning that there would be no relaxation in the Government's fight against inflation. (This was also a pun on the title of Christopher Fry's play *The Lady's Not For Burning*, about Joan of Arc.)

1. to **paper over the cracks** – to pretend that agreement on all important issues has been reached. 'Now that the election is approaching, the party managers are papering over the cracks to impress the voters.' Papering over the cracks is a common device for concealing the structural weaknesses of a house from a buyer.
2. to **go/appeal to the country** – to call a general election.
3. a **floating voter** – a voter at a general election who has not decided which party to vote for. Having no strong opinions, he will be pushed in this direction or that like someone floating on the water.
4. to **win by a landslide** (American colloquialism) – to win an election by an overwhelming majority of seats. A landslide denotes a fundamental shift in the political and social attitudes of the electorate. In 1945 in Britain, Labour won by a landslide; in 1980, Ronald Reagan won the presidential election in one of the biggest landslides in the history of America.
5. to **rig the poll** – to conduct a poll fraudulently, as by managing the poll in one's own interests instead of putting it under the control of an independent authority.
6. to **climb/jump on the bandwaggon** – to join a popular trend for the sake of material advantage. 'When Krugerrands rose quickly in value, many investors jumped on the bandwaggon and bought as many as they could in the hope of making an easy profit.' The reference is to the custom in America of putting a band on a waggon to advertise a politician's campaign at election time. When it becomes clear who is going to win, many of the local leaders will 'jump on the bandwaggon' to show their support in the hope of obtaining a well-paid job in the newly elected administration.
7. to **kick** someone **upstairs** – to promote someone who has proved unsatisfactory to a position of nominal importance without responsibility where he can do no harm. This is done when it would be embarrassing to dismiss or demote him. Senior Cabinet Ministers are sometimes 'kicked upstairs' to the House of Lords to save them from humiliation.
8. a **hue and cry** – an outcry, public protest and opposition to an unpopular measure of the government.

   to **raise a hue and cry** – to organize opposition to an unpopular measure. 'The opposition raised a hue and cry against the government's decision to increase the salaries of the top civil servants.' Originally (*c.* 1584), the hue and cry was a system for the pursuit and arrest of criminals in which all citizens were obliged to take part (from French 'huer', meaning to shout).
9. a **witch-hunt** – a campaign against a group of dissidents within a party for advocating views that are contrary to official policy. There have been similar witch-hunts against homosexuals who occupy positions of trust in the security services. The term takes its name from the witch-hunts in the Middle Ages when thousands of young women in Europe were denounced for practising witchcraft, and burned at the stake.

1. to **be beaten at the hustings** – to lose an election to Parliament. The hustings are the open-air meetings at which the rival candidates argue their case. Husting is an Icelandic word formed by 'hus', meaning house, and 'thing', meaning an assembly.

25. WAR AND PEACE

WAR

1. **all's fair in love and war** – conventional morality does not apply to the most important activities in life.
2. to be **in the wars** – to suffer from a number of minor mishaps to one's health, all at the same time. 'A cut lip, a stiff neck and now a sore throat! You *are* in the wars, Tim!'
3. **on the war-path** – in an aggressive mood, in search of one's enemy in order to start a fight with him.
4. a **war of nerves** – constant attacks on the nerves of one's opponent, as by making propaganda against him and writing abusive letters to him. 'John and his neighbour are fighting a war of nerves against each other.'
5. a **cold war** – a diplomatic and economic struggle reflecting a high state of tension between the two power blocs which stops short of armed conflict. 'There are signs that the cold war between the West and Soviet Russia will soon be resumed.'
6. a **shooting war** – an outbreak of fighting. A shooting war is often contrasted with a cold war, when the hostility of the adversaries is limited to economic and diplomatic measures.

BATTLE, FIGHT

7. a **pitched battle** – a battle in which large forces on both sides are committed. This phrase is used in contrast with 'skirmishes' or 'guerilla warfare'.
8. **half the battle** – the first steps in accomplishing a difficult task which often decide the outcome. 'We have got the best equipment for the job; that is half the battle.'
9. to **fight a losing battle** – to engage in a struggle which one cannot hope to win. 'We all fight a losing battle with age; it's better to grow old gracefully.'
10. a **running battle/fight** – a long-protracted dispute. 'William has had a running battle/fight with his local council about the rates ever since he bought his house.' The phrase comes from naval warfare. A running battle is one that takes place between two hostile fleets while they are on the move, one advancing and the other retreating.
11. to **fight shy of** – to avoid, to keep away from. 'Paul fought shy of the law courts because the costs were so ruinously high.'
12. to **put up a good fight** – to fight hard, to be a worthy opponent. 'Although we lost the match, we put up a good fight, losing by three goals to one.'
13. to **spoil for a fight** – to seize on any pretext for a fight. 'When you pay our landlord the rent, be careful how you speak to him. He is spoiling for a fight with you.'
14. to **take the fight out of** someone – to defeat one's enemy so severely that he has no wish to continue the fight.

    to have **plenty of fight left in one** – despite a bad defeat, to be willing and able to continue the fight.
15. a **fighting chance** – a fair chance, a reasonable chance. 'Harry is very ill, but he still has a fighting chance of pulling through.'
16. to **fight it out** – to settle a dispute by fighting. 'Those boys have been quarrelling the whole term and no amount of argument is going to settle the matter. The best thing is for them to fight it out.'

1. **fighting fit** (colloquial) – in excellent physical condition. 'Andrew is fighting fit and ready to start work again.' This phrase derives from cock-fighting.
2. to **show fight** – to accept a challenge, to indicate one's willingness to fight. 'We've had a letter from the defendant. He disputes your claim and he is showing plenty of fight.'
3. to **fight tooth and nail** – to fight with the utmost ferocity. 'Our son has been accused of stealing from another boy. We are going to fight tooth and nail to defend him.'
4. to **go on the offensive** – to change one's tactics from defence to attack in a contest or argument. 'Now we have refuted Anderson's accusations, it's time we went on to the offensive and attacked him.'
5. to be **on the defensive** – to be extremely sensitive to criticism, to imagine an insult when none is intended. 'I haven't accused you of anything, Henry. Why are you so much on the defensive?'
6. to **throw** someone **on the defensive** – to seize the initiative from one's opponent and turn from defence to attack. 'The manager was complaining about my work, but I threw him on the defensive by reminding him that he had absented himself for two weeks without permission.'
7. to **blunt the attack** – to weaken the attack of one's opponent, to reduce its effect. 'At the meeting, Johnson was very critical of Hazel Smith's record, but she was able to blunt his attack by showing that he had a private grievance against her.'
8. to **go for the jugular** – to attack one's opponent in the most vulnerable place. 'Harold Wilson, ex-Premier, said that during his political career he always went for the jugular.'
9. to **open (up) a new front** – to shift one's attack to a new target, to approach a problem from a new angle. 'The replacement of a human heart by an artificial one opens up a new front in the treatment of heart diseases.'
10. to **take the line of least resistance** – (1) when on the attack, to avoid obstacles so as to keep moving forward; a very effective strategy in World War II. (2) to avoid opposition of any kind and to submit to other people's demands. 'Henry always took the line of least resistance with his wife and did whatever she wanted.'
11. to **beat a retreat** – to withdraw, to abandon a position one has taken up. 'When Roger heard that there was going to be a collection, he beat a hasty retreat.'
12. to **make a tactical retreat** – to retreat with the object of advancing later in more favourable circumstances. 'Simmonds is not pressing his claim to our land, but I think he is only making a tactical retreat. He is trying to obtain more evidence, then he will go back to the Court.'
13. to **steal a march on** – to obtain an advantage over an opponent by making a sudden surprise move. 'Davis & Hay have stolen a march on us by starting their spring sales on the same day as we open our new shop.'
14. to **give** someone **his/her marching orders** – to dismiss, to terminate someone's employment abruptly. 'Claude didn't get in until three o'clock this morning. If she does that again, I shall give her her marching orders.'
15. a **trouble-shooter** – an expert in industrial/diplomatic relations who is called in to mediate between the parties to a dispute. 'We shall need a trouble-shooter to settle our dispute with the boss.'
16. to **shoot down** – to demolish, to refute

an argument. 'If you put forward that argument, the judge will shoot it down at once.'

1. to **shoot a line** (slang) – to tell a wildly exaggerated story in order to create an impression or mislead. 'Jerry was shooting a line that his parents are friends of the American president, but no one believed him.'
2. to **shoot from the hip** – to be quick with an answer. 'I'm not going to get into an argument with Sue again; she is very sharp, and she shoots straight from the hip.' This comes from the American Wild West, when firing the first shot was essential for survival.
3. **quick on the draw** – quick to attack, or defend oneself from, an enemy. The reference is to the drawing of their pistols by American cowboys when their lives would depend on the speed of their reaction to the approach of an enemy.
4. to **go over the top** – to act rashly, wildly. 'At the auction, Mary had £50 to spend, but when she saw a painting by her favourite artist, she went over the top and bid £100 for it.' The reference is to World War I when soldiers had to go over the top of their trenches in order to move forward and attack their enemy.
5. to **leave oneself wide open** – to offer an easy target to one's opponent/enemy. 'If you complain about the noise your neighbour makes, you will leave yourself wide open when you give a party for your son's twenty-first birthday.'
6. a **pincer movement** – an attack from two opposite directions. Often used humorously. 'Let's make a pincer movement on Father about our summer holidays. You tell him you are fed up with the South Coast, and I'll show him some photographs of Crete.'
7. a **Pyrrhic victory** – an apparent victory which in fact is no victory at all. The phrase comes from the victory won by King Pyrrhus at Asculum in 279 BC which cost him many of his best men. After the battle Pyrrhus remarked: 'One more such victory and we are finished.'
8. a **sitting target** – a target that is vulnerable to attack. 'The teaching profession is a sitting target for criticism and always has been.' cf. 'a **sitting duck' 68/16**.
9. **bang/plumb on target** – right in the centre of the target, a perfect aim.
10. **an uphill struggle** – something that costs a great deal of effort and shows very little result. 'It's an uphill struggle teaching Henry Greek; he has no aptitude for languages.'
11. to use **brute force** – to use physical strength rather than one's intelligence. 'Jones was the better boxer of the two but was overwhelmed by brute force.'
12. to **hold the fort** – to accept responsibilities in the absence of the person in charge. 'I have to meet my friend this afternoon. Could you hold the fort for me until I get back?' A military phrase meaning to hold one's position and not retreat.

PEACE

13. to **hold one's peace** – to keep silent. 'I shall hold my peace until I have had the opportunity to study the facts of the case.'
14. to **make one's peace** – to put an end to a quarrel. 'It's time you made your peace with Betty. You and she have always been such good friends.'
15. a **peace offering** – a gift made with the object of ending a quarrel and restoring a friendship.
16. **peace at any price** – the avoidance of war or violence, whatever the cost.

The phrase applies not only to nations but also to private relationships. 'It's no good asking Father to support you in your row with the headmaster. Father is for peace at any price.'

1. **peace of mind** – inward serenity. 'Please telephone us as soon as you arrive. We shall have no peace of mind until we hear from you.'

26. WEAPONS

WEAPON

1. a **double-edged weapon** – a weapon which cuts both ways so that it may harm as well as benefit the user, particularly in an argument. 'If you reduce your children's pocket money, you will save money but they will hate you. It's a double-edged weapon!'

GUN

2. to **carry too many guns** – to possess strong superiority over one's opponent. 'In the debate, the proposers of the motion carried too many guns for us: they had a better grasp of the facts, and they were more experienced in public speaking.'
3. to **go down with all guns firing** – to suffer defeat fighting manfully to the very end. 'Robin was knocked out in the fifth round, but he went down with all guns firing.'
4. to **stick to one's guns** – to defend one's position against strong opposition. 'Alan has been asked by his boss to withdraw his complaints, but he is sticking to his guns.'
5. to **go great guns** – to act with energy and efficiency. 'Grandfather is going great guns and his business is booming.'
6. to **spike** someone's **guns** – to spoil someone's plans, to prevent him realizing them. 'When we heard the Simpsons were planning to buy the house next door to us to extend their shop, we spiked their guns by buying the house ourselves.' The spike (obsolete term for nail) was pushed into the barrel of the gun to stop it firing properly.
7. to bring up **the heavy guns/artillery** – the important people, the leaders. 'At the by-election, all the heavy guns were brought up to support the rival candidates.'
8. to **gun for** someone – to plot revenge on someone. 'Davey is gunning for us for taking his customers away from him.'
9. **calibre** – the relative worth of someone's mind or character. 'Sally is a nice girl with plenty of common sense but I shouldn't have thought she was university calibre.' Literally, the internal diameter of a gun.

POWDER, LOCK, STOCK, BARREL

10. to **keep one's powder dry** – to hold oneself ready for action as soon as the need arises. 'Colonel Williams is sure to attack you in the local newspaper. In the meantime, all you can do is to wait and keep your powder dry.' Powder meant gunpowder, which it was necessary to keep dry for effective use (somewhat dated).
11. **not worth powder and shot** – not worth making the effort (rather old-fashioned but still in use). 'It's not worth powder and shot writing to the Minister. There is nothing he can do to help you.'
12. **lock, stock and barrel** – everything, with nothing excluded. 'Mr Hobson was obliged to sell the house and contents, lock, stock and barrel.' The lock, stock and barrel are the three parts of a gun.

SWORD AND LANCE

13. to **cross swords with** – to fight or quarrel with. 'Jackson is a hot-tempered man; I wouldn't cross swords with him, if I were you.'

1. to **measure swords with** someone – to test one's strength against someone else. In duels, the swords were measured by the seconds in order to check that they were of the same length.
2. to **beat one's sword into a ploughshare** – to turn from war to peaceful pursuits. From the Old Testament: 'They shall beat their swords into ploughshares, . . . nation shall not lift up sword against nation . . .' (Isaiah II, 4).
3. to **break a lance with** – to have an argument with. 'It's a pleasure to break a lance with Tom; he is a very good-humoured man.'

DAGGER, KNIFE AND STILETTO

4. **at daggers drawn** – in open enmity, ready to attack one's enemy. 'The two brothers have been at daggers drawn for many years.' When the dagger has been drawn from its scabbard, it can be used at once without any further preparation.
5. to **look daggers at** – to look with hatred or fury at someone. 'Mrs Jessop looked daggers at her little son when he repeated to her guest what she had been saying about him behind his back.'
6. to **have one's knife in** someone – to bear malice towards someone, to bear a strong grudge against him. 'The manager has got his knife in me; he is making my life a misery.'
7. to **put the knife in** – to deal one's enemy a fatal blow. 'When you published Kenneth's letter, you put the knife in; his career is finished.'
8. **the knives are out for . . .** a number of people are waiting for the opportunity to strike at their enemy. A phrase that is often used in politics, for example about an ex-prime minister who is blamed for the defeat of his party at the polls.
9. **stiletto heels** – high pointed metal heels on women's shoes. 'Marie-Louise, will you please take off your shoes. Your stiletto heels are cutting our carpet into ribbons.'

SABRE, STEEL AND HILT

10. to **rattle the sabre / sabre rattling** – to make threatening noises, to attempt to frighten one's opponent/enemy into doing what one wants. 'Don't let Mr Ash frighten you. It's only sabre rattling.'
11. to **use cold steel** – to use bayonets or knives. 'Wars are no longer won by cold steel but by superior fire-power.'
12. **up to the hilt** – completely, to the very limit. 'Under the guarantee, your rights are protected up to the hilt.' The allusion is to the penetration of the full length of the sword into a body right up to the handle (hilt).

ARMS

13. **up in arms** – in open revolt, as by demonstrating, shouting insults, etc. 'The students were up in arms when they heard that their privileges had been withdrawn.'
14. **armed to the teeth** – fully armed, armed with a variety of weapons so that one is prepared for any attack.

SHOT AND TRIGGER

15. **like a shot** – at once, without the slightest hesitation. 'I would change jobs like a shot if I were twenty years younger.'
16. a **long shot** – an attempt to find an answer with very little information to assist one. 'It may be a long shot but I think Harry will marry again soon.'

1. a **shot in the dark** – a wild, random guess, one that has as little chance of being right as hitting a target in the dark.
2. **no more shots in the locker** – at the end of one's resources. The derivation of the phrase is from the lockers on board a warship in which the ammunition was stored.
3. to **call the shots** – to make the decisions. 'If you want anything done, you'd better ask Mary's housekeeper. She calls the shots in this house.'
4. a **shot in the arm** – a strong encouragement, a stimulus. 'North Sea Oil has been a shot in the arm for the economy of Great Britain.' A shot in the arm means an injection which stimulates the patient and gives him fresh energy.
5. to **have a shot** – to have a try and see how well you do. 'Table tennis is such an easy game. Why don't you have a shot at it?'
6. **trigger-happy** – willing to use force on the slightest pretext. 'The workers have gone on strike without warning us. They are in a trigger-happy mood.'
7. to **trigger off** – to precipitate, to be the immediate, as opposed to the fundamental, cause. 'It is feared that a big increase in wages for the miners might trigger off similar wage claims throughout the country.'

BULLET AND BOMB

8. to **bite the bullet** (colloquial) – to accept with courage the prospect of a fight or unpleasant experience. 'Now that Father is dead, we must bite the bullet and learn to put up with hardship.'
9. to **come as a bombshell** – to astonish, to dumbfound. 'The news that their father had left home came as a bombshell to his wife and children.'
10. to **cost a bomb** – to cost a huge amount of money. 'A Persian carpet for our sitting-room would cost a bomb. It's out of the question.'
11. to **go like a bomb** – (1) to sell in huge numbers. 'Our fur-lined boots are going like a bomb now the cold weather is coming on.' (2) (of transport) to travel very fast.

ARROW, BOLT, BOW

12. to **shoot one's last arrow** – to be left without resources in a contest. 'There are no further steps you can take against Mr Brown; you have shot your last arrow.'

    to **shoot one's bolt** – to spend one's resources prematurely in a contest. 'Jack attacked his opponent with all his strength but, by the fifth round, he had shot his bolt, and retired soon afterwards.'
13. **bolt upright** – absolutely straight. It is used to describe a sitting position. Bolt was the old English word for a short arrow for a cross-bow; hence, bolt upright means as straight as an arrow, and often expresses surprise.
14. to **draw the long bow** – to exaggerate.

OTHER WEAPONS

15. **hoist with his own petard** (literary) – injured or harmed by one's own weapon; ensnared in a trap intended for someone else. 'The strikers threatened to bankrupt their boss unless their wages were doubled. Their demand was granted, but the firm went bankrupt and they all lost their jobs. They had been hoist with their own petard.' (Shakespeare, *Hamlet*, III, iv: 'For 'tis sport, to have the engineer / Hoist with his own petard'.) The petard was a small bomb which was exploded to make a breach in a wall. Sometimes the military engineer

firing the petard was blown up with it.

1. **cannon-fodder** – men who are regarded by the high command as unimportant enough to sacrifice in war. 'I would keep out of the infantry if I were you; they are only cannon-fodder.' Fodder is the food fed to the animals on a farm.

2. to **hold a pistol to** someone's **head** – to use a dangerous threat to achieve one's ends. 'I shall have to accept the workers' demands or close the factory. They are holding a pistol to my head.'

3. to **bury the hatchet** – to end a feud with one's enemy. The reference is to the old custom of the American Indians who buried all their weapons so that they might not be reminded of past quarrels when they smoked the pipe of peace with their old enemies.

4. a **hatchet man** – a person who is expert at destroying the reputation of an opponent. 'Harvey is a marvellous hatchet man but he never says anything constructive.'

   a **hatchet job / the hatchet work** – the task of destroying the reputation of an opponent.

5. a **battle-axe** – a domineering, aggressive woman, one who likes to take charge of any activity. A battle-axe with its long handle was used as a weapon in the Middle Ages. It is not clear why the term should be applied only to women.

6. to **take up the cudgels** on behalf of a person or cause – to defend a person or cause with great energy and determination. 'Now that the editor of the local newspaper has taken up the cudgels for your campaign, you have a good chance of success.' The cudgel is a thick stick or club.

7. a **chink in** someone's **armour** – a defect or weakness in someone which makes him vulnerable to attack. 'Robin was very sure of himself, but he had a chink in his armour: mention the name Yates and he would start shouting and swearing.' cf. **'Achilles' heel' 195/8**, **'a glass jaw' 86/9**, **'to have feet of clay' 104/10**.

27. TOOLS

TOOLS

1. **it's a poor workman who quarrels with his tools** (proverb) – the inefficient and idle often put the blame for their failure on their tools, or the conditions in which they work. 'Jack blamed the school textbooks for failing his examinations although his class-mates were successful. It's a poor workman who quarrels with his tools.'
2. to **down tools** – to refuse to work, to go on strike.

SCREW

3. to **put a screw / the screws on** someone – to put pressure on someone, usually with the object of extracting money. In former times, the thumbscrew was a common instrument of torture. By turning the screw, one could increase the pressure on the victim until the pain became unbearable. Hence: to **tighten the screw,** to **give the screw another turn,** and to **screw** something **out of a person.**
4. to **have a screw loose** (slang) – to be slightly mad, not quite sane. Often used humorously to express incredulity at someone's actions.
5. to **screw up one's courage** – to make up one's mind to do something courageous or daring, to overcome one's reluctance to act. 'Colin screwed up his courage and asked his boss for a rise in his wages.'
6. to **have one's head screwed on the right way** – to be sensible and intelligent. The very opposite of 'to **have a screw loose' 211/4**.

NAIL

7. **as hard as nails** – unrelenting, without feeling or sentiment.
8. to **pay on the nail** – to pay on the exact date that money becomes due.
9. to **drive a nail into one's coffin** – to make a blunder which will destroy one's reputation or happiness. 'If you resign from the Party, you will only be driving a nail into your coffin.'

   to **drive a nail/another nail/a final nail into** someone's **coffin** – to do someone an injury which will destroy his reputation or happiness. 'I've had a disastrous year anyway, but Joan's memoirs have driven the final nail into my coffin.'
10. **as dead as a door-nail** – dead beyond any doubt. It can apply to causes and campaigns, as well as people. 'The campaign for spelling reform is as dead as a door-nail.' cf. **'as dead as mutton' 161/14**, **'as dead as Queen Anne' 193/15**.
11. to **nail a lie** – to produce certain, unquestionable proof of a lie. 'That's one lie we have nailed. I wonder how many more lies the witness has told.'
12. to **hit the nail on the head** – to find exactly the right answer to a problem in one or two words.

HAMMER AND TONGS

13. to **come under the hammer** – to be sold by an auctioneer, to be put up for auction. The auctioneer indicates his acceptance of a bid by striking the table with his hammer.
14. to **hammer a point home** – to emphasize a point one has made in an argument by repeating it with great force.
15. to **hammer out** a scheme – to decide on a scheme after the most thorough and intensive examination of the difficulties, often in the course of discussion and argument.

1. to go for someone **hammer and tongs** – to quarrel furiously with someone. 'At the meeting the hecklers were going for the speaker hammer and tongs until the chairman threatened to have them turned out.'

   to **go hammer and tongs at** a job – to work at a job with all one's might.

2. to **take a sledgehammer to crack a nut** – to use unnecessary force to achieve one's object. 'Surely, to disconnect a customer's electricity because he owes the Electricity Board £3 was taking a sledgehammer to crack a nut.'

3. **not to touch** someone **with a pair of tongs** – to avoid someone at all costs, said of someone with an evil reputation. cf. **'not to touch with a bargepole' 182/1**.

SPADE AND RAKE

4. to **call a spade a spade** – to speak plainly and bluntly, to tell the plain truth without bothering with polite phrases. 'In Yorkshire we don't use flowery language; we call a spade a spade.'

5. **the spadework** – the hard, detailed work. 'Peter's research workers took two years on the spadework before he was able to start on his book.'

6. **as thin as a rake** – very thin. The comparison is probably based on the thin prongs of the rake.

7. to **rake up** the past, the ashes, old quarrels, etc. – to remind someone of disagreeable events in the past, to revive unpleasant memories. 'Why rake up the past? I thought it was all over and forgotten.'

8. to **rake in** the money – to make money very fast, to make huge profits. 'George's shop is raking the money in with their new product.'

9. a **rake-off** – an introduction fee, a commission. A rake-off implies that there is something dishonest about the transaction; for example, when an information bureau, which states that it gives the public free and independent advice, takes commissions from the businesses it recommends.

OTHER TOOLS

10. to **throw a spanner in the works** – deliberately to obstruct or ruin the results of someone's efforts. 'You threw a spanner in the works, didn't you, telling the manager your father wasn't paying him enough.'

11. to **have an axe to grind** – to allow one's private interest to affect the advice one gives. 'The principle of reducing fares to reverse the decline in the number of passengers was supported by many independent transport specialists with no political axes to grind' (The *Observer* Profile, 12 December 1982).

12. to **axe a job** – to abolish a job in order to save money. The job may be in the private or the public sector.

    to **be axed** – to lose one's job, to be made redundant for the sake of economy. 'Paul is afraid he'll be axed from the navy; he'll be fifty next April.'

13. **the nuts and bolts** – the practical considerations. 'We have talked enough about theory. It's time we considered the nuts and bolts.' The nuts and bolts are what hold the machinery together. They play a humble but essential part in any enterprise.

14. **by hook or by crook** – by any means whatsoever, lawful or unlawful. 'Hugh will make money by hook or by crook; he won't let anybody stop him.'

15. to **swallow hook, line and sinker/anchor** – to believe every detail of a story. 'Ted is the most credulous per-

son I have ever met. He swallowed my explanation hook, line and sinker.' From the fish that swallows the angler's hook, line and sinker, 'swallow' being a colloquialism for 'believe'.

1. to be **hooked on** – to be caught, to become addicted to a person or object. One can be hooked on a drug, tobacco, a hobby, a sport, or anything else that gives pleasure. A woman may hook a man and marry him.
2. to **let** someone **off the hook** – to release someone from an obligation, promise or admission of guilt. 'Now you have accepted Jackson's apology, you have let him off the hook.'
3. to be **on tenterhooks** – to be in a state of acute suspense, waiting for news/results. 'We've been on tenterhooks the whole morning waiting for the results of the X-rays.' The term 'tenterhooks' means tenting or canvas that has been stretched by hooks, thus producing a state of tension.

TROWEL

4. to **lay** something **on with a trowel** – to flatter grossly, to exaggerate one's praise. 'You were laying it on with a trowel, weren't you, when you told Angela she had a divinely beautiful voice!' The phrase comes from Shakespeare, 'Well said; that was laid on with a trowel' (*As You Like It*, I, ii, 113).

WEDGE

5. **the thin end of the wedge** – a small concession which is used to obtain a very big and costly one. 'If we give our workers an increase of 5 per cent in a bad year when we've made a loss, how much will they want in a good year? It's the thin end of the wedge.'

TACKS

6. to **get down to brass tacks** – to concentrate on the essentials. 'Let's get down to brass tacks, shall we? How much is each of you prepared to put into the project?'

28. NUMBERS

NUMBER, NUMBERS

1. an **opposite number** – someone who holds a corresponding post in another firm, company, etc.
2. a **back number** – (1) someone who is no longer active in his work, retired or semi-retired. 'I'd have been glad to advise you, but I haven't practised for the last ten years. I'm afraid I am a bit of a back number!' (2) any magazine or newspaper which has appeared prior to the current issue.
3. **one's number is up** – all hope for a person has been abandoned, one is doomed. 'His number is up' – he is finished, doomed.
4. to take **care of number one** – to put one's own interest before that of other people, an egoistic outlook.
5. **time out of number** – again and again, so frequently as to be uncountable.
6. **one's days are numbered** – one is approaching the end of one's life, or time in office, etc.
7. **in round numbers** – an approximate number, a number which is measured in tens, hundreds, thousands, and which does not include the numbers in between.
8. **safety in numbers** – protection provided by numerical superiority. 'I don't mind my daughter going out with a group, but I don't want her to be alone with one man. There is safety in numbers.'

SINGLE

9. to do something **single-handed** – to accomplish a task without anyone else's help. Literally, to do something with only one hand.

QUARTER

10. to have a **bad quarter of an hour** – to have a very unpleasant experience for a short period.
11. **no quarter was given** – no mercy was shown, no man's life was spared. One interpretation is that 'quarter' refers to the quarters, i.e. the lodging, given to prisoners of war by the victorious army. Hence 'no quarter given' meant 'no prisoners taken'.

HALF

12. to **go halves** – to take an equal share with somebody else.
13. to **do** something **by halves** – to do something without finishing it, superficially, unenthusiastically. Also used in the negative: 'He doesn't do a thing by halves' – he is extremely thorough in everything he does.
14. **not half** (cockney) – very much indeed, with great pleasure. '"Would you like a glass of beer?" "Not half!"'
15. to **meet half-way** – to make concessions to another person's position in a disagreement, to make a fair compromise. 'I do think you might meet us half-way, Lilian. We have agreed to go with you to the theatre, but why must it be the evening performance? What's wrong with the matinee?'
16. **one's better half** (colloquial) – a humorous reference to one's wife.
17. to **have half a chance** – a very slight chance. 'If I had half a chance, I would go to America.'
18. to **have half a mind** – to feel somewhat inclined to do something, but without any real conviction.
19. a **half-baked idea** – an idea that has not been properly thought out; colloquially: a stupid idea.

a **half-baked boy/girl** (slang) – a foolish, stupid boy or girl.

1. to **go off at half-cock** – to execute a plan before the necessary preparations have been completed. 'Our attack went off at half-cock. We should have waited until we had won the support of our colleagues.' The phrase is taken from the inadvertent firing of a gun when the hammer is set at half-cock.
2. the flag **at half-mast** – the flag that flies half-way down as a sign of respect for an important person who has died.
3. **half-way house** – a compromise between two conflicting systems. 'The college was a half-way house between a school and a university. There were no regular lessons but we were not allowed out without permission.'

ONE

4. **A.1.** – (1) the best possible. (2) in a military sense, enjoying perfect health.
5. to **be at one** – to be in full agreement (in the case of several people, to be unanimous).
6. to be **one too many for** someone – to outmatch somebody, to outwit him. 'When it comes to business, your sister is one too many for me.'
7. to **be the last one to** – to be the least likely to. 'You're the last one I would have expected to behave like that.'
8. to **have a one-track mind** – to be totally absorbed in a single topic. 'Harry has a one-track mind; he only thinks about sex.'
9. **one-sided** – to the advantage of one person and not the other, e.g. a **one-sided agreement** – an agreement which favours one party and not the other.

   to **be one-sided** – to be unfair or prejudiced.
10. to **go one better** – to outdo someone else. 'When Jack heard I had invited Mervyn to tea, he invited him to dinner. Jack always goes one better than me!'
11. **one-off** – once only. 'His novel has been selling very well but I doubt whether he can repeat his success. It was a one-off effort.'
12. to **take one with another** – to balance the advantages and disadvantages.
13. **it's all one to him** – it's all the same to him, he doesn't care.
14. **back to square one** – back to the very beginning of some task or enterprise as a result of a setback. 'My secretary has left my one and only manuscript in the taxi, so I'll have to write the book all over again. It's back to square one!' The allusion is to the game of Ludo when a player is sent back to square one if he lands on the wrong square.
15. a **one-armed bandit** – a gambling machine in which coins are inserted, usually 'fixed' so that the gambler loses his money. Hence the name 'bandit'.
16. to be a **one-man band** – to do all the work oneself without employing staff.

FIRST

17. **first come, first served** – whoever arrives first has a right to be served first. '"Why do you always serve Mr Wood before me?" "Because Mr Wood always arrives before you. First come, first served."'
18. **first and last** – more important than any other consideration.
19. **there's always a first time for everything** – just because something has not happened in the past is no reason for thinking it will never happen in the future.

1. **at first sight** – the first impression, superficially. 'He fell in love with her at first sight.'

2. **first thing** – before doing anything else. 'I'll let you have the results first thing Monday morning.'

   not to know the first thing about something – to know nothing whatever about something. 'My father doesn't know the first thing about cooking.'

3. to **give the first refusal** – to give a person the first opportunity of accepting an offer, before others are considered. 'He's given us the first refusal of his house.'

4. to **get a first** – to obtain a first-class honours degree on graduation at a university.

5. **first fruit** – first benefits from one's work. From the first fruit that is ripe for picking.

ONCE

6. **once and for all** – for the last time. 'Once and for all, the answer is no! I'm not going to pay you any more money.'

7. to **give** someone or something **the once-over** – to give someone or something a quick or superficial examination.

8. **once/twice removed** – refers to family relationships between cousins. My cousin once removed is my first cousin's child. My cousin twice removed is my second cousin's child.

TWO

9. to **put two and two together** – to draw an obvious conclusion.

   two and two make four – an obvious conclusion from the facts.

10. **two's company, three's none** – when there are three in a company there is always a tendency for two of them to make friends at the expense of the third. cf. **'three's a crowd' 217/14**.

11. a **two-edged compliment** – a comment which can be understood in two contradictory ways, one of which is to the disadvantage of the person praised. An example might be: 'He has a phenomenal memory. He can remember every word of his old speeches.'

12. to have **two strings to one's bow** / to have **a second string to one's bow** – to have two means of achieving an objective. If the first fails, you can try the second. The allusion is to the second string that bowmen kept in reserve.

13. **not to care two hoots** – to be totally indifferent.

14. **not to give two pins for** someone – not to have any care or regard for that person.

SECOND

15. to **come off second best** – to lose a fight or a contest.

16. to be **second-rate** – to be in an inferior class, e.g. a second-rate mind, a second-rate painter, a second-rate teacher.

17. to **be a good/bad second** – to run close behind the leader / a long way behind the leader.

18. **one's second self** – another person whose character, tastes and outlook are identical to one's own.

19. **second nature** – what can be done instinctively, without thought.

   to **become second nature** – to become habitual, almost instinctive. 'Bobby lies for the sake of lying. It has become second nature to him.'

20. to **second-guess** (American) – to give oneself credit for predicting an event correctly after it has already happened. 'Larry Speakes spent much of

last week angrily criticizing doctors who were now "second-guessing" about the original decision not to test the President immediately in 1984' (*Observer*, 21 July 1985). cf. 'to **be wise after the event' 119/2.**

1. to **play second fiddle** – to play a subordinate part, to be second in command. 'I am tired of playing second fiddle to William. I am every bit as good as he is.'
2. to **have second thoughts** – to change one's mind. 'He was going to buy the house but, when he saw the neighbourhood, he had second thoughts.'
3. **second sight** – the possession of extrasensory perception.

DOUBLE

4. to **see double** – to hallucinate under the influence of drink, drugs or disease.
5. to **be** someone's **double** – to resemble someone so closely that one can be mistaken for the other.
6. **double-talk** – talk that is calculated to mislead. Promises made dishonestly.
7. to **double-think** – this is a variation on double-talk and means the ability to hold two contradictory opinions simultaneously. From George Orwell's *1984* (written in 1948).
8. **double-quick** – at great speed. The phrase is derived from the command 'double', meaning run.
9. **double time** – twice the normal rate of pay; for example, double the normal wage when the work is done outside the usual working hours.
10. to **double back** – to turn round and retrace one's footsteps.
11. a **double-barrelled name** – two surnames joined by a hyphen.
12. **in double harness** – two people working together.

THREE

13. a **three-cornered fight** – a contest (e.g. for Parliament) in which three candidates participate.
14. **three's a crowd** – when two people want to be together, a third person will be in the way. cf. **'two's company, three's none' 216/10**.
15. **'Yes, Sir, yes, Sir, three bags full!'** – sometimes said of a person who is only too anxious to please, indicating a servile or submissive attitude. Taken from the nursery rhyme: 'Baa, Baa, black sheep, have you any wool?'
16. **the three R's** – Reading, Writing and Arithmetic, the three subjects which are taught in all elementary schools and are considered an essential part of anyone's education.
17. **the three wise monkeys** – these are a symbol of discretion because they see no evil, hear no evil and speak no evil.

THIRD

18. **third degree** – the pressure put on suspects by the police in some states by means of exhausting interrogation and intimidation in order to obtain information and confessions.

FOUR, FOURTH

19. **a foursome** – two partners who play against two other partners, especially at golf.
20. to **make up a four** – to join three others in a game, as in Bridge or tennis.
21. **the fourth dimension** – an imaginary dimension in addition to length, breadth and height.
22. **the fourth estate** – the Press, the other three estates being the Monarchy, Parliament and the Church.

FIVE, FIFTH

1. **two and two make five in your case** – you have drawn the wrong conclusion.
2. **the fifth column** – a wartime phrase meaning those people in an occupied country who collaborated with the invaders.

SIX, SIXTH

3. **six of one and half a dozen of the other** – there is no difference at all between one course of action and another.
4. **at sixes and sevens** – bewildered or hopelessly confused, chaotic. The phrase comes from the figures on the dice which were once used in gaming.
5. to **hit for six** – to deal an enemy a crushing blow. 'We hit the newspaper for six! For libelling us, the Court awarded us damages of £40,000 plus all our costs.' This is a cricketing metaphor: a batsman scores six runs when he hits the ball over the boundary line without it touching the ground first.
6. **six of the best** – six strokes with the cane, a school punishment. The phrase is sometimes used as the headline of a newspaper report: 'Six of the best – Mrs Todd gave birth yesterday to sextuplets. All are doing well.'
7. **sixth form** – the top form in any school.
8. **sixth sense** – a supernatural sense, a special intuition in addition to the five senses (sight, hearing, touch, smell, taste).

SEVEN, SEVENTH

9. the **seven deadly sins** – in the Christian religion these are: pride, envy, anger, lust, sloth, avarice and gluttony.
10. **seven-league boots** – this phrase which is derived from fairy tales means boots which will carry the wearer seven leagues (21 miles) at a step.
11. **in (the) seventh heaven** – a state of exaltation, bliss or ecstasy. The seventh heaven in the Muslim religion is the dwelling of Allah; in Judaism it is the home of God and the highest angels. cf. **'on Cloud Nine' 30/1**.

EIGHT

12. to have **one over the eight** – to get drunk, so called because eight drinks are usually enough to intoxicate anyone.

NINE

13. to be **dressed up to the nines** – to be dressed for a special occasion, to be dressed to perfection. 'Up to the nines' is a corruption of medieval English 'to the eyne' – 'to the eyes', meaning from head to foot. cf. **'dressed to kill' 169/8**.
14. **a stitch in time saves nine** (proverb) – a prompt correction saves a lot of labour and time later.
15. a **nine-days wonder** – something very sensational or scandalous which will be forgotten after a short time.
16. to **bowl over like ninepins** – to overcome with little or no resistance. 'The unexpected results of the election bowled them over like ninepins. They all sat silent and dejected.'
17. **possession is nine points of the law** – a legal maxim meaning that it is easier to defend one's possession of an object than to dispossess someone else.

TEN, TENTH

18. **ten out of ten** – full marks, ten marks being the maximum marks given in English schools. 'I gave Andrew ten

out of ten for his last novel. It was faultlessly written.'

1. **ten to one** – nine chances in ten that something will happen.
2. the **submerged tenth** – the lowest and most under-privileged social class.

ELEVEN, ELEVENTH

3. **elevenses** – tea or coffee or other refreshments taken at eleven o'clock in the morning.
4. **at the eleventh hour** – at the last possible moment, only just in time to save the situation.

TWELVE, DOZEN AND TEEN

5. a **baker's dozen** – thirteen. Formerly, bakers were fined for giving short weight. In order to avoid the trouble of weighing their loaves, they threw in one extra to make sure their loaves were up to the required weight.
6. to **talk nineteen to the dozen** – to talk very fast without stopping in order to prevent others from interrupting, to be excited.
7. **in one's teens** – a boy or girl aged from 13 to 19 years of age.

THIRTEEN

8. **thirteen at table** – this is considered unlucky by many people who believe that the first person to rise from a table of thirteen will die. The superstition is based on 'The Last Supper' when Jesus and the twelve Apostles were seated at the table, and Judas Iscariot, the thirteenth man, went out and hanged himself after betraying Christ.

SEVENTEEN

9. **sweet seventeen** – the age of sweetness and charm in a girl.

NINETEEN

10. the **nineteenth hole** – the bar in a golf club, a humorous phrase because there are only eighteen holes on a golf course.

TWENTY, TWENTY-ONE AND TWENTY-TWO

11. the **Roaring Twenties** – the period immediately following World War I when young men and women were enjoying a new freedom. Girls wore short skirts, smoked and danced the Charleston.
12. a **21st birthday party** – a coming of age party when the boy/girl is acknowledged by the parents to have reached adulthood.
13. a **Catch-22 situation** – a dilemma from which it is impossible to escape. 'The public are calling for less crowding in our prisons; at the same time they are demanding longer prison sentences for crimes of violence. It is a Catch-22 situation.' From *Catch 22* by Joseph Heller (1961).

THIRTY AND FORTY

14. the **hungry Thirties** – the 1930s were a period of depression and unemployment when many workers went hungry.
15. **forty winks** – a nap taken after lunch.
16. **fair, fat and forty** – refers to the middle-aged spread in women (Sir Walter Scott, *St Ronan's Well*, Ch. 7).

FIFTY AND SIXTY

17. **fifty-fifty** – in equal proportions, half and half, often used in reference to chance. 'The chances of his recovering from the operation are only fifty-fifty.'

1. the **wrong/right side of fifty** – over fifty years of age / under fifty years of age.
2. the **Swinging Sixties** – the 1960s which ushered in the 'permissive Society', 'the pill' and the 'mini-skirt'. It was a new era when young people threw off traditional restraints on sexual behaviour and expression. The word 'swinging' is connected with the swinging hips of the young woman.

NINETY

3. the **Naughty Nineties** – the period from 1890 to the end of the century which was dominated by the aesthetic philosophy of 'Art for Art's Sake' of Wilde, Beardsley and others. The exponents of this philosophy were notorious for their dandyism and decadence.

HUNDRED

4. **a hundred-and-one reasons** – many, many reasons which the speaker does not wish to enumerate.
5. **I've told you a hundred times** – I've told you over and over again. 'If I've told you once, I've told you a hundred times.'
6. **not in a hundred years** – never.
7. **not a hundred miles away** – very near here, closer than one might think. The phrase is used when the speaker does not wish to give an exact location.

ONE THOUSAND

8. **one in a thousand** – very remarkable. 'She's one in a thousand' – she has a very splendid character.
   a wife in a thousand – an outstandingly good wife.
9. **a thousand and one** – a huge number. 'He has a thousand and one ideas.'

MILLION

10. a **chance in a million** – either no chance at all or a very slim chance, a tremendous fluke.
    not one chance in a million – completely impossible.

29. SCHOOL AND EDUCATION

SCHOOL

1. to **tell tales out of school** – to talk maliciously about a person's private affairs behind his back. 'I don't want to hear any more. Don't tell tales out of school.' In this context 'out of school' means after class, when the tale-bearer has the opportunity to speak to the teacher alone.
2. a **hard school** – a strict training. 'He was brought up in a hard school which stood him in good stead later when he explored the Antarctic.'
3. a man **of the old school** – someone whose education and point of view is based on traditional principles and loyalties. 'He is a strict disciplinarian and expects his men to work hard, but he never asks them to do more than he does himself. He is a man of the old school.'
4. a **different school of thought** – a different body of opinion. When a problem has not been resolved with any certainty – in philosophy, science or art – then rival groups or schools may form which advocate a variety of theories, as for example the empirical, idealistic and marxist schools in philosophy.

CLASS

5. **top/bottom of the class** – to excel / to do badly in a particular field or subject. 'I would recommend Mr Vernon for the post; he is good at management and top of the class in administration.'
6. **in a class of one's own** – to be incomparably better than one's companions in a particular subject or skill. 'If you want a specialist in tax law, I would suggest we brief Mr Williams QC; he is in a class of his own.'

LESSON

7. an **object lesson** – a model of how something should / should not be done. 'The way the little boy acted when the burglar attacked his mother is an object lesson to us all.'
8. to **teach** someone **a lesson** – to punish or make someone feel sorry. 'The losses you made on the Stock Exchange last year should have taught you a lesson.'

   let that be a lesson to you – let's hope you will take warning from this unpleasant experience.

ANSWERS

9. a **straight answer** – a clear, simple and unambiguous answer. 'Are you going to lend me the money or not? I'd like a straight answer.'
10. to **know all the answers** – (1) to be an expert. (2) to take a smug satisfaction in one's knowledge and cleverness. 'George doesn't trouble to follow the lessons, he thinks he knows all the answers.'
11. to **answer back** – to answer insolently when corrected or rebuked. 'If you answer the teachers back, you will soon be in trouble.'

READING AND WRITING

12. to **read between the lines** – to draw conclusions about the writer's feelings from the manner and tone of the work and not from his actual words. 'Reading between the lines of Miss Prout's reference, I have the impression that her employer was not satisfied with her work, although he doesn't actually say so.'
13. to **read** something **into** a document,

letter, etc. – to put words into a work to suggest a meaning that was not intended by the author. 'We said the brochures should be ready by the end of March, but we didn't promise anything; you are reading more into our letter than we intended.'

1. to **write** something **off** – to acknowledge that something no longer has any value. 'Malcolm's house was burned to the ground and he has written it off completely.' This is a book-keeping phrase for cancelling the value of an item shown in the accounts as an asset.

   to **write** someone **off** – (1) to acknowledge that someone is no longer capable of useful work in his/her occupation. 'It is too early to write Edwards off; he has had a disappointing season but he is still capable of championship tennis, once his health improves.' (2) to dismiss someone's chances of survival. 'After three days of intensive search, there is no trace of the missing mountaineers and their chances of survival have been written off.'

SUMS

2. to **do one's sums** – to make one's calculations or estimate. 'In the course of the Minister's speech, it soon became clear that he had not done his sums.'

   to **get one's sums right** – to make a correct calculation or estimate. 'The borough treasurer was criticized by the Chairman for not getting his sums right.'

3. to **reckon without one's host** – to make one's plans or calculations without taking other people's views into account, to ignore possible opposition. Originally, to calculate the bill at an inn without asking the landlord for the bill.

4. to **take** someone's **measure** – to judge someone's character and abilities, his strengths and weaknesses. 'If I have taken Lever's measure, he is just the man we want for the job.'

5. to **stand up and be counted** – to declare one's principles openly, whatever the cost to one's career or reputation. 'If you wish to help our cause, it is time for you to stand up and be counted.' cf. 'to **have the courage of one's convictions' 119/4**.

6. **count me out** – I do not agree with you and do not wish to be counted among your supporters.

GEOMETRY

7. to **draw the line** – to set a limit to one's tolerance. 'I don't mind Carol bringing her friends home but I draw the line at strangers she's picked up in the bus.'

8. to **draw a parallel** – to point to similarities between two (historic) events or phenomena. 'It is difficult to draw a parallel between the ancient and the modern world.'

9. to **go off at a tangent** – to introduce an irrelevant subject in the course of a discussion. 'It's impossible to discuss anything with Molly; she will keep going off at a tangent.'

CIRCLE

10. to **go round in circles** – to think for a long time about a problem without getting any nearer to a solution. 'We've been arguing for the last half-hour about what we are going to do and we are just going round in circles.'

11. to **come full circle** – to return to one's starting point. 'After making and losing a fortune in America, Tom

returned to his old job at Barclays. He had come full circle.'

1. a **vicious circle** – a chain of events in which the cause of the difficulty / disorder produces an effect which intensifies the cause. 'I didn't have enough lodgers to pay the rates (tax) on my house. To pay the rates I had to sell some of the furniture. Without the furniture I lost some of my lodgers. As a result, I have less money than before to pay the rates; so I have to sell more of my furniture again. It's a vicious circle.'

SQUARE

2. to **square the circle** – to try to do the impossible. 'You'll never solve the problem; it's like trying to square a circle!'
3. **fair and square** – with the utmost frankness. 'I told Marion fair and square what I thought of her behaviour.'
4. a **square deal** – fair treatment. 'Tom always gave his workers a square deal.'
5. to **square accounts** – to revenge oneself on someone. 'Wallis has treated me with contempt in front of my friends; I intend to square accounts with him.'
6. to **square an account** – to pay a bill.
7. **all square** – a golfing phrase, meaning that the score is even. 'Dick won the eleventh hole to make them all square.'
8. **on the square** – (1) honest, straightforward, dependable. 'Miles has always been on the square with me; you can trust him to act fairly.' (2) to be a Freemason. Freemasonry is a secret religious society which goes back to medieval times when a group of stonemasons are believed to have founded it.

HISTORY

9. to **make history** – to do something important, for which one will be remembered. 'Professor Beloff has made history by establishing the first private university in Britain.'

   to **go down in history** – (of events, people) to be sufficiently important to be remembered or recorded. 'Alexander Bell has gone down in history as the inventor of the telephone.'
10. **ancient history** – something that is already familiar to everyone, nothing new. 'You've already told me that John and Mary are getting married; that's ancient history!'

GEOGRAPHY

11. to **put a place on the map** – to bring a place to the attention of the public, to make a place well-known. 'When the American film star returned to her birthplace, she put the small village on the map.'

ART

12. to **keep a low profile** – to avoid attracting attention, to be inconspicuous. 'I had no idea my proposal would arouse so much hostility. I had better keep a low profile for the next few months.'
13. **no oil painting** – not at all good-looking. 'Fred has plenty of girlfriends, although he is no oil painting.'

SLATE

14. to **wipe the slate clean** – to give someone another chance and overlook past offences. 'The judge told the prisoner that if he accepted the job offered him, he would wipe the slate clean.' The idiom has its origin in the former

custom in schools of chalking up on a slate the names of pupils who had misbehaved. When the pupils had been punished, the slate was wiped clean.

COPYBOOK

1. to **blot one's copybook** – to make a serious mistake, which damages one's record. 'If you hadn't blotted your copybook borrowing the boss's car, you would have been promoted by now.'

MARKS

2. to **give** someone **full marks** for – to give someone credit for a faultless achievement. 'Christine Bowles deserves full marks for the excellence of her latest biography.'

   to **give** someone **no marks** – to give someone no credit for his work. One can award marks on a ten-point scale in the same way as marks are awarded in English schools. 'I give the local council only five out of ten for its plan to clean up the town centre.'

SNEAK AND EGG ON

3. a **sneaking sympathy** – a sympathy for someone or something that one is reluctant to admit. 'I have a sneaking sympathy for middle-aged housewives who are brought before me for shoplifting although, as a magistrate, I shouldn't talk like that.' The word 'sneak' means to complain about a fellow pupil behind his back to the teacher, and make trouble for him.

4. to **egg** someone **on** – to encourage someone to do wrong, as for example by breaking rules. 'You shouldn't have egged Stephen on to play that joke on Mr Gibbs. Now he'll be in trouble.' The derivation is from Icelandic 'egg' meaning edge, so that the literal meaning is to put someone on the edge.

RULES AND PUNISHMENTS

5. a **hard and fast rule** – a rule that is strictly enforced and cannot be changed or varied in any circumstances. 'We have a hard and fast rule about wearing uniform at our school and we cannot make an exception for your son.'

6. to **rule with a rod of iron** – to use the utmost severity in maintaining order. 'Jack told us how his step-father ruled the family with a rod of iron; the teachers at school were quite gentle by comparison.'

7. to **kiss the rod** – to accept punishment meekly and submissively. 'If the boss expects me to kiss the rod the way the others do, he is making a mistake.'

8. to **haul over the coals** – to rebuke severely. 'I was hauled over the coals for taking the day off yesterday. I won't do that again!' The phrase meant originally to torture a person by holding him over burning coal.

9. to **be whacked** (colloquial) – to be exhausted. 'I feel completely whacked after spending the day with Jill shopping in the West End.' To 'whack' is slang for to beat or cane. cf. **'dead beat' 43/3**.

10. a **fair whack** (colloquial) – a fair share. 'If the Company can afford an increase of 15 per cent for the directors, I don't see why we shouldn't get a fair whack of the profits too!'

11. a **whacking/thumping/whopping lie** – a huge, obvious lie. 'That's a whacking lie of the Manager to say I am idle; I'm the first to arrive at the office and the last to leave.' The explanation for these phrases may be that whacking/thumping/whopping were regarded as a fit punishment for telling lies. The

verbs 'whack', 'thump' and 'whop' mean to beat.

1. a **whipping-boy** – someone who is made responsible for the mistakes and faults of another. 'The Cranes got badly sun-burned on their Pacific cruise and tried to make the travel agency the whipping-boy for their mishap for not warning them how hot the climate would be in those parts.' The whipping-boy was a boy who was educated with a prince and whipped whenever the prince deserved punishment, because tutors were not permitted to hit a child of the royal blood.

BOY

2. a **new boy** – someone who is new to a position of employment or a place of work. 'I'd be grateful if you could please explain the office routine to me; I'm a new boy here.' Boys in their first term at school (in particular, boarding school) are referred to as new boys.
3. the **old boy network** – an association of ex-public school boys, i.e. old boys, who obtain jobs for one another on the basis of their common background, rather than merit.

30. WORK AND OCCUPATIONS

WORK

1. to **have one's work cut out** – to accomplish a task only with the greatest difficulty. 'We shall have our work cut out to get the house ready in time for the wedding reception.' Literally, to work to a plan prepared by someone else.
2. to **make light work of** – to accomplish a task very easily, with little effort or trouble. 'Vivien made light work of her O-level papers; they were much easier than she had expected.'
3. to **work to rule** – to obey the rule-book (i.e. one's working instructions), with exaggerated care, so as to bring about a slow-down in the service; a tactic of the trade unions for putting pressure on the employer.
4. to **work wonders / to work like magic** – to have an astonishing effect. 'That medicine the doctor prescribed for me has worked wonders for my rheumatism; I have no pain now.'
5. to **make short work of** someone/something – to dispose of someone or something very quickly and easily. 'Rupert jumped on the burglar from behind and made short work of him.' 'The children made short work of the Christmas pudding, which disappeared very quickly.'
6. to **work off steam** – to find an outlet for one's energy or feelings. 'In the afternoons, the boys work off steam on the football field.'
7. a **nasty piece of work** – someone of bad character, false and cruel. 'I am sorry you are going out with Beaney. He is a nasty piece of work.'
8. a **glutton for** work/punishment – someone who welcomes the opportunity of working hard for long hours. 'Don't tell me you've brought your work home after nine hours at the office; you are a glutton for work!'

JOB

9. to **have a job** (colloquial) – to have difficulty in doing something. 'I had a job making Pierre understand me. My French is very weak and he doesn't know any English.'
10. an **inside job** – a burglary committed with the assistance of an employee or relation of the person robbed. 'It must have been an inside job, otherwise how could the thieves have known where the jewellery was hidden?'
11. a **put-up job** – something arranged beforehand with a deceitful or criminal purpose. 'We were burgled two days after the new window-cleaner started work. The police think it was a put-up job.'
12. **just the job** – exactly what is wanted. 'Your car is just the job for London – cheap to run, and small enough to park anywhere.'
13. **it's a good job** – it's a good thing; it's lucky that. 'It's a good job you weren't at home when Jim called; he was in such a bad temper.'
14. to **make the best of a bad job** – to try to gain as much advantage as possible from an unsatisfactory situation. 'At least the post will give you the opportunity to learn Spanish. Why don't you make the best of a bad job instead of grumbling all the time.'
15. to **give** something **up as a bad job** – to abandon an attempt to do something because it is too difficult or impossible. 'Having failed the driving test three times, Ralph gave it up as a bad job.'

1. **jobs for the boys** – the giving of the best positions by those in authority to their relations, friends and supporters. Selection for the jobs is based on favour not merit.

PROFESSION

2. **the oldest profession** – prostitution.

OCCUPATIONS: THE CHURCH

3. to **go into the church** – to be ordained as a priest in the church.
4. a **broad church** – an organization which tolerates a wide range of ideas and policies among its supporters. 'The traditional Labour Party has always been a broad church with room for social democrats and Marxists.'
5. **as poor as a church-mouse** – very poor, because there is little or no food in most churches for mice to feed on. As the Germans have the same phrase in their language: 'So arm wie eine Kirchenmaus', it is possible that the Saxons introduced it to Britain in the fifth- or sixth-century invasions.
6. **high priest** – the leading exponent of a theory or doctrine. 'Sigmund Freud was the high priest of psychoanalysis.'
7. **take a pew** – make yourself comfortable, sit down. Often said casually by the host to a visitor who can only stay a short time. The pew is the bench that is fixed to the floor of the church for seating the congregation. It has no place in a private house, so its use is a little facetious.
8. **the Vicar of Bray** – a sixteenth-century vicar who changed his views in accordance with the views of each new government. The phrase is occasionally used to describe anyone who changes his views for profit.
9. **like the curate's egg** – a euphemism for something that is bad or unsatisfactory. It derives from a joke in *Punch*: a young curate on being asked whether his egg was good replied: 'It is good in parts.' He was too polite to tell his host that his egg was bad.
10. **benefit of clergy** – a privilege enjoyed by members of the Church in the Middle Ages which exempted them from criminal prosecution in the King's Courts, the Ecclesiastical Courts being much more lenient. The privilege was much abused and almost anybody who could read was able to claim 'benefit of clergy'.
11. the **parish pump / parish pump politics** – (1) a preoccupation with trivialities. (2) a derogatory term for local government and council meetings. 'I am tired of parish pump politics. We should be talking about our wages, not petty problems like canteen meals.'
12. to **give** someone **short shrift** – to treat someone curtly, impatiently. 'The Colonel gave his men's complaints short shrift.' 'Short shrift' was originally the short time allowed a prisoner for making his confession before execution. 'Shrift' meant confession and derives from Anglo-Saxon 'scrift', with the same meaning.
13. to **bear one's cross** – to bear suffering, affliction or annoyance. The suffering is usually the fault of someone else. 'To be under-estimated by men is the biggest cross I have had to bear' (Barbara Taylor Bradford, *Woman of Substance*).
14. an **odour of sanctity** – an overpowering atmosphere of piety and virtuous living. 'Although I was made welcome at the vicarage, there was an odour of sanctity about the place which made me uncomfortable.' The

allusion is to a legend in the Middle Ages that when the saints were buried, their bodies gave off a sweet-smelling odour, which came to be known as the odour of sanctity.

1. to **make a martyr of oneself** (derogatory) – to make unnecessary sacrifices in order to win sympathy and pity from one's friends. 'Why shouldn't you take a holiday like the rest of the staff? Are you trying to make a martyr of yourself?'

2. a **holier-than-thou** attitude/expression – to behave as though one were more virtuous than one's companions. 'Yes, I didn't get home until half-past two this morning, but you have come in later than that, so you needn't look at me with that holier-than-thou expression.'

3. **the holy of holies** – the most private room in a house. 'This is my husband's holy of holies where he can work without fear of being disturbed.' The Holy of Holies was the name given to the innermost apartment of the Jewish Temple where the Ark of the Covenant was kept. Only the high priest could enter this room on the Day of Atonement (Yom Kippur).

4. a **holy terror** – someone who causes a public disturbance by his rowdy misbehaviour. The term is often applied to a child who gets out of control and runs wild. 'That boy has become a holy terror to the whole neighbourhood, running his bicycle up and down the pavement all day long.'

5. to **take holy orders** – to be ordained as a priest in the Anglican Church. 'My son has just taken holy orders. He always wanted to be a priest.'

6. to **preach to the converted** – to waste one's persuasive powers on someone who is already of one's own opinion. 'I should like blood sports to be made illegal just as much as you. You are preaching to the converted.'

7. to **count one's blessings** – to remember all the advantages that one enjoys, especially when complaining about the annoyances of present-day conditions. 'Yes, it must have been disappointing not getting the job, but you should count your blessings: good health, a happy home, and a nice circle of friends.'

8. a **mixed blessing** – something that should bring joy but suffers from serious drawbacks. 'We were delighted when Mervyn gave us the puppy, but it has proved a mixed blessing; it has done so much damage to the furniture and curtains.'

9. to **give one's blessing to** – to give one's approval of. 'Although Julie is only sixteen, her parents have given us their blessing, and we are to be married in May.'

10. a **blessing in disguise** – what at first appears to be a misfortune turns out later to be a boon. 'Perhaps your son's failure to get into a university may be a blessing in disguise. He'll have no difficulty getting a job, and by the time he's 21 he'll have three years of practical experience behind him.'

11. to **take as Gospel** – to believe something to be true with absolute certainty. 'You must believe me; I'm telling you the Gospel truth.' The Gospel consists of the first four books of the New Testament (by Matthew, Mark, Luke and John) which describe the life and teaching of Christ.

12. to **give/quote chapter and verse** – to produce evidence in support of one's statements. 'I can't quote chapter and verse for what I am saying; you'll just have to believe me.' The whole of the Bible is divided into chapters and verses; so that when a priest gives 'chapter and verse' as the authority for his statements, they can be immediately verified.

13. a **baptism of fire** – someone's first test,

often painful. 'I have to visit a patient, so Dr Wake will have to take surgery; that will be his baptism of fire.' A baptism of fire is the first experience a soldier has of gun-fire.

1. **for one's sins** (humorous) – as a punishment for one's wrong-doing. 'I'm a teacher, for my sins.' Although the phrase is used humorously, it often implies dissatisfaction with one's occupation.
2. to **cover a multitude of sins** – to include a great number of undesirable possibilities. 'She calls herself a consultant on personal problems, but that could cover a multitude of sins.'
3. to be **thankful for small mercies** – to be thankful for the small advantages and consolations that can be set against a misfortune or setback. 'Almost all the furniture was destroyed but we were able to save the jewellery. I suppose we should be thankful for small mercies.'
4. **'That's your funeral!'** (colloquial and impolite) – that is your misfortune. 'You can't expect me to reduce your bill because your house has been burgled; that's your funeral!'

THE LAW

5. to **take the law into one's own hands** – to seek justice by using force or the threat of force without resorting to the law courts.
6. to be **a law unto oneself** – to live in accordance with one's own principles and ignore the law. In practice, this amounts to putting oneself above the law. 'You can't apply ordinary standards to that man. He is a law unto himself.' From Romans II, 14 (New Testament): 'These, having not the law, are a law unto themselves.'
7. **the rule of law** – the application of the law to all alike (institutions, local government, etc.), irrespective of differences in power or wealth.
8. to keep **on the right side of the law** – to obey the law but without troubling whether one's actions are honest or moral.

   to be **on the wrong side of the law** – to disobey the law. It is possible to get on the wrong side of the law unintentionally or through ignorance.
9. **the long arm of the law** – criminals are never safe from the law which has all the resources of the state behind it.
10. **in the eyes of the law** – the legal position, as distinct from the common-sense point of view. 'If a stranger enters your room and sits on your bed, he has done you no wrong in the eyes of the law unless he uses force.'
11. to **lay down the law** – to be dogmatic and prejudiced on matters of opinion. 'It's no fun arguing with you; you lay down the law every time, and that's the end of the discussion.'
12. to keep **within the letter of the law** – to obey the law in every particular while defeating its spirit. 'There's nothing I can do about the noise my neighbour makes; he switches his radio off every night at the stroke of ten. In that way he can keep within the letter of the law and, at the same time, prevent me getting any peace.'
13. **the law of the jungle** – no law at all because, in the jungle, the strongest animals prevail over the weaker. Some economists have compared the Free Market economy with the law of the jungle.
14. a **loophole in the law** – a way of avoiding the effect of the law without breaking it, when the language of the law is inaccurate or ambiguous.
15. to **call in the law** – to request the assistance of the police to protect one's rights against criminal action.
16. the **unwritten law** – a law which is

generally recognized, although it has not been committed to writing. Custom has the force of law in many parts of the world, even when it is not part of the written law. There is also an unwritten law of criminals, such as the trial and execution of men and women who betray their accomplices to the police.

1. to **have the law on** someone – to prosecute, to take legal proceedings against. 'I'll have the law on you for the damage you have done to my property.'
2. to go **beyond the law** – to go beyond the reach of the law, outside the jurisdiction. 'We can't sue him now. He is in Brazil and beyond the law.'
3. to **go to law** – to take proceedings in a court of law in defence of one's rights. 'I don't *want* to go to law, but I shall have to if he doesn't offer me fair compensation.'
4. **necessity knows no law** – someone who is desperate cannot be expected to keep the law.
5. **'The law is an ass'** – the laws of the land are often unfair and stupid. The quotation is from *Oliver Twist* by Charles Dickens, when the beadle protested at being dismissed from his post.
6. the **law does not concern itself with trifles** – the courts will not listen to petty grievances, such as claims for a few pence or complaints that the neighbours' children make rude gestures over the garden fence. The derivation is from the Roman maxim '*de minimis non curat lex*'.
7. to be **laughed out of court** – to make such an absurd claim that it arouses derision instead of sympathy. 'The demands of the union leaders were so ridiculous that they were laughed out of court by the workers themselves.'
8. to put oneself **out of court** – to take any action which disqualifies one from receiving a benefit or advantage. 'By talking like that to the secretary about the boss, you have put yourself out of court for any promotion.' In a lawsuit, a party may 'put himself out of court' if he behaves improperly, for example if he tries to bribe the judge or jury or threatens the other party with physical violence.
9. **special pleading** – an unfair way of arguing which consists in giving the words (e.g. of a contract) an unreal meaning to suit one's own case.
10. an **open and shut case** – a case whose outcome can be predicted with absolute certainty. 'There is no such thing as an open and shut case. Going to law is always a gamble.'
11. a **cast-iron case** – an irrefutable case, one that cannot possibly be disproved. 'You have a cast-iron case; I would advise you to sue without further delay.' Cast iron is iron in a molten condition which is poured into a mould, where it is cooled and sets solid.
12. to be **as sober as a judge** – to be absolutely sober. Judges have a reputation for sobriety and seriousness.
13. a **Philadelphia lawyer** – one who is celebrated for his acuteness and quickness.
14. a **barrack-room lawyer** (derogatory) – a soldier without legal training who uses the Queen's Regulations to promote his own interests and make life uncomfortable for his military superiors. Such people are always disliked by their commanding officers.
15. to **keep one's own counsel** – to keep one's thoughts to oneself. 'There are times when it is wiser to keep one's own counsel. Even the best of friends may talk.' cf. 'to **play one's cards close to one's chest' 99/7**.
16. **the devil's advocate** – an official appointed by the Catholic Church to

refute the claims put forward for admitting a person to the calendar of saints. Counsel at conference with their clients sometimes play the part of devil's advocate to test them and, if possible, to anticipate the arguments of the other side.

1. an **honest broker** – an intermediary who brings two parties in dispute together in a fair and impartial manner without showing favour to either side. 'At the Congress of Berlin in 1876, Bismarck played honest broker to Russia and Turkey.'
2. **no respecter of persons** – to treat everyone equally, notwithstanding differences in rank or importance. 'Your senior position won't help you; the judges are no respecters of persons.' A biblical reference, Acts X, 34: 'Then Peter opened his mouth and said, Of a truth I perceive that God is no respecter of persons.'
3. a **gentleman's agreement** – an agreement that has no legal force but is based solely on the honour of the parties involved. 'We have a gentleman's agreement. When you are dealing with Malcolm, that is as good as a signed contract.'
4. a **sore trial** – a painful, disagreeable experience. 'The children were a sore trial to their mother and gave her no peace, only annoyance and hard work.'
5. **trial and error** – the use of experiment to find the correct solution to a problem by eliminating all the incorrect ones.
6. a **trial of strength** with – a contest to determine which of the two participants is the stronger. 'In 1972 and 1973 the government and the miners had a trial of strength; the miners won both times.'
7. to **have a raw deal** – to suffer an injustice. 'Only £100 compensation for all your injuries! You've had a raw deal.' The phrase comes from the dealing out of cards (at card games).
8. to **put** someone **in the dock** – to make accusations against someone.

   not to be in the dock – not to have to defend oneself against an accusation. 'You are forgetting that *we* are not in the dock; *you* were responsible for what happened, not us.'
9. to make a **snap judgement** – to make a quick judgement without taking all the facts into account. 'It wouldn't be fair to you to give you a snap judgement on the telephone. If you would like to make an appointment, that will give me time to study your case.'
10. to **sit in judgement on** (derogatory) – to criticize and pass judgement on the behaviour of other people. 'You have no right to sit in judgement on Mary for coming home late; you aren't her father, and it's no concern of yours when she gets in.'
11. to **do oneself justice** – to realize one's true potential, to do work which reflects one's true abilities. 'When Roy takes an examination, he is always in such a state of nerves that he never does himself justice.'

    to **do** someone/something **justice** – to be fair in one's treatment and judgement of someone or something. 'Your portrait of Sue is a reasonable likeness but, in my opinion, doesn't do justice to her charm and vivacity.' 'I'd better not eat anything now or I shan't be able to do justice to your mother's delicious cooking this evening!'
12. **poetic justice** – a misfortune which punishes a wrong-doer just as if it had been intended by divine providence. 'It was poetic justice that, after refusing his best friend a loan of £50, Mason was mugged on his way home and was robbed of twice that amount.'
13. to **hold no brief for** – to have nothing to say in defence of. 'I hold no brief

for Stewart, but he has a right to a fair trial.' The brief is the bundle of papers relating to a client's case which is passed over to Counsel by the solicitor.

1. to **read the riot act** – to threaten someone (usually a child) with severe punishment unless he stops his misconduct immediately. 'We were having a wonderful party, when the landlord suddenly appeared and read us the riot act. He threatened to give us notice if we didn't stop the commotion.' Under the Riot Act (1715) if twelve or more people make a riot, a magistrate may read the Riot Act to them, calling on them to disperse. If the riot continues for more than one hour, they are then guilty of a felony.

2. **the small print** – conditions which may not be noticed by one party to a contract because they appear in the small print. 'The typewriter had a 24-month guarantee. However, when I read the small print, I discovered the guarantee was null and void unless I had it serviced by the suppliers every year at a cost of £70 a time!'

3. **without prejudice** – without making any admission. If a letter in a legal dispute is marked 'without prejudice' the contents are treated as confidential, and the letter may not be shown to the judge. The writer of the letter can then make an offer, without fear that his letter will be used against him in court if his offer is refused by the other party.

4. to **sign one's own death-warrant** – to bring about one's own destruction or collapse. 'You have depended on your brother for your livelihood for the last twenty years. By quarrelling with him, you have signed your own death warrant.' Before execution of a convicted murderer, it was necessary for the responsible authority to sign the death-warrant.

5. to **send** someone **down** – to send someone to prison after he has been convicted and sentenced.

MEDICINE

6. to **doctor** something – to add to, to dilute or otherwise interfere, as by poisoning, with the quality of wine, spirits or other drinks. The term usually has a sinister meaning.

7. to **doctor the accounts** – to falsify the accounts in order to make them appear better (or worse) than they really are.

8. **just what the doctor ordered** – exactly what is needed. 'A glass of iced lemonade? After two hours of tennis in the hot sun, that's just what the doctor ordered!'

9. to **hold a surgery** – of a Member of Parliament: to listen to the complaints of his constituents and, if necessary, take up their case with the appropriate Minister. The phrase has its origin in the doctor's surgery where the patients go for treatment.

10. to **nurse one's energy** – to keep one's energy in reserve, to save it for an important occasion.

11. to **nurse a grievance** – to feel resentment against someone or something. 'Having been dismissed from the Foreign Office, Peter nursed a grievance against it all his life.'

THE NAVY AND AIR FORCE

12. to be **a good sailor** – to adjust quickly to the movement of a ship at sea, without being sea-sick. cf. 'to **find one's sea-legs' 181/13**.

    to be **a bad sailor** – to be frequently sea-sick. 'Nelson was a bad sailor all his life.'

13. **a sailor has a wife in every port** – sailors have always had a reputation

for promiscuity, owing to their long absences from home.

1. **Tell that to the marines!** – Don't expect me to believe that! The phrase was originally: 'Tell that to the horse marines!' There is no such thing as a horse marine, so it is a joke phrase.
2. to be a **sky pilot** (colloquial) – a clergyman.
3. to **drop the pilot** – to dismiss an expert adviser. The classic example was the dismissal of the German Chancellor, Bismarck, by Kaiser Wilhelm II in 1891.
4. a **pilot scheme** – an experiment to test the demand for a product without incurring heavy expenditure on its production or sale. 'Before you spend a lot of money on your invention, you should try a pilot scheme to see whether there is any interest in the idea.' A pilot is a guide who steers ships into and out of harbour.

THE ARMY

5. to **come the old soldier** – to offer advice on how to do a job instead of doing it oneself, to claim superior knowledge because of one's long experience of the work. 'You needn't come the old soldier with me. I've been in the job as long as you.'
6. to **soldier on** – to persevere, despite setbacks and defeats. Soldiers are expected to fight on, even when they suffer defeats. 'The Government is expected to soldier on until the end of its term, although it has lost its majority in the House, and popular support in the country.'
7. **soldiers of fortune** – men who offer their services to any state; mercenaries.
8. to **swear like a trooper** – to use lurid language when swearing such as an ordinary soldier is supposed to do.
9. to **get a rocket** (slang) – to receive a severe reprimand. 'Mary got a rocket from her boss for coming back from her holiday two days late.' 'Rocket' is a military term for a self-propelled missile.
10. to **fall into line** – to conform to routine or custom. 'Naturally, you'll be expected to fall into line in your uncle's office, just like the rest of the staff.'

    to **fall out of line** – not to conform to routine or custom. Both phrases are military, deriving from the falling into/out of line of soldiers on parade.
11. **when the balloon goes up** (slang) – when events become critical. 'Have you any idea what you'll do if the balloon goes up and the company goes bust?'
12. **spit and polish** – emphasis on appearances rather than on more serious matters. 'We do 90 per cent of our business on the telephone, so we don't have to waste time on spit and polish, or trying to impress our customers with expensive wallpaper.'
13. to **pass muster** – to reach an acceptable standard, to pass inspection. 'I'm afraid I'm not a brilliant cook but the dinner should pass muster.' The 'muster' was the assembling of men for inspection, and introduction into the army or navy.
14. to **muster up one's courage/strength** – to summon up or marshal one's courage or strength. 'I could barely muster up courage to ask for a rise, although I had a right to one.' Soldiers were mustered up or collected for the defence of the country.
15. the **top brass** – the most important people in an organization. 'The top brass are coming up from London to inspect the factory, so we had better clean the place up.' In the army, the generals and staff officers at the War Office are often referred to as the top brass.

1. to **pull rank** – to remind people in an organization of one's senior position. 'I didn't like the way the managing director's wife pulled rank at the office party. I didn't see why I should give up my seat to her.' In the army, officers pull rank when they act with stiff formality off duty.
2. to **close ranks** – to unite in defence of a common interest. 'Commuters are at last closing ranks against the policies of British Rail because of the high fares.' A military phrase for uniting in the face of attack by the enemy.
3. to **break ranks** – to fail to maintain unity with one's comrades. 'If we break ranks now, that will be the end of our fight for a fair wage.' Soldiers break ranks when they retreat against orders.

THE POLICE

4. **off** someone's **beat** (colloquial) – outside one's subject. 'I'm sorry, chemistry is off my beat; I'm a physicist.' The phrase comes from the police constable's beat – the area he has to patrol when he is on duty.
5. **not to have a clue** (slang) – to be unable to account for a fact, problem, etc. 'I haven't a clue why I have been picked for this job.' A clue is a fact which may point to the solution of an investigation, in particular the investigation of a crime.

OTHER OCCUPATIONS

6. to **shepherd** someone – to guide, take care of. 'The verger shepherded us to our pews immediately behind the bridegroom.'
7. to **shepherd one's flock** – (of a priest) to attend to the spiritual needs of his parishioners.
8. the **poacher turned gamekeeper** – said of anyone with a dubious record who has been appointed to a post of trust and responsibility. 'The Irish were among the most lawless of the earlier immigrants to the US. But today the majority of American policemen are of Irish stock. The poacher turned gamekeeper!'
9. to be **as hungry as a hunter** – to be very hungry. Hunters are presumed to be hungry because of all the exercise they are obliged to take in order to catch their quarry.
10. to be **an old maid** – to be a spinster long past marriageable age.
    to be **old-maidish** – to be like an old spinster in character: fussy, prudish, gossipy.
11. **What's cooking?** (slang) – I wonder what is going to happen. What are they scheming? 'When I went into the dining-room, I could tell from the expression on the men's faces that something was cooking.'
12. a **butcher** – someone who uses brute force instead of intelligence. 'The operation was a disaster. The man behaved like a butcher, not a surgeon.'
13. **stick to your last** – concentrate on your own speciality, and don't tell me how to do mine. 'Administrators should stick to their lasts' (Winston Churchill during World War II). The phrase comes from the old adage: Cobbler, stick to your last. The last is a wooden model of a foot used by shoemakers for shaping boots and shoes. cf. **'every man to his trade' 237/1**.
14. **tailor-made** – specially designed to suit a person's particular needs. 'These language courses have been tailor-made for business executives.'
15. **like a tailor's dummy** – an effeminate or immaculately dressed man, a dandy; used in a disparaging sense.
16. **not to care a tinker's cuss** – not to

attach any value to . . . 'I don't care a tinker's cuss for her principles.'

1. to **tinker with** – to deal superficially with. 'It is only tinkering with the problem to give her sedatives. She should be examined by a specialist to find out the root cause of her illness.'

2. a **busman's holiday** – to spend one's time on holiday doing the same work as one does for a living. 'The teacher spent his summer holiday teaching at his friends' school in Italy. It was a real busman's holiday for him.'

3. an **empire-builder** – a civil servant who seeks to increase the size of his department at the expense of the taxpayer. It was originally used to describe the soldiers, explorers and administrators who extended the frontiers of the British Empire.

4. to be **taken to the cleaners** / to be **cleaned out** – to lose all one's money in business or gambling. 'We have been properly taken to the cleaners this time; we haven't a penny left.'

5. to **make a clean sweep** – to rid oneself completely of a thing or person that no longer serves a useful purpose. 'I have made a clean sweep of all my old papers that have been taking up too much space.'

6. to **come out in the wash** – of mistakes, difficulties and so on, to be soon forgotten, although they were embarrassing at the time. The reference is to the stains which disappear in the wash.

7. **'That won't wash!'** – 'Nobody is going to believe that!' The phrase is used with reference to explanations or excuses that are weak and unconvincing. 'That excuse Philip made for not keeping his appointment won't wash. If his train had really been stuck two hours in the tunnel, the story would have been in the papers.'

8. **everything is grist to his mill** – he can turn to good advantage everything you offer him. 'Your husband is a celebrity now, Mrs Holmes, so anything you tell us about him will interest our readers – everything is grist to our mill.'

9. to **put** someone **through the mill** – to subject someone to harsh training or unpleasant experiences. 'The army recruits were really put through the mill for the first three months of their training.'

   to **go through the mill** – to undergo harsh training or unpleasant experiences. cf. 'to **go/put through the hoop**' **260/8**.

10. to be **on a treadmill** – to be employed on exhausting never-ending work. 'The meals run into one another. No sooner have I cooked one meal than I have to start on the next. I am on a treadmill.' In the old days, treadmills were used in prisons as a punishment.

11. **yeoman service** – steady, effective service, a help in time of need. 'My manager has given me yeoman service for many years. I shall be sorry to lose him.' The phrase comes from Shakespeare: 'It did one yeoman's service' (*Hamlet*, V, ii, 36), and refers to the military service of the yeomen in England's armies. The yeomen in Shakespeare's days were small middle-class farmers.

12. to **jockey for position** – to manoeuvre for advantage. Newly elected councillors jockey for positions in the most important committees, just as jockeys jostle one another for the best positions on the racecourse.

13. a **cowboy outfit** (American colloquialism) – an unscrupulous business which exploits and swindles its customers. And so one reads of **'cowboy airlines'**, **'cowboy contractors'**, **'cowboy language schools'** (meaning the bad ones).

BEGGAR, THIEF, HEWERS AND CARRIERS

1. to **beggar description** – to be so remarkable or appalling that no words can describe it. 'The conditions in which the family are living are absolutely horrible; they beggar description.' The phrase 'It beggared all description' appears in Shakespeare's *Antony and Cleopatra* (II, ii, 199) with reference to Cleopatra, but is always used today in a bad sense.
2. to **go begging** – to be unwanted. 'Large numbers of jobs which no one seems to want are going begging at top London hotels' (*Daily Mail*, 23 May 1983).
3. to **beg the question** – to assume what one is trying to prove. 'The statement that travelling is good because it broadens the mind begs the question whether travelling does broaden the mind.'
4. **as thick as thieves** – on very close, friendly terms with one another. There is a similar phrase in German: 'dicke Freunde', meaning thick, i.e. close friends.
5. a **den of thieves** – a meeting place for criminals of all sorts. The phrase can be used as a term of abuse for a place.
6. **no honour among thieves** – criminals will not hesitate to give one another away to the police if they believe it is to their advantage.
7. the **hewers of wood and carriers of water** – used humorously today to emphasize the lowliness of a person's calling. 'It's no good asking me to explain your X-rays. I'm only a hewer of wood and carrier of water.' The hewers of wood and carriers of water were the bondsmen, i.e. slaves, referred to in the Old Testament (Joshua IX, 21).

CUSTOMER

8. an **ugly customer / rough customer** – a bad character who may become violent unless he gets what he wants.
9. a **slippery customer** – a deceitful person who will cheat and swindle to achieve his object.

SHOP

10. to **shop** (slang) – to get somebody into trouble by reporting him to the authorities. 'I don't want to shop you, but I will do so if I catch you stealing the men's food again.'
11. to **talk shop** – to restrict one's conversation to one's own specialized subject. 'When two doctors get together, they always talk shop.'
12. **the other shop** – the rival establishment.
13. to **come to the wrong shop** – to apply to the wrong person.
14. to **shut up shop** – (1) to stop work, to cease business for the day. 'It has turned half-past five. It's time we shut up shop.' (2) to go out of business.
15. to be **all over the shop** – to lie untidily all over the place.
16. **shoplifting** – stealing articles from a shop. 'Shoplifters always say they did it on the spur of the moment!'
17. **shop floor** – the workers on the factory floor, as opposed to the office workers and management.

    shop floor politics – action by the trade-union officials in a factory to obtain higher wages for the shop floor or factory workers by, for example, ordering a go-slow, or calling a strike.
18. to **shop around** – to go from shop to shop in search of the best bargain. 'You are paying too much for your meat. You should shop around like me.'

TRADE

1. **every man to his trade** – keep to your own job and don't meddle in other people's. cf. **'stick to your last' 234/13.**
2. to be **in trade** – to engage in an unlearned, commercial occupation, as distinct from a profession.
3. **the tricks of the trade** – methods, dodges, short cuts and so on which are only learned with experience. 'That's a trick of the trade you can't learn out of a book or at college.'
4. to **trade on** – to take unfair advantage of someone's weakness to further one's own ends. 'He trades on his lameness to win sympathy.'
5. to **trade in** – to use an old article in part exchange for a new one, paying the difference in value in cash. 'I traded in my old car for a new one and got a 25 per cent discount.'
6. to **trade up** – to improve the quality of one's merchandise, thereby justifying an increase in prices. 'As they were unable to extend their premises, the chairman proposed a policy of trading up.'
7. **in the trade** – among people employed in the trade.
8. **known in the trade as . . .** – to use a word that is peculiar to the trade in question. For example: in the theatre, actors and actresses, who are out of work, are said to be 'resting'; in business, salesmen who praise their merchandise 'talk up' its value; and advertisers, who exaggerate the value of their products and services, are said to 'puff' them.

BUSINESS

9. to **make** something **one's business** – to make it one's own responsibility. 'I will make it my business to see that he gets the job finished in good time.'
10. to **mean business** – to show that one's intentions are serious. 'He must mean business. He has paid £500 on account.'
11. to have **no business** in a place / **no business** to do something – to have no right to be in a place, no right to do a particular thing.
12. **Mind your own business!** – attend to your own affairs and don't concern yourself with mine.
13. to **send** someone **about his business** – to dismiss curtly, to end an interview abruptly.
14. **unfinished business** – scores still to settle with one's enemies.
15. **not to be in the business of** – to have no intention of . . . 'We are not in the business of dismantling the coal industry' (Norman Siddall, ex-Chairman of the National Coal Board).
16. a **bad business** – said when something has gone badly wrong. 'On his arrival he was robbed of all his money; a bad business!'

AT WORK

17. a **sleeping partner** – a partner who has invested capital in a firm but plays no part in its management. 'It's no good going to Mr Parsons for advice; he is only a sleeping partner.'
18. **the top of the ladder** – the summit of one's career or profession. 'If you want to get to the top of the ladder, you must work like a demon, and be completely ruthless.' Benjamin Disraeli likened the premiership to 'the top of the greasy pole'.
19. to be sent on a **fool's errand** – to be sent on a pointless errand, one that has no purpose.
20. to **get the message** (slang) – to understand a warning or threat. 'I was polite but I made it clear we couldn't wait

any longer for our money. He got the message all right.'

1. to be **in a rut** – to lead a boring, monotonous way of life which is difficult to change because it is so well established. 'I'm doing exactly the same work now as I was doing fourteen years ago. It's too late now for me to get out of the rut.' The reference is to the groove made by cart-wheels in a soft road.
2. to **sack / to get the sack** – to dismiss / to be dismissed. 'Harry got the sack for taking time off without permission.' In earlier times, workmen brought their tools in a sack to their place of work and on dismissal they were given back their sacks; hence, to get the sack.
3. a **rich man's hobby** – an occupation that enjoys a certain prestige but brings no money in. Before World War II, farming was described as a rich man's hobby because it was so uneconomic. The Bar was also so described shortly after the war because briefs were so scarce.

THE MUSIC SHOP

4. **music to one's ears** (colloquial) – the pleasure one feels on receiving a piece of good news, especially news of the discomfiture of an old enemy. 'I hear Matthew has had to resign from the Ministry. That must be music to your ears, Tom!' cf. **'meat and drink' 161/10**.
5. to **face the music** – to answer for the consequences of one's actions. 'We have just received a complaint about you from the Dean of your College, Jack; you will have to face the music next term.'
6. to **blow one's own trumpet** – to praise oneself publicly, to boast about one's achievements. 'You have to blow your own trumpet in business. If you don't, no one else will.'
7. to **beat the drum for** someone – to campaign noisily on somebody's behalf, to advertise his services energetically. 'While I'm in Hong Kong, I'll beat the drum for you; so you'll get plenty of publicity.'
8. to **drum** something **into** someone – to impress an idea forcefully on someone. 'It's been drummed into them ever since they were small that their country is the best in the world.'
9. to be **drummed out** – to be dismissed in a humiliating manner. 'It is shameful the way Dean cheats his customers. He would have been drummed out of any decent company years ago.' The reference is to the dismissal of an officer from his regiment for dishonourable conduct; the dismissal takes effect in front of the soldiers with the drums beating.
10. to **fiddle / to be on the fiddle** – to swindle, often by falsifying the accounts. 'I'm sure that Robert is on the fiddle; otherwise he couldn't afford all those holidays on the Riviera on his salary.'
11. **as fit as a fiddle** – to be in excellent health. 'I've worked for twenty years without a holiday and I'm as fit as a fiddle!' cf. **'as sound as a bell' 146/18**.
12. to **harp on the same string** – to make the same point over and over again. 'I wish you wouldn't harp on the same string every time I light a cigarette. I know smoking is bad for the health, but I won't give it up!'
13. to **whistle in the dark** – to talk optimistically in order to keep up one's courage. 'Have you got any evidence, Frank, for believing things are going to improve, or are you just whistling in the dark?'
14. to **whistle for it** – to ask in vain for the repayment of one's money. 'I'm afraid you've seen the last of your money, Paul. You can whistle for it as far as Richard is concerned.'

1. to **blow the whistle on** – to denounce publicly an illegal or dishonest activity. 'It's time the authorities blew the whistle on these chain-letters, because they really amount to taking money under false pretences.' The reference is to football when the referee blows his whistle to stop foul play.
2. to **pull out all the stops** – to make a tremendous effort. 'When the airport told us Mary's luggage had been lost, Father pulled out all the stops to get it back for her.' The stops refer to organ stops. When the organist pulls out all the stops, the organ is being played at full volume. The church organ is the most powerful of all musical instruments.
3. to **soft-pedal** – to understate the importance of, to moderate. 'The workers are soft-pedalling their demands in case the company goes bankrupt and they lose their jobs.' When the soft pedal is down, the piano plays more quietly.
4. to **strike the right note** – to behave in a manner that is suited to the occasion. 'In his address to the men, the army chaplain struck just the right note; he was serious without being grim and friendly without being familiar.' The reference is to a musical note.
5. to **strike a chord** – to remind one of something. 'This book I am reading strikes a chord; I must have read it before, many years ago.'
6. to **compare notes** – to exchange ideas and opinions. The reference is to musical notation.
7. **out of tune with** – out of sympathy with, having nothing in common with. 'I don't think Paul enjoyed the African tour; he was out of tune with his companions.'
8. to **call the tune** – to impose one's will. 'You must do what your uncle asks. He is paying for your training so he has a right to call the tune.' From the proverb: He who pays the piper calls the tune.
9. **to the tune of** (colloquial) – the excessive amount of . . . 'Martin was charged by the hotel to the tune of £650 a week.'
10. to **be / not to be tuned in to** – to be / not to be in sympathy with. 'The teacher was not tuned in to the feelings of his pupils.' The reference is to the tuning in of a radio to a frequency.

VOCAL AND DANCE MUSIC

11. to **change one's tune** – to change one's manner, usually after being disappointed or humiliated; but it can also be used when one has been proved wrong. 'Father said I would never make a painter, but he'll have to change his tune now that I've won first prize at the County Exhibition.'
12. to **sing** someone's **praises** – to speak very highly of someone, to praise him enthusiastically. 'Julie was singing your praises this afternoon. You must have made a very good impression on her.'
13. to **sing** (to the police) (slang) – to inform on one's criminal associates. The larger part of police evidence is supplied by the criminals themselves in the hope of getting lighter sentences.
14. to **sing for one's supper** – to do some unaccustomed work to pay one's keep. 'If Jackie wants to stay on with us after she has finished here, she will have to sing for her supper. I'm not giving her free board and lodging.'
15. to **go for a song** – to be sold for a very small sum. 'The house went for a song because the owner had to raise money quickly.'
16. to **make a song and dance about** – to make an unnecessary fuss about. 'I

don't know why Mrs Scott should have made such a song and dance about her daughter coming home at three o'clock in the morning. Angela is nineteen years old and not a little girl any longer.'

1. to **dance attendance on** someone – to be over-anxious to please and assist someone. 'I don't know why Lady Miriam should expect me to dance attendance on her all day. I'm only a friend of the family, not her servant.'
2. to **lead** someone **a (pretty) dance** – to put someone to a great deal of trouble before agreeing to what he wants. 'I must say Mr Vincent led me a pretty dance. I've never worked so hard in my life to win a customer.'
3. to **waltz home** – to win easily. 'With two of Fulham's team off the field with injuries, the Rangers should have waltzed home.'

THE PRESS

4. to have **a good/bad press** – to be reported on favourably/unfavourably in the newspapers. 'The Government have been getting a bad press recently for their handling of the unemployment problem.'
5. **the gutter press** – newspapers that depend on scandal, sex and violence to promote their sales.
6. a **press campaign** – an organized attempt by newspapers to promote a cause rather than report – and comment on – the news.
7. **on the record** – officially authorized for publication. When information has been given on the record, it is 'attributable', i.e. the name of the informant may be given, and he will accept responsibility for the story.

   off the record – not authorized for publication, given in confidence and 'non-attributable', meaning that the name of the informant may not be used by the newspaper.
8. to **sit on a story** – to delay publication of a story. A newspaper may sit on a story in order to obtain confirmation from an independent source, or to await a more favourable opportunity for publication.
9. **a tall story** – a story that is so improbable that it will not be believed by the readers of the newspaper. 'That's a tall story! Show me your evidence.'
10. to **kill a story** – to suppress publication of a story. This may happen if the government objects to publication on security grounds, or if the editor believes that publication could damage the interests of the country.
11. to **meet a deadline** – to have a story ready for publication by a specified date. The 'deadline' refers to the Andersonville prisoner-of-war camp in the American Civil War, which had a 'deadline' marked out round its perimeter; any prisoner of war caught crossing the deadline would be shot on sight.
12. to **dot the i's and cross the t's** – to pay meticulous attention to detail so as to make oneself absolutely clear. From the confusion which arises when the letters 'i' and 't' are not properly written.
13. to **mind one's p's and q's** – to be on one's best behaviour, to take great care not to cause offence. 'If you are having tea with Aunt Jane, you had better mind your p's and q's; she takes offence very quickly.' The p's and q's refer to the type that the compositor sets up for printing.
14. a **free lance** – an independent, self-employed person, who works on his own initiative and is his own master. A free lance journalist or reporter contributes articles to a number of national or provincial newspapers

without being tied to any particular one.

1. **in the know** – having access to information that is not available to the ordinary citizen. Being in the know depends primarily on having reliable sources of information.

THE BOOK TRADE

2. **in my book** – it is a matter of principle, in my opinion. 'In my book, you don't complain about the staff to the boss until you have discussed it with them first.' The book is an imaginary book of rules that everyone follows.
3. to **bring** someone **to book** – to make someone answer for his misdeeds. 'We must bring these criminals to book; they deserve severe punishment.'
4. to **throw the book at** someone – to charge someone with as many offences as one possibly can. For example, a housebreaker who attacks the landlord can be charged with unlawful entry, trespass, malicious damage to property, assault and battery. The book consists of the various sections of the Statutory Law under which the accused is charged.
5. to **read** someone **like a book** – to know exactly what someone is thinking, even before he has spoken. 'When Sally comes to my office, it is always to ask for money. No matter how carefully she leads up to the subject, I can read her like a book.'
6. to **cook the books** – to falsify the accounts for a dishonest purpose. 'I don't believe the company made anything like that profit. Peter has been cooking the books so that he can get a good price for the business.' A clever cook can conceal the basic ingredients of a dish by adding all kinds of spices.
7. to **suit / not to suit one's book** – to serve one's own interest – not to serve one's own interest. 'It may not suit his book to take the carpet back. He may not find another customer for it so quickly.'
8. to **go by the book** – to act in strict accordance with the rules and regulations, without taking personal factors into account. 'Edward would have been happier in the Civil Service than in business. Whatever the circumstances, he always goes by the book.'
9. a **closed book** – a subject about which one knows nothing, a mystery. 'Astronomy is a closed book to me.'
10. to **speak volumes / to speak volumes for** – (1) to be full of meaning. 'When the landlady showed Ralph his room, he was too polite to make any comment, but the expression on his face spoke volumes.' (2) to do a person or thing credit. 'Jack failed his examination three times before he finally passed; that speaks volumes for his determination.'

31. MONEY AND VALUABLES

MONEY

1. **money down the drain** – money wasted. 'Why do you spend all your money on a hobby like model trains; it's all money down the drain.'
2. to be **in the money / to be rolling in money** – to be extremely rich.
3. to have money **burn a hole in one's pocket** – to be in possession of more money than one is used to and to be unable to stop oneself spending it. 'James can't wait to spend all that money you gave him; it is burning a hole in his pocket.'
4. a **money spinner** – a means of making money quickly with very little effort. It usually refers to ideas or projects.
5. a **licence to print money** – a business that is so profitable that it is like having permission to print money. These words were spoken by Lord Thomson when he took over the Independent Broadcasting Authority at its inception in 1967. cf. 'to **coin money' 243/2**.
6. **hush-money** – money paid to someone in return for keeping silent about a crime.
7. **ready money** – money that is immediately available.
8. to **knock some money off** – to offer a reduction in price.
9. to **spend money like water** – to spend large sums of money recklessly without considering the cost.
10. to **throw good money after bad** – to try to recover money one has invested in an unsuccessful business by paying in still more, even though there is no chance of getting the money back. 'I wouldn't lend Henry any more money now he's lost so many of his customers. It would be throwing good money after bad.'
11. to **throw money at** something – to finance (usually at the taxpayers' expense) a business or enterprise which is losing money. 'You won't make the company efficient by throwing money at it. The only solution is to replace the management.'
12. **money is no object** – the amount of money spent is of no importance in comparison with the object desired.
13. to **put one's money where one's mouth is** – to give practical assistance to a cause one has been openly supporting by, for instance, contributing money to it. 'You have made so many speeches denouncing cruelty to animals. Isn't it time you put your money where your mouth is?'
14. to **give** someone **a run for his money** – to put someone to a great deal of trouble before he gets what he wants. 'The visiting team beat us in the end but we gave them a run for their money.'
15. to **have a run for one's money** – to get plenty of enjoyment for one's efforts, even if one doesn't achieve everything one hoped for.
16. **for my money** – if I had to make the choice. 'For my money, this bottle of champagne is better value than the others, even though it is a good deal more expensive.'

CASH

17. to **cash in on** – to take advantage of. 'The dwarf cashed in on his abnormality to advance his career in the theatre.'
18. **hard cash** – money that consists of banknotes and coins as opposed to cheques. 'The advertising agency won't accept cheques any more, only hard cash.'

CHANGE

1. to **get no change out of** – to get no help or satisfaction from. 'We complained to our neighbour about the behaviour of his children but we got no change out of him.' cf. 'to **get no joy from**' **123/7**.

COIN

2. to **coin money** – to make so much money from one's business that it is almost the same as minting it oneself. cf. 'a **licence to print money' 242/5**.
3. to **pay back in the same coin** – to retaliate by using the same method. 'Jukes has attacked us in his advertising overseas; we will pay him back in the same coin.'
4. **the other side of the coin** – the opposite standpoint, showing the disadvantages as against the advantages. 'Flying has enormous advantages over other means of transport; it is not only much faster but much less tiring. The other side of the coin is that it is boring and takes all the novelty out of travelling.'
5. to **coin a phrase** – to invent a phrase in order to express a new idea. Hundreds of new phrases are coined every year, such as: software, meaning the contents of a computer program; hardware, the computer itself; video TV, for the storing and reproduction of TV programmes; to hijack, to seize an aeroplane for political or economic ends. All these phrases have been made out of existing words which are used in a new form.

MINT

6. **in mint condition** – as good as new, perfect. 'These books are as good as the day they were printed; they are in mint condition.' The reference is to coins newly produced at the Royal Mint.

CHEQUE

7. a **blank cheque** – permission to do whatever one considers desirable or necessary. 'I've been given a blank cheque to modernize the company's equipment.'

PENNY

8. to **make an honest penny** – to make an honest living through hard work.
9. to **turn up like a bad penny** – a bad character who returns just when one was hoping to be rid of him.
10. **the penny drops** – the point of a remark is at last understood after a great deal of difficulty. 'I don't know how many times I told my husband that I was bored with fishing, but when he found me asleep over the rod one day, the penny dropped at last. He never took me fishing again.'
11. to **go/be two a penny** – to be in such plentiful supply that the pay offered is very small. 'You had better think of another way to make a living; artists are two a penny.'
12. **a penny for your thoughts** – what are you thinking about? May I know, or is it private? The person addressed is usually lost in thought. The phrase goes back to the sixteenth century.
13. **not to have / to be unable to rub two pennies together** – to be penniless, without any money; often said of someone who started without any money and got rich quickly. 'When I first met Tom three years ago, he couldn't rub two pennies together; look at him now!'
14. **not to care two pence for** – to be totally indifferent to. 'I don't care two pence what Martin thinks.' Two pence is almost valueless today.
15. to **cost a pretty penny** (colloquial) – to cost a considerable sum of money. 'It

will cost you a pretty penny to take Jackson to Court if you lose.'

1. to **spend a penny** – to pay a penny for the use of a public toilet. The price has risen in the last few years, but the phrase remains the same.
2. **penny wise pound foolish** – by trying to save a little one can lose a large sum. 'Herbert insisted on taking the bus to London Airport instead of a taxi. As a result, he missed his flight and had to pay £150 extra for a later one. Penny wise pound foolish!' cf. 'to **spoil a ship for a ha'porth of tar' 179/4**.
3. a **penny-farthing organization** – an organization that is managed inefficiently for lack of money or resources. 'We would have won the election if we had had a computer and a properly staffed office instead of the penny-farthing organization we had to make do with.' The farthing was worth one quarter of the old penny, and was abolished when the decimal currency was introduced in 1971.
4. **more kicks than halfpence** – criticism or punishment instead of gratitude. 'I get more kicks than halfpence for looking after my sister's dog when she is away on holiday. She always complains that I spoil the dog and give it too much to eat.'

SHILLING

5. to **cut off with a shilling** – to disinherit a son. In the old days it was the custom for a father, who had been displeased with his son, to pay him a shilling and tell him to leave.

DOLLAR

6. to **bet one's bottom dollar** – to be absolutely certain that something is going to happen or not going to happen. 'If my stockbroker recommends a share, you can bet your bottom dollar that it will go down.' The bottom dollar is the dollar at the bottom of a stack of banknotes, so if one bets one's bottom dollar, that means all the money in one's possession.
7. the **million /64 million dollar question** – the question that everybody would dearly like to know the answer to.

GOLD

8. a **gold-digger** – an adventuress who obtains money from men by making use of her physical attraction.
9. **as good as gold** – very well behaved. Often said of a child who has been looked after by a relative or friend in the absence of the parents.
10. a **gold-mine** – a lucrative source of income. 'This business could be a gold mine if it were properly developed.'
11. **worth one's weight in gold** – someone whose services are considered invaluable. Often said of a trusted servant, or employee who cannot be easily replaced.
12. to **have a heart of gold** – to be a kind, generous, forgiving person whose qualities are much appreciated.
13. **a crock of gold** – a large reserve of money which will support one in old age.

    the crock of gold at the end of the rainbow – a treasure that is unattainable, a mere dream.
14. **fool's gold** – a worthless product or venture which is mistaken by foolish or ignorant people for something of great value. 'A firm which fell victim to a "fool's gold" swindle has collapsed with debts of £500,000 and the loss of 50 jobs' (*Daily Mail*, 21 January 1985). Literally, iron pyrites which, being yellow in colour, are sometimes mistaken for gold.

SILVER

1. to **cross one's palm with silver** – to bribe someone.
2. **thirty pieces of silver** – the money paid to Judas Iscariot for betraying Jesus Christ. This phrase is used as a symbol of betrayal.

DIAMOND

3. **a rough diamond** – someone whose kindness is concealed by a rough, unpolished manner. 'Jane's boy-friend is a bit of a rough diamond, but he's very nice when you get to know him.' A rough diamond is a diamond before it has been cut and polished.
4. **diamond cut diamond** – a contest between two equally sharp or cunning people. 'The two experts argued fiercely with each other the whole afternoon. It was diamond cut diamond.' The diamond is the hardest substance in the world, so it can only be cut by another diamond.

32. GAMES AND SPORTS

GAME

1. **the name of the game** is . . . – the outstanding feature or characteristic is . . . ; often said of a business, institution or school. 'The name of the game at our school is science.'
2. **two can play at that game / that's a game that two can play at** – in a contest, the opponent can use the same weapon or tactics. 'If you complain to the landlord about the noise, I will complain about the people you bring in at all hours; that's a game that two can play at.'
3. a **dirty game** – unfair, unethical behaviour. 'That's a dirty game of yours, threatening your men with dismissal unless they work overtime.'
4. to **have the game in one's hands** – to enjoy a decisive advantage over one's opponent. Said of card games when one has a winning hand.
5. to **know what** someone's **game is** – to understand what someone is scheming. 'You don't deceive me; I know what your game is!'
6. to **give the game away** – accidentally to betray one's purposes. 'Philip told the girl there was a spider just behind her, but his smile gave the game away.'
7. to be **game to the end** – to show courage to the end. 'Hammersmith were easily beaten by the Rangers, but they were game right up to the end of the match.'
8. to **play the game** – to be fair and honest in one's dealings with other people.
9. to **play a waiting game** – to act with caution, waiting for one's opponent to make a mistake.
10. to be **on one's game / off one's game** – to be in good form / to be below one's usual form, when playing a game.
11. **the game is up** – the deception has been exposed. 'The game is up; would you like to make a statement now?'
12. to **put** someone **off his game** – to spoil someone's game, to cause him to play badly. 'I wish you wouldn't photograph me all the time; you are putting me off my game.'
13. a **winning game** – a venture with a strong probability of success. 'Judging by his past successes, Paul is playing a winning game.'

    a **losing game** – a venture with little chance of success. 'You are playing a losing game competing with such a large and well-established company.'
14. a **deep game** – a secret plan or scheme. 'Stephen is playing a deep game; he won't talk about it to anyone.'
15. a **mug's game** – an activity which would only appeal to a fool. 'Crime is a mug's game; criminals always get caught in the end.'
16. a **completely new ballgame** – a totally different situation in which to continue the contest or struggle. 'I have just heard the police will be charging your son with pushing drugs in addition to being in possession of them. We are now in a completely new ballgame.'
17. a **game of chance** – a gamble whose outcome depends on chance, not on skill. 'If you play a game of chance, you can always blame your bad luck when you lose.'
18. to **beat** someone **at his own game** – to compete successfully with someone in his own specialized field. 'Heinrich Schliemann, the discoverer of the ancient city of Troy, had had no training in archaeology, but he beat the experts at their own game.'

1. **'So that's the game!'** – So that's what you are trying to do!
2. to **play games with** someone – to conceal, in a teasing or cruel manner. 'Stop playing games with me and tell me what you want!'
3. **on the game** – engaged in prostitution.
4. **fair game** – a legitimate target for attack or ridicule. 'Recruits in the army are fair game for the non-commissioned officers.' The phrase comes from the shooting of birds in the open season when they have a chance of escaping and are therefore fair game.
5. **game, set and match** – the decisive point which wins an argument or debate. 'So you do agree with me! Game, set and match to me.' This is the final point in tennis that wins the player a match in a tournament or championship.
6. a **slanging match** – a fierce argument conducted in abusive language.

SPORT

7. to be **a good sport** – to act honourably and fairly, not to complain when one is beaten.

   to be **a bad sport** – to act dishonourably and unfairly, to complain and make excuses when one is beaten.
8. **a sporting chance** – a fair or reasonable chance. 'The examiner didn't give me a sporting chance to answer his questions. He went on to the next question before I could get the words out.'

TO PLAY

9. to **play oneself in** – to get accustomed to the conditions before attempting anything bold or daring. 'The new Minister only expressed his opinion after he had played himself in and learned the routine of the department.'
10. to **play** someone **up** – (1) to tease or annoy. 'That little girl is playing her mother up; she is only pretending to be ill so that her mother will give her some extra attention.' (2) in the medical sense: when a part of the body causes pain from time to time. 'In the damp weather my left leg plays me up.'
11. to **play down** – to make little of, to discount. 'When I complained to the doctor about the pain in my elbow, I could tell he was trying to play it down.'
12. to **play hard to get** – to feign reluctance or unwillingness. 'Yvonne has refused your invitation to dinner again! Don't be discouraged; she is only playing hard to get.'
13. to **play safe** – to be extremely cautious, to avoid any risk. 'If you want to be sure of catching your aeroplane, you had better play safe and allow yourself two hours to get to the airport.'
14. to **play up to** – to flatter, with the object of gaining some advantage. 'I wonder why Campbell has been playing up to Lady Soames all the evening; he never does anything without a reason.'
15. to **play along with** – to pretend to co-operate with someone for a limited period. 'If you have any proof that your boss is breaking the law, let us know. In the meantime, play along with him.'
16. **played out** – out of date, no longer in fashion. 'There are signs that TV is played out as the main source of entertainment in the home now that video has come in.'
17. to **play fast and loose** with someone – to alternate warmth with coldness in a person's affection. 'John has been

playing fast and loose with Susan for months; she should find herself another boy-friend.'

1. to **play the fool** – to amuse oneself and one's companions joking and clowning.
2. to **play it cool** / to **keep one's cool** – to act calmly, in a restrained manner. 'Whatever you do, don't lose your temper with Paul; just play it cool.'
3. to **play havoc with** – to damage, ruin or destroy. 'Tony's chicken-pox has played havoc with his complexion. I hope he will lose the scars one day.' Havoc is derived from the military command 'Havock' of medieval times, meaning 'Kill all without quarter'.
4. to **play upon words** – to pun, to make a joke by using a word in a double sense. e.g. Question: 'When is a door not a door?' Answer: 'When it is ajar.' (ajar = only a little open; a jar = a container, e.g. a jar of jam.)
5. to **play one person off against another** – to make mischief between two people, often in order to divert their annoyance from oneself. 'Don't take any notice of what Stanley says; he is trying to play us off against each other.'
6. to **play upon** someone's **feelings, sympathy, etc.** – to arouse someone's feelings in order to make use of him. 'Don't let him play on your sympathy, Monica. He is only trying to get some money out of you.'
7. **foul play** – an act of violence (or treachery) which may result in murder. 'The girl has been missing seven days from her home; the police suspect foul play.'
8. to **toy with** an idea – to consider a possibility but only half seriously. 'I toyed once with the idea of emigrating to Canada, but rejected it almost at once because of the climate.'

FOOTBALL AND OTHER BALL GAMES

9. to **kick off** – to start. 'The quizmaster kicked off by asking the first contestant where he came from.' The phrase comes from football, when the centre forward gives the ball the first kick to start the game.
10. to **kick over the traces** – to throw off all restraint. 'George is £2,000 in debt. He has been kicking over the traces again.' The traces are the harness a horse tries to get rid of so that it can kick more freely.
11. **a kick-back / a kick-back commission** – the commission paid to someone for introducing a client to an agency. The commission is usually split in equal shares between the agency and the person making the introduction. The 'kick-back' is not disclosed to the client, such payments being probably illegal. The phrase comes from football when a player kicks the ball back to one of his own side to prevent the other side getting possession of it.
12. a **political football** – a cause which is good in itself but which has become a political issue so that it is no longer judged on its own merits. 'What a pity, vivisection has become a political football.'
13. **the ball is in your court** – it is your turn to take the next step (in a negotiation, dispute, etc.). 'They have offered us £500 compensation. Are you going to accept or refuse their offer? The ball is in your court.' The reference is to tennis when the ball falls in a player's court and it is in his turn to hit the ball back.
14. to **play ball** (American colloquialism) – to co-operate with. 'If he won't play ball, we can always find someone who will.'
15. to **have the ball at one's feet** – to have the initiative, to have the opportunity one has been waiting for. 'Now that

the boss has put him in charge, Andrew has the ball at his feet.'

1. **on the ball** – alert, quick, and very keen. 'I am very pleased with my new assistant. You don't have to say anything to him twice; he is on the ball all the time.'
2. to **keep the ball rolling** – to keep the interest alive. 'At the meeting, the chairman kept the ball rolling by inviting each person to ask questions.'

CRICKET

3. **'That's not cricket!'** – that's not fair, not honourable. 'When I caught Sam listening in to their conversation on the extension, I told him in no uncertain terms that that was not cricket!'
4. to **catch out** – to find someone in the act of doing wrong. 'Tim was caught out by his teacher playing truant yesterday.' In cricket, a batsman is dismissed if the ball he has hit is caught by a fielder; he is then said to be caught out.
5. to **play a straight bat** – to act in an honest, straightforward manner. 'You can trust Mike; he always plays a straight bat.'
6. **off one's own bat** – without asking for anyone's assistance or permission. 'You shouldn't have invited Mr and Mrs Robinson to dinner off your own bat like that. You should have spoken to your parents first.' From cricket, meaning the score made by one player in a game.
7. to **bat on a sticky wicket** – to take action in unfavourable conditions. 'We have been batting on a sticky wicket all the morning; it was obvious that the judge was against us.' From cricket, when the ground is damp from the rain, and the bowler has the batsman at a disadvantage.
8. **a long stop** – a last resort, a person one can rely upon when everyone else has failed. 'Would you mind guaranteeing my loan from the bank? You can be the long stop.' In cricket, the long stop is the player who stands behind the wicket keeper to stop the ball if he misses it.
9. to be **100 not out** – to be a hundred years old and still alive. The reference is to a player's innings when a batsman has made 100 runs and is still in the game.
10. to **have had a good innings** – to have had a long life, marriage or career. 'I suppose I can't complain; I'm eighty years old and sound in health and mind. I've had a good innings.' The innings is the time the batsman spends at the wicket scoring runs.
11. to be **bowled out / bowled over** – to be taken completely by surprise, to be unable to explain one's actions. 'Poor Angela, she was bowled out by the first question on the TV show, and it was such an easy one, too.' The phrase comes from cricket, the batsman being dismissed when the ball hits his stumps.
12. to be **stumped** – to be baffled, to be unable to solve a problem or answer a question. 'When my pupils asked me for the meaning of "mundungus", I was stumped for an answer. I only remembered later that it meant bad tobacco.'

GOLF

13. to **stymie / to be stymied** – to obstruct or hinder / to be obstructed or hindered. 'I was planning to sell the house, but my sister has stymied me by letting some rooms.' A stymie is a golfing term meaning that a player can stymie his opponent's ball by interposing his own between it and the hole.

KITE

1. to **fly a kite** – to put forward an idea (usually in a ministerial speech) to test public reaction. If the reaction is favourable, the idea may be adopted; if it is not, the idea can be disowned. A kite is a framework of paper and cardboard that is flown at the end of a string, in the wind. The kite gives an indication of the direction and strength of the wind. The toy is so called because it hovers like the bird of the same name.

BOXING

2. to **keep up / to drop one's guard** – to keep one's defences in a state of readiness / to neglect one's defences. 'History shows that countries that drop their guard are often overrun by stronger and more aggressive ones.'
3. to **pull one's punches** – to struggle half-heartedly. 'If we are to compete successfully with Phillips, we can't afford to pull our punches; we must be ruthless.' A boxing term meaning to strike with less than one's full weight, to strike with a light blow.
4. to **beat** someone **to the punch** – to obtain an advantage over someone before he has time to do the same to you. 'Our book came out a week before Turner's. I'm glad we beat him to the punch.'
5. to **win a round** – to inflict a temporary but not a decisive defeat on the enemy. 'We have won a round, but we still have a hard struggle ahead of us.' A boxing match between amateurs is divided into 3 rounds, and between professionals 6–15 rounds.
6. to **win on points** – to win a useful advantage without crushing one's opponent. 'At the College debate, we won narrowly on points.' In a boxing match the contestants are given points at the end of each round, and the one who has scored more points at the end of the fight is the winner, unless the match has been terminated by a knock-out.

SKATING

7. to **put/get one's skates on** (colloquial) – to hurry up.
8. to **skate over** – to deal superficially with. 'When I discussed our project with my partner, he expressed his approval while skating over the difficulties.'

ROWING

9. **not to pull one's weight** – to leave one's share of the work to others. 'If Baxter doesn't pull his weight, we would be better off without him. He is putting too much strain on the rest of us.' A rowing phrase for moving the oar through the water without putting one's weight behind the stroke.
10. to **put one off one's stroke** – to distract someone from what he is doing. 'I wish you wouldn't criticize my driving; you are putting me off my stroke.'

ARCHERY

11. **wide of the mark** – inaccurate, wrong. 'The auctioneer's estimate was wide of the mark. He overvalued the necklace by nearly half.'
12. to **hit/miss the mark** – to get something right/wrong. 'How extraordinary! When Madame Vernet told Julie's fortune, she hit the mark every time.' The mark is the target in archery.
13. to **overshoot the mark** – to exceed the limit. 'You overshot the mark, didn't you? You spent £300 more than your grant.'
14. **nearer/closer to the mark** – almost

correct. 'When you said that unemployment would go above four million, you were nearer the mark than you realized.'

SHOOTING

1. to **shoot the (traffic) lights** – to drive a vehicle past the lights when they are showing red or amber.
2. to **shoot off** – to commence proceedings. 'Tom shot off by welcoming the delegates to the conference.'

HUNTING

3. to give someone **a fair crack of the whip** – to give someone a fair opportunity, a fair share, e.g. of time or attention. 'You can say a lot in five minutes. I thought the chairman gave you a fair crack of the whip.'
4. to be **at bay** – to be beset by a danger from which there is no escape. 'The robbers are at bay and the police are calling on them to give themselves up.'

   to **keep at bay** – to prevent a danger from materializing when one is already under threat, but usually for only a short time. 'The medicine won't cure the arthritis in your thumb but it will keep it at bay.' The 'bay' means the baying of the hounds in pursuit of their quarry.
5. **in full cry** – in eager pursuit. 'A pity you said that about Sandra in your book. Her relations and friends are in full cry.' The reference is to the barking of the hounds as they approach their quarry.

ANGLING

6. to **rise to the bait** – to respond to a hint, temptation or provocation in the way hoped for. 'Whenever I want to infuriate Dennis, I make a violent attack on modern art. He rises to the bait every time.' The reference is to fish which rise to the surface of the water for food.

CYCLING

7. to **ride in tandem** with – to work in perfect harmony with. 'The twins ride in tandem; they manage the office without a hint of disagreement, and smile approval of each other throughout the day.'
8. to **back-pedal** – to withdraw quickly from an offer or statement one has made. 'Simpson promised he would look after our dog if we wanted to take a holiday, but now he is back-pedalling on his offer.'

RIDING

9. to **take for a ride** – to make a fool of, to cheat. 'I wish I hadn't paid Hughes all that money in advance; he has taken me for a ride.'
10. to **ride roughshod over** someone – to show a complete lack of consideration for a person's wishes or feelings, to treat him with harshness. 'The landlord has ridden roughshod over us; we asked him for a month's notice, and he has given us twenty-four hours to get out.' The shoes of a horse that is roughshod have the heads of the nails projecting to prevent slipping.
11. to **ride for a fall** – to bring disaster on oneself by behaving in an arrogant or provocative manner. 'Since Brian became the boss he has made a lot of enemies among the staff; I'm afraid he is riding for a fall.'
12. to keep someone **on the trot** – to keep someone busy, always on the move. 'The sightseers kept me on the trot all day long. I am exhausted.'
13. to **trot out** – to exhibit for approval.

'When I asked the official for information about language schools in London, she trotted out a number of brochures, commenting on each with great enthusiasm.' The phrase comes from trotting a horse to show off its paces in front of a customer.

1. to **win in a canter / an easy canter** – to win easily, without having to make any real effort. 'Hazel Smith won the election in an easy canter.' A canter is short for a Canterbury gallop, the slow easy pace that the pilgrims are supposed to have ridden on their way to Canterbury.
2. to **saddle with / to be saddled with** – to burden someone with responsibility for / to be burdened with a responsibility for. 'On the death of my father, I was saddled with the debts of his estate.'
3. to **remain in the saddle** – to remain in a position of authority. 'Despite the attempts by the clergy in the diocese to remove him, the bishop remained in the saddle until his death.'
4. to keep someone **on a tight rein** – to keep someone under strict control. 'Andy's father keeps him on a tight rein; he has to account to his father for every penny he spends.'
5. to be **back in harness** – to be restored to one's employment or office. Often said of someone returning to work after recovering from an illness. 'I am so glad to be back in harness. I'm miserable when I'm away from my work.'
6. to **die in harness** – to continue to work until the day of one's death. 'I hope I die in harness; I shouldn't know what to do with myself if I retired.'
7. to **win one's spurs** – to win recognition for outstanding ability. Originally, to gain a knighthood in recognition of one's courage in battle. The knight was then presented with a pair of gilt spurs. cf. 'to **win one's colours' 15/6**.

SWIMMING AND DIVING

8. to **swim with / against the stream** – to think or act in accordance with / contrary to the views of the majority. 'Original thinkers seldom swim with the stream.'
9. **it's sink or swim** – in a desperate situation, one must resort to desperate remedies. 'I had to dismiss half our staff this morning; we are simply not earning enough to pay the wages; it's sink or swim for us.'
10. to be **in the swim** – to be active in – or aware of – what's going on. 'You didn't know that Lloyd has resigned from the government? You can't be in the swim any more.'
11. to **dive in at the deep end** – to be put to the test without any preparation. 'I'm a great believer in diving in at the deep end. The sooner young barristers get into court the better.'

JUMPING

12. to be **for / to be due for the high jump** (slang) – to incur a severe punishment. 'If Mrs Brown finds out that Yvette has been wearing her clothes, she will be for the high jump.'
13. to **jump at an opportunity** – to accept an opportunity eagerly. 'I am sure that Diane would jump at the opportunity of learning French in such pleasant surroundings.'
14. to **jump the gun** – to take premature action, with the object of gaining an unfair advantage. 'You jumped the gun, didn't you, calling here at this hour of the morning? Mrs Graham will be making a statement to the press at three o'clock this afternoon.' The reference is to a sportsman who starts the race before the gun has been fired.
15. to **jump to conclusions** – to draw an inference from insufficient evidence.

'Aren't you jumping to conclusions? Just because I have taken Jenny out a couple of times this week, it doesn't mean that I want to marry her.'

1. to be **one jump ahead** – to be in a position to anticipate the words or actions of someone else. 'I know exactly what he is going to say before he is half-way through his sentence. I am always one jump ahead of him.'

SKIPPING

2. **to skip** – to do without, to dispense with. 'Shall we skip the introduction and start the game?' The literal meaning is to jump lightly over something.

RUNNING

3. to **run rings round** someone (slang) – to outmatch someone decisively. 'Amanda is a useful tennis player but her brother Ted can run rings round her.' From athletics, when one competitor runs so much faster than his rival that he can make a circle round him and still reach the winning post first.

4. **in the long run** – ultimately, looking a long time ahead. 'In the long run it is surely better to have your own house, even if it means having to pay a big mortgage for it.'

   in the short run – in the near future, looking only a short time ahead. 'In the short run, it is better to enjoy oneself while one can.'

5. **hit-and-run** – to knock someone down and drive away without stopping. 'They should increase the penalties for hit-and-run offences.'

6. a **running commentary** – a continuous account of an event while it is taking place. 'While the two boys were fighting together outside the girls' bedroom, Margaret gave her sister a running commentary.'

7. to **make the running** – to take the lead, to be the most prominent in any activity. 'All the Robsons were talented writers, but it was the mother who made the running with her magnificent biographies.'

8. to be **in/out of the running** for – to have a chance / no chance. 'Martin's headmaster has just told us that Martin is in the running for a scholarship, but he won't say more at the moment.'

9. to be **run down** – to be lacking in vitality and energy, easily tired. 'You look run down to me; you could do with a good holiday.'

10. to **run** someone **down** – to speak ill of / to find fault with someone. 'Joe is always running me down; I wonder what he's got against me?'

11. the **runner-up** – a competitor who comes second to the winner. 'Contrary to all expectations, Miss United Kingdom, the hot favourite for the Miss World Contest, had to be satisfied with being the runner-up to Miss France.'

12. to **run out of steam** – to lose vigour / momentum. 'Our new magazine did very well at first – we had lots of new ideas we wanted to experiment with – but after the first six numbers, we ran out of steam.'

13. to be **on the run** – to be in flight from. 'The jail-breakers are on the run, but it is only a question of time before they are caught.'

14. to **run** someone / something **close** – to rival, to compete strongly with. 'You are always saying how stupid our Director is, but I must say his Deputy runs him very close!'

15. to **run away with an idea** – to make a hasty assumption which is not supported by the facts. 'You shouldn't run away with the idea that because

you haven't been elected chairman, we don't appreciate your services to the association.'

1. to be **an also-ran** – to be a failure. 'Hugh was an also-ran in everything he tried to do and deeply resented his failure.' The phrase refers to horse racing: an also-ran is a horse that comes past the winning post after the first three.

2. **the first hurdle** – the first obstacle to one's plans. 'The first hurdle will be to obtain planning permission from the local council before we start building the new extension.'

LEAPING

3. **by leaps and bounds** – with great rapidity. 'Since Tom has been taking private lessons in maths, he has progressed by leaps and bounds.'

4. a **leap in the dark** – a hazardous undertaking whose results cannot be predicted. 'When Baden-Powell started the Boy Scout movement in 1908, he could have had no idea that it would be such a success; it was a leap in the dark.'

5. to **leap to mind** – to suggest itself immediately to one, usually through an association of ideas. 'When William told us that his school-days had been the happiest time of his life, the memory of his being tossed in a blanket in the school dormitory leapt to my mind.'

CLIMBING

6. to **climb down** – to withdraw an assertion or accusation one has energetically upheld, to accept a defeat. 'You had better climb down while there is still time, or you may find yourself in court.'

CHESS

7. an **opening gambit** – the first step in a dispute or contest. 'Harvey's opening gambit was to call an emergency meeting.' In chess, the phrase means the offer of a sacrifice in the opening of a game in order to obtain a positional or tactical advantage. The idiom and the chess term do not therefore correspond in meaning. The 'opening gambit' (gambito) was first recorded in 1561 by the Spanish chess player, Ruy Lopez.

8. to **checkmate** – to make a move which puts an end at once to one's opponent's plans. 'Our main competitors have checkmated us by taking us over.' Checkmate is a chess term meaning a decisive attack on the opponent's King which brings the game to a finish.

9. **only a pawn (in the game)** – only a person of very minor importance who is manipulated by stronger forces. 'We none of us have any say in our future; we are just pawns, nothing more.' In chess, the pawns are the weakest pieces which are often sacrificed in attacks on the opponent.

10. a **stalemate** – a position in which neither party to a dispute can take effective steps against the other. In chess, stalemate occurs when one of the players is unable to move any of his pieces.

CRIBBAGE

11. to **leave in the lurch** – to desert someone in need of one's help. 'James was only asking for a small loan. How could you have left such an old friend in the lurch!' In cribbage, the loser was said to be 'in the lurch' when the winner scored 61 before he had scored 31.

GAMES OF CARDS

1. to be **a card / quite a card** – to be a notable character, to be eccentric. 'Old Mr Williams is quite a card, isn't he? He walks his dog up and down the road at all hours of the day and night.'
2. **one's leading/trump card** – one's strongest point, one's main strength. 'Jane's leading card was her charm. She played it time and again to good effect.'
3. to **play one's best card** – to employ the best means at one's disposal to get the desired result. 'In the court action Ian played his best card by calling a surprise witness.'
4. to **play one's cards well** – to act with skill and good judgement, to make the most of one's chances. 'At the interview, Jack played his cards well by trying to show how he could be useful to the company.'
5. to **hold all the cards in one's hands** – to be in a position to dictate the conditions. 'You will have to do as he says; he is holding all the cards in his hands.'
6. to **show one's cards** – to show one's intentions. 'I wouldn't show your cards if I were you. In business it is often best to keep one's intentions to oneself.'
7. **on the cards** – likely to happen, possible. 'It's on the cards that Julian will be getting married soon.' The phrase comes from fortune-telling, when the future is read in the cards.
8. to **have a card up one's sleeve** – to have some surprise or secret in reserve, unknown to one's adversary. The idiom is taken from cheating at cards, when a player conceals an ace up his sleeve.
9. to **stack the cards** against someone – to place obstacles in the way of someone's success. 'If you start a business, I'm afraid you will find the cards stacked against you. You have very little capital, and hardly any experience.'
10. to **put one's cards on the table** – to make one's intentions clear. 'Richard told me he was going to put his cards on the table but I had the impression that he was hiding something from me.'
11. **one's long suit** – one's principal strength. 'I'll be glad to help your daughter with her O-levels in history. History was always my long suit.'
12. to **follow suit** – to do exactly the same as the person immediately preceding you. 'When their host began to attack the government, Brian got up and left the room; soon afterwards, the other guests followed suit.' In many card games, a player is obliged to play a card of the same suit as the last card that has been played.
13. to **trump** someone's **ace** – to counter a strong argument / action of one's opponent with an argument / action that is even stronger. 'When the application of William Morris, the motor car manufacturer, to join a golf club was refused by its members, he trumped their ace by buying the club.'
14. to **trump up a charge** – to concoct a charge against someone by producing false evidence. 'All these charges against me have been trumped up. There isn't a word of truth in any of them.' The word derives from the French 'tromper' meaning to deceive.
15. to **come / turn up trumps** – to prove surprisingly helpful. 'Our neighbour has never had anything to do with us, but when Nancy had a bad fall, he turned up trumps, rang the hospital and gave her first aid.'
16. to **play one's last trump** – to use one's last asset. 'When Mark was made redundant as a chemist, there was noth-

ing for it but to play his last trump and return to his old school as a teacher.'

1. **a poker face** – a face that shows no expression so that one's feelings remain concealed. 'I never know whether Henry is pleased or annoyed; he has a real poker face.' The phrase comes from the card game of the same name.

BOARD

2. to be **above-board** – to be honest, respectable. The 'board' is the table on which the card games were played. When the players had their hands 'above board', they couldn't change the cards or cheat. It follows that, if someone is 'above-board', you can rely on him not to cheat you.
3. to **sweep the board** – to vanquish all one's opponents and win all the prizes.

DICING

4. **no dice** (slang) – no luck, no success. 'Sorry, no dice. I can't lend you any money this time.'
5. **as straight as a die** – absolutely honest and fair. A 'die' was originally the single form of dice, but is obsolete except in the phrases 'straight as a die' and 'the die is cast'.
6. **the die is cast** – the gamble has been taken and is irrevocable. The words used by Julius Caesar in 49 BC when he crossed the Rubicon.

THE FAIRGROUND

7. **in full swing** – of social events, going off well, a success. 'When we arrived, the party was already in full swing.'
8. **what you lose on the swings you gain on the roundabouts** – there is nothing to be said for or against a particular course of action because the advantages and disadvantages are evenly balanced. 'You eat better at the Victoria Hotel, but then it's much further from the beach than the Cavendish; what you lose on the swings you gain on the roundabouts.'

33. THE THEATRE

SHOW

1. to **steal the show** – to capture all the attention. 'At the garden party, the innocent charm of her beautiful teenage daughter stole the show from the hostess.'
2. **the show must go on** – one must fulfil one's obligations whatever the cost to one's own feelings. 'I am so sorry that your husband has lost his job, but you cannot cancel your campaign now; the show must go on.' There is a tradition in the theatre that the show must go on, whatever happens, except in the case of accident or illness.
3. to **give the show away** – to tell everyone what is going to happen. 'Father will be making an announcement after dinner to the guests, but I won't tell you what about; that would be giving the show away.'
4. **good show** – well done, splendid. 'So you will be able to come to the party. Good show!' (rather dated but still in use).

   it's a bad show – disappointing news, very wrong. 'It's a bad show Alan wasn't given leave to come; what a mean way to treat him.'
5. to **get the show on the road** – to put an idea into effect, to get something organized. 'You deserve the credit for getting the show on the road.' The 'show' was originally the theatrical company on tour.
6. **only a side-show** – an activity of only incidental importance. 'The company's work in Australia is only a side-show; the bulk of the business is in London.' In a circus, there used to be side-shows like the 'strong man', the bearded lady and the freaks who were on display in the intervals of the performance but were not part of it.
7. a **show-down** – a show of strength to settle a dispute and force a person to withdraw or apologize. 'If that lout doesn't stop annoying my sister, I'll have a show-down with him.' The reference is to poker when the players lay down their cards on the table face upwards to show the strength of their hands.

SCENE

8. **behind the scenes** – out of the public view. 'There is always a lot of manoeuvring behind the scenes before a new government is formed.' A theatrical term for all the work done behind the stage by the electricians, make-up artists, costume designers and so on (which the audience does not see).
9. to **make a scene** – to give way to one's emotions, especially anger or grief, in a dramatic manner. 'The bill is much too high, but for goodness sake let's pay it rather than make a scene.'
10. to **set the scene for** – to describe the background to an event (historic, literary, sporting, etc.). 'Before he began his lecture on the Battle of Jutland, Mr Walker set the scene for the naval cadets by describing the background to the action.'
11. to **come on the scene** – to appear, to make one's presence felt. 'Until Marx and Engels came on the scene, no one had attached any importance to the class war.'

STAGE

12. **stage-fright** – the fear experienced when speaking in front of an audience. 'Although John prepared his sermons with great care, he always had a moment or two of stage-fright when he addressed the congregation.'

A theatrical term for the nervousness of actors / actresses on the stage, especially when they are appearing for the first time. cf. **'first-night nerves' 259/3**.

1. a **stage-whisper** – a whisper that is intended to be heard by others, as a whisper on the stage is intended to be heard by the audience. 'During the headmaster's end-of-term speech, his wife would entertain the boys with her stage whispers which could be heard all over the assembly room.'
2. to **stage-manage** – to plan in detail an operation or important event. 'At the annual conference of the party, one delegate complained that the speeches had been stage-managed.' In the theatre, every detail of the production is stage-managed.
3. to **stage a recovery / a come-back** – to repeat one's earlier success, after retirement or failure. 'The majority of athletes who try to stage a come-back are unsuccessful.'
4. to **upstage** a rival – to divert attention from a rival, to put him at a disadvantage. 'The managing director resented the way Forbes was trying to upstage him at the board meeting.' An actor is upstaged when he is obliged to turn his back on the audience in order to speak to his colleague upstage, i.e. at the back of the stage. When this happens, the attention of the audience is centred on the rival upstage, and the actor at the front of the stage is at a disadvantage.

PART

5. to **throw oneself into a part** – to accept with enthusiasm a duty that has been laid on one. 'Having been unexpectedly appointed chairman of the Housing Committee on the local council, Patrick threw himself into the part with all his energy.'
6. to **look the part** of – to resemble a particular type of person in manner and appearance. 'You may hate being a captain in the Royal Artillery, but you certainly look the part.'
7. to **play a part** – (1) to assist in an activity or project, to co-operate in. 'Tom played an important part in starting the local youth club.' (2) to assume a false role, to pretend to be somebody one is not. 'Jeremy plays the part of the caring nephew to perfection, but don't let him fool you; it's her money he's after.'

PLAY, PIECE AND ROLE

8. **as good as a play** – as entertaining as a performance at the theatre. 'It was most amusing to watch Hobson wriggling under your cross-examination – as good as a play.' A comment allegedly made by Charles II on a debate in the House of Lords.
9. **the villain of the piece** – the real cause of the evil. 'There is no doubt that inflation is the villain of the piece; it has bankrupted thousands of small businesses and even put state industries in danger.' A theatrical phrase for the wicked character in a drama.
10. to **cast** someone **in the role of the villain** – to fix blame on someone, to hold him responsible for a wrong. 'Since you have cast me in the role of the villain, I hope you will give me the opportunity to reply to your accusations.' The reference is to the distribution of roles among the actors/ actresses in a theatre company.

ACT

11. to **put on an act** – to dissimulate, to act in a way that is deliberately misleading. 'That boy is putting on an act; I don't believe he has hurt himself at all.'

1. to **get in on the act** – to imitate someone else in the hope of obtaining the same advantages. 'I have been making a good living from my mushroom growing, and now I see that my neighbour is getting in on the act, too.'
2. to **get/put one's act together** – to get oneself organized. 'You had better get your act together before you lose any more customers.' This phrase comes from the circus when the members of a troupe get their act ready for the performance.

SOME MORE FROM THE THEATRE

3. **first-night nerves** – an attack of nerves that some people experience when taking part in a public event, especially when it is for the first time. 'Winston Churchill often suffered from first-night nerves on the eve of an important debate in the House of Commons.' 'First-night nerves' refers to the nervousness felt by the actors/actresses the first night a play is performed in public. cf. **'stage-fright' 257/12**.
4. to **take one's cue from** – to follow someone else's example. 'When we were staying with the Garners, we noticed that the children took their cue from the eldest boy; when he began to laugh, they would all laugh, too.' In the theatre the cue is a gesture or word spoken by one actor which serves as a warning signal for another to say his words.
5. **a dress-rehearsal for** – a final preparation for. 'In the early part of the twentieth century, five years at a public school was a dress-rehearsal for military service on the Western Front.' A dress-rehearsal is the final rehearsal when actors wear the costumes in which they will appear at the performance.
6. to be **in the limelight** – to be the centre of public attention. Limelight usually has the meaning of an intense but passing attention. 'My son was in the limelight for a few days for challenging the school bully, but the excitement soon died down.' The limelight was used in the nineteenth century for lighting the stage. It would focus on one actor on the stage, leaving the others in the dark. Limelight is produced by heating lime in a hot flame.
7. to **play to the gallery** – to court the applause of the uneducated by showing off in front of them. 'Although Borotra was one of the most brilliant tennis players of all time, he sometimes played to the gallery.' The cheapest seats in the theatre are in the gallery.
8. to **ring the curtain down** – to put an end to; used in connection with life, marriage, career, happiness, business, plans, etc. 'The scandal rang the curtain down on a promising career.' In former times a bell was rung at the end of each act as a signal for the curtain to be lowered.
9. to **pull strings** – to make use of private influence to obtain favours. 'I've had no promotion, although I've been ten years in the service. Can't you pull a string for me?' From puppeteering, i.e. the manipulation of puppets by pulling the strings.
10. **If I had a magic wand . . .** – a picturesque way of expressing a vain wish. 'If I had a magic wand, I would do away with unemployment this very moment.' In fairy stories and pantomimes, the fairy godmother accomplishes good by waving her magic wand and making a wish which is immediately realized.

TRICKS

11. **a bag of tricks / the whole bag of tricks** (colloquial) – all a person's tools or

equipment. 'I've no idea where the plumber has gone, but I'm sure he'll be back; he has left his whole bag of tricks in the bathroom.' The term comes from the conjuror's bag in which he carries his equipment for the performance of his tricks.

1. to **do a vanishing trick / one of his vanishing tricks** – to disappear suddenly when it suits someone's purpose. 'The day before the rent was due, Andy did one of his vanishing tricks.' The allusion is to the magician's art of causing a person to disappear and reappear again.
2. **that should do the trick** – that should serve our purpose. 'I've stopped the bleeding and bandaged the wound; that should do the trick until you get him to hospital.'
3. to **have a trick** – to have a habit or mannerism. 'It sounds as if the man you were talking to was Paul, because Paul has the same trick of repeating himself.'
4. to **be/get up to one's old tricks again** – to use a device (generally dishonest) that one has used successfully in the past. 'So Philip has been up to his old tricks again. It's extraordinary how many people fall for his hard-luck story.'
5. to **know a trick or two / a thing or two** – to acquire a certain cunning in the course of one's experience. 'You learn a trick or two after twenty years in business.'
6. to **play a confidence trick on** someone – to tell someone a falsehood to get money out of him. So called because the success of the trick depends on winning the confidence of the victim.

THE CIRCUS

7. to **walk a tight-rope** – to act with the greatest possible caution in an extremely delicate situation. 'The two teenage boys are always quarrelling with each other, so their mother has to walk a tight-rope between them.'
8. **to go/put through the hoop** – to undergo / to subject someone to a harsh discipline. 'The lieutenant really put us through the hoop when we joined the ship.' At circuses, lions, tigers and leopards are put through the hoop for the entertainment of the audience. cf. 'to **go through the mill' 235/9**.
9. to **have / not to have a crystal ball** – to have / not to have the means to predict the future. This phrase is often used ironically, for example: 'If I knew, Inspector Francis, how much money my company will be making this time next year, I should be only too pleased to let you know. Unfortunately, I don't have a crystal ball.' The reference is to the crystal ball used by fortune-tellers.

34. WORD AND WORDS

WORD

1. **a man of his word** – a trustworthy man who will do what he promises.
2. **a word to the wise** – one word of advice or even a hint is enough for an intelligent man. The derivation is from the Latin 'verbum sat sapienti', a word is enough to the wise.
3. **as good as one's word** – to do exactly what one has promised. Often said when the promise is unlikely to be kept. 'I didn't think for one moment Bob would keep his promise but he was as good as his word'.
4. to **break one's word** – to fail to do what one has promised. cf. to **go back on one's word.**
5. **from the word go** – right from the very beginning. 'From the word go Smithers has made trouble for us.'
6. to **give one's word** – to pledge one's honour on the truth of one's word.
7. to **give the word to** – (of officers in the armed services and the police) to command – 'The Major gave his men the word to open fire on the enemy.'
8. to **go back on one's word** – to change one's mind about keeping a promise in a way which causes great indignation. 'You can't go back on your word now; without the loan you promised us, we shall lose all our savings.'
9. to **have a word with someone** – to have a brief conversation with someone.
10. to **have the last word** – (1) to insist one is in the right in an argument. 'Denis is so argumentative; he will always have the last word.' (2) to take the final decision. 'I like your cost-cutting idea but you had better talk it over with the Manager; he has the last word.' (3) the most authoritative source of information on a subject. 'Gilbert has the last word on the life of Winston Churchill, having written many volumes on his chosen subject.'
11. **his word is law** – he must be obeyed. 'When we were children, our father expected us to do what he told us without questioning his orders. His word was law.'
12. **I don't believe a word of it** – the whole story is a lie from start to finish.
13. **in a word** – very briefly. 'Our son is bored with the office work, he dislikes his colleagues and he quarrels with the boss. In a word, he hates the job.'
14. to **keep one's word** – to do what one has promised.
15. to **leave word** – to leave a message. 'They left word for Anne at the hospital to come back later.'
16. **mum's the word** – don't talk about it to anyone. This is a secret between the two of us; 'mum' is used here to describe the expressive sound made by a person when his lips are closed. The word 'mum' is related to the verb mumble, to speak weakly, and to mummers who, in earlier times, entertained at Christmas parties in dumb shows.
17. **my word** – an explanation of surprise. 'My word!, this is the second time you've had a rise in your wages this year. Aren't you doing well!'
18. **my word is my bond** – my word is as good as a signed contract. 'You can rely on my promise, even though it is not in writing. My word is my bond.'
19. **not the word for it** – an inadequate or unsufficiently strong description. 'Impolite is not the word for it, he was downright insulting!'

1. **not to get in a word edgeways** – to find it impossible to take part in a conversation because the other person is talking continuously.

2. to **preach the word** – to preach the gospel of Jesus Christ.

3. to **put in a good word for someone** – to praise or recommend someone to a third party, who is in a position to help him. 'I would like the job Mrs Hornby is advertising. When you see her tomorrow, can you put in a good word for me.'

4. **say the word** – you only need to ask, and your wishes will be carried out. 'Say the word, and I'll marry you tomorrow.'

5. **send word** – send a message. 'As soon as you arrive, send word that you are safe.'

6. **spread the word** – inform as many people as possible. 'Jack Dickson will be speaking at the town hall at eight o'clock on Saturday. Spread the word.'

7. to **take someone at his word** – to act on the literal meaning of someone's words without making sure that he means to be taken seriously. 'I told Stephen to be sure to visit us if ever he came to Spain. Two weeks later, he arrived at our villa with six suitcases. He had taken me at my word.'

8. to **take someone's word for it** – to believe that he is speaking the truth without making further inquiries. 'Don't take my word for it – you can see for yourself.'

9. the **buzz word** – the fashionable word. 'The buzz word is 'community', e.g. 'community services', 'community care', 'community health', the 'European Community', the 'Chinese community', the 'community centre', and 'community singing'.

10. the **last word in** – the very best and most up-to-date. 'The hotel is the last word in luxury and elegance.'

11. the **operative word** – the most important word. 'You can take any route you like but please drive carefully. The operative word is carefully.'

12. **upon my word** – an exclamation expressing surprise (usually unpleasant) or impatience. 'Upon my word, what is the matter with our Managing Clerk? He is always ill – he must be a hypochondriac!'

13. the **word is** – a rumour, usually well founded, that something will happen. 'The word is that next month we shall be ordered overseas.'

14. **word came** – information was received.

15. **word for word** – literally. 'I translated the passage word for word from German into English.'

16. **word of honour** – (first person). I pledge my honour that I am telling the truth. cf. to **give one's word 261/6**.

17. **word perfect** – able to recite every word of a poem, part etc. without a mistake.

18. **word splitting** – (derogatory) making subtle distinctions, for example distinguishing between 'governance' and 'government', 'gentlemanly' and 'gentlemanlike', 'preciseness' and 'precision'. cf. to **'split hairs' 79/10**.

WORDS

19. a **man of few words** – a man who avoids conversation whenever he can. Sometimes used as a euphemism for an unsociable person.

    a **man of many words** – a garrulous person, one who prefers three words when one would have done.

1. **actions speak louder than words** – 'The clergyman had often preached against the sin of drunkenness. One day, he was arrested for being drunk and disorderly. Actions speak louder than words.'

2. to **bandy words** – to enter into an argument with someone. 'Don't bandy words with that man. He is a violent character.

3. **be lost for words** – to be so astonished or shocked that one is unable to put one's feelings into words. cf. **words fail me 263/17.**

4. **big words** – boastful words. 'We shall beat the champions easily.' 'Big words.'

5. **empty words** – meaningless words. 'Sam telephoned this morning to apologize for his behaviour last night.' 'Empty words!'

6. **famous last words** – a humorous comment predicting disaster for an impractical undertaking. 'With modern technology, we can climb Everest in half the time it took Hillary in 1953.' 'Famous last words!'

7. **hang upon someone's words** – to pay slavish attention to what someone is saying. 'Sharon is full of admiration for Paul and hangs upon his words.' 'Words' may be replaced by 'lips' with the same meaning.

8. to **have words with** – to quarrel with. 'Ever since my sister had words with our neighbour, he hasn't spoken to us.'

9. **in other words** – put in another way in order to summarize what the speaker/writer has said or to deduce his true intention from the words he has used. 'Anne is sorry she can't come with us to France but the crossing always makes her feel sick and the trip would be too expensive.' 'In other words, she doesn't want to come with us!'

10. **let the words stand** – make no change. 'The editor is satisfied with the original wording of your article. Let the words stand.'

11. **mark my words** – listen carefully to what I am telling you. 'Mark my words, the boy will ruin himself before he is forty,' said by George V about his son, Edward Prince of Wales, shortly before the death of the King.

12. **not in so many words** – not actually said, although it was clearly meant. 'Did Margaret refuse your offer of help?' 'Not in so many words, but it was obvious from her manner that she did not want any help from me.'

13. **not to mince one's words** – to speak bluntly without troubling to be tactful. 'I won't mince my words: you are rude to the staff and insolent to the Manager; you will have to go.'

14. **too (adjective) for words** – too (adjective) to be expressed in words. 'Because of the epidemic we can't leave the hospital. It is too sickening for words.' Many adjectives can be used with this idiom, most of which express the speaker's feelings, e.g., beautiful, ugly, frightful, boring, annoying, exasperating, sickening, disgusting and disappointing.

15. **waste words on someone** – waste time and effort speaking to someone. 'Don't waste words on that man; he isn't interested in our complaint.'

16. **to weigh one's words** – to choose one's words with the greatest care. 'When you are being interviewed for a job, you must weigh your words before answering the questions they put to you.'

17. **words fail me** – I cannot express my feelings in words. 'When I try to describe my experience in the prison camp, words fail me.' cf. **be lost for words 263/3.**

INDEX

Possessives and plurals of nouns follow immediately after the singular unless there is a spelling change within the word. Thus **day's** *and* **days** *follow* **day** *and precede* **daylight**; *but* **men** *follows* **memory**, *not* **man** *and* **man's**.

B

F

I

J

K

T

Y